Mediation as an Inclusive and Sustainable Method of Resolving Conflicts

IUS, LEX ET RES PUBLICA
STUDIES IN LAW, PHILOSOPHY AND POLITICAL CULTURES

Edited by Barbara Janusz-Pohl

VOL. 40

Kinga Anna Gajda / Marta Pietras-Eichberger /
Małgorzata Skawińska (eds.)

Mediation as an Inclusive and Sustainable Method of Resolving Conflicts

PETER LANG

Berlin · Bruxelles · Chennai · Lausanne · New York · Oxford

Bibliographic Information published by the Deutsche Nationalbibliothek
The Deutsche Nationalbibliothek lists this publication in the Deutsche Nationalbibliografie; detailed bibliographic data is available online at http://dnb.d-nb.de.

Library of Congress Cataloging-in-Publication Data
Names: Gajda, Kinga Anna, editor. | Pietras-Eichberger, Marta, 1979- editor. | Skawińska, Małgorzata, 1981- editor.
Title: Mediation as an inclusive and sustainable method of resolving conflicts / [edited by] Kinga Anna Gajda, Marta Pietras-Eichberger, Małgorzata Skawińska.
Description: New York : Peter Lang, 2025. | Series: Ius, lex et res publica. studies in law, philosophy and political cultures, 2191-3250 ; 40 | Includes bibliographical references.
Identifiers: LCCN 2025015848 (print) | LCCN 2025015849 (ebook) | ISBN 9783631922385 (hardback) | ISBN 9783631922392 (ebook) | ISBN 9783631939451 (epub)
Subjects: LCSH: Mediation. | Dispute resolution (Law) | Conflict management.
Classification: LCC K2390 .M4333 2025 (print) | LCC K2390 (ebook) | DDC 347/.09–dc23/eng/20250403
LC record available at https://lccn.loc.gov/2025015848
LC ebook record available at https://lccn.loc.gov/2025015849

The publication has been supported by a grant from the Faculty International and Political Studies under the Strategic Programme Excellence Initiative at Jagiellonian University.

Cover image is courtesy of Benjamin Ben Chaim.

ISSN 2191-3250
ISBN 978-3-631-92238-5 (Print)
ISBN 978-3-631-92239-2 (E-PDF)
ISBN 978-3-631-93945-1 (E-PUB)
DOI 10.3726/b22994

Published by Peter Lang GmbH, Berlin (Germany)

info@peterlang.com

This publication has been peer reviewed.

www.peterlang.com

Contents

List of tables

Introduction

Mediation has increasingly become an indispensable mechanism for conflict resolution, widely recognised for its efficacy across a broad spectrum of legal systems and cultural contexts. Distinguished by its capacity to foster inclusivity and sustainability, mediation offers a structured yet flexible approach to resolving disputes that emphasises voluntary participation, confidentiality and the active engagement of all parties in reaching a consensual resolution. Unlike adversarial litigation, mediation prioritises the preservation of relationships and the promotion of long-term cooperation, attributes that are critically important in today's interconnected and rapidly evolving global landscape.

The primary objective of this publication is to investigate whether mediation, as a method of Alternative Dispute Resolution (ADR), serves as an inclusive and sustainable approach to resolving conflicts. A collaborative effort was established to address this research question, involving academics and practitioners from the international socio-economic business environment, each specializing in ADR. This publication is the outcome of these collaborative efforts.

Another key objective of the publication is to enhance the interdisciplinarity of research on mediation by fostering collaboration between representatives from both academic and practical fields. It focuses on mediation within the European Union (EU) and beyond. The book explores mediation as a broad and versatile phenomenon, demonstrating its applicability across a variety of conflict types and adaptability in different contexts – ranging from disputes between states to conflicts within private sector. For this very reason, the publication also includes an analysis of mediation from the perspective of its role in international law, particularly its application in shaping relations between states (e.g. Hungarian–Balkan relations), as well as its significance and origins rooted in philosophy and culture. The interdisciplinary approach allowed for viewing mediation not only as a solution embedded in law at the national and international levels but also as a process influenced by the cultural, historical and philosophical factors present in different communities.

The publication undertakes a comprehensive examination of mediation, analysing its development and application across various jurisdictions, including Australia, India, Italy, Iceland, Lithuania, Poland, Singapore, Switzerland, Ukraine and Hungary. It seeks to elucidate how these diverse societies have integrated mediation into their legal frameworks, adapting the practice to align with local cultural, historical and social dynamics. This deeper exploration of the roots of mediation suggests that it may indeed originate from human nature itself and serves as a tool for a sustainable approach to conflicts, which are better understood as divergences of interests between parties. Rather than viewing conflicts as a binary struggle between good and evil, mediation embraces an inclusive framework that acknowledges and values the diversity of perspectives and needs, fostering resolutions that are more equitable and reflective of the complex nature of human interactions.

The purpose is to provide a nuanced understanding of how mediation operates within these different environments, highlighting both the successes and challenges inherent in its implementation. The subsequent objective of this book is to critically explore the evolution, implementation and efficacy of mediation as a conflict resolution mechanism across a range of legal, social and cultural contexts. By analysing the experiences of these various jurisdictions, cultures and approaches, this book aims to identify best practices and common challenges that influence the success of mediation globally.

As global attention increasingly shifts towards more sustainable and inclusive methods of conflict resolution, this exploration is particularly pertinent. By examining the distinct ways in which mediation is practiced in different regions, the book provides critical insights that are invaluable for legal practitioners, scholars and policy makers striving to advance the use of mediation as a preferred method for dispute resolution.

In this publication, the view is adopted that inclusivity entails accessibility for all potentially interested parties in a conflict, regardless of their status, the legal system in place in a given territory, or any other criteria that could hinder or potentially obstruct access to a swift, affordable, autonomous and sustainable method of dispute resolution. In the contemporary world, there is a noticeable shift from a vertical approach to conflict resolution – where methods and conditions for resolving a dispute are imposed through court or arbitration rulings – towards collaborative or integrative methods that rely on the willingness of the parties to manage their conflict.

Research Questions and Thesis

The primary ideas guiding the authors during the research include:

- What factors contribute to the effectiveness of mediation frameworks in various jurisdictions, and what challenges do they encounter?
- How have legal, social, cultural or historical factors interacted to shape the dynamics of mediation models in different regions?
- In what ways can effective mediation practices from diverse contexts be applied to refine and enhance mediation processes globally, ensuring adaptability in both state and private sector conflicts?

The central thesis of the publication asserts that the effectiveness of mediation as a method of conflict resolution is significantly influenced by a complex interplay of legal, cultural, social and historical factors. Furthermore, by assimilating best practices from diverse jurisdictions and tailoring them to local contexts, mediation can be refined to better fulfil the objectives of inclusivity and sustainability. The book argues that such an approach not only enhances the resolution of disputes but also aligns with global standards for sustainable development, thereby establishing mediation as an essential instrument for fostering a more equitable and just society.

The interdisciplinary approach taken by the authors, many of whom are practising mediators from various countries and legal cultures, has led to the hypothesis that there is no universal 'recipe' for the concept of mediation within a single country, despite the existence of certain recurring principles. These principles include voluntariness, autonomy of the parties, confidentiality, mediator neutrality, cost-effectiveness and the flexibility of the mediation process. While these standards are widely recognised as essential to effective mediation, their application and success can vary significantly depending on the legal, cultural and even historical context of each jurisdiction. What proves effective in one legal system may not necessarily yield the same results in another, due to these varying factors.

Given the interdisciplinary nature and the focused scope of this publication, a variety of research methods have been employed. For chapters that primarily analyse mediation through the lens of the legal frameworks in individual countries, the dogmatic method was predominantly applied. Conversely, for chapters that explore the non-legal aspects of mediation, such as its cultural significance and origins, historical and comparative methods were utilised.

The selected countries were chosen to represent a broad spectrum of jurisdictions, encompassing Member States, other European countries and non-European countries. This strategic selection facilitated a focused examination of mediation practices across different legal, cultural and historical contexts, rather that attempting to cover every possible jurisdiction. Given the complexity of conflicts, which often extend beyond personal disputes to encompass organizational, inter-organizational and even inter-state disagreements, it is essential to adopt a holistic approach when analysing mediation. The inherent complexity of these conflicts, which can involve diverse stakeholders with varying interests and power dynamics, necessitates a comprehensive perspective which recognises that conflicts do not exist in isolation but are interconnected within broader systems. Therefore, addressing conflicts effectively requires an understanding that cutting out specific areas, such as family or commercial mediation, from the broader conflict resolution ecosystem, could be counterproductive. Instead, it is crucial to view these areas as part of a larger, interconnected framework where lessons from one area can inform and enhance practices in others.

The publication is divided into two parts: the first focuses on mediation within the broad context of international environments, considering culturally rooted aspects of mediation, while the second part deals with mediation in light of national regulations in selected countries. In the second part, the authors analyse legal acts and the evolving practices within the examined legal systems, as well as attempt to identify specific solutions developed within particular legal cultures. This approach is reflected in the structure of this book, where the initial chapters address fundamental aspects of mediation.

In Chapter I of Part I, the cultural conditions of mediation in a global context are discussed. In Chapter I titled 'Intercultural Competence in Mediation: A Cultural Studies Perspective on Understanding, Adapting and Integrating Conflict Resolution Strategies', Kinga Anna Gajda examines the critical role of intercultural competence in mediation processes across diverse global contexts. Intercultural mediation has emerged as an essential tool for managing conflicts and fostering mutual understanding in increasingly multicultural societies marked by rapid cultural change and heightened individualism. This method addresses disputes stemming from cultural differences, language barriers and diverse communication styles. It is proving particularly significant in nations with high immigration rates, such as the United States, Canada and Australia, and in European countries focused on immigrant integration. Kinga Anna Gajda delineates four primary approaches to mediation within cultural frameworks: the metacultural approach, which overlooks cultural differences; the transcultural approach, which imposes universal values; the multicultural approach, which highlights the uniqueness of each culture and the intercultural approach, which promotes dialogue and positive change through authentic cultural interaction. The intercultural approach is emphasised as the most effective, as it blends universalism and relativism to facilitate genuine engagement and understanding. Mediators using this approach bridge cultural gaps, resolve disputes and foster tolerance by interpreting diverse perspectives. Chapter I underscores the importance of intercultural competencies in mediation, which are crucial for enhancing communication and conflict resolution between culturally diverse parties. Mediators must possess a deep understanding of cultural diversity and identity formation to effectively recognise and interpret cultural differences. Essential skills include adapting communication styles to meet the needs of all parties, empathetic listening and building trust to create a conducive environment for resolution. Proficiency in negotiation, conflict resolution and the strategic use of media and technology are also vital. Ongoing self-reflection and education are necessary for mediators to address biases and continuously improve their intercultural skills. Intercultural competencies are intertwined with the practice of mediation, focusing on managing cultural differences and fostering mutual understanding. Mediators need advanced skills to interpret cultural perspectives, minimise misunderstandings and support effective communication, which involves understanding language nuances, non-verbal signals and cultural norms. Training and experiential learning, such as international exchanges, are essential for developing these competencies and enhancing mediation effectiveness. Chapter I further explores how culture, encompassing shared symbols, beliefs, values and social practices, profoundly impacts communication and behaviour, influencing how individuals from different backgrounds interact and resolve conflicts. Effective mediation requires awareness of these cultural differences and the application of techniques such as active listening, empathy and culturally sensitive dialogue. Mediation can also contribute to cultural transformation by introducing new norms and symbols to promote intercultural understanding and reduce conflicts. Religious and cultural perspectives significantly shape conflict interpretation and resolution approaches, necessitating that mediators navigate these differences respectfully. Facilitating interfaith and intercultural dialogue is crucial for achieving deeper understanding and sustainable solutions. Mediators must be attuned to cultural contexts to build trust, avoid misunderstandings and adapt methods to fit cultural preferences. Chapter I also introduces various models of intercultural mediation, including those identified by Katharina Kriegel-Schmidt, such as cultural knowledge, communicative action, cultural constructions and power disparities. These models assist mediators in understanding and managing cultural differences through various strategies. Mitchell R. Hammer's additional models – Transformational, Facilitation, Simplex, Resource, and Dialogue – further illustrate approaches tailored to different intercultural contexts and conflict types. Facilitative mediation, prevalent in Western cultures, involves a neutral mediator assisting parties in reaching their agreements by understanding deeper interests rather than merely legal claims. This approach emphasises autonomous decision-making, resulting in solutions that are often more satisfactory and durable. In contrast, Eastern cultures may favour evaluative mediation, where the mediator provides expert guidance, due to values of collectivism, hierarchy and indirect communication. Cultural differences such as individualism versus collectivism and high versus low context communication impact mediation dynamics significantly. Integrating Western and Eastern mediation elements can enrich practices by combining the strengths of each approach. Effective intercultural mediators must adapt their strategies to respect cultural differences, address power imbalances and foster inclusive, culturally sensitive solutions.

In Chapter II, the analysis focuses on the function of law in the context of interpersonal relationships, particularly when conflicts arise. In Chapter II titled 'Law and Habilitation to Dialogue: The Challenge of Mediation from a (Paduan) Legal–Philosophical Perspective', Federico Reggio explores the necessity of re-envisioning the role of law moving beyond traditional norm-centred approaches. Instead, he advocates for perspectives that emphasise the relational value of law, viewing it in dynamic terms, according to which the main purpose of law is to (re-)enable interpersonal relationships when conflict occurs. The author also highlights that the latter approach has a long tradition at Padua University, where, for almost one century, the teachings of the philosophy of law have placed particular emphasis on this aspect of law. Nevertheless, while originally such perspective tended to consider that such dynamic and relational character of the law should be guaranteed by the legal process, the recent evolution of instruments of mediation shows that there are other spaces, within legal systems, which can fulfil this function. Mediation, therefore, offers the chance to bring to a different level the proposal of rethinking the role of law in terms of 'habilitation to dialogue', as Chapter II seeks to explain.

Chapter III delves into the concept of mediation in international public law. In Chapter III, Marta Pietras-Eichberger investigates the development and application of mediation within the framework of international public law, highlighting its historical evolution and contemporary relevance. Although mediation is an ancient practice, its formal codification in international law began with the 1899 Hague Convention, which recognised it as a peaceful mechanism for resolving international disputes. Chapter III explores how mediation is integrated into various international legal frameworks, including the United Nations Charter and numerous regional agreements, using legal dogmatics and comparative analysis. Marta Pietras-Eichberger traces mediation's historical roots to ancient civilizations such as Egypt, Greece and the Mari Kingdom, dating as far back as 1800 BC. The modern resurgence of interest in mediation, particularly notable in the 1970s in the United States, has had a significant impact on global practices and is interconnected with various cultural traditions, including those in China. Chapter III also reviews key regional and multilateral treaties that incorporate mediation, such as the 1936 Inter-American Treaty on Good Offices and Mediation, the 1948 Pact of Bogota and the 1963 Charter of the Organisation of African Unity. These treaties underscore mediation as an essential tool for peaceful dispute resolution and often include guidelines for the selection and qualifications of mediators. Despite the absence of a uniform definition and standardised criteria for mediators, Marta Pietras-Eichberger emphasises mediation's role in preventing the escalation of conflicts and facilitating dialogue between disputing parties. Mediation is portrayed as a voluntary and flexible method that enables parties to manage their disputes autonomously. Chapter III concludes that while the fundamental principles and objectives of mediation are consistent across international conventions and domestic laws, their application varies based on the nature of the dispute. Notably, issues related to sovereignty and territorial integrity are often excluded from mediation, which generally serves as a preliminary step towards more formal conflict resolution mechanisms.

Chapter IV is dedicated to the philosophical and historical analysis if mediation, focusing on the techniques and methods used in mediating conflicts. Titled 'Types of Arguments Used in Negotiations Topical–Rhetorical Aspects of Mediation: An Attempt at Theoretical Reflection in the Light of Chaïma Perelman's Legal Arguments', Chapter IV is authored by Anna Moskwa. In this chapter, Anna Moskwa delves into the intricate role of argumentation within the contexts of mediation and negotiation, particularly through the lens of Chaïm Perelman's theories on legal argumentation. She emphasises the growing recognition of interpersonal communication techniques across theoretical, empirical and practical dimensions as crucial in shaping social behaviour. This shift highlights the significance of persuasion and rhetorical skills, traditionally associated with legal contexts, in various modern domains. Anna Moskwa underscores that effective interpersonal communication, as conceptualised by Zbigniew Nęcki and Jerzy Stelmach, is central to regulating social interactions and influencing outcomes. This involves employing persuasive techniques that extend beyond formal logic to include rhetorical and dialectical strategies. These skills are increasingly relevant in legal adjudication and managing conflicts in diverse areas such as business, politics and personal relationships. Chapter IV explores the historical evolution and contemporary practice of mediation, tracing its origins from ancient civilizations to modern applications. Early forms of mediation, found in Roman law and various ancient cultures, have evolved into contemporary methods institutionalised in countries like Great Britain and the United States. The rise of ADR reflects a response to inefficiencies in traditional litigation, emphasizing mediation as a voluntary, confidential process aimed at facilitating mutual agreements rather than imposing binding decisions. Anna Moskwa discusses the characteristics of mediation, including its voluntary nature, confidentiality and the parties' control over the resolution process. She contrasts mediation with adjudicatory methods, highlighting its role in fostering agreement through negotiation rather than enforcing decisions. Despite its value, mediation faces limitations, such as its applicability in cases involving significant social interests or where impartiality is challenging. Perelman's 'new rhetoric' is central to Moskwa's discussion, emphasizing the importance of rhetorical techniques in argumentation. This approach challenges the absolutism and dogmatism of traditional formal logic, advocating for a flexible, open philosophy that seeks practical, balanced resolutions. Perelman's notion of the 'universal auditorium' reflects an ideal audience for ensuring fairness and universal relevance in arguments, though it remains an idealised construct. Chapter IV concludes that successful negotiation and mediation rely on advanced communication, rhetorical and negotiation skills from all parties involved. Stalmach's Argumentative Code for lawyers, including principles such as clarity, conviction and respect for accepted practices, provides a framework for effective argumentation. Techniques such as analogy, contrast and historical arguments, along with legal topics like evidence requirements and the balance between formal and material justice, guide negotiators in developing fair and ethical resolutions. Overall, Moskwa's analysis highlights the importance of integrating rhetorical strategies into mediation and negotiation processes to achieve fair and practical outcomes, thereby acknowledging the complexity and variability of real-world disputes.

The first part of the book concludes with Chapter V, which explores the role of the state as a mediator in international relations. Titled 'The Balkans

Powder Keg Reloaded. Hungary and the Western Balkan Region at the Crossroads of European Integration', this chapter authored by Viktor Glied and Andrea Schmidt examines Hungary's evolving role and influence in the Western Balkans amid the challenges faced by the EU since the 2008 global financial crisis. These challenges include the migration crisis, Brexit, the war in Ukraine, and the impact of COVID-19. As the EU discusses further integration and enlargement, particularly concerning the Western Balkans, Hungary took on the rotating EU presidency in July 2024. Hungarian officials, like Prime Minister Viktor Orbán and Foreign Minister Péter Szijjártó, emphasised Hungary's strategic interests in stabilizing and developing the Western Balkans, arguing that the EU needs these countries more than these countries need the EU. Chapter V analyses Hungary's controversial role as a mediator within the EU, particularly following Orbán's visits to Kyiv and Moscow, which raised questions about Hungary's intentions. Despite Hungary's claims of pursuing a 'peace mission', its actions, including threats to veto EU financial support for countries supplying arms to Ukraine, have led to some scepticism. Hungary's foreign policy is marked by its ambition to act as a bridge between East and West, leveraging its geographical and historical ties to the Balkans to mediate in regional conflicts, such as the ongoing Serbia–Kosovo dispute. Chapter V further explores Hungary's historical connections to the Balkans, shaped by centuries of interaction with powerful empires, and how these ties inform its current foreign policy. Hungary's approach is described as pragmatic, focusing on national interests while navigating complex regional dynamics. The country seeks to increase its influence in the Balkans through economic investments and by promoting European integration for the region, particularly in light of competition from non-EU actors like China and Turkey. Chapter V concludes by highlighting the challenges Hungary faces in balancing its commitments to the EU with its relationships with Eastern partners, including Russia. Hungary's foreign policy is seen as a mix of realism and idealism, emphasising energy security, national sovereignty and the desire to act as a mediator in regional conflicts. However, this approach has also led to criticisms and potential isolation within the international community, particularly concerning Hungary's stance on the Serbia–Kosovo conflict.

In the subsequent chapters, while the authors do place the institution of mediation within the context of selected international legal frameworks, their focus shifts to the origins and analysis of national legal acts, identifying key mediation practices that could potentially serve as international standards. The second part of the publication opens with Chapter VI titled 'Mediation for Sustainable Resolution of Commercial Disputes within the Polish Legal Framework: A Path to Sustainable Development', where Małgorzata Skawińska explores the growing significance of mediation as a tool for sustainable business practices within Poland's evolving legal and economic landscape. As businesses face growing environmental, social and governance (ESG) requirements, mediation emerges as a constructive method for resolving disputes that align with sustainable development principles. Małgorzata Skawińska emphasises that mediation, grounded in voluntariness, confidentiality, impartiality and flexibility, allows businesses to address disputes in a way that is not only efficient but also supportive of long-term goals. Chapter VI highlights how mediation can transform business conflicts into opportunities for dialogue and collaboration, thereby fostering a more sustainable and ethical business environment. Małgorzata Skawińska argues for the integration of inclusivity and sustainability into mediation practices as essential for achieving durable and equitable outcomes. These principles ensure that all parties' perspectives are considered, leading to resolutions that are fair and reflective of the diverse interests involved. Małgorzata Skawińska further explores the legal framework for mediation in Poland, noting that while there is no statutory definition of mediation, the principles of inclusivity and sustainability are inherently embedded within the provisions of the Polish Code of Civil Procedure (CPC). This legal structure supports the use of mediation as a fair, effective and sustainable method for resolving commercial disputes, contributing to a stable and cooperative business environment. Chapter VI also advocates for future legislative reforms, such as introducing mandatory mediation in commercial disputes, the development of an electronic system for mediation requests and tax incentives for companies that utilise mediation. These measures, coupled with increased promotion and education about mediation, are seen as crucial for enhancing its role within the Polish legal system. In conclusion, Skawińska underscores the importance of recognizing inclusivity and sustainability as core principles of mediation.

By doing so, businesses can better navigate the complexities of ESG regulations and contribute to a more stable and progressive economic landscape, ultimately promoting long-term success and resilience in the global economy.

Continuing the discussion on mediation within the context of domestic law, the book offers a comprehensive analysis of this institution within the Italian legal system. Mediation in Italian law is explored in two consecutive chapters.

Isidoro Barbagallo's chapter, Chapter VII, titled 'Civil and Commercial Mediation in Italy – Part One: Origins and Functioning for a Comparative View', offers a detailed exploration of the evolution and current state of mediation within the Italian legal system, contextualised within an international framework. Chapter VII begins by tracing the historical roots of mediation, noting its origins in Western legal traditions, particularly in Roman law as codified in the XII Tables, which mandated attempts at conciliation before litigation could proceed. This foundational principle of pre-litigation conciliation has remained a persistent feature of Italian legal practices throughout history. In the mid-twentieth century, the formalization of ADR emerged, with significant developments occurring in common law systems, notably in the United States during the 1970s. The introduction of the Alternative Dispute Resolution Act of 1998 defined ADR as involving neutral third parties to facilitate dispute resolution through methods such as mediation and arbitration, which later influenced global ADR practices. In Europe, the movement towards formal ADR mechanisms began in the early 1990s, with the United Kingdom and France leading the way. The EU further advanced ADR through various directives and recommendations aimed at enhancing cross-border dispute resolution and promoting mediation practices, including Directive 2008/52/EC on mediation in civil and commercial matters. Italy, with its historical tradition of conciliation, formalised civil and commercial mediation through Legislative Decree No. 28/2010. This decree, part of Law No. 69/2009, introduced a structured mediation process involving impartial third parties. Despite initial challenges, including a period of unconstitutionality, the framework was later refined by Legislative Decree No. 69/2013 and Law No. 98/2013, which reinforced mediation's role in civil and commercial disputes. Mediation bodies in Italy operate independently of the judicial system and are often affiliated with bar associations, chambers of commerce, or private entities. These bodies must adhere to specific professional, organisational and financial standards and are regulated by the Ministry of Justice. Mediators are required to undergo extensive training and adhere to ethical standards, although not all mediators are lawyers. Recent reforms, particularly the 'Cartabia Reform' (Legislative Decree No. 149/2022), introduced significant updates to the mediation process. Ministerial Decree No. 150/2023, effective from November 2023, brought new training and qualification requirements for mediators, aiming to enhance the effectiveness and inclusiveness of mediation. Chapter VII discusses various types of mediation, including voluntary mediation, which parties may initiate with or without legal assistance; mandatory mediation, required by law for specific matters such as property disputes or medical malpractice claims and delegated mediation, ordered by a judge during ongoing proceedings.

Isidoro Barbagallo emphasises the increasing use of ADR in Italy, with statistics indicating a rise in mediation adoption from 3.6% in 2015 to 7.1% in 2023. Mediation is recognised for offering a faster, more cost-effective alternative to traditional litigation, helping to alleviate the burden on the judicial system and improve the efficiency of dispute resolution. Chapter VII also addresses the role of technology and artificial intelligence (AI) in mediation. While AI holds the potential for supporting mediation, Barbagallo stresses that human judgement remains essential, cautioning against over-reliance on technology.

In conclusion, Chapter VII provides a comprehensive overview of civil and commercial mediation in Italy. It highlights the impact of recent reforms in enhancing mediation's effectiveness and inclusiveness and underscores the need for ongoing adaptation to technological advancements. Mediation continues to evolve as a vital tool for efficient dispute resolution – both within Italy and internationally.

The discussion on mediation in Italian law is further enriched by Chapter VIII titled 'Mediation of Civil Affairs in Italy – Second Part: Tax Benefits in the Fiscal Approach to Support Sustainability', in which Valeria Botti provides a detailed examination of the tax incentives related to mediation in Italy, emphasising their role in enhancing the sustainability and efficacy of ADR mechanisms. Botti highlights that the regulatory framework for civil and commercial mediation in Italy was established by Legislative Decree No. 28

of 4 March 2010, which implements European Directive 2008/52/EC. This directive aims to facilitate access to ADR and promote amicable settlements. Botti explains that the mediation process, introduced by Decree No. 28/2010, involves a neutral third party assisting in resolving disputes. Chapter VIII details how the 'Cartabia Reform', enacted through Legislative Decree No. 149 of 10 October 2022, and further refined by subsequent regulations, including the decrees of 1 August 2023, has significantly altered the landscape of mediation in Italy. The reform enhances the fiscal sustainability of mediation by expanding and clarifying tax incentives. The author notes that, under Article 17 of Decree No. 28/2010, all activities and documents related to mediation are exempt from document taxes and other fees, and settlement agreements are exempt from a registration tax of up to €100,000. This exemption provides a notable advantage over judicial proceedings, where similar documents are subject to taxation. Botti underscores that this tax exemption is a key factor in promoting mediation as an alternative to court processes. In the context of real estate transactions, Botti points out that mediation offers tax neutrality for deals up to €100,000, resulting in significant savings compared to traditional transactions. Supreme Court Ruling No. 11617/2020 further clarifies that tax benefits apply specifically to the mediation agreement and not to subsequent notarial acts. Furthermore, Botti details the provisions of Article 20, which introduces a tax credit mechanism for mediation. Successful mediation settlements can yield a tax credit of up to €600, with additional credits available for court-ordered mediation and legal assistance. The tax credit system is designed to offset the costs of mediation and encourage its use by reducing the financial burden on the parties involved. Botti critically assesses the practical implementation of these tax credits, noting past difficulties such as delays in certification and limited uptake. The Cartabia Reform aims to address these issues by simplifying the process for obtaining and utilizing tax credits, thereby improving the financial viability of mediation. In conclusion, Botti argues that the tax benefits associated with mediation are crucial for promoting its adoption and sustainability. By reducing the burden on the judicial system and encouraging amicable resolutions, these incentives contribute to both economic efficiency and social integration. Chapter VIII underscores that tax incentives for mediation are a vital tool for enhancing the effectiveness of dispute resolution in Italy.

In the same spirit, but with particular attention to Switzerland's role as a permanently neutral state in the peace process, Chapter IX, titled 'Mediation in Switzerland: A Comprehensive Overview', is authored by Lara Pair and Małgorzata Skawińska. Chapter IX provides an in-depth analysis of the evolution and formal integration of mediation within the Swiss legal system. Initially, mediation in Switzerland was an informal practice primarily used for resolving community and family disputes outside the judicial system. However, it has progressively gained formal recognition, influenced by international frameworks such as the United Nations Commission on International Commercial Law (UNCITRAL) Model Law and the EU Mediation Directive. A significant development in this evolution was the incorporation of mediation provisions into the Swiss CPC. The CPC outlines the procedures for proposing, conducting and integrating mediation into the civil justice system. It mandates that courts encourage mediation, underscores its voluntary nature and ensures the suspension of litigation during mediation. Additionally, it provides for the confidentiality and enforceability of mediation agreements. The acceptance and growth of mediation have been further supported by various Swiss legal institutions, professional organisations and public awareness campaigns. Key players, such as the Federal Office of Justice (FOJ) and the Swiss Association for Mediation, have been instrumental in promoting and standardising mediation practices both within Switzerland and internationally. This comprehensive support has established mediation as a credible and integral component of dispute resolution in the Swiss legal framework. The professionalisation of mediation is emphasised as crucial for maintaining high standards and effectiveness. Mediators in Switzerland must meet specific educational and professional criteria to achieve certification, which includes completing accredited training programmes, gaining practical experience and adhering to ethical codes. Organizations like the Swiss Chamber of Commercial Mediation (SCCM) oversee the certification process, ensuring the maintenance of professional standards. Chapter IX distinguishes between mediation and conciliation, noting that while both involve third-party assistance, mediation focuses on facilitating dialogue without decision-making authority, whereas conciliation involves the evaluation of conflicts and proposal of solutions based on legal principles. Mediation is characterised by its voluntary nature, autonomy of parties and confidentiality, while conciliation often precedes legal proceedings and involves mandatory participation in many cantons. Swiss courts actively support mediation by integrating it into formal legal proceedings, although judicial recommendations for mediation are non-coercive. Courts have the authority to suspend proceedings for mediation and can offer practical assistance, such as providing lists of accredited mediators. However, courts ensure that mediated agreements comply with mandatory legal provisions but do not assess their fairness unless they involve statutory standards. Federal offices, such as the FOJ, play a crucial role in promoting and regulating mediation within Switzerland. The FOJ oversees mediator training programmes, supports research on mediation practices and conducts public awareness campaigns. The Federal Department of Foreign Affairs (FDFA) further extends Switzerland's influence internationally by supporting mediation efforts, collaborating with international organisations and facilitating training for global mediators. Chapter IX also highlights specific case studies demonstrating Switzerland's effective role in international mediation. Notable examples include the Colombian peace process, the Sudanese Comprehensive Peace Agreement and the Iran Nuclear Deal, where Switzerland's neutral facilitation was pivotal in achieving significant agreements. Overall, Switzerland's approach to mediation, marked by its commitment to neutrality and institutional support, has positioned the country as a leader in both domestic and international dispute resolution. Chapter IX underscores how Switzerland's model of mediation, supported by a robust legal framework and professional standards, contributes to global peace and stability.

Chapter X addresses the legislative reforms in the field of mediation in Lithuania. By employing the dogmatic method, the authors have analysed the latest changes in Lithuanian law concerning mediation.

Chapter X provides a comprehensive analysis of the evolution of mediation in Lithuania, with a particular focus on recent amendments to the Law on Mediation and its implications for the mediator profession. Mediation is presented as a sustainable and efficient method of dispute resolution that offers an alternative to litigation by emphasising transparency, accountability and social responsibility through direct dialogue and stakeholder engagement. The sustainability of mediation is highlighted by its confidentiality, ability to preserve relationships and capacity to address the emotional components of disputes, thereby providing a personalised approach that enhances efficiency and accessibility.

Chapter X situates mediation within a broader European context, noting the increasing regulation of the profession across the continent, which supports its development by establishing standards for mediator credentialing and quality assurance. In Lithuania, efforts have been underway for nearly two decades to integrate mediation into the legal framework and enhance the credibility of the mediator profession. Chapter X evaluates whether recent legislative reforms in Lithuania provide a robust foundation for the continued development of the profession and whether these measures could serve as a model for other countries facing similar challenges. The authors outline the historical context and development of mediation in Lithuania, reviewing its progress up to the current legislative changes. They examine the regulatory model adopted in Lithuania, assessing its evolution and evaluating the extent to which the legal and social environment supports mediation as a distinct profession. Korsakovienė and Tvaronavičienė provide an overview of recent legislative initiatives aimed at strengthening the mediator profession, including the granting of self-governance rights to the Lithuanian Chamber of Mediators, which is expected to enhance the profession's recognition and service quality. They discuss potential challenges in implementing self-governance for mediators and offer insights that could be valuable for other countries seeking to strengthen their mediator professions.

Chapter X highlights that mediation has been part of Lithuania's legal system for almost two decades, but significant traction has only been achieved since 2017 due to legislative reforms. Lithuania initially faced challenges in establishing a robust dispute-resolution culture due to political, economic and social upheavals. The introduction of the Lithuanian CPC in 2003 was a pivotal moment, mandating conciliation before litigation and laying the groundwork for ADR. A major advancement occurred with the adoption of the Concept of Mediation Development in 2015 and the subsequent amendments to the Law on Conciliatory Mediation in 2017. These amendments, effective as of January 2019, introduced mandatory family mediation as a pre-litigation step, included provisions for state-funded mediation services and established an official List of Mediators. Chapter X notes that the evolution of mediation in Lithuania has been marked by a gradual process of institutionalisation, with the integration of judicial and out-of-court mediation into a unified system. Despite these positive developments, challenges remain, including issues related to the professional identification of mediators, the need for further development in mediation practices and the ongoing requirement for high-quality training. The recent legislative changes, including the latest amendments approved by the Seimas in June 2024, aim to improve the effectiveness of mediation processes and enhance the quality of services. These changes grant the Lithuanian Chamber of Mediators new management functions, adjust the state funding model for mandatory mediation and introduce new training requirements. In conclusion, the article underscores that while the institutionalization of mediation in Lithuania is progressing positively, it continues to face challenges. Effective self-governance, coupled with strategic planning, adequate resources and continuous dialogue with stakeholders, will be essential for the future development of the mediator profession in Lithuania and could potentially serve as a model for other jurisdictions.

The origins of private mediation are also presented within the legal system of Iceland. In Chapter XI, Małgorzata Babula provides a comprehensive analysis of the historical and legislative development of the mediation system in Iceland. She delineates the evolution of the Icelandic mediation framework, particularly highlighting the establishment of the state mediator's office as a response to changing social and economic conditions. Babula traces the origins of the mediation system back to the early twentieth century, when Iceland's fishing towns transitioned from informal partnerships to formal employment relationships. This shift led to the emergence of trade unions advocating for workers' rights and subsequent strikes starting in 1916. In response to these labour conflicts, the Icelandic Parliament enacted the Act on Attempts to Settle Labour Disputes in 1925. This legislation, supported by broad political consensus, introduced the role of the state mediator, appointed by the Minister of Labor, to facilitate the resolution of disputes between employees and employers. If disputes could not be resolved through mediation, the mediator was tasked with proposing settlement solutions for a vote by the parties involved. Chapter XI further details the reinforcement of the mediator's role through the 1938 Act on Trade Unions and Labor Disputes, which remains in effect alongside other relevant legislation such as the Information

Act, Administrative Law, Public Finance Act and the Act on the Rights and Obligations of State Employees. Under the 1938 Act, the state mediator is appointed for a 5-year term by the Minister of Social Affairs and the Labour Market and is required to report annually. The mediator, who must be an Icelandic citizen with no criminal record, operates from the capital and may appoint deputies if needed. The government has the authority to establish special conciliation committees for significant disputes, which are endowed with similar rights and obligations as the mediator. Babula emphasises that the mediator's salary is regulated and adjusted based on public salary statistics. The mediator's responsibilities include resolving disputes, monitoring the labour market and maintaining a register of collective agreements. If mediation fails, the mediator can propose new settlement solutions for a vote or attempt further mediation within 14 days. Mediators are expected to adhere to a professional code of ethics promoting honesty, impartiality and effectiveness, with violations subject to reporting to the ombudsman. This ethical framework has been developed with input from various stakeholders, including the Union of State Employees and the Institute of Ethics at the University of Iceland. Chapter XI also addresses the challenges of aligning Icelandic mediation procedures with EU law. Although Iceland is not an EU member, it complies with many EU regulations through the European Economic Area (EEA) agreement. However, delays in implementing Directive 2013/11/EU on ADR led to legal proceedings before the EFTA Court in 2019. As a result, Icelanders now have access to online dispute resolution platforms, such as the Housing Complaints Commission and the Consumer Complaints Commission, further illustrating the adaptability and ongoing development of the Icelandic mediation system.

Chapters XII to XIV primarily focus on the historical and cultural roots of mediation in the non-European legal system, while also discussing contemporary mediation regimes applicable to the analysed countries. In Chapter XII titled 'Mediation: An Indian Perspective', Sayali Ganu-Dabake discusses mediation as a voluntary dispute resolution process where parties engage a neutral mediator to reach a mutually acceptable solution. The author underlines mediation's historical roots in India dating back to ancient times when resolving disputes through dialogue was the preferred method. Although in India mediation does have historical roots, it lost prominence during British colonial rule, which prioritised the judicial system. To alleviate the burden on courts, various ADR mechanisms were introduced, with mediation being the most recent. Chapter XII outlines the introduction of the Mediation Act of 2023 by the Indian Parliament, which aims to promote mediation as a peaceful dispute-resolution method. This act emphasises resolving disputes within a specific timeframe while maintaining the voluntary nature of the process. The formalisation of mediation through this legislation reflects the Indian government's intent to promote it as an effective ADR mechanism. Chapter XII delves into India's historical context of mediation, key provisions of the Mediation Act of 2023, the mediation process outlined in the Act, institutional mediation and the impact of the Act on existing laws. Ganu-Dabake claims mediation offers several advantages over other dispute resolution methods like litigation or arbitration, such as its voluntary nature, flexibility, party control and confidentiality. The 2023 Act, alongside India's accession to the Singapore Convention on Mediation, highlights the growing importance of mediation in India, particularly in the context of economic growth and the country's promotion on the global market. The Act establishes a legal framework for mediation procedures, defining key concepts such as 'mediation', 'mediator' and 'mediation agreement'. The Act mandates pre-litigation mediation in civil and commercial disputes, except in cases requiring urgent interim relief. The author details the procedures for appointing, replacing and removing mediators, as well as the principles for avoiding conflicts of interest. A key element of the Act is the confidentiality of the mediation process and the legal recognition and enforceability of mediation agreements, which can be enforced like court judgements. Additionally, the Act establishes the Mediation Council of India, responsible for promoting mediation and overseeing mediator education and certification. Certain disputes, such as those governed by criminal law or involving minors, are excluded from mediation under the Act's First Schedule. Mediators play a crucial role by assisting parties in reaching a voluntary agreement without imposing a solution. They must disclose potential conflicts of interest and cannot later act as arbitrators in the same dispute. The Act impacts existing laws, introducing a new mediation regime and amending laws such as the Indian Contract Act, the Arbitration and Conciliation Act and the Consumer Protection Act. Pre-litigation mediation is mandatory in commercial cases, with exceptions for urgent interim relief. Chapter XII concludes that the Mediation Act of 2023 represents a significant step in integrating mediation into India's legal system. However, its success depends on effective implementation and further amendments to address gaps, particularly in international mediation.

In Chapter XIII titled 'Mediation in Australia: Development and Successful Practice in Both Aboriginal and Western Society and Their Possible Collaboration', Iwona Pruszyńska provides a comprehensive analysis of mediation practices within Aboriginal and Western contexts and explores potential collaborative approaches between these frameworks. She initiates the discussion by referencing Tim Costello's insights on storytelling from 'Tips from a Travelling Soul-Searcher', which underscores storytelling as a universal human experience that reinforces fundamental values and fosters communal growth. This foundation helps contextualise the evolution and current state of mediation practices in Australia. Pruszyńska outlines the historical development of mediation in Australia, noting that while contemporary mediation is often associated with the 1990s, its roots extend to Aboriginal practices and the social justice movements of the 1980s. Chapter XIII highlights that the modern mediation movement emerged alongside significant global events, such as Nelson Mandela's release and the reunification of Germany, initially drawing on the Harvard Negotiation model, which reflects Australia's pragmatic and rational approach. Chapter XIII examines how socio-economic factors, particularly the rise of economic rationalism, have influenced mediation practices in Australia. Economic rationalism emphasises individual autonomy and market-driven values, which impact the framing of disputes, often prioritising contractual and self-interest perspectives over communal concerns. Pruszyńska discusses the complexity of Australia's multicultural landscape, which adds layers of difficulty to mediation practices due to cultural diversity. This diversity necessitates a broad spectrum of mediation approaches – from high-level diplomatic efforts to community-based initiatives – complicating efforts to standardise ethical standards and competency requirements. The legal framework for mediation in Australia is described as fragmented, with varying state regulations, court rules and private regulations. Despite its initial role as an alternative to the traditional adversarial legal system, mediation had become central to Australian legal processes by 1998, with official endorsement from the

Attorney-General. Chapter XIII details the three main types of mediation in Australia: private, court-connected and judicial mediation. Private mediation operates independently and requires mutual consent, court-connected mediation is initiated by the court but does not involve further judicial participation, judicial mediation occurs within the court system – often involving judges. Pruszyńska also discusses the National Mediator Accreditation System (NMAS), established between 2007 and 2008, which serves as the de facto standard for mediator accreditation in Australia. While accreditation is voluntary, it imposes rigorous requirements, including character assessments and ongoing professional development. Chapter XIII highlights the evolving role of mediators in Australia, noting the increasing involvement of former judges, and the rise of evaluative mediation, which bears similarities to conciliation. These trends reflect ongoing developments in the field of mediation. A contrast is drawn between Aboriginal mediation practices, which focus on community harmony and relationship healing, and Western models that often emphasise punishment and contractual detail. Aboriginal practices are noted for their flexibility and holistic approach, involving community elders and integrating broader community engagement. Pruszyńska suggests that incorporating Aboriginal values, such as cooperation and respect for elders, could enhance Western mediation practices, particularly within Australia's multicultural context. Finally, Chapter XIII addresses challenges related to the judicialisation of mediation, which threatens the voluntary and informal nature of the process. Issues such as mandatory participation and rigid court regulations are discussed as potential risks to mediation's flexibility. Pruszyńska also highlights the need for mediators to bridge the gap between intuitive understanding and systematic knowledge of conflict, emphasising the importance of contextual adaptation. Chapter XIII concludes on an optimistic note, acknowledging current challenges while anticipating continued growth and advancement in the field of ADR in Australia.

In Chapter XIV titled 'Mediation as a Method of Resolving Conflicts in Singapore', Yue-En Chong discusses the historical and contemporary significance of mediation in Singapore. Mediation, with roots in traditional Asian cultures, declined with urbanisation but was revitalised in the 1990s under Western influence, particularly with the support of the judiciary, including former Chief Justice Yong Pung How. Mediation is a voluntary, confidential process where a neutral mediator helps disputing parties reach a mutually acceptable resolution, offering benefits like cost and time efficiency, privacy and the preservation of relationships. Since the 1990s, mediation has become integral to Singapore's legal system, with developments like the establishment of the Singapore Mediation Centre (SMC) and the Singapore International Mediation Centre (SIMC). The Mediation Act 2017 and the Singapore Convention on Mediation have further solidified Singapore's role in international mediation. In family justice, mediation is closely tied to the 'therapeutic justice' framework, promoting a holistic approach to dispute resolution that minimises conflict and encourages healing. The government's support, combined with grassroots initiatives like the Society of Mediation Professionals (SMP), has helped create a robust mediation system in Singapore that not only resolves disputes but also fosters long-term relationships and participant well-being.

The book concludes with Chapter XV devoted to the analysis of the status of mediators in selected jurisdictions. In this chapter titled 'Frames of Regulation of the Mediator Profession: Is Access to the Profession Inclusive?', Alina Serhieieva examines the critical role that regulatory frameworks play in influencing the inclusion and recognition of mediators within the broader professional landscape. This study explores the various regulatory frameworks that govern the mediator profession across different jurisdictions, examining how these frameworks impact professional inclusion. Through a comprehensive literature review and detailed case studies, Chapter XV identifies key trends, challenges and best practices in mediator regulation. The findings highlight the importance of balanced regulatory approaches that ensure high standards of practice while promoting accessibility and inclusivity within the profession. The study concludes with policy recommendations aimed at enhancing the regulation of mediators, thereby fostering a more inclusive and effective professional environment. This research significantly contributes to the ongoing discourse on professional regulation and offers valuable insights for policymakers, professional bodies and mediators themselves.

This holistic approach is fundamental when proposing changes *de lege ferenda*, emphasising the need to consider the entire ecosystem of conflict resolution rather than focusing narrowly on individual issues.

State of the Law as at 1 January 2025.

PART I

Mediation in an International Environment

Intercultural Competence in Mediation: A Cultural Studies Perspective on Understanding, Adapting and Integrating Conflict Resolution Strategies

Kinga Anna Gajda[1]

Introduction

Modern global societies, characterised by cultural diversity and dynamic intercultural interactions, often face challenges in managing conflicts and promoting mutual understanding. Intercultural mediation is emerging as an extremely important tool aimed at mitigating disputes and building constructive relationships between people and groups representing different cultures. The modern era is an era of 'now culture' and 'rush culture' (Bertman 1998), characterised by a lack of time and an obsession with innovation, as well as a renegotiation of fundamental references to universal values. Ongoing economic wars between wealth imbalance countries may also have political and social consequences. Individualism is promoted, with an inability to perceive oneself as part of a social group with humanity, leading to indifference to the needs and suffering of plants, animals and other human beings. Collaboration costs are prescription (Portera 2023) and promotes an 'I don't care' culture (Portera 2020). Meeting people with different cultural paradigms of uncertainty avoidance, risk taking, values, behaviours and worldviews complicates professional relationships as well as language barriers, different communication styles, expectations and problems that may arise can cause new conflicts (Portera et al. 2020). Therefore, mediators and mediation processes face a challenge.

Globalisation, multiculturalism and economic, political and cultural interdependence raise important questions about mediation, especially in countries with high immigration such as the United States, Canada and

1 Prof., Head of the Institute of European Studies, Jagiellonian University, email: <kinga.gajda@uj.edu.pl>.

Australia (Portera 2023). In Europe, the integration of immigrants has been a key element of social policy since the Treaty of Amsterdam (1997). The European Year of Intercultural Dialogue in 2008 highlighted the multicultural nature of many countries, and the need for intercultural dialogue. Agostino Portera (2020) identified four main approaches to mediation in a cultural context: (1) The metacultural approach assumes ignoring cultural differences during mediation, which is wrong and potentially dangerous because each interaction is culturally conditioned; (2) The transcultural approach is based on universal values and methods, which may lead to the imposition of one's cultural norms and the assimilation of minorities; (3) Multicultural approach emphasises the uniqueness of each culture and their right to autonomy, which promotes respect and strengthening cultural identity, but may lead to stereotyping and ignoring other important problems of clients; (4) Intercultural approach recognises the dynamics of culture and identity, promoting dialogue, confrontation and positive change through real interaction and communication. It enables open reflection on cultural concepts and their adaptation. Intercultural mediation aims to promote mutual understanding and cooperation. Intercultural mediators facilitate dialogue between people from different cultures, enabling the exchange of views and experiences. They intervene in conflict situations, assisting parties in constructively resolving disputes and negotiations. By translating and interpreting various cultural perspectives, mediators support the building of understanding and acceptance of differences. Intercultural mediation contributes to educating people about cultural diversity, promoting tolerance and openness to other cultures. Through organising meetings, seminars and workshops, intercultural mediation fosters active participation in social and economic life, encouraging the integration of diverse cultural groups. All these activities aim to create an atmosphere of mutual respect, cooperation and harmony between cultures, which is crucial in a globalised world where cultural diversity is increasingly prevalent and significant (Hogan et al. 2014).

The intercultural approach is considered the most appropriate because it combines the positive aspects of universalism and relativism, promoting authentic interaction and personal and social development. Intercultural mediation is considered the most promising approach to integration and conflict management, focusing on cultural meanings and combining elements of psychology, sociology, communication sciences and political science. The 2019 World Health Organisation (WHO) report (Verrept 2019) confirms the high effectiveness of intercultural mediators in overcoming language and cultural barriers and their irreplaceable role in providing health care for refugees and migrants.

The concept of intercultural mediation refers to the process in which a neutral third party intervenes in a conflict to support the disputing parties in reaching an agreement and finding a solution that considers their needs and values. The central goal of mediation is not only to solve specific problems, but also to promote dialogue, reduce tensions and create conditions conducive to cooperation and harmonious relations.

In an intercultural context, mediation becomes a key tool that not only helps resolve disputes, but also promotes mutual understanding and ac–cep–tance of cultural diversity. However, intercultural mediation involves a number of challenges, including the need to consider cultural diversity and the dynamics of change that intercultural contexts are subject to. Intercultural mediators must not only have conflict mediation skills, but also sensitivity to cultural contexts and specific behavioural norms. Different cultures may differ not only in how they understand conflict, but also in their preferred methods of resolving it. Intercultural mediation implies that certain elements of differences associated with cultural or ethnic belonging influence the mediation process. In a mediation session, when parties come from different cultures, their starting points, assumptions about the mediation process and expectations of the mediator's role strongly impact the process of symbolic exchange and the construction of meaning (Ting-Toomey 2010). Therefore, intercultural mediation requires flexibility and the ability to adapt to changing situations and the needs of the parties to the conflict. The cultural context is important both for understanding the conflict and for the mediation process. Different cultures have different expectations about what is appropriate behaviour during a conflict and how the search for a solution should proceed. For example, in some cultures an open and direct communication style may be preferred, while in others a more subtle approach is more desirable.

Research on intercultural mediation, regarding the effects of adapting mediation to cultural needs and contexts, is crucial for effective conflict management in a globalised world. The value of intercultural mediation lies in its ability to resolve conflicts and to create dialogue and cooperation, which is essential for the harmonious functioning of modern multicultural communities. Hans Verrept (2019), the author of the report for WHO, emphasises that intercultural mediation facilitates communication, improves the therapeutic relationship by increasing intercultural understanding, reduces the perceived level of discrimination and contributes to adapting services to the cultural needs of community members. The role of crossing cultural barriers is central to the work of intercultural mediators. They perform this function by explaining and contextualising messages and situations for both participants and may also clarify cultural values and norms. Intercultural mediators act as integration agents. Stella Ting-Toomey (2010) emphasises that in order to behave appropriately during a mediation session, competent mediators must have adequate knowledge of the cultural values of both parties to the conflict and apply cultural and situational norms in understanding the overall history of the conflict. To be perceived as effective, intercultural mediators must have flexible linguistic, verbal and non-verbal skills to manage the mediation process effectively and know when to 'lead' or 'let' the conflicting parties take the initiative. It is also important to have differential knowledge in the understanding that both culturally based and personal motives are at work during a mediation session.

In light of rapidly changing supervisory realities, the application of intercultural mediation is becoming more and more valuable and equal. This mediation not only supports the resolution of disputes but also supports the creation of lasting foundations for peaceful and harmonised global communities.

The Role of Intercultural Competence in Intercultural Mediation

Intercultural competencies play a crucial role in intercultural mediation by facilitating effective communication and conflict resolution between individuals or groups from different cultural backgrounds. An intercultural mediator must possess a deep understanding of cultural diversity and the processes of cultural identity formation. This understanding is essential for accurately recognising and interpreting cultural differences in the context of conflicts and interactions.

Effective communication skills with individuals from diverse cultures are vital for intercultural mediation. A mediator should be able to adapt their communication style to meet the needs and expectations of the different parties involved, avoiding misunderstandings arising from language or cultural differences. Additionally, an intercultural mediator must have the ability to listen empathetically and understand the feelings, needs and perspectives of all parties. This is key to building trust and creating an environment conducive to conflict resolution.

Competence in negotiation and conflict resolution is indispensable for an intercultural mediator. The mediator must be able to identify and address conflicts stemming from cultural differences while respecting the diversity and specificity of each party. Intercultural mediation often involves the use of media and technology to facilitate communication and resolve conflicts. Therefore, a mediator should be aware of media preferences and skilfully use mediation tools in a culturally sensitive manner.

Self-reflection and ongoing education are critical competencies for an intercultural mediator. Mediation requires an awareness of one's biases and limitations, as well as a commitment to continuous learning and improving intercultural skills. In summary, intercultural competencies in mediation are essential for effectively functioning as a mediator who not only resolves conflicts but also builds bridges of understanding and mutual respect between different cultures. They provide the foundation for an ethical and professional approach to working with diverse social and cultural groups.

Intercultural competencies and intercultural mediation are closely linked, as both concepts focus on effectively managing cultural differences and bridge-building between diverse cultural worlds. Intercultural competencies encompass the skills, knowledge and attitudes that enable individuals to function effectively and appropriately in intercultural situations. These competencies are crucial in today's globalised world, where cultural diversity is commonplace. Intercultural mediation, on the other hand, is the process of facilitating communication and resolving conflicts between individuals from different cultures. It aims to find mutually acceptable solutions for all parties involved in a conflict.

Intercultural competencies are the fundamental building blocks of effective intercultural mediation. Mediators must possess advanced intercultural skills to understand the perspectives of all parties, minimise misunderstandings arising from cultural differences and support communication processes. These competencies develop empathy and acceptance of different values, beliefs and practices, which are critical in intercultural mediation. Mediators must be able to understand and respect various viewpoints.

Effective communication is at the heart of both intercultural competencies and intercultural mediation. Knowledge of languages, as well as the ability to interpret non-verbal communication signals, is crucial for avoiding misunderstandings. Intercultural competencies include conflict resolution skills that are indispensable in intercultural mediation. Knowledge of common sources of intercultural conflicts and strategies for their resolution is the basis for effective mediation.

In practice, intercultural mediation requires mediators to be aware of cultural norms and values. Mediators must be aware of the norms and values of different cultures to correctly interpret the behaviours and intentions of the parties involved in a conflict. Intercultural mediation requires flexibility and a readiness to adapt mediation methods to the cultural specifics of the parties in conflict. It also presents various challenges. Mediators must be aware of their own stereotypes and prejudices and work to minimise them, so they do not negatively impact the mediation process.

Cultural complexity is another challenge. Modern societies are multicultural, meaning that mediators often have to work with more than two cultures simultaneously, increasing the complexity of the mediation process. Education and training are crucial for developing intercultural competencies and mediation skills. Educational and training programmes can support the development of these skills through workshops, cross-cultural communication training, conflict resolution and mediation.

Experiential intercultural experiences, such as participating in international exchange programmes, internships abroad and other forms of direct contact with different cultures can significantly enhance intercultural competencies. (Ladmiral 2014; ten Thije 2023; Vaupel 2014)

Cultural Influences and Perspectives in Intercultural Mediation: Theoretical Frameworks and Practical Models

Culture is based on a shared system of symbols, beliefs, values, norms and social practices. Beliefs mean a group of individuals' shared perception of the world, including their understanding of the concepts of truth and falsehood. Values refer to what is generally considered good or bad, important or unimportant. Norms, on the other hand, define what is considered appropriate behaviour in a given group, thereby shaping the expectations that people have of each other and themselves. Social practices refer to the predictable patterns of behaviour that members of a culture typically follow (Lustig & Koester 2013). This definition of culture implies that culture significantly influences the behaviour of its individual members, which is important in the context of intercultural communication and mediation. If culture influences behaviour in general, it inevitably influences the way individuals communicate and interact. Since both verbal and non-verbal communication are shaped by the cultural environment, it seems inevitable that when individuals from different cultures apply their own interpretive frameworks, cross-cultural omissions, misunderstandings and even conflicts may arise (Hogan et al. 2014).

Culture and all its elements play a key role in the intercultural mediation process, defining the contexts in which conflicts arise and are resolved. In the context of intercultural mediation, culture plays a key role for several reasons (Cloke 2023). Culture determines how individuals perceive and interpret conflicts. Differences in the perception of space, time or communication styles can lead to misunderstandings and conflicts. Understanding these differences is crucial to effective mediation. Culture influences the dynamics of conflict through decision-making norms, communication styles and ways of expressing emotions. Mediators must be aware of these differences and skilfully manage the mediation process to achieve positive results. Therefore, intercultural mediation requires the use of specialised techniques, such as active listening, empathy and the ability to conduct dialogue, which consider cultural differences and help discover unearth cultural meanings. Mediation can lead to cultural transformation by introducing new norms or symbols that help reduce conflicts and build positive intercultural relationships. This is why culture is extremely important in intercultural mediation. Understanding and considering cultural diversity not only enables more effective conflict management, but also promotes deeper understanding and mutual respect between parties. Mediators, with cultural sensitivity and possessing the ability to integrate cultural differences, can support mediation processes that lead to lasting and positive solutions to conflicts.

Religious and cultural perspectives can differ significantly in how their lenses interpret a conflict situation and the causes and solutions to problems. Mediators must be aware of these differences and be able to manage them to effectively help resolve disputes (Abu-Nimer & Seidel 2023). Many cultures and religions have specific social norms and values that shape how conflicts are resolved. Mediation should consider these norms, respect the values of the community and seek solutions that are acceptable to all parties. In intercultural mediation, it is important to create space for interfaith and intercultural dialogue. Such dialogue can lead to deeper understanding and more sustainable and lasting solutions to conflicts. Intercultural mediation seeks to understand and consider cultural differences to effectively manage conflicts and promote understanding between parties (Kriegel-Schmidt 2023). Mediation is about helping parties in a conflict communicate and find a solution. Understanding the cultural contexts from which the parties come is crucial to effective communication and conflict resolution. It is based on trust and acceptance of the parties. Understanding and respecting cultural differences help mediators build trust, which is crucial for the effectiveness of the mediation process. Mediators should have an in-depth understanding of the cultural differences that may influence the way parties perceive the conflict, communicate their needs and expectations and make decisions. This knowledge helps avoid interpretation errors and misunderstandings (Menkel-Meadow 2023). In some cultures, mediation may be more accepted than other forms of conflict resolution, such as court. Therefore, understanding how culture influences the preferred methods of resolving disputes is important to the effectiveness of the mediation process. Moreover, cultural differences may lead to conflicts resulting from different value systems, social norms and expectations towards mediation. Mediators must be aware of these differences and skilfully navigate them to support constructive conversations and negotiations. Understanding cultural specifics can lead to more satisfying and lasting conflict resolutions that consider the needs and expectations of all parties involved. Therefore, cultural sensitivity, humility and inclusiveness play an important or even key role in mediation.

Intercultural sensitivity is the ability to communicate and interact effectively in diverse cultural contexts. It includes a positive approach to understanding and appreciating cultural differences and the ability to adapt to new cultures (Chen & Starosta 2000). Guo-Ming Chen and William J. Starosta (1997, 2000) define intercultural sensitivity as a person's ability to develop positive emotions in the process of intercultural communication. According to them, intercultural sensitivity consists of six elements: self-esteem, self-control, open-mindedness, empathy, engagement in interaction and a non-judgemental attitude. With globalisation and the increase in international cooperation, intercultural sensitivity is becoming an essential element in fostering effective interpersonal and professional relationships. Cultural sensitivity (Menkel-Meadow 2023) plays a key role in mediation, especially in intercultural contexts where the parties to the conflict may differ not only in language and origin, but also in deeply rooted norms, values and methods of communication. Cultural sensitivity includes the ability to adapt mediation techniques to the needs and cultural preferences of the parties to the conflict. This may mean using appropriate communication strategies, such as direct versus indirect communication, or using mediators who speak the appropriate languages or the use of translators. Cultural sensitivity requires the ability to listen empathetically and understand the cultural perspectives of each party. The mediator should be aware of differences in the perception of time, hierarchy and the importance of Candour in communication. Cultural sensitivity in mediation requires not only theoretical knowledge, but above all practical communication and interpersonal skills. An effective intercultural mediator can break down cultural barriers, support conflict parties in discovering common points of understanding and forge lasting solutions that consider the diversity and cultural specificity of each party. Humility (Yokotsuka 2023) means being open to the perspective of the other party, especially how its culture, values and experiences influence the way it perceives the conflict and expectations towards mediation. Instead of imposing solutions, mediators who want to be humble try to understand what is important to each side. Humility means being open and empathetic to the experiences and emotions of conflict participants. Mediators strive to create a safe space in which parties can express their needs and concerns related to cultural differences. A humble attitude requires awareness of one's own prejudices and stereotypes. Mediators should avoid simplifying the culture of the participants in the conflict and not assume that they know every aspect of the culture from which the participants come. Mediators should strive for communication equality and fair treatment of all parties, regardless of their cultural background. Humility in intercultural mediation is the ability and willingness to recognise and respect cultural diversity, to constantly learn and to support equality and empathy in the mediation process. This is a key element in supporting effective and inclusive mediation, especially in the context of cultural and linguistic differences between participants.

Inclusiveness (Collins 2023; Muwanzi & Goredema 2023), in intercultural mediation, refers to the practice of engaging and considering the diverse perspectives and needs of all parties involved in the mediation process, regardless of their cultural, ethnic, gender or social differences. Inclusiveness ensures that all groups interested and affected by the conflict have representation at the negotiating table. This means that the voices of minorities, women, youth, older people and other marginalised groups are heard and considered. Inclusiveness in mediation is about considering the needs and interests of all parties equally to ensure fair and balanced solutions. This means that mediators must strive to identify and address hidden needs and concerns that may not be immediately apparent. Inclusiveness requires creating an environment in which all participants feel safe and encouraged to express their thoughts and feelings. Inclusiveness also means ensuring that no mediation participant is discriminated against or excluded from the decision-making process. Mediators must act as neutral participants, ensuring balance of power and procedural fairness. Mediation should promote open communication and active listening. For mediation to be truly inclusive, language and communication barriers must be removed. This may mean providing translators, conducting meetings in local languages or using various forms of communication so that each participant can fully participate in the process. Inclusiveness in intercultural mediation is not only limited to the mediation process itself, but also includes the implementation and monitoring of agreements. It is important that solutions are sustainable and truly consider the needs of all parties involved.

Intercultural mediation is not only knowledge and intercultural competences, but also strategy and action models. Katharina Kriegel-Schmidt (2023) presents four models that enable mediators to flexibly develop intervention strategies and that can be adapted to specific cases and intercultural challenges. A cultural knowledge perspective on the actions of all mediation actors focuses on understanding the explicit and implicit information that the parties have about relevant actions in their cultural context. Mediators can help make tacit knowledge explicit through detailed questions and exploration of cultural contexts. The perspective of communicative action of all mediation subjects focuses on the analysis of language, communication styles and communication rules built into different cultures. Mediators must understand how these differences can lead to communication dissonance and how they can affect the effectiveness of mediation. The perspective of the cultural constructions of all mediation subjects examines how different cultures construct identities and meanings. Mediators must be sensitive to individuals' emotional attachment to their cultural constructs, and how these constructs may influence conflict perception and resolution. The perspective of power disparities among all mediation subjects considers how unequal power relations may affect the mediation process. Mediators must be aware of how differences in status, resources and access to power can affect conflict dynamics and the effectiveness of mediation. According to the author, the combination of these perspectives enables mediators to understand and effectively manage cultural differences in the intercultural mediation process. Adopting a holistic approach to culture and using appropriate intervention strategies are crucial to achieving harmony and understanding between parties in intercultural conflicts. There are also different mediation models that are adapted to specific needs and intercultural contexts. Mitchell R. Hammer (2005) lists several main models of intercultural mediation. Hammer points to the transformational model, which assumes that mediation should lead to transformations in the attitudes and relationships between the parties to the conflict. It focuses on personal development and communication between the parties, aiming to understand and accept cultural differences and jointly search for solutions that meet the needs of both parties. The second one Hammer mentions is the facilitation model, which focuses on supporting communication and interaction between the parties, enabling them to independently identify problems and jointly reach solutions. The mediator acts as a neutral facilitator, helping the parties to communicate and create constructive proposals for a solution. The third one is the Simplex model, which assumes a simplified approach to mediation. It is adapted to the cultural specifics and requirements of the parties to the conflict. It focuses on the simplicity of procedures and on enabling the parties to quickly and effectively resolve the dispute by reaching a compromise. The resource model focuses on identifying and using cultural resources and culture-specific conflict resolution strategies. The mediator helps the parties recognise and use their cultural strengths and resources that can support the mediation process. The last one is the dialogue model. This model emphasises open dialogue between the parties to the conflict and building understanding through mutual understanding and acceptance of cultural differences. Mediation in this model focuses on creating a space for a deep exchange of views and experiences, which leads to building trust and finding a solution together. Each of these models has its advantages and can be used in various intercultural situations depending on the specificity of the conflict, the needs of the parties and the cultural contexts. However, a key element of each model is the mediator's ability to understand and consider cultural differences and to manage the mediation process in a way that supports forging lasting consensus and harmony between the parties to the conflict.

Facilitative Mediation across Cultures: Bridging East–West Practices and Perspectives

Mediation has become a widely used method for resolving disputes both in the West and the East. Currently, the most commonly applied approach is facilitative mediation (Tang & Tan 2022). Facilitative mediation is a conflict resolution process where the mediator acts as a neutral intermediary, supporting the parties in communicating and independently reaching an agreement. The key feature of this mediation is the mediator's impartiality and neutrality, refraining from making partisan decisions or imposing settlements. Instead, the mediator assists the parties in clearly expressing their positions, needs and interests, and then collaboratively seeking solutions that satisfy those needs (Brown 2004; Manning 2006; Zumeta 2018).

The facilitative mediation process is based on identifying the deeper interests and needs of each party rather than focusing solely on positions or legal claims. The mediator supports the parties in creatively problem-solving, encouraging exploration of various options and possibilities that can lead to win–win solutions. A fundamental principle of this approach is party self-determination – the parties make decisions regarding the final agreement, with the mediator facilitating the process by supporting clarity in communication and avoiding conflict escalation. Compared to other approaches, such as evaluative mediation where mediators may actively provide opinions on legal aspects of the dispute, facilitative mediation gives parties greater control over the process and final outcome. Thus, solutions achieved through facilitative mediation are often more satisfactory and durable because they stem from the parties' autonomous decisions rather than imposed resolutions (Zumeta 2018).

Interestingly, facilitative mediation is predominantly used in Western cultures. In contrast, Asian cultures, characterised by collectivism and respect for hierarchy, may perceive Western facilitative mediation as less aligned with their values. In such cases, evaluative mediation is proposed, where mediators base their guidance on experience and expertise. Cultural differences highlighted by Geert Hofstede (2011), such as individualism–collectivism, power distance and the importance of maintaining relationships, influence mediation dynamics. An essential role in international mediation is played by communication strategies and ways of expressing emotions observed in different cultural contexts. Hammer (2005), referring to Hofstede's division, discusses differences in direct and indirect communication. He writes that individuals from different cultures vary in how they express disagreements. Those who prefer direct communication emphasise clarity and explicitness, using straightforward language and favouring face-to-face conversations. Conversely, indirect communicators rely on ambiguity, analogies and metaphors and sometimes use intermediaries to convey messages. This difference is often linked to cultural values such as individualism (emphasis on personal goals) versus collectivism (emphasis on group harmony). Individualism and collectivism are cultural values that significantly shape conflict resolution styles. Individualistic cultures prioritise autonomy and competitive communication styles, favouring direct conflict resolution. In contrast, collectivist cultures emphasise group harmony and may employ accommodating or avoidance strategies to maintain interpersonal harmony. This difference affects how emotions are perceived and managed during conflicts. Individualism refers to a culture's tendency to emphasise individual identity over group identity, individual rights over group interests, and emotions centred on the individual rather than community. Conversely, collectivism emphasises group identity over individual identity, group interests over individual desires and concern for others' identities over concern for one's own identity (Ting-Toomey 1988). These individualistic and collectivistic tendencies manifest in daily interpersonal, familial, educational and professional interactions, explaining why conflict parties from Western cultures typically employ more direct and confrontational conflict tactics, whereas Eastern cultural groups prefer more conciliatory or even avoidance tactics. In Western culture, greater emphasis is placed on preserving one's own face during conflict, whereas in Asian culture, greater weight is given to concern for the own group and other party's face, which surpasses concern for one's own identity (Ting-Toomey 2010).

Another dimension influencing communication is the context dependency of communication. High-context cultures rely on implicit understanding and non-verbal cues, often preferring indirect conflict resolution strategies to maintain social harmony. Low-context cultures emphasise clear, explicit, verbal communication and direct approaches to conflict resolution. Cultures also differ in their styles of emotional expression. Emotional expression varies significantly across cultures. Emotionally expressive cultures openly display feelings through gestures, body language and verbal expression. In contrast, emotionally restrained cultures tend to suppress or mask emotional expression, valuing composure and avoiding open display of emotions during conflicts. Research highlights how these cultural dimensions (individualism/collectivism, high/low context communication, emotional expressiveness/restraint) shape conflict resolution styles. For example, individualistic cultures prefer direct and competitive conflict resolution strategies, whereas collectivist cultures prefer indirect and harmonious approaches. Cultural differences in the perception and utilisation of space and time can lead to conflicts. Variations in the perception of personal versus communal space or punctuality versus flexibility in time management are common sources of such conflicts (Cloke 2023; Hammer 2005). Hammer (2005), in his article 'The Intercultural Conflict Style Inventory: A Conceptual Framework and Measure of Intercultural Conflict Resolution Approaches', critiques existing theoretical frameworks such as individualism/collectivism and high/low context communication for their adequacy in explaining cultural differences in emotional expression. Hammer emphasises the need for a more nuanced understanding of cultural diversity in conflict styles beyond broad cultural categories.

Differences in approaches to conflict management between members of the in-group and out-group also significantly impact how collectivists from East Asia take action. Representatives of Eastern cultures are more inclined to resolve conflicts with members of external groups while avoiding conflicts with close members of the in-group, unlike representatives of Western cultures. In confrontations with members of external groups, they employ strong competition and aggression tactics, whereas, for example, Americans usually do not draw a sharp distinction between internal and external conflict boundaries and engage in direct and competitive conflict tactics in professional disputes (Ting-Toomey 2010).

In Western facilitative mediation, emphasis is placed on individual autonomy and direct communication, whereas in collectivistic Asian cultures, the priority is harmony, indirect communication and respect for authority. Mediators in Asia often have to play a more active role, providing guidance in the context of differences in power perception and relational aspects, which deviates from Western norms of mediator neutrality (Bond 2023). Western approaches to intercultural mediation refer to frameworks and mediation methods mainly originating from Western countries such as the United States, which are exported and promoted worldwide. These approaches are typically based on assumptions and values that may be culturally specific to Western countries. A comparison of Western and Eastern models of intercultural mediation reveals significant differences in approaches to conflict resolution. The Western approach places a strong emphasis on collaboration and participatory decision-making processes, engaging participants in actively resolving disputes. Western mediators also attempt to address power imbalances through problem-solving workshops and strategies that strengthen weaker sides. In this model, mediators are perceived as neutral, uninvolved parties, which is crucial for fair and just conflict resolution. Conflict resolution is based on a rational approach, often based on cost–benefit analysis, where mediators assist parties in finding fact-based solutions that meet their interests. Western mediation models typically comply with specific ethical and legal-administrative standards, ensuring legal and ethical certainty for both mediators and participants. The mediation process is often confidential and non-public, meaning that information regarding the conflict is kept confidential and not disclosed without the parties' consent. Mediation focuses on identifying the real problems and interests of the conflict parties rather than on emotions or relationships between people.

The Eastern approach to mediation is based on hierarchical structures, where mediators are often perceived as authorities or representatives of the community. The mediation process reflects existing power asymmetries between the conflict parties, which can lead to difficulties in achieving balance and justice in agreements. Local communities play a key role, exerting pressure on conflict parties to reach an agreement. Mediation considers the rich history and social context of the conflict, influencing decision-making and negotiations. The Eastern approach also considers emotions and relationships between parties, which can lead to a more holistic conflict resolution. Mediators in this model may not be perceived as neutral parties but as individuals tasked with supporting one party or acting in the community's interest. Compared to the Western approach to conflict resolution, which is based on formal and judicial processes, the Asian approach focuses on maintaining social balance and honour, as well as involving socially strong leaders as mediators (Abu-Nimer 1996). Additionally, third-party intervention in the Asian often takes on an immediate nature and is based on traditional social norms and values. Resolving conflicts in the context of the Asian requires a deeper understanding of the cultural and social contexts in which these conflicts occur and the adaptation of intervention methods to specific local realities. As noted by Ting-Toomey (2010), mediation participants from Asia may prefer a generous approach, expecting the mediator to be an authoritative, benevolent figure ready to propose a solution to the problem. They are often sensitive to face-saving and may not feel comfortable sharing information directly. For mediators, it is important to spend more time in the introduction phase, explaining the role of mediation and ensuring the confidentiality of the process. Patience and appropriate types of questions are also important to encourage conflict participants to be open.

Western mediation models emphasise cooperation, participation and equality, while Eastern approaches often rely on hierarchical mediation structures and strong engagement of local communities. The Western approach focuses on rational, analytical problem-solving with an emphasis on mediator neutrality, whereas Eastern models integrate the social and emotional context of the conflict, with greater community engagement and pressure.

Adapting mediation approaches to accommodate cultural nuances is crucial for effective conflict resolution. Mediators must adeptly handle linguistic and behavioural differences, interpret non-verbal signals and adjust mediation techniques to respect and protect the parties' faces in conflict. Understanding these differences enhances mediator effectiveness and ensures culturally sensitive dispute resolution, ultimately contributing to achieving positive mediation outcomes tailored to diverse cultural contexts. Hence, there is a growing need for the development of more flexible and culturally sensitive mediation approaches that acknowledge cultural diversity and the contextual specifics of conflicts. It is also recommended to combine Western and Asian mediation models. Despite fundamental differences between approaches to conflict resolution in the Asian and the West, there are valuable principles that can be exchanged and adopted to enrich both methods (Abu-Nimer 1996). The Western approach emphasises cooperation and joint decision-making, which can significantly contribute to achieving lasting agreements. Such a participatory decision-making approach can be beneficial for an Asian context by promoting inclusive approaches and shared decision-making among conflict parties. Both approaches grapple with asymmetry in power relations between factions. The Asian approach effectively utilises social and communal pressure to influence conflict parties towards resolution. This strategy can be adopted in the Western context as a complement to legal procedures with social pressure, enhancing the importance and acceptance of community-resolving agreements. It is important not to impose foreign conflict resolution principles on societies in the Asian or the West without a thorough understanding of their social contexts. Although certain adjustments may be beneficial, each adaptation should respect and integrate with the cultural and social values of the involved parties. A holistic approach by Asian mediators, considering historical and social nuances, contrasts with the often specific and focused strategies of Western third parties. Integrating elements from both approaches can enrich conflict resolution practices by expanding the scope of understanding and intervention effectiveness. By respecting cultural differences, exploring these shared principles can contribute to advancing conflict resolution practices in both the Asian and the West. Emphasising inclusion, addressing power imbalances, community engagement and appropriately adjusting strategies are crucial for effective conflict resolution worldwide.

Competent intercultural mediators must consciously shift their reference points from habitual perspectives to viewing things from a 'third culture' perspective. They must shift their own cultural viewpoints and be willing to change perspectives between individualistic and collectivistic viewpoints or between small and large power distances (Molinsky 2007).

Summary

Intercultural competences are crucial for effective intercultural mediation, which aims to facilitate communication and resolve conflicts between people or groups from different cultural backgrounds. Mediators must have a deep understanding of cultural diversity and cultural identity formation processes to effectively manage differences between conflicting parties. It is crucial that mediators are able to calibrate their communication style to different cultural needs, listen empathetically and build trust. Additionally, they must be adept at negotiations and be able to use appropriate mediation tools, considering the cultural preferences of the parties.

Continuous self-reflection and education are essential for mediators to overcome their biases and continually develop their skills. Cultural sensitivity, i.e. the ability to adapt mediation techniques to the needs and cultural preferences of the parties, is also crucial. Mediators must be aware of differences in social norms, values and communication methods, and be able to manage these differences to effectively resolve conflicts. At the same time, inclusivity ensures that all parties, including marginalised groups, are represented and included in the mediation process.

In practice, intercultural mediation uses various models. A key element of any model is the mediator's ability to understand and manage cultural differences, leading to lasting and positive conflict resolutions. Mediation has become a popular method of dispute resolution in both the West and the East, with the most-commonly used approach being facilitative mediation. In this model, the mediator acts as a neutral intermediary, helping the parties communicate and reach an agreement themselves, rather than imposing solutions. The key to facilitative mediation is the parties' autonomous decision-making, which leads to more satisfactory and lasting solutions.

Both Eastern and Western mediation models have their strengths, and their integration can enrich mediation practices. It is crucial to adapt approaches to cultural and contextual specificities, which requires cultural sensitivity and the ability to adapt strategies to a variety of conflict contexts.

Bibliography

Abu-Nimer, Mohammed, and Seidel, Timothy (2023). 'The Political Dimensions of Culture and Religion in Mediation'. In Dominic Busch, Claude-Helene Mayer, & Christian Boness (eds), *International and Regional Perspectives on Cross-Cultural Mediation*, pp. 111–118. Frankfurt am Main: Peter Lang.

Abu-Nimer, Mohammed (1996) 'Conflict Resolution Approaches: Western and Middle Eastern Lessons and Possibilities', *The American Journal of Economics and Sociology*, 55 (1), 35–52.

Bertman, Stephen (1998). *Hyperculture: The Human Cost of Speed*. Westport, CT: Praeger.

Bond, Greg (2023). 'Culture and Mediation: A 2020s Perspective on Early Criticism of Western Paradigms'. In Dominic Busch (ed.), *The Routledge Handbook of Intercultural I*, p. 29. New York, London: Routledge.

Brown, Carole J. (2004). 'Facilitative Mediation: The Classic Approach Retains Its Appeal', *Pepperdine Dispute Resolution Law Journal*, Issue 2, 279–295.

Chen, Guo-Ming and Starosta, William J. (2000). 'The development and validation of the intercultural sensitivity scale', *Human Communication*, 3 (2000), 1–15.

Chen, Guo-Ming and Starosta, William J. (1997). 'A Review of the Concept of Intercultural Sensitivity', *Human Communication*, 1, 1–16.

Cloke, Kenneth (2023). 'Transforming Conflict Cultures through Mediation'. In Dominic Busch (ed.), *The Routledge Handbook of Intercultural I*, pp. 180–188. New York, London: Routledge.

Collins, Haynes (2023). 'The Politics of Intercultural Space: Inclusive, Unobtrusive, and Failed Mediation'. In Dominic Busch (ed.), *The Routledge Handbook of Intercultural I*, pp. 145–152. New York, London: Routledge.

Geert Hofstede (2011). 'Dimensional Zing Cultures: The Hofstede Model in Context'. In *Online Readings in Psychology and Culture, Unit 2*. <http://scholarworks.gvsu.edu/orpc/vol2/iss1/8>, accessed 11 July 2024.

Hammer, Mitchell R. (2005). 'The Intercultural Conflict Style Inventory: A Conceptual Framework and Measure of Intercultural Conflict Resolution Approaches', *International Journal of Intercultural Relations*, 29 (6), November, 675–695.

Hogan, Ciara, Rentel, Nadine, and Schwerter, Stephanie (2014). 'Introduction'. In Ciara, Hogan, Nadine Rentel, and Stephanie Schwertner (eds), *Bridging Cultures: Intercultural Mediation in Literature, Linguistics and the Arts*, pp. 7–18. Stuttgart: ibidem-Verlag.

Kriegel-Schmidt, Katharina (2023). 'Putting Culture into a Perspective in Intercultural Mediation'. In Dominic Busch (ed.), *The Routledge Handbook of Intercultural I*, pp. 85–92. New York, London: Routledge.

Ladmiral, Jean-René (2014). 'Intercultural Communication'. In Ciara, Hogan, Nadine Rentel, and Stephanie Schwerter (eds), *Bridging Cultures: Intercultural Mediation in Literature, Linguistics and the Arts*, pp. 37–54. Stuttgart: ibidem-Verlag.

Manning, Carolyn M. (2006). 'Transformative and Facilitative Mediation Case Studies: Improving Relationships and Providing Solutions to Interpersonal Workplace Conflict', *The Arbitrator & Mediator*, 25 (2), 81–90.

Menkel-Meadow, Carrie (2023). 'Cross-Cultural Disputes and Mediator Strategies'. In Dominic Busch (ed.), *The Routledge Handbook of Intercultural I*, pp. 30–42. New York, London: Routledge.

Molinsky, Andrew (2007). 'Cross-Cultural Code-Switching: The Psychological Challenges of Adapting Behavior in Foreign Cultural Interactions', *Academy of Management Review*, 32 (2), 622–640.

Muwanzi, Joseph and Goredema, Dorothy (2023). 'The Relevance of Inclusivity in Mediation and Negotiation Processes: A Reflection', *Research and Analysis Journals*, 6 (07), 1–6.

Myron, W. Lustig and Koester, Jolene (2013). *Intercultural Competence: Interpersonal Communication Across Cultures*. Boston: Pearson.

Portera, Agostino, Moodley, Roy, and Milani, Marta (2020). *Intercultural Mediation Counselling and Psychotherapy in Europe*. Newcastle: Cambridge Scholars.

Portera, Agostino (2020). 'Intercultural Competences in Mediation, Counselling and Psychotherapy'. In Agostino Portera, Roy Moodley, and Marta Milani (eds), *Intercultural Mediation Counselling and Psychotherapy in Europe*, pp. 10–30. Newcastle: Cambridge Scholars.

Portera, Agostino (2023). 'Intercultural Mediation from a European Perspective'. In Dominic Busch (ed,), *The Routledge Handbook of Intercultural I*, pp. 163–171. New York, London: Routledge.

Tang, Nicolas and Tan, Cheryl (2022). 'Comparing Mediation Strategies in Asia and the West', *Farallon Law Corporation*, 9 June, <https://fl.sg/resource/comparing-mediation-strategies-in-asia-and-the-west/>, accessed 11 July 2024.

ten Thije, Jan D. (2023). 'Intercultural Mediation as Intercultural Competence'. In Dominic Busch (ed.), *The Routledge Handbook of Intercultural I*, pp. 301–309. New York, London: Routledge.

Ting-Toomey, Stella (1988). 'Intercultural Conflicts: A Face-Negotiation Theory'. In Young Yun Kim and William B. Gudykunst (eds), *Theories in Intercultural Communication*, pp. 213–235. Newbury Park, CA: Sage Publications.

Ting-Toomey, Stella (2010). 'Intercultural Mediation: Asian and Western Conflict Lens'. In Dominic Busch, Claude-Helene Mayer, and Christian Boness (eds), *International and Regional Perspectives on Cross-Cultural Mediation*, pp. 79–98. Frankfurt am Main: Peter Lang.

Vaupel, Angela (2014). 'There is No Normal Way of Doing Things: Interculturality and the Development of Intercultural Competence'. In Ciara, Hogan, Nadine Rentel, and Stephanie Schwerter (eds), *Bridging Cultures: Intercultural Mediation in Literature, Linguistics and the Arts*, pp. 21–36. Stuttgart: ibidem-Verlag.

Verrept, Hans (2019). What are the roles of intercultural mediators in health care and what is the evidence on their contributions and effectiveness in improving accessibility and quality of care for refugees and migrants in the WHO European Region? World Health Organization, Regional Office for Europe, <https://iris.who.int/handle/10665/327321>, accessed 13 July 2024.

Yokotsuka, Shin (2023). 'Cultural Humility in Intercultural Mediation'. In Dominic Busch, ed., *The Routledge Handbook of Intercultural I*, pp. 51–58. New York, London: Routledge.

Zumeta, Zena (2018). 'Styles of Mediation: Facilitative, Evaluative, and Transformative Mediation', *Mediate.com*, 27th February, <https://mediate.com/styles-of-mediation-facilitative-evaluative-and-transformative-mediation/>, accessed 11 July 2024.

CHAPTER 2

Law and Habilitation to Dialogue: The Challenge of Mediation from a (Paduan) Legal–Philosophical Perspective

Federico Reggio[1]

Introduction

There are several reasons why mediation should catch the interest of legal philosophers. They are not just limited to the two features which are normally associated with mediation, namely its usefulness in offering a deflationary alternative to the judicial system, and its capacity to pacify interpersonal relationships in a way that a judicial sentence is almost never able to provide parties with.

Indeed, both the above-mentioned characteristics of mediation highlight the two relevant sides of its appeal as an alternative. Nevertheless, the way mediation seeks to offer an 'alternative' approach implies a deeper and holistic rethinking, on the one hand, (I) of the law in its pacifying character and, on the other hand, (II) of legal methodology as a process meant to transform conflict into a dialogical interaction capable of finding common grounds, and, if possible, bottom up, consent-based solutions to controversies.

Such rethinking challenges an established approach to legal theory, according to which law should be mostly understood in its capacity to ensure social order through a more or less articulated scheme of prescriptions, made effective by the possibility of activating legal remedies, mostly based on forms of enforcement[2]. Despite a variety of (very) different articulations (from modern natural law theories, through legal positivism, to legal realism, to quote some of the best known and notable ones), such approach is commonly characterised by considering the law mostly within the framework of a set of legal rules.

---

1 Department of Private Law and Critique of Law, University of Padova, email: <fererico.reggio@unipd.it>.

2 The literature on this point is very vast and articulate. See, for a mere first overview, Bix 2015; Raz 2009; Schauer 1991; Marmor & Sarch 2019. In the Italian Literature, theories of law that consider law mostly as a set of rules, the validity of which can be justified in different ways according to different approaches (nature law theories, legal positivism, legal realism) have been defined as 'normativistic' or 'norm-centred': for a critical overview, see Moro 2022; Zanuso 2022.

Some interesting literature underlines that mediation is more than just 'an alternative way' to deal with legal controversies. The mediative approach to conflict resolution, in fact, relies on a different logic, or even on a different legal paradigm (Harris Crowne 2001), which aims at facing the challenge of interpersonal conflict through a 'negotiated order' rather than an 'imposed order'[3]. In mediation, bottom–up, agreed-upon solutions are preferred to top–down, imposed ones.

This perspective obviously focusses on the different way in which mediation promotes an interpersonal confrontation between conflicting parties. Instead of a highly agonistic and antagonistic, adversarial confrontation, typical of a legal trial, mediation seeks to promote a more informal and participatory dialogue, aimed at settling a dispute through mutual agreement. Moreover, in the latter form of interaction, there is a space also for elements which are not normally considered in a judiciary process, such as narratives[4] based on experiences, emotions (Irvine & Farrington 2016), feelings and expectations. This involves – rather than renouncement of legal rationality – a widening and reframing of it, in a way that is typical of dialogue as an ideal 'place' in which both the *pathos* (emotional component) and the *ethos* (behavioural component) find connection and expression in the *logos* (connective, dialogical rationality), as John W. Cooley had suggested in his pioneering works on the methodology of mediation[5].

The above-mentioned considerations briefly show how mediation and dialogue are intertwined, and how this peculiar focus captured a restlessness within many contemporary societies regarding the theory and practice of

3 This expression has been frequently used by Giovanni Cosi in his philosophical studies on mediation. For an overview, see Cosi 2007. See also, more recently, Monoriti 2023.

4 Here, I am using the noun 'narrative' in a broad and non-specific sense, although I am aware of a 'narrative' approach to mediation, which embodies a particular view and set of methodologies. For an introduction, see Cobb 1994.

5 See Cooley 1993. A critique of the modern 'narrowing down' of legal rationality during the early Enlightenment was undertaken by Giambattista Vico (1668–1744), who argued in favour of a wider idea of legal reasoning capable of giving space also to emotions, creativity, arguments based on common sense and 'verisimilitude'. This approach was a minority view in his time, and has been since revaluated. See, e.g. 't Hart 1982–1983; Shaffer 1990; Grassi 1976; Reggio 2012b.

law and, more specifically, the way legal systems were meant to deal with interpersonal conflict. The progressive affirmation of ADR tools, including mediation, did not take place, in fact, only for utilitarian reasons or for hetero-directed legal policies, but rather for addressing needs that were (and still are) related to the legal systems and to the law in general, and that the latter were not able to fully meet[6]. The divergence between the way people experience interpersonal conflict (and the need for solutions), and the way legal systems normally deal with conflict[7] has sometimes appeared as a sort of expropriation of conflict and its management, and sometimes as an inadequate way of addressing people's actual needs[8].

In a sense, then, there seems to be an underlying proposition to this phenomenon to rethink the law's pacifying role and its methodological approach to interpersonal conflict in a way that involves dialogue as a central aspect of legal experience, rather than a sort of (unnecessary) addendum to it.

Law and Dialogue. Suggestions from the 'Process-Based' Tradition within the Italian Legal Philosophy

The above-mentioned considerations cross paths with a certain approach that emerged in the Italian legal doctrine, the gravitational centre of which is based on the teachings of philosophy of law at the University of Padova. This approach, which has been proposed for almost a century (mostly but not only) at Padova University's School of Law, is called the 'process-centred perspective of law' (in Italian, *La prospettiva processuale del diritto*) (Cavalla 1991; Cossutta 2019; Moro 2012; Zaccaria 2006).

---

6 Also, on this point there is a vast literature. I would like to suggest some selected publications. See, for example, Abel 1982; Auerbach 1983; Bush and Folger 1994; Morineau 1998. See also, in the Italian literature, Cosi and Foddai 2003; Arielli and Scotto 2003; Reggio 2017.

7 This topic is seen as the 'original' question from which the whole ADR movement stemmed. See, for instance, the famous 'Pound' discourse on the dissatisfaction with the administration of justice, and its further rebounds in the North American legal doctrine. See Pound 1937, and, for a recent evaluation, Friedman 2007.

8 The claim that conflicts are 'a property' of private parties emerged within the criminological debate in the late '70s, later influencing the early debate on *restorative justice*. On this point, see Christie 1977, and, more recently, Woods & Suzuki 2000.

If we agree with the fact that, as we remarked earlier, mediation presupposes a different approach to legal experience, namely a perspective which is not merely norm-centred and prescription-based, then a brief confrontation with the 'process-centred perspective of law' can offer some remarkable conceptual standpoints for reflecting on the features and challenges of mediation from a legal–philosophical perspective. The above-mentioned perspective, in fact, clearly reconnects law's fundamental function to the importance of transforming interpersonal conflict in a way that relies on human relationality and on a dialogic rationality[9].

According to the tradition of the 'process-centred perspective of law', the law should not be understood only as a set of legal rules, mostly of prescriptive nature, as norm-centred approaches suggest (for instance, within the contemporary traditions of legal positivism or legal realism)[10]. The 'process-centred perspective', as its name suggests, purports that the legal dimension is philosophically justified (and therefore valid) when it dynamically enables a conflict to be solved in a way that is not based on violence or arbitrariness. For this purpose, it must allow the possibility of a dialogic confrontation between parties. As the main proponents of this approach argue, such function can be mostly found in the legal process, seen as the centre of legal experience[11] and as the 'place' where conflict can be transformed into a controversy (Gentile 1987; Zanuso 1993), and therefore in a situation based on dialogical confrontation and dialectical reason (Cavalla 2017; Moro 2012; Zanuso & Fuselli 2011).

In this sense, the 'conclusion' of the process is not founded only on the authority of a decision in its voluntaristic character, but rather relies on rationally controllable and acceptable developments, based on the correct use of legal argumentation in its dialectical character (Cavalla 2008; Fuselli 2023).

9 I personally emphasise this element as a true distinctive characteristic of this approach, slightly shifting the focus from the concept of 'process' towards the dynamics of dialogue-building: see, again, Reggio 2017.

10 Law, to abide to its essential function, must instead be understood in its basic function of transforming interpersonal conflict, which cannot happen only through a mere application of legal rules and procedures due to the intrinsically controversial nature of both human interaction and regulations. See, again, Cavalla 2017.

11 This theory was systematically thematised by Enrico Opocher (1914–2004), under the influence of the philosophical reflections of Giuseppe Capograssi (1889–1956). See Capograssi 1959a; Opocher 2005; Opocher 1983.

In a more recent writing, one of the most important exponents of this perspective, Francesco Cavalla (1939-), underlined the idea of *complex, necessary and specific nature of law*. According to his view, the necessary and specific role of law is associated with the idea of law as an alternative to violence, including the risk of self-asserting one's reasons by avoiding confrontation and expression of arguments and evidence to sustain each other's claims. Such characteristics, however, reveal also the complex nature of the legal dimension, in which three elements appear necessary and reciprocally implicated, with none of them sufficient on its own: (1) the law; (2) the legal process and (3) dialogue (Cavalla 2022).

According to the philosopher, law without dialogue, and without the possibility of contesting and discussing its implications (which are always controversial, as the ancient and pre-modern philosophy reminds us in many different ways), is a mere command. Law without the process is an abstract and general prescription, unable to confront with the issues stemming from the concreteness of human experience (which is, again, controversial, despite the modern 'dream' of solving or preventing it through a variety of legal and political 'engineerings'). The legal process without the law risks becoming a mere act of authority, if not of arbitrariness. Moreover, without a true dialogue and confrontation (between the parties, but also with judges, who are called to motivate their decisions), also the legal process risks being reduced to a mere decision of the case incapable of habilitating a true confrontation of reasons underlying parties' claims which, again, would make the final decision sustainable. Finally, also dialogue, without the law and the legal process, falls beyond the legal dimension. Yet again, dialogue is not just an act of communication, but most of all a human dimension which requires mutual recognition, respect and openness to confront with someone else's reasons, and in this sense a dialogue is at the foundation of humanity's social dimension, both as a precondition and as a value which needs to be preserved (also by the law). Dialogue may saturate the legal dimension with an attention to people and relationships, which 'saves' the law from being a purely formal abstraction, incapable of confronting real-life issues.

Some questions arise at this point.

The first one is regarding the compatibility of the above-mentioned perspective with the rise of consensual ADR tools, and more specifically with mediation, which is mostly understood and presented as an 'alternative' to the judicial process.

This question leads to a second one, regarding the meaning of the word 'process': in other words, one may ask whether this understanding of a process is limited to the judicial trial; or, instead, are there ways to embrace a larger idea of a process-based idea of law, including other instruments as well, which are not heteronomous but autonomous (as mediation is)?

To answer this question, we need to understand that an interpretation of 'process' as limited to the legal trial which happens within the judiciary systems encounters a variety of problems. These problems may even contest the meaningfulness of the overall proposal of the 'process-centred' approach, the core of which has to be sought in the idea of the 'necessary, specific and complex nature of the law'. Accordingly, we will have to consider the possibility of reframing the idea of 'process-centred perspective' within the concept of '*law as habilitation to dialogue*'. As I will try to argue, such reinterpretation saves the philosophical core of the process-centred perspective, thereby opening its conceptual proposal to those approaches that look at the issue of transforming conflict in a way that does not necessarily involve a formal trial and the decision of a judge, or a jury[12].

A Process-Centred Approach – Beyond the Limitation(s) of the Judicial Process? Critical Remarks

Some elements that characterise the judicial, and, above all, 'adjudicative' dimension of the trial highlight how such procedural instrument is limited in its real capacity to address and resolve the inter-subjective conflict projected onto the dispute.

Such limitations are visible in both modern and contemporary theory, as well as in legal practice, but we can try to focus mostly on three points, on which we will reflect below: (I) the tendency to consider the legal norm as a rigid and polarising regulatory canon; (II) the dispute as a 'polarisation'

12 This paragraph is based on a more elaborate analysis, published in Fuselli et al. 2022: 'Il diritto tra "conversione del conflitto in controversia" e "abilitazione al dialogo". La prospettiva processuale del diritto alla prova degli strumenti ADR consensuali'.

of disputed claims and (III) the overly rigid delimitation of the boundaries of the dispute.

The legal norm as a rigid and polarising regulatory canon

While the critical reflections that have emerged in recent years – whether in the context of critical positivism or, for example, as a result of the lessons learned in hermeneutics – certainly provide a warning against naive readings of the very concept of 'application' of law, one cannot overlook the role that substantive legal norms play within arguments of the parties in the process (Poscher 2019).

Substantive rules, in other words, tend to be seen, and invoked in arguments of the parties, as a pre-established regulatory canon, with respect to which clear contrasts are often established. In short, with respect to a rule (or a combination of rules), there seems to be a strong alternative, because one is either inside or outside the applicative/interpretive sphere of the rule itself, and based on this clear opposition the claims and arguments of the parties are, to a large extent, confronted. Therefore, the demarcation line set by the rule(s) tends to be exclusionary towards alternatives: this is evident both where the rule is invoked to sanction a borderline between lawful and unlawful, and where it is invoked in support of a given thesis, with respect to which one is 'within' or 'without' the scope of application of the selected case (Reggio 2012a). The result is that a reference to the law takes on a structurally 'polarising' connotation in the context of controversial argumentation, especially in court, exasperating contrasts that, in other contexts of conflict analysis and interpretation of the law, actually turn out to be much less clear-cut.

In this sense, this creates a sort of prism that prevents the possibility of finding mutually acceptable solutions. The most glaring example of the above observations can be seen precisely in the context of mediation practice, in which – as it is usual for institutions of a consensual-conciliatory nature – the attitude towards the rule is more flexible and creative, as is especially visible in civil disputes (concerning disposable rights). In fact, frequently during a mediation 'opposition' on legal rules which appeared to be mutually exclusive, later condenses around more mutually compatible positions. This is precisely the result of the attitude that mediation helps adopting towards legal regulations. The search for a solution capable of meeting the interests and needs of each party is in itself, firstly, a source of flexibility and, secondly, requires flexibility towards legal regulation to be adopted.

Here, spaces and methodologies offered by (negotiation and) mediation tools allow for a special margin of analysis of the *res controversa*. It all starts from a reading of the controversy which accepts its complexity as a multi-layered phenomenon, involving a multiplicity of aspects (personal, relational, economic and legal). The next step, of course, is to understand that such opening up of perspectives may imply a different way to interpret the 'solution' of the dispute as not only aimed at 'adjudicating wrongs and reasons' but also, and more importantly, at composing interests, needs and prerogatives in such a way as to seek a possible integration[13].

Consequently, there are wider possibilities of finding a solution that satisfies both parties, with the result of enabling a creative approach to legal regulatory schemes which may suit the case. The latter, in fact, can be 'moulded' to fit the interests and needs of the parties with an opportunity of finding a consensus around issues that fall within the realm of lawfulness and practicability, which, however, be still innovative and constructed around that specific 'harmonisation'[14]. Freed from the constraints of norms taken as a pre-established regulatory canon, a good negotiation or mediation practice opens up a prospect of 'legislating' a set of regulatory rules capable of settling the dispute through a new order of relations. These rules will, in any case, be formulated in legally lawful, feasible, determined terms and built around the needs of the parties and the case[15].

In order to find a mutually satisfactory solution that is rationally recognised as commonly acceptable, it is fundamental not to get trapped in the set of normative and interpretative references that each party can invoke in support of a possible judicial argument. Instead, it is necessary to search for the best 'rule of the case' in which the parties' substantial interests and needs are best formalised and summarised, also in their legal representation.

---

13 On the multi-layered structure of conflict, see Lederach 2003.

14 This is also one of the cornerstones of the first Harvard approach to negotiation, for instance. See Fisher et al. 1981.

15 The idea of mediation as a dialogic and consensual construction of the 'norm of the case' is one of the core claims expressed in Reggio 2017.

In this model of reasoning, the rule logically (but also factually) 'follows' the procedure. Consequently, it emerges as a result that has proved capable of combining, as a result of a reasoned dialogue, the positions, needs and interests that the parties have highlighted in their arguments. If this is not necessarily a point of distance from the process-centred perspective of law – which does not place the rule as the first premise of legal reasoning – there is indeed a partial difference in the way conflict transformation is conceived. What consensual instruments, like mediation, ask for is to 'suspend judgement' on the adjudicative side of the trial and to allow an attempt to be made to find a solution based on agreement. Moreover, as we will see, if both the process-centred perspective and mediation rely on the development of a dialogue founded on argumentative rationality, the dialogue at which mediation aims differs from the agonistic and antagonistic logic of the dialectic of the trial. What is shared between the two, however, is the search for 'best reasons' capable of resolving the dispute (Slob 2002).

As a result, the final agreement at which mediation aims is a 'rule between the parties', inscribed in the principle of freedom of forms typical of private autonomy. On the other hand, in a judicial settlement it would be difficult to shy away from using the legal rule as an 'interpretative canon' that binds the parties and the judge to a decision relating to the 'type' identified in abstract terms in the legal prescription. The legal process, therefore, risks to further enhance a polarising effect thereby fostering an opposition between the parties to a dispute. This topic will be explored below.

The dispute as 'polarisation' of disputed claims

The legal process – especially as structured and disciplined nowadays – proves to be a source of 'polarisations' which do not always facilitate the search for a solution capable of resolving the underlying conflict. Indeed, sometimes the outcome of the process may prove to have the effect of 'widening the wound' of the conflict itself, revealing the 'cutting' nature of judicial decision. The 'sword', a typical iconographic attribute of modern justice, thus runs the risk of making the trial not an alternative to force, but a monopolisation of its exercise in the hands of an institutional subject neglecting the need for a real settlement of the fracture that the conflict has created on the interpersonal level.

Let us consider, first of all, that the trial is based 'always on a radical questioning' which implies a defensive response, so that 'in the legal trial the questioning and answering are always a challenge that qualifies the procedural opposition and that, at every stage and level of the trial itself, cannot be interrupted without being accompanied by the risk of losing' (Moro 2012).

Moreover, one should not overlook the significance that 'non-contestation' may assume both at the level of strategy (think of a claim that is asserted and not contested by the claimant) and at the level of proof. In both cases, contestation is necessary to avoid exposing oneself to unfavourable outcomes (regardless of whether there is really disagreement on the point). This 'dynamic', derived from a set of rules, mostly procedural ones, but inscribed in the very structure of the trial, reveals the agonistic nature that characterises the trial confrontation, but also poses a serious question as to how much it exasperates the *krisis* underlying the conflict[16].

Conversely, in the mediation context confidentiality – implying, *inter alia*, the inability to use statements made during mediation without the consent of the party entitled to a confidentiality guarantee – allows statements or concessive strategies to be implemented, without them constituting arguments that would expose those who use them to exacerbating consequences in terms of the final outcome of the dispute. It is precisely the enabling of concessions and admissions that allows a rapprochement – both in content and empathy – which can make it possible for the parties to overcome that mutual closure and sharp opposition stemming from the conflict.

In practice, then, it should come as no surprise that *agonism* translates into systematic *antagonism*, which not infrequently makes the courtroom the place where 'unarmed duels' (or rather, ones armed with papers, pleadings and counter-arguments) take place. In addition, even if the courtroom confrontation is a way to avoid violence and to give voice to adversarial confrontation, this does not mean that it helps to soothe rips and wounds in the relations of conflicting parties. In fact, the parties are very often completely absent

16 On the possibility of overcoming the *krisis* of the conflict through a true encounter and dialogic confrontation, see Morineau 1988; on the agonistic–antagonistic nature of the legal process as a way to transform the energies clashing in the conflict, see Moro 2014.

(because they are legally represented) and therefore unable to participate in the proceedings in an active and conscious manner. The contemporary process seems, therefore, precisely to tend to 'ritualise' conflict by perpetuating its underlying relational oppositions for a long time. This is one of the aspects that mediation seeks to counteract by offering a participatory model in which parties are involved in trying to shape a commonly agreed-upon solutions based on a communicative common ground which tries to enhance cooperation rather than adversarial confrontation (Hale 1998; Stewart & Milt 2002).

The overly rigid delimitation of the contours of the dispute

The legal process is characterised by a rigid *petitum*. This means that the range of issues which can and must be discussed and decided is rigidly framed by parties' claims. This principle has the function of preventing judge's decisions from being autonomous and content-wise separate from the cross-examination of parties (a risk inherent in the so-called 'surprise' or 'third way' judgements)[17]. In practice, however, we may ask ourselves whether this may not, in fact, prevent the trial from adequately 'exploring' solutions that may – obviously, following a discussion with the parties – deviate from what the parties have identified in (mutual) claims.

On the other hand, according to the best practice of negotiation and mediation, the involvement of parties in the search for a creative and mutually satisfying solution necessarily involves a flexible reading of the object of the dispute. Not seldom does broadening or narrowing down of the object of dispute turn out to be a useful tool for a satisfactory settlement thereof (Cooley 1994; Cooley 1998; Getzels 1975; Kinsey et al. 1993). Flexibility, then, presents itself as a resource, mostly in opposition to the rigid legal procedures which characterise the trial.

In the wake of the above-mentioned approach to contestation, the adversarial process runs the risk of embodying an excessively 'demolitionist' contest that is incapable of bringing out truly shared discourses, rather than a 'dialogical search for a fair solution to the dispute, in which the disputants and

17 The Latin legal rule of '*nec ultra nec extra petita*' sets this limit as 'the' framework within which the legal process authorises a discussion and a judgement.

the third judge are necessarily called upon to collaborate' (which is the way the 'process-centred' approach sees as the 'core' of the process) (Moro 2012).

Certainly, one cannot overlook the epistemic value that cross-examination also has in the trial as the process where a dialectical reasoning helps testing arguments for soundness and congruity enabling the identification and consolidation of what 'survives' the 'scrutiny of refutation'.

However, it is precisely at this point that some supporters of consensual ADR instruments, and mostly of mediation, criticise the process for its *win–lose* structure, so ill-suited to seeking and bringing out real 'syntheses' between the parties' arguments (Spangler 2003). In other words, while the dialectical character of the process may be necessary when the issue at stake is about ascertaining facts or deciding upon logically incompatible claims, in the experience of legal disputes many situations logically allow the opportunity for a truly common solution to be outlined between claims without the need for an either/or kind of reasoning. As the rise and affirmation of different ADR tools show, the legal process is neither the only, nor always the most appropriate way to approach a dispute between parties[18]. On the other hand, the setting and specific conflict analysis and dialogue-building methodologies of, for instance, mediation may expose parties' claims as not fully incompatible. Indeed, a different way to approach each party's issues (including a deeper analysis of each one's personal and relational situations, interests, needs, etc.) may help to show that a 'synthesis of the contraries' is sometimes possible and capable of being translated into a mutually agreed-upon conclusion of the case.

In this sense, the challenge of consensual ADR instruments – and first and foremost of mediation – should not be sought in the different centre of gravity it proposes regarding the 'will' (thinking of a 'redistribution' of the will to the parties instead of devolving it to an institutional third party). In my view, the gist of the question lays in the special way in which mediation enhances dialogue between the parties in order to seek a legal solution to the dispute and, hopefully, also to the underlying conflict. It should be noted

18 Therefore, rather than reading 'ADR' as 'Alternative Dispute Resolution', I agree with the proposal of translating the acronym as 'Appropriate Dispute Resolution'. See, e.g. Smith 1996; Wood 2016; Wolfe 2001.

that this is a path 'made possible' by the law, but which, in turn, far from closing the legal dimension to abstract normativity alone, allows the latter to offer an authentic alternative to the danger of using force alone to solve.

All this leads us to formulate a question already adumbrated in course of the discussion so far, namely that 'processuality', as a dimension of the judiciary in its pacifying function[19], is not only delivered in the trial, but can also manifest itself through other juridical 'forms', including those, such as mediation, having an autonomous and non-heteronomous character. To this end, the emergence of consensual models, and in particular – due to its peculiarities – of mediation, can help to grasp some of the intrinsic limits of the legal process, confirming the intuition according to which the category of 'processuality' should probably be rethought in its conceptual breadth, and perhaps also in its overall nature.

The increasing relevance of mediation should stimulate a significant opportunity to highlight how the 'processual' character of law is inscribed in the structural co-implication of law itself with intersubjective relationality. As a consequence, we can argue for the irreducibility of processuality to the trial, especially where emphasis is placed on its (voluntaristic) character of a 'judgement' aimed at adjudicating wrongs and reasons through an affirmation of a specific rule whose validity is determined by the assertion of its cogency in an imperative manner.

Law as 'Habilitation to Dialogue' – A Few Insights

While challenging the idea of a trial as the 'application of norms and procedures' presided over by an 'adjudicative' and heteronomous logic and carried out within a highly formalised procedure delegated to professionals and institutional subjects, mediation plays a significant role in fostering a critical reflection on the procedural institute and its relationship with law[20].

19 The importance of rediscovering law's pacifying function in a variety of forms has been recently argued in Greco 2021.

20 It is impossible to think of a full substitution of the legal process, whose function remains necessary, but not necessarily the one and only available. In the structural conflictuality of human existence, it is impossible and lacking realism to think of the consensual way of solving disputes as being capable of absorbing all kinds of controversies. See, for instance, some critical thoughts expressed by Fiss 1984.

If both in common and civil law systems the emergence of alternative models to the trial gives rise to criticism of depersonalising outcomes of the procedural institute as it is conceived and practised, it is possible to hypothesise that paradoxically the emergence of mediation also is a response to a need for a model of law that is more attentive to the experiential dimensions of intersubjectivity and dialogue.

The theme that lies at the heart of our questions posed in this chapter, in comparison with the Paduan philosophical–legal tradition, concerns the real possibility that the trial may always constitute the best implementation modality of a juridical perspective that conceives of law as the guardian and promoter of human *socialitas*, explicated first and foremost in the relational and dialogic character of human beings (and here dialogue is understood not only as an anthropological condition of structural relationality, but also as communication in action) (Reggio 2013).

The question is topical but has ancient roots, indeed. In fact, if we look at the pre-modern western legal conceptions, we can see that a close link between law and conflict resolution was already present in many Indo-European cultures and is still visible in the legacy of thought of the Greek classicism, and of the Roman world. In both cultures, indeed the centrality of the procedural dimension as a way for enabling the resolution of the conflict is clear (Moro 2021; Reggio 2022). However, one should also not forget the importance of consent-based ways of conflict resolution[21].

Confronting with this legacy, it emerges that 'the way of law' – as an alternative to 'the way of violence' is characterised by plurality of instruments by

21 Jacqueline Morineau, founder of the 'humanistic mediation' approach, found inspiration in Greek Tragedies to outline her triadic model of mediation (Morineau 1998). Other connections have been outlined between Greek Tragedy and instruments of conflict transformation outlined within the paradigm of *restorative justice*: see, e.g. Soulou 2022. Also, see the reference to the biblical tradition, Ost 1999, 2007. On the Roman legal world, see Milazzo 1990 and Burdese 1995. For a reference to the ancient world, see also Reggio 2021. Again, the already cited John William Cooley rooted the methodology of mediation in ancient rhetoric, thereby emphasising how the ancient approach to argumentation was embedded in the legal methodology, which according to the author includes also consensual instruments of conflict resolution: see Cooley 1993, 1994.

which the legal dimension tries to deal with the occurrence of conflict in a way that does not replicate the logic of violence, but rather seeks to transform it. As the 'process-centred perspective' understands, mostly by reconnecting to the classical tradition of legal thinking, rules and procedures *per se* are never enough to ensure order. If conflict is unavoidable – as a reflex of human structural limitedness and diversity – what is avoidable, instead, is resorting to violence and prevarication as a way to solve conflicts. In this sense, the true 'core' and philosophical justification of law resides in its capacity to *manifest, protect and restore* intersubjective dialogicality.

Manifesting, protecting and restoring all allude, not by chance, to three typical moments of the function of law, as they were construed by 'originators' of the Paduan Philosophy of Law, such as Giuseppe Capograssi. This conceptual triad recalls the three dimensions that characterise the core of law according to philosopher and jurist Giambattista Vico (1668–1744), whom Capograssi himself cited in various parts of his philosophical reflection (Capograssi 1925, 1959b).

The reference to Vico offers a valuable cue to understanding how the relationship between law and intersubjective dialogicality is not exclusively expressed within the need, albeit necessary, to 'convert conflict into controversy', but through forms and modalities that enable the parties to promote and protect the intersubjective relationship, which is also given within juridical dimensions other than those projected onto the controversy.

It is no coincidence that, starting from his legal works, Giambattista Vico, by reconnecting the legal dimension to the need to protect the (natural) societal dimension and, with it, to the function of preventing and resolving conflict in forms that are not abandoned to violence, had emphasised how the latter's function was not exhausted in one mode or form[22].

Starting from his reflection on 'fantastic universals', so strongly connected with mythological narratives that go back to the remote antiquity of western civilisation, Vico had in fact claimed that resolution of conflict was not entrusted solely to the dimension of the trial (to which he reconnected the

22 In fact, the law for Vico is 'eternal' in its principle but 'runs in time', to underline its capacity of historically and contextually assuming a variety of forms. For a first reconstruction of Vico's legal philosophy, see Bellofiore 1954.

symbol of *Vesta's fire*), but also to spaces in which law manifested itself through negotiation (to which he reconnected the symbol of *Mercury's caduceus*, which brought calm to the souls of the conflicting parties by inviting them to dialogue and confrontation)[23]. The 'negotiation dimension and the judicial dimension, therefore, are not grasped only in their reciprocal alternation, but in their constituting different modalities potentially aimed at the same end of preventing violence and recomposing the inter-subjective fabric torn by it' (Reggio 2021a,b).

More than the dimension of the will – whether it be manifested heteronomously in the judgement, or autonomously in the agreement – what characterises the path of law, is its capacity to present itself as an alternative to a self-referential and ultimate use of force as the sole criterion for resolving conflict. This alternative operates not only through the forms of controversy, but also through everything that *enables dialogue*, understood as much in its ethical–anthropological projection on the relationship as in its component of manifestation of the capacity to connect the variety of human manifestations with the *(dia)logos*, as the rationality which enables connections and discourses (Cavalla 1996).

On the contrary, on closer inspection, if it is the *logos* itself that enables the opportunity for connecting and reconnecting what the conflict has led to split, or even to silence, the pacifying value of law does not end in the monological illusion of norms nor in the cut made by the de-cider, whether it is made by a third party or by the parties themselves. Law as an instrument capable of bringing the *logos* into difference, law that becomes, precisely, *dia-logos*, is such because it enables and re-enables the *logos* itself where it has been forgotten, silenced or trampled upon.

The current emergence of mediation is better understood within this philosophical frame, thereby revealing a contemporary 'nostalgy' and need for rediscovering the law's function of '*habilitation to dialogue*' as 'the' path of law. Mediation, in this sense, does not constitute the only way to actualise this idea of law, but probably emerges as a phenomenon that puts emphasis

23 Such passage has been recently re-read in Mazzoleni 2019.

on a character of the legal dimension which had been long downsized and underrated by the modern and contemporary approach to conflict resolution.

Mediation as Maieutic of Dialogue

Summary

If, at the end of this brief philosophical dissertation, we are convinced that law is intertwined with the function of transforming inevitable conflicts in a way that makes violence evitable, and which does not embrace or imitate the prevaricatory structure of violence, then we return to recognizing that rules are never enough. There must be ways to organise interpersonal confrontation, and these cannot be reduced to mere procedural rituals, but they all need to offer a space for true dialogue to take place.

Law, therefore, is necessarily embedded with *dia-logos*, and, consequently, with legal argumentation.

Still, legal systems adopt a variety of tools for attempting to transform conflict in a dialogical way: some are heteronomous (like the judicial trial or arbitration), some others are autonomous (like mediation and negotiation); some are more, some less formalised; some involve an agonistic and ritualised confrontation, some others a more cooperative and informal way to engage in interpersonal communication.

The way mediation embraces the challenge of making the 'river' of conflict transformation place itself in the 'waterway' of *(dia)logos* is unique, because it involves a collaborative, participatory, flexible and less formalised approach to communicative interaction and, consequently, to both legal reasoning and legal argumentation.

According to the perspective that this chapter tries to purport, mediation is better understood if its voluntary and consensual element, its specific attention to narratives, stories and emotions, its capacity of widening the spectrum of analysis to interests and needs are all framed within the fact that mediation seeks to develop a reasoned and reasonable dialogue[24] and

24 As Sara Greco purports, mediation is a form of reasonable dialogue, based on a plurality of elements: 1. Ideally, it is a dialogue that 'in critical confrontation, takes into account the humanity of the participants, their person'. 2. Participants in a genuine

relies upon the latter to enable the possibility of a common solution, based on a common ground and common arguments (and reasons).

I believe, therefore, that, moving towards the methodological implications of my philosophical analysis, it is necessary to emphasise the connection between mediation and argumentation. This is an interpretative strand which should be further developed both in theory and in practice[25].

This is also a very important challenge, if we do not want mediation to be reduced merely to a factual and voluntaristic element of agreement: an accepted solution does not necessarily coincide with an acceptable one, and a common argument does not necessarily coincide with the best argument which parties were able to mutually outline, as the result of a reasoned and well-argumented dialogical confrontation.

A promising field for further research, therefore, would be to explore preconditions which make dialogue possible, as well as argumentative tools that enable its occurrence and ensure its best development in line with (or despite) specificities of each case and of each person involved. On closer inspection, in fact, it is on this boundary with the above-mentioned dialogic dimension that law reveals its necessary, specific and complex nature. However, it is also there that, above all, law reveals its most authentic and human side, which is not about a mere projection of authority, but, rather an ability to create and

argumentative dialogue accept that 'their position is not the only possible position' and thus agree to question and challenge themselves. 3. The fact that there are different points of view in a dialogue does not mean that 'there is no criterion for reasoning together' or that 'everything applies' regardless of content. Reasoned dialogue presupposes a commitment to a content-based examination of each other's positions and arguments. 4. Argumentative dialogue is ideally critical. The parties are committed to a reasonable solution to their disagreement. 5. It must revolve around certain issues that can be clearly defined by the parties, while also verifying the understanding of the topic discussed. See Greco 2017.

25 The connection between classic argumentation and mediation has been suggested in the pioneering work of John W. Cooley, whose most complete work can be found in Cooley 2006. Following this approach, I have personally developed the idea of mediation as a Socratic 'maieutics of dialogue'. See, e.g. Reggio & Sartor Hoffer 2017, 2019. Also, Sara Greco has recognised this aspect of mediation, putting an emphasis on the possibility of connecting mediation's methodology with a pragma-dialectical approach: see Greco 2011.

recreate peaceful and meaning connections after the inevitable occurrence of conflict. Thereby, law shows that violence is evitable and that it is exactly the way of the law.

Bibliography

Abel, Richard (1982). *The Politics of Informal Justice*. New York: Academic Press.

Arielli, Emanuele and Scotto, Giovanni (2003). *Conflitti e Mediazione. Introduzione a Una teoria Generale*. Milano: Bruno Mondadori.

Auerbach, Jerome S. (1983). *Justice without Law?: Non-Legal Dispute Settlement in American History*. Oxford: Oxford University Press.

Bellofiore, Luigi (1954). *La Dottrina del Diritto naturale in G. B. Vico*. Milano: Giuffrè.

Bix, Brian (2015). 'Rules and Normativity in Law'. In Michał Araszkiewicz, Paweł Banaś, Tomasz Gizbert-Studnicki and Krzysztof Płeszka (eds), *Problems of Normativity, Rules and Rule-Following*, pp. 125–146. London: Springer.

Burdese, Antonio (1995). 'Pacisci, Convenire, Contrahere', *Publicationes Universitatis Miskolciensis, Sectioiuridica et Politica*, 10, 3–16.

Baruch Bush, Robert and Folger, Joseph (1994). *The Promise of Mediation: Responding to Conflict through Empowerment and Recognition*. San Francisco: Jossey Bass.

Capograssi, Giuseppe (1925). 'Dominio, Libertà, Tutela nel De Uno', *Rivista Internazionale di Filosofia del Diritto*, 3 (III), 437–451.

Capograssi, Giuseppe (1959a). 'Giudizio, Processo, Scienza, Verità', *Giuseppe Capograssi, Opere, V*, pp. 58–76. Milano: Giuffrè.

Capograssi, Giuseppe (1959b). 'L'attualità di Vico', *Giuseppe Capograssi, Opere*. Milano: Giuffrè.

Cavalla, Francesco (1991). *La Prospettiva Processuale del Diritto. Saggio Sul Pensiero di Enrico Opocher*. Padova: Cedam.

Cavalla, Francesco (1996). *La Verità Dimenticata. Attualità dei Presocratici Dopo la Secolarizzazione*. Padova: Cedam.

Cavalla, Francesco (ed.) (2008). *Diritto, Processo, Verità*. Milano: Franco Angeli.

Cavalla, Francesco (2017). *L'Origine e il Diritto*. Milano: Franco Angeli.

Cavalla, Francesco (2022). 'Diritto, Principio e Processo. La Tragedia greca'. In Stefano Fuselli and Paolo Moro (eds), *Al Principio. Invitoalla Filosofia del Diritto*, pp. 129–163. Milano: Franco Angeli.

Christie, Nils (1977). 'Conflicts as Property', *British Journal of Criminology*, 17(1), 1–15.

Cobb, Sara (1994). 'A Narrative Perspective on Mediation: Toward the Materialization of the Storytelling Metaphor'. In Joseph Folger and Tricia Jones (eds), *New Directions in Mediation: Communication Research and Perspectives*, pp. 48–62. London: Sage.

Cooley, John W. (1993). 'Classical Approach to Mediation – Part I: Classical Rhetoric and the Art of the Persuasion in Mediation,' *University of Dayton Law Review*, 19, 83–131.

Cooley, John W. (1994). 'Classical Approach to Mediation – Part II: The Socratic Method and Conflict Reframing in Mediation', *University of Dayton Law Review*, 19 (2), 589–632.

Cooley, John W. (1998). 'Joke Structure: A Source of Creative Techniques for Use in Mediation', *University of San Francisco Law Review*, 33, 85–108.

Cooley, John W. (2006). *The Mediator's Handbook. Advanced Practice Guide for Civil Litigation*. Boulder (CO): National Institute for Trial Advocacy Press.

Cosi, Giovanni (2007). *Invece di Giudicare. Scritti Sulla Mediazione*. Milano: Giuffrè.

Cosi, Giovanni and Foddai, Maria A. (eds) (2003). *Lo Spazio della mediazione*. Milano: Giuffrè.

Cossutta, Marco (2019). 'L'avvenire del diritto e la sua prospettiva processuale', *Tigor. Rivista di Scienze della comunicazione e di Argomentazione giuridica*, 2, 73–78.

Di Grazia, Thomas (2016). *Light on Peacemaking. A Guide to Appropriate Dispute Resolution and Mediation Family Conflict*. New York: Business Expert Press.

Fisher, Roger, and Ury, William (1981). *Getting to Yes. Negotiating Agreement Without Giving in*. London: Penguin Books.

Fiss, Owen M. (1984). 'Against Settlement', *Yale Law Journal*, 93, 1073 ff.

Friedman, Barry (2007). 'Popular Dissatisfaction with the Administration of Justice: A Retrospective (and a Look ahead)', *Indiana Law Review*, 5, 1193–1214.

Fuselli, Stefano (2023). *La Verità nel Processo. Percorsi di Logica ed Epistemologia*. Milano: Franco Angeli.

Fuselli, Stefano, Moro, Paolo and Pariotti, Elena (eds) (2022). *Universa Universis Patavina Libertas. Filosofia del Diritto a Padova Tra innovazione e Tradizione. Per Celebrare gli 800 Anni Dell'Ateneo*, pp. 59–104. Padova: Primiceri.

Gentile, Francesco (1987). 'La controversia alla radice dell'esperienza giuridica'. In Pietro Perlingieri (ed.), *Soggetti e Norma, Individuo e Società*, pp. 141–152. Napoli: Esi.

Getzels, Jacob W. (1975). 'Problem-Finding and the Inventiveness of Solutions', *The Journal of Creative Behaviour*, 9 (1), 12–28.

Grassi, Ernesto (1976). 'The Priority of Common Sense and Imagination: Vico's Philosophical Relevance Today', *Social Research*, 43, 553–580.

Greco, Sara (2011). *Argumentation in Dispute Mediation*. Amsterdam: John Benjamin Publishing Company.

Greco, Sara (2017). *Dal Conflitto al Dialogo*. Firenze: Maggioli.

Greco, Tommaso (2021). *La Legge della Fiducia. Alle Radici del Diritto*. Roma-Bari: Laterza.

Hale, Katherine (1998). 'The Language of Cooperation: Negotiation Frames', *Mediation Quarterly*, 16 (2), 147–162.

Harris Crowne, Caroline (2001). 'The Alternative Dispute Resolution Act of 1998: Implementing a New Paradigm of justice', *New York Law Review*, 76, 1768–1811.

Irvine, Charlie and Farrington, Laurel R. (2016). 'Mediation and Emotions: Perception and Regulation'. In John Stannard and Heather Conway (eds), *The Emotional Dynamics of Law and Legal Discourse*, pp. 211–239. Oxford: Hart Publishing.

Kinsey, William, Fuller, Rex M. and McKinney, Bruce C. (1993). 'Mediator Listening, Dispute Reframing, and Mediation Outcome: A Pilot Study', *International Listening Association Journal*, 1, 74–91.

Lederach, John P. (2003). *The Little Book of Conflict Transformation*. Intercourse (PA): Good Books.

Marmor, Andrei and Sarch, Alexander (2019). 'The Nature of Law'. In Edward E. Zalta (ed.), *The Stanford Encyclopedia of Philosophy*, Fall Edition, <https://plato.stanford.edu/archives/fall2019/entries/lawphil-nature/>.

Mazzoleni, Emil (2019). 'Universali fantastici giuridici. Narrazioni Normative in Giambattista Vico', *Dirittopenale e Uomo*, 9, 1–22.

Sturm, Fritz (1990). 'Il Pactum e le sue Molteplici applicazioni'. In: *Contractus et Pactum Tipicità e Libertà negoziale nell'esperienza Tardo Repubblicana, Atti del Convegno di Dirittoromano e di Presentazione della Littera Florentina (Copanello, 1–4 giugno 1988)*, pp. 149–180. Napoli: Esi.

Monoriti, Angelo (2023). *Dall'Ordine imposto all'Ordine negoziato*. Milano: Giuffrè.

Morineau, Jacqueline (1998). *L'Esprit de la Mediation*. Toulouse: Eres.

Moro, Paolo (ed.) (2012). 'Il Diritto Come Processo', *Principi, Regole e Brocardi per la Formazione critica del Giurista*. Milano: Franco Angeli.

Moro, Paolo (2014). *Alle Origini del Nòmosnella Grecia Classica. Una Prospettivadella Legge per il Presente*, pp. 20–78. Milano: Franco Angeli.

Moro, Paolo (2021). 'Lo Scudo di Achille. Il Processo Come Archetipo di Pace', *Mediares. Rivista Su trasformazione dei conflitti, Cultura della riparazione e Mediazione*, 1, 22–46.

Moro, Paolo (2022). 'La Prospettiva processuale del diritto oggi'. In Stefano Fuselli and Paolo Moro (eds), *Al Principio. Invitoalla Filosofia del Diritto*, pp. 391–412. Milano: Franco Angeli.

Opocher, Enrico (1983). 'Il Diritto nell'Esperienza pratica: la Processualità del Diritto', *Lezioni di Filosofia del Diritto*, p. 285 ff. Padova: Cedam.

Opocher, Enrico (2005). *Lezioni metafisiche sul diritto, a Cura di Franco Todescan*. Padova: Cedam.

Ost, François (1999). *Du Sinaï au Champ-de-Mars. Lautre et le Même au Fondement du Droit*. Bruxelles: Lessius.

Ost, François (2007). *Mosè, Eschilo, Sofocle. All'Origine dell'Immaginario giuridico*. Bologna: Il Mulino.

Poscher, Ralf (2019). 'Hermeneutics and Law'. In Michael N. Forster and Kristin Gjesdal (eds), *The Cambridge Companion to Hermeneutics. Cambridge Companions to Philosophy*, pp. 326–353. Cambridge: Cambridge University Press.

Pound, Roscoe (1937). 'The Causes of Popular Dissatisfaction with the Administration of Justice', *Journal of American Judicature Society*, 10 (4), 20 ff.

Raz, Joseph (2009) *The Authority of Law*. Oxford: Oxford University Press.

Reggio, Federico (2012a) '"Norma del Caso" e soluzioni concordate della controversia in ambito civile. Alcune riflessioni su una: "Zona Limite" Della positività giuridica'. In Paolo Moro and Claudio Sarra (eds), *Teoria e Prassi nella formazione giudiziale del Diritto Positività e Giurisprudenza*, pp. 217–251. Milano: Franco Angeli.

Reggio, Federico (2012b). 'A "Discarded Image". Rediscovering Vico's Lesson as a Topical Heritage for the Contemporary Reflection on Law and Justice,' *L'Ircocervo*, 1, 1–29.

Reggio, Federico (2013). 'Dialogical Justice. Philosophical Considerations for Re-thinking the Reaction to Crime in a Restorative Way'. In John Blad, David Cornwell and Martin Wright (eds), *Civilizing Criminal Justice. An International Restorative Agenda for Penal Reform*, pp. 315–346. Hook-Hampshire (U.K.): Waterside Press.

Reggio, Federico (2017). '*Concordare la Norma. Gli strumenti consensuali di soluzione della controversia in ambito civile. Una Prospettiva filosofico-metodologica*'. Padova: Cleup.

Reggio, Federico (2021a). 'La Pax Attraverso il Pactum. Note a margine della figura di Pietro Patrizio, Negoziatore di età Giustinianea'. In Massimo Antonazzi and Paola Betti *Negoziatori* (eds), *Italiani. Analisitecnica di Negoziatiefficaci*, pp. 193–228. Roma: Eurilink University Press.

Reggio, Federico (2021b). '*Il Paradigma scartato. Saggiosulla Filosofia del Diritto di Giambattista Vico*', pp. 218–219. Padova: Primiceri.

Reggio, Federico (2022). 'Dirittocontroversia e Processo: Due Immaginidall'Iliade (Focus IV)'. In Stefano Fuselli and Paolo Moro (eds), *Al Principio. Invitoallafilosofia del Diritto*, pp. 120–125. Milano: Franco Angeli.

Reggio, Federico and Sartor Hoffer, Marina (2017). 'Educating to Dialogue: Connecting an Argumentative Approach to Mediation and Educational Transactional Analysis. Some Transkills Signposts for Promoting Complex, Inclusive and Participative Societies'.

In: *Proceedings of the 34th International Academic Conference of The International Institute of Social and Economic Sciences*, Florence 13–17 September 2017. Prague: International Institute of Social and Economic Studies, pp. 214–231.

Reggio, Federico and Sartor Hoffer, Marina (2019). 'Maieutic for Dialogue: Connecting an Argumentative Approach to Mediation and Educational Transactional Analysis'. In Patrizia Lattarulo, Francesco Palermo, Vincenzo Provenzano and Thomas Streifeneder (eds), *The Regions of Europe Between Local Identities, New Communities and Territorial Disparities*, pp. 379–396. Milano: Franco Angeli.

Schauer, Frederick (1991). *Playing by the Rules*. Oxford: Oxford University Press.

Shaffer, John D. (1990). *Sensus Communis: Vico, Rhetoric, and the Limits of Relativism*. London: Duke University Press.

Slob, Wouther (2002). *Dialogical Rhetoric. An Essay on Truth and Normativity After Postmodernism*. Dordrecht-Utrecht: Springer.

Smith, Roger (1996). *Achieving Civil Justice. Appropriate Dispute Resolution for the 1990s*. Edinburgh: Scottish Legal Action Group.

Soulou, Katerina (2022). 'The Heritage of Greek Tragedies as Source of Inspiration for Restorative Justice in Theoria and in Praxis', *Mediares*, 1, 47–58.

Spangler, Brad (2003) 'Win–Win, Win–Lose, and Lose–Lose Situations'. In Guy Burgess and Heidi Burgess (eds), *Beyond Intractability.* University of Colorado: Conflict Information Consortium.

Stewart, John and Milt, Thomas (2002). 'Dialogic Listening: Sculpting Mutual Meanings'. In John Stewar (ed.), *Bridges Not Walls*, pp. 184–201. New York: McGraw-Hill.

't Hart, August C. (1982–1983). 'La Metodologia giuridica vichiana', *Bollettino del Centro di Studi Vichiani*, XII–XIII.

Wolfe, Jeffrey S. (2001). 'Across the Ripple of Time: The Future of Alternative (Or Is It Appropriate) Dispute Resolution', *Tulsa Law Review*, 36, 785–812.

Wood, William R. and Suzuki, Masahiro (2000). 'Are Conflicts Property? Re-Examining the Ownership of Conflict in Restorative Justice', *Social & Legal Studies*, 29 (6), 903–924.

Zaccaria, Giuseppe (2006). *Omaggio ad un Maestro. Ricordo di Enrico Opocher.* Padova: Cedam.

Zanuso, Francesca (1993). *Conflitto e Controllo sociale nel pensiero Politico-Giuridico moderno.* Padova: Cleup.

Zanuso, Francesca (2022). 'La Fragile Zattera di Ulisse. Alcune riflessioni sul ruolo della Norma Positiva nella composizione del Conflitto'. In Stefano Fuselli and Paolo Moro (eds), *Principio. Invitoalla Filosofia del Diritto*, pp. 305–336. Milano: Franco Angeli.

Zanuso, Francesca and Fuseli, Stefano (eds) (2011). *Il Liscio di Atena. Funzioni, Strumenti ed Esiti della controversia giuridica*. Milano: Franco Angeli.

CHAPTER 3

The Concept of Mediation in International Public Law

Marta Pietras-Eichberger[1]

Introduction[1]

The topic of mediation is a relatively new research issue, especially at the public international law level, including the law of the European Union (EU). The concept of mediation has existed for centuries, but codification and standardisation of provisions relating to mediation in international law started in the late nineteenth century. The first provisions on mediation were contained in the Hague Convention of 1899[2]. Mediation is also one of the peaceful means of resolving international disputes set out in Chapter VI of the United Nations Charter[3] and in certain multilateral international agreements of a regional nature. The very concept of mediation in international law derives from alternatives to resolution of international disputes and conflicts by force.

The purpose of this chapter is to show that mediation is not only based on solutions adopted in the internal laws of individual countries, but also originates from international law, both codified and in the form of a set of standards. The specific objective is to demonstrate that, despite different categories of disputes being resolved by means of alternative dispute resolution (ADR), which mediation is a part of – both at the international state-to-state level and at the local natural/legal person-to-person level – the aims and principles of mediation are almost the same.

1 PhD, Institute of European Studies, Jagiellonian University, mediator, attorney at law, email: <marta.pietras-eichberger@uj.edu.pl>

2 1899 Convention for the Pacific Settlement of International Disputes, <https://docs.pca-cpa.org/2016/01/1899-Convention-for-the-Pacific-Settlement-of-International-Disputes.pdf>, accessed 1 July 2024.

3 United Nations Charter (1947). 'Statute of the International Court of Justice and Agreement Establishing the Preparatory Commission of the United Nations signed in San Francisco on 26 June 1945', *Official Journal of Poland of 1947*, 23 (item 90).

The main research method employed in Chapter III will be legal dogmatics consisting of a legal (logical linguistic) analysis of definitions and procedures regarding mediation as stipulated in binding international agreements. Chapter III also aims to compare definitions, ideas and functions of mediation as found in various binding legal instruments at the universal and regional law level, by using a comparative method. In addition, non-binding documents with the status of good practices, recommended standards and recommendations adopted mainly at the United Nations (UN) level will be analysed.

As early as 1800 BC, mediation and arbitration were used in the territory of Mari Kingdom (in modern Syria) to resolve dispute with other kingdoms. Diplomacy as a form of mediation/negotiation between rulers was used in ancient Egypt, Greece, and in 1000 BC the Western Zhou Dynasty created the position of a mediator. Just two examples of important mediation processes that had an impact on the history of mankind include: ending the 30-Years' War in 1648 with the active role of Count Maximilian mediating on the side of the Holy Roman Empire, and the mediation efforts of Teddy Roosevelt, which in 1906 led to the peace agreement that ended the Russo-Japanese War (Barrett & Barrett 2004).

Sunday Akinolu Fagbemi underlines that the use of mediation to resolve disputes has a long history and takes slightly different forms depending on geographical location and cultural aspects. However, the current global interest in mediation as a conflict management technique can be traced back to the Modern Mediation Movement in the United States, which in the 1970s spread to Australia and then to Europe and South Africa. Fagbemi also points out that mediation is historically embedded in Chinese legal culture (Fagbemi 2020).

Mediator goes back to the Latin word 'mediate', meaning to be in the middle, to mediate a dispute (Taslim 2017). Mediation and other forms of ADR are used by people, organisations, states, governments and corporate enterprises; so the group of stakeholders is virtually unlimited (Naureen et al. 2023). Indeed, ADR techniques can be used both to resolve disputes between a public entity and private corporations, as exemplified by the case study of the conflict that arose during the construction of the San Ramos bypass by Britco for the US Army Corps of Engineers (Senan et al. 2018). Chapter III will focus primarily on mediation between states, although in recent years there have been noticeable attempts, especially on the regional level, to codify and institutionalise principles of mediation between actors other than states.

It seems that consideration of the codification of mediation in international law should begin with the Convention for the Pacific Settlement of International Disputes of 1899, which established the Permanent Court of Arbitration (PCA) as the first permanent intergovernmental organisation focused on resolving international disputes through peaceful means.

Subsequently, in 1907, the peace conference in The Hague adopted a convention under essentially the same title, Chapter II of which entitled 'Good Offices and Mediation', is devoted entirely to these two alternative ways of resolving disputes. Importantly, the chapter highlights the significance of mediation during warfare[4].

Adopted in San Francisco on 26th June 1945, the Charter of the United Nations, in Article 33, Chapter VI 'Pacific Settlement of Disputes', explicitly mentions mediation as one of the alternative means of resolving disputes, continuance of which are likely to endanger the maintenance of international peace and security. It thus requires states to resort to peaceful means of dispute resolution as a matter of priority. This article contains an open-ended catalogue of ADR means, giving states freedom to choose one of the means listed in the article, or to use 'other peaceful means of their own choice'.

The flexible and open-ended structure of the catalogue of peaceful dispute resolution measures in Article 33 of the UN Charter underlines the idea and spirit of mediation as one of possible, not legally imposed measures of resolving disputes. The UN engages in mediation through the Secretary-General or through the General Assembly, which recommends that the Security Council continue mediation. The same Article 33 of the UN Charter grants the Security Council the initiative to call upon parties to settle their dispute by means of one of the ADR measures listed therein (Handbook 1992). In addition to mediation, Article 33 of the UN Charter mentions negotiation, enquiry, conciliation, arbitration, judicial settlement, resort to regional

4 Convention for the Pacific Settlements of International Disputes adopted in The Hague on 18 October 1907, <https://cil.nus.edu.sg/wp-content/uploads/2017/07/1907-The-Hague-Convention-for-the-Pacific-Settlement-of-International-Disputes-1.pdf>, accessed 1 July 2024.

agencies or arrangements and the above-mentioned other peaceful means of their own choice. This means, firstly, that the Security Council, according to Article 24(1) of the UN Charter, is responsible for the maintenance of international peace and security, and, in this respect, has the power to impose certain courses of action on states in order to avoid escalation of a dispute. Secondly, the use of ADR may be mandatory for states. Of course, certain UN challenges connected with the crisis between permanent members of the Security Council and their inability to effectively agree on moral, political and legal assessments of current disputes and/or conflicts between states give rise to doubts about enforcing states' commitment to peaceful dispute settlement.

When it comes to mediation clauses in international law, one should also mention regional multilateral treaties that directly or indirectly refer to the concept and objectives of mediation in relations between states.

The Inter-American Treaty on Good Offices and Mediation was adopted by the Inter-American Conference for the Maintenance of Peace[5] and ratified by fourteen states from South America, Central America and the USA (but in relation to Cuba and the USA, the treaty never entered into force). In Article 1 of this Treaty, institutions of mediation and good offices are linked. Interestingly, the Treaty does not provide a definition of mediation or good offices, indicating only that they apply to disputes between states that are parties thereto which cannot be resolved by diplomatic means. In a situation of dispute, Article 1 recommends parties to use the mediation of a citizen of any of the US countries chosen from a list of people distinguished by reason of his/her high character or juridical learning. According to Article 2 of the Treaty, each state has the right to designate two persons for the list regardless of its population potential or territory. Therefore, the principle of equality in the number of persons representing a country on the so-called general list was used. From the perspective of contemporary standards concerning the educational requirements of mediators, the emphasis on 'high juridical learning' is interesting. Article 3 of the 1936 Inter-American Treaty provides for a rather

5 Inter-American Treaty on Good Offices and Mediation, signed at Buenos Aires on 23 December 1936, League of Nations Treaty Series 1938, vol. CLXXXVIII, No. 4353, <https://treaties.un.org/doc/Publication/UNTS/LON/Volume%20188/v188.pdf>, accessed 2 July 2024.

complicated method of selecting the mediator/the person lending his good offices in the absence of agreement between the countries in controversy. This is an example of delegates being chosen to select the actual mediator. This indirect method is intended to allow a mutually acceptable person to be selected.

Subsequent articles of the analysed Treaty define rules of mediation by indicating a minimum and a maximum time for reaching a peaceful settlement of the dispute, i.e. from 3 to 6 months. Article 4 stipulates that after 6 months, if there is no consensus between the parties on how to resolve the dispute, a procedure of conciliation based on other applicable Inter-American agreements is triggered. Article 5 provides for contracting parties to bear their own costs and to share equally in common costs or honoraria.

Not adapted at the level of a specific geographical region, but at the level of Arab culture states, Article 5 of the Pact of the League of Arab States prohibits the use of force to settle disputes between countries[6]. In disputes that do not involve the independence of a state, its sovereignty or its territorial integrity, if both disputing parties apply to The Council of the League to settle the dispute, the decision of The Council on the proposal to settle the dispute will be effective and obligatory. Article 5 of the Pact goes on to use the term mediation explicitly to refer to mediation by the aforementioned Council in any dispute that may lead to war between two Member States of the League of Arab States, or a Member State and a non-LAS state. This is, therefore, a classic mediation to reconcile states in dispute. The Pact includes the institution of mediation and of arbitration in one article. Arbitration and mediation decisions are made by a majority vote.

The Pact of Bogota was signed in 1948 by the US states to settle disputes between states by peaceful means[7]. The Pact was concluded during the Ninth International Conference of American States based on Article XXIII of the Charter of the Organization of American States[8]. In Article 2 of this Pact,

6 The Pact of the League of Arab States concluded in Cairo on 22 March 1945, *Arab Law Quarterly*, 1992, 7 (2), pp. 148–152.

7 The American Treaty on Pacific Settlement (Pact of Bogota) signed in Bogota on 30 April 1948, U.S. Department of State, <https://2009-2017.state.gov/p/wha/rls/70580.htm>, accessed 6 July 2024.

8 Charter of the Organization of American States, signed in Bogota on 30 Apri1 1948 (entry into force 13 December 1951), <https://www.scribd.com/document/262897822/OAS-Charter-1948>, accessed 6 July 2024.

countries committed to settling disputes between themselves first through regional procedures before submitting them to The Security Council of the United Nations. The same article provides for two means of peaceful dispute settlement, i.e. direct negotiations by diplomatic channels or, alternatively, such special procedures which, in the disputing states' opinion, will permit them to arrive at a solution. Under Chapter II of the Pact of Bogota, the special procedures concerned include good offices and mediation. Articles IX to XIV provide general definitions and general guidelines for both procedures, which are practically the same.

Article XI of the Pact indicates that the mediator or mediators are to be selected by the parties by mutual agreement from among eminent citizens of any US state or a party to the controversy. Therefore, there are no formal criteria regarding the educational background of mediators. Article XII broadly defines the purpose of mediation as the simplest and most direct manner of dispute settlement avoiding formalities. The entire mediation process is fully confidential, which is underlined not so much by the absence of any obligation for the mediator(s) to make a report of the mediation, but by the direct statement that no report is to be made of the mediation.

It should be underlined that Article VIII of the Pact explicitly states that pacific means that the solution of controversies cannot delay the exercise of the right to individual or collective self-defence.

In 1963, under the auspices of the African Union, the Charter of the Organisation of African Unity (OAU) was adopted, in which Member States pledged to settle all disputes between themselves by peaceful means[9]. Article XIX of this Charter establishes a Commission of Mediation, Conciliation and Arbitration, the composition and conditions of service of which are set out in a separate protocol forming an integral part of the Charter[10].

9 The Charter of the Organisation of African Unity, established in Addis Ababa on 25 May 1963, <https://au.int/sites/default/files/treaties/7759-file-oau_charter_1963.pdf>, accessed 8 July 2024.

10 The Protocol of the Commission of Mediation, Conciliation and Arbitration, adopted in Cairo on 21 July 1964, *International Legal Materials*, 1964, 3 (6), 1116–1124, <https://www.jstor.org/stable/2068984>, accessed 9 July 2024.

Article XI of the 1964 Protocol established the seat of the Commission in Addis Ababa, Ethiopia; Article XII limited its jurisdiction to disputes between countries, thus excluding the possibility of ADR between other subjects of international law. In the case of a controversy arising between countries, parties may choose one of three modes of settlement: mediation, conciliation or arbitration.

It is worth noting that the Protocol's provisions on conciliation and arbitration are much more extensive than those on mediation. Shared provisions are contained in Part II of the Protocol, 'General Provisions', which sets out in very general terms how to initiate an ADR procedure. Article XIII of the Protocol indicates that the procedure begins with a presentation to the Commission of the dispute by parties or party concerned or by the Council of Ministers (African Union body) or by the Assembly of Heads of State and Government.

Article II of the aforementioned Protocol stipulates that member of the Commission, established under The Charter of OAU, are to be appointed from among persons with recognised professional qualifications. At the same time, it is not specified which qualifications are concerned. Further on, Part III stipulates that one or more members of the Commission are designated by the President, who, according to Article VI of the Protocol, is elected by the Assembly of Heads of State and Government for a term of 5 years. There are no additional stipulations regarding the manner, procedure or criteria for selection of mediator(s). Under Article XXI of the Protocol, the mediator's role is limited to reconciling the views and claims of parties to the dispute. The mediator presents parties with a proposal for resolving the dispute in writing as soon as possible. If parties accept the mediator's proposal, it becomes the basis for a memorandum of understanding between the parties.

On 1st December 1959 in Washington, DC, twelve countries signed the Antarctic Treaty, in which they undertook to use Antarctica for peaceful purposes and to prevent it from becoming the object of international discord[11]. The treaty prohibits states from using the area south of 60° south latitude for nuclear tests and disposal of radioactive waste material. Only one

11 The Antarctic Treaty, signed in Washington on 1 December 1959, *Official Journal of 1961*, 46 (item 237), Annex.

article (Article XI) is devoted to the means of peaceful settlement of disputes. Paragraph 1 of this article requires parties to settle disputes arising from the application or interpretation of the provisions of the Treaty by peaceful means. The catalogue of measures is open-ended, leaving the parties freedom to settle disputes not only by negotiation, inquiry, mediation, conciliation, arbitration and judicial settlement, but also by any other peaceful means. Pursuant to Article XI(2) of the Treaty concerned a dispute, with the consent of all parties to the dispute, may be referred to the International Court of Justice (ICJ) for settlement. However, if a dispute is not settled by the ICJ, the parties should seek a peaceful resolution of their dispute. It is noteworthy that mediation, as well as other means of peaceful dispute resolution, are applied to the most difficult issues concerning the exploration of a disputed area, rich in valuable deposits and potentially used for nuclear testing during the cold war, before the official court route before the ICJ. The Antarctic Treaty of 1959 was signed by both the United States of America and the Union of Soviet Socialist Republics.

Another document in which the international community refers to mediation as one of the peaceful means of resolving international disputes between countries is the 1970 Declaration on Principles of International Law concerning friendly relations and co-operation among states in accordance with the Charter of the UN[12]. The Declaration solemnly proclaimed seven principles of international law, including the principle of settlement of disputes between states by peaceful means in point 2. In six sub-points, this principle underlines the obligation of states to use peaceful means to settle international disputes, which in addition to negotiation, inquiry, mediation, conciliation, arbitration and judicial settlement, also include the use of regional agencies or regional arrangements, as well as other means at the choice of parties to a dispute. If no settlement of the dispute is reached by one of the above means, parties have the duty to settle the dispute by

12 Declaration on Principles of International Law concerning Friendly Relations and Co-operation among States in accordance with the Charter of the United States, adopted by the General Assembly of the United States in New York on 24 October 1970, A/RES/2625, <https://documents.un.org/doc/resolution/gen/nr0/348/90/pdf/nr034890.pdf?token=NppnJn5gwgRGAxW20W&fe=true>, accessed 25 July 2024.

other peaceful means. The 1970 Declaration is directly linked with the UN Charter and emphasises the peaceful resolution of the most serious disputes that could lead to the use of force against territorial integrity or the political independence of a state.

In similar wording, the Final Act of Conference on Security and Cooperation in Europe of 1975[13] requires states to settle disputes by peaceful means. The catalogue of means of peaceful settlement of disputes is open-ended and includes negotiation, enquiry, mediation, conciliation, arbitration, judicial settlement or other peaceful means of their own choice, including any settlement procedure agreed to in advance of disputes to which states are parties.

The Manila Declaration on the Peaceful Settlement of Disputes reiterates the idea of using exclusively peaceful means to resolve disputes between states[14]. The declaration mentions peaceful means of dispute resolution set out in Chapter VI of the Charter of the UN. The Manila Declaration does not elaborate on the provisions of specific peaceful means of dispute resolution, including mediation, but indicates that legal disputes should be referred by parties to the ICJ.

The most comprehensive, albeit regional, piece of legislation devoted entirely to mediation as an ADR method is Directive 2008/52/EC on certain aspects of mediation in civil and commercial matters[15].

EU Member States were required to implement the Directive into their national laws, and twenty six of them did so, with the exception of Denmark and the United Kingdom of Great Britain and Northern Ireland – an EU member at the time. Poland implemented the Directive concerned by amending the

---

13 The Final Act of the Conference on Security and Cooperation in Europe signed in Helsinki on 1 August 1975, <https://www.osce.org/files/f/documents/5/c/39501.pdf>, accessed 25 July 2024.

14 The Manila Declaration on the Peaceful Settlement of Disputes, the annex to the General Assembly resolution 37/10, adopted in New York on 15 November 1982, <https://peacemaker.un.org/node/93>, accessed 25 July 2024.

15 Directive 2008/52/EC of the European Parliament and the Council of 21 May 2008 on certain aspects of mediation in civil and commercial matters, OJ L 136/3 on 24 May 2008, <https://eur-lex.europa.eu/legal-content/en/ALL/?uri=CELEX:32008L0052#:~:text=DIRECTIVE%202008/52/EC%20OF%20THE%20EUROPEAN%20PARLIAMENT>, accessed 10 July 2024.

Civil Procedure Code Act of 17 November 1964 and the Civil Code Act of 23 April 1964 and by issuing the Order of the Minister of Justice No. 24/09/PR of 3 April 2009 establishing the Public Council to the Minister of Justice for Alternative Methods of Conflict and Dispute Resolution.

The preamble of Directive 2008/52/EC provides a very broad outline of objectives and the value of mediation as a cost-effective and quick method of extrajudicial dispute resolution. The Directive, unlike universal international law instruments of both a binding and non-binding nature, is addressed to states with a view to issuing relevant domestic legislation, but it concerns the mediation of cross-border civil disputes and commercial disputes between natural and legal persons. It, therefore, does not cover conflicts between objects of international law, i.e. mainly states, which, through escalation, may threaten security, peace or justice at the EU level.

Directive 2008/52/EC introduces definitions of mediation and mediator at the EU level. Article 3(a) of the Directive defines mediation as a structured, voluntary process in which at least two parties, with the assistance of a mediator, seek to resolve a dispute. This definition encompasses a facilitative model of mediation, which suggests that the parties themselves should reach a resolution of the dispute (ADR Report 1998). Mediation may be initiated by parties to a dispute themselves, by a court or may be prescribed by the internal law of an EU Member State. It should be noted, however, that the Directive emphasises the voluntary nature of mediation; therefore, the obligation to submit to mediation under national legislation may be enforced provided that the right of access to a judicial system is ensured. Further on, according to Article 3(b) of the Directive, a mediator is any third person who is asked to conduct a mediation. The Directive stipulates that it is not the profession exercised by the mediator in a given Member State that matters, but the manner in which the mediation is conducted, which should be effective, impartial and competent. It is up to the Member States to define standards that a mediator must meet in order to ensure the quality of mediation.

As Oksana Melenko (2020) points out, even though the number of disputes resolved by means of an alternative out-of-court-procedure is growing, there are still many legislative gaps that negatively affect the perception of mediation. Additionally, in many countries the process of ADR institution establishment has only just begun or is still ongoing (Melenko 2020).

Another important binding piece of international law is the Singapore Convention on Mediation, which harmonised and codified standards for enforcement of mediation settlement agreements in international commercial cases[16]. The Singapore Convention aims to strengthen mediation as an effective and efficient means of resolving disputes between commercial entities, relative to other methods of alternative means of international dispute resolution. The Singapore Convention does not apply to settlements concluded in the context of employment, family and inheritance law disputes, even if they meet the criterion of an international dispute. The Singapore Convention introduces a fairly general definition of mediation by stipulating that it is a process leading to an amicable resolution of a dispute with the assistance of a third person or persons.

It should be noted that in 1958 the New York Convention on the Recognition and Enforcement of Foreign Arbitral Awards was adopted, and in 2005 the Hague Convention on Choice of Court Agreements were adopted, so the Singapore Convention fills the gap in recognition of solutions adopted under other dispute resolution methods. It, therefore, raises the profile of mediation vis-à-vis arbitration and court awards.

One should note the results of the comparative study of all ADR methods conducted by Oksana Melenko. As a result of her work, she ranked mediation the highest in terms of benefits for parties. She identified only two weaknesses of mediation, i.e. lack of guarantees to affect the terms of the mediation procedure, and lack of formalised criteria, including those related to legal education, to be met by mediators (Melenko 2020). Authors of the Alternative Dispute Resolution Practitioners Guide (Brown et al. 1996) also call for creation of procedures for regular evaluation of mediators' work to ensure high quality mediation.

Interestingly, critics of mediation and other forms of ADR argue that these methods undermine the role of courts in the dispute resolution process, and

16 United Nations Convention on International Settlement Agreements Resulting from Mediation (Singapore Convention on Mediation), adopted in New York on 20 December 2018, open to signature in Singapore on 7 August 2019, <https://uncitral.un.org/sites/uncitral.un.org/files/media-documents/EN/Texts/UNCITRAL/Arbitration/mediation_convention_v1900316_eng.pdf>, accessed 27 July 2024.

that resolution itself, by relying on non-legal criteria, may threaten compliance and lead to privatisation of the legal system (Naureen et al. 2023). Some dangers associated with the use of mediation are also mentioned by Carrie Menkel-Meadow (2004), who points to the lack of state oversight of the extrajudicial dispute resolution process and the associated inequality of the parties, which may lead to forcing the socially weaker party to accept a solution imposed by the economically stronger party (Menkel-Meadow 2004). The imbalance of power between parties and the associated inability of an inherently neutral mediator to intervene is increasingly being noted by mediation practitioners (Benedikt et al. 2020). This risk may also materialise in disputes between superpower states and, for example, states with little economic, military or other potential, entailing the abuse of their position by stronger states. A mediator may not influence the solution accepted by parties even if, from an objective point of view, it is unfair to one of them. Therefore, it appears that mediation may not be the best method to end, for example, the armed conflict between Russia and Ukraine that began in 2022.

On the other hand, the essence of mediation is that it is private, confidential and shielded from the public. Its aim is to facilitate a mutually acceptable resolution of a dispute, with the role of a mediator being the opposite to that of a judge who imposes a solution on parties. A mediator's role is to bridge communication barriers between disputing parties, or to improve communication by helping parties understand each other's claims through, for example, facilitating information flow or curbing emotions that can arise during both individual and state disputes (Mnookin 1998).

Importantly, due to the flexibility of mediation regulations, the role of a mediator may develop during the mediation process, as was the case, for example, in the 1962 case of New Guinea which was referred to mediation by the UN Secretary-General. Originally, the mediator's role was to prepare the ground for formal negotiations, but ultimately the mediator worked out entire agreements with the parties through informal and secret discussions (Handbook 1992).

Summary

To sum up, there is no unanimous and comprehensive definition of mediation, nor is it clearly separated from other ADR means. A solution recurring in international law links definitions of mediation and good offices, or mediation and conciliation as peaceful/alternative means of dispute resolution between states.

Certainly, mediation as a method of peaceful settlement is more than a complement to negotiation. In UN practice, it has become a distinctive method for facilitating dialogue between parties to an international dispute, redirecting parties towards a peaceful dispute resolution. Mediation reduces tension in an international dispute; thus, it has a precautionary role preventing the rupture of pacific relations between states (Handbook on the Peaceful Settlement of Disputes between States 1992). As in mediation between parties other than states, the main function of mediation between states is to reconcile opposing claims of parties and to promote a solution that will be, to some extent, satisfactory to all (usually two) parties to the dispute.

Interestingly, requirements, or perhaps more precisely the lack of specific requirements that must be met by persons selected as mediators, is also apparent in the legal texts analysed. In fact, the only recurring criterion is that a mediator should be selected from among 'eminent citizens of the state' (Art. XI Pact of Bogota 1948). Sometimes an additional condition in the form of a certain background and/or experience is stipulated. Absence of clear criteria to be met by persons performing the function, or perhaps rather the profession of mediator, may have both a negative impact on the quality of mediation, and a positive one as it provides a very high degree of freedom to choose a person trusted by all parties – especially at the state level.

An important recurring aspect of the use of peaceful means of dispute resolution between states in many international documents is the freedom to choose the specific means, the consent of all parties to a dispute to use that particular means and, importantly, the absence of a hierarchy of peaceful means of dispute resolution. The idea behind the use of peaceful means of dispute resolution boils down to choosing a particular means that suits the circumstances of the dispute and other aspects that are important to parties. While analysing provisions relating to the concept and principles of mediation in international law, two features of this method of dispute resolution come to the fore: it is voluntary, and parties are fully independent in managing their conflict, and the ways to end it, or deciding to move to another ADR method.

Finally, it should be assumed that the main objectives, values and general principles of mediation are almost identical to the conventions adopted within international organisations and by individual states implementing Directive 2008/52/EC. Of course, the subject matter of mediation differs. While domestic laws mainly regulate mediation relating to civil and commercial law matters, treaties cover mediation between states in disputes that may threaten peace or security. With a large dose of caution, it should be assumed that disputes between states concerning sovereignty and territorial integrity are excluded from mediation. Such clear exemption is found in the Pact of the League of Arab States. In the light of other conventions, it appears that mediation is regarded as a preliminary method that lays the ground for more formalised methods of ending a conflict.

Bibliography

Ahammad, Taslim (2017). 'Mediation as Alternative Dispute Resolution', *The Asian Age*, 1–3. https://www.researchgate.net/publication/322888087_Mediation_as_alternative_dispute_resolution/citations#fullTextFileContent (Accessed: 25 July 2024).

Barrett, Jerome T., and Barrett, Joseph P. (2004). '*A History of Alternative Dispute Resolution. The Story of a Political, Cultural and Social Movement*'. San Francisco: Jossey-Bass.

Benedikt, Antoni, Susło, Robert, Paplicki, Mateusz, and Drobinik, Jarosław (2020). 'Mediation as an Alternative Method of Conflict Resolution: A Practical Approach', *Family Medicine & Primary Care Review*, 22 (3), 235–239.

Brown, Scott, Cervenak, Christine, and Fairman, David (1996). '*Alternative Dispute Resolution Practitioners Guide*', <https://pdf.usaid.gov/pdf_docs/PNACB895.pdf>, accessed 26 July 2024.

Fagbemi, Sunday A. (2020). 'Assessing the Efficacy of Mediation as a Form of Alternative Dispute Resolution (ADR) Mechanism in Nigeria', *Humanities, Management, Arts, Education & The Social Sciences Research Journal*, 8 (2), 1–20.

Handbook on the Peaceful Settlement of Disputes between States (1992). OLA/COD/2394, <https://legal.un.org/cod/books/HandbookOnPSD.pdf>, accessed 1 July 2024.

Melenko, Oksana (2020). 'Mediation as an Alternative Forum of Dispute Resolution: Comparative-Legal Analysis', *European Journal of Law and Public Administration*, 7 (2), 46–63.
Menkel-Meadow, Carrie (2004). 'From Legal Disputes to Conflict Resolution and Human Problem Solving: Legal Dispute Resolution in a Multidisciplinary Context', *Journal of Legal Education*, 62(1), 7–29.
Mnookin, Robert H. (1998). 'Alternative Dispute Resolution'. *Harvard Law School, Discussion Paper* No. 232, <www.law.harvard.edu/programs/olin_center/papers/pdf/232.pdf>, accessed 26 July 2024.
Naureen, Akhtar, Nadeem, Saadat Ali, and Habib, Rao Imran (2023). 'Alternative Dispute Resolution: Concept, Criticism and Future of Arbitration on Mediation', *Global Legal Studies Review*, VIII (II), 36–42.
Senan, Mohammad Hasan, Alzaghini, Nadine, and Srour, Issam (2018). 'Mediation Tactics and Effectiveness in Dispute Resolution'. In Abdul-Malak, M., Khoury, H., Singh, A., and Yazdani, S. (eds), *Responsible Design and Delivery of the Constructed Project*. ISEC Press 2018.
The Law Reform Commission (2010). 'Report Alternative Dispute Resolution: Mediation and Conciliation', <https://www.lawreform.ie/_fileupload/Reports/r98ADR.pdf>, accessed 18 July 2024.

Legal Sources

Charter of the Organization of American States, signed in Bogota on 30 April 1948 (entry into force 13 December 1951), <https://www.scribd.com/document/262897822/OAS-Charter-1948>, accessed 6 July 2024).
1899 Convention for the Pacific Settlement of International Disputes, <https://docs.pca-cpa.org/2016/01/1899-Convention-for-the-Pacific-Settlement-of-International-Disputes.pdf>, accessed 1 July 2024.
Convention for the Pacific Settlements of International Disputes adopted in The Hague on 18 October 1907, <https://cil.nus.edu.sg/wp-content/uploads/2017/07/1907-The-Hague-Convention-for-the-Pacific-Settlement-of-International-Disputes-1.pdf>, accessed 1 July 2024.
Declaration on Principles of International Law concerning Friendly Relations and Co-operation among States in accordance with the Charter of the United States, adopted by the General Assembly of the United States in New York on 24 October 1970, A/RES/2625, <https://documents.un.org/doc/resolution/gen/nr0/348/90/pdf/nr034890.pdf?token=NppnJn5gwgRGAxW20W&fe=true>, accessed 25 July 2024.

Directive 2008/52/EC of the European Parliament and the Council of 21 May 2008 on certain aspects of mediation in civil and commercial matters, OJ L 136/3 on 24 May 2008, <https://eur-lex.europa.eu/legal-content/en/ALL/?uri=CELEX:32008L0052#:~:text=DIRECTIVE%202008/52/EC%20OF%20THE%20EUROPEAN%20PARLIAMENT>, accessed 10 July 2024.

Inter-American Treaty on Good Offices and Mediation, signed at Buenos Aires on 23 December 1936, League of Nations Treaty Series 1938, vol. CLXXXVIII, No. 4353, <https://treaties.un.org/doc/Publication/UNTS/LON/Volume%20188/v188.pdf>, accessed 2 July 2024.

The American Treaty on Pacific Settlement (Pact of Bogota) signed in Bogota on 30 April 1948, U.S. Department of State, <https://2009-2017.state.gov/p/wha/rls/70580.htm>, accessed 6 July 2024.

The Antarctic Treaty, signed in Washington on 1 December 1959, *Official Journal of 1961*, 46 (item 237), Annex.

The Charter of the Organisation of African Unity, established in Addis Ababa on 25 May 1963, <https://au.int/sites/default/files/treaties/7759-file-oau_charter_1963.pdf>, accessed 8 July 2024.

The Final Act of the Conference on Security and Cooperation in Europe signed in Helsinki on 1 August 1975, <https://www.osce.org/files/f/documents/5/c/39501.pdf>, accessed 25 July 2024.

The Manila Declaration on the Peaceful Settlement of Disputes, the annex to the General Assembly resolution 37/10, adopted in New York on 15 November 1982, <https://peacemaker.un.org/node/93>, accessed 25 July 2024.

The Pact of the League of Arab States concluded in Cairo on 22 March 1945, *Arab Law Quarterly*, 1992, 7 (2), pp. 148–152.

The Protocol of the Commission of Mediation, Conciliation and Arbitration, adopted in Cairo on 21 July 1964, *International Legal Materials*, 1964, 3 (6), 1116–1124, <https://www.jstor.org/stable/2068984>, accessed 9 July 2024.

United Nations Charter (1947). 'Statute of the International Court of Justice and Agreement Establishing the Preparatory Commission of the United Nations signed in San Francisco on 26 June 1945', *Official Journal of Poland of 1947*, 23 (item 90).

United Nations Convention on International Settlement Agreements Resulting from Mediation (Singapore Convention on Mediation), adopted in New York on 20 December 2018, open to signature in Singapore on 7 August 2019, <https://uncitral.un.org/sites/uncitral.un.org/files/media-documents/EN/Texts/UNCITRAL/Arbitration/mediation_convention_v1900316_eng.pdf>, accessed 27 July 2024.

CHAPTER 4

Types of Arguments Used in Negotiations Topical – Rhetorical Aspects of Mediation: An Attempt at Theoretical Reflection in the Light of Chaïma Perelman's Legal Arguments

Anna Moskwa[1]

Introduction

One can notice lately an unusual increase of interest in techniques exerting influence on people and in various dimensions (theoretical, empirical as well as practical). Through communication, we can explain mechanisms shaping the social behaviour of man. Interpersonal communication refers to issues connected with the use of a linguistic system in the regulation of social contacts and the creation of the course of interaction (Nęcki 2000; Stelmach 2003).

Persuasive functions of linguistic statements in interpersonal communication have their legal–judicial origin; it is a classic area of legal skills. Moreover, as Jolanta Jabłońska-Bonca and Kamil Zeidler rightly indicated, nowadays, one perceives that these special communication skills are more and more needed in extra-judicial discourse, which are necessary in adjudication, not only of judicial disputes, but also in relieving tensions resulting from conflicts of interests in the free market, in economy and trade, in political life, in workplaces, in family relations, etc. They observed that in these spheres, not only the substance but also the communication, rhetoric, negotiation and mediation qualifications of lawyers have become more important (Jabłońska-Bonca & Zeidler 2023). Communication between people makes the misuse of communication natural, which refers to persuasion and manipulation (Zirk-Sadowski & Łukowski (ed.) 2012). Logic, dialogue and rhetoric all play a role. Treating a way of thinking as a rhetorical process provides us with a new perspective going beyond the sphere of the individual brain (Cartesian perspective), indicating as well that dialogue

1 PhD, Judge of the District Court in Rzeszów, email: <amoskwa@o2.pl>

is the nature of thinking. Anyone seeking to investigate mental processes should pay particular attention to conversational interactions (Lewiński 2012). As Michel Meyer states, living in a communicative society, in which 'individuals express themselves, debate, must be liked and convince others', all spheres (the law, politics, philosophy, literary analysis and the sphere of everyday life) are connected in rhetoric (Meyer et al. 2010).

For this reason, my considerations in this chapter will go in this direction, while I focus on topical–rhetorical aspects of mediation in the light of Chaïm Perelman's legal arguments.

Alternative Methods of Dispute Resolution – Negotiations

As the law emerged in antiquity, becoming an essential means of social control on the one hand, and a means of settling conflicts on the other, mediation and other forms of dispute resolution – not necessarily by bodies of administration of justice – also have an ancient origin, going back to Ancient Egypt, China and Japan. They were also known in European practice and thought. We find these forms in primitive law, and their more subtle forms emerged in Roman law and played a part in our legal culture. Examples include such institutions as *arbitrum ex compromisso* (entrusting of dispute to an arbitrator) and *arbitrum bon iviri* (an opinion of an honest man or according to a decision of an honest man) (Arkuszewska & Plis 2014; Sołtysiak 2012; Zienkiewicz 2005).

Nowadays, institutional forms were shaped in Great Britain, and then they were transferred to the United States. The term Alternative Dispute Resolution (ADR) was created there, and its basic forms were distinguished, where, since the turn of the nineteenth century, they began to develop individually, supplementing types of dispute resolution to lawsuits (Kobielska 2023; Korybski 1993; Lusińska 2023). They emerged in relation to a crisis of judicial dispute settlement, which manifested itself in the judiciary at the end of the 1960s.

It leads to a question: an alternative towards what? In the literature on the subject, there is no unanimous answer to the question put in such a way. There are several variants. In the first, it is accepted that such a way of dispute resolution is an alternative which departs from a classical lawsuit. In the second, it is assumed that every method becomes an alternative which aims at enabling the end of dispute in a conciliatory way (it also embraces decisions taken by judges aimed at concluding an amicable agreement). The essence of the alternative consists in the free possibility of resignation from judicial proceedings taking place before a common law court and using other commonly attainable methods (e.g. arbitration). The most radical solutions assume exclusion from the ADR not only of judicial proceedings but also of extra-judicial arbitration, as methods (and other mechanisms approximating to it) based on the so-called adjudicative model, i.e. consisting in issuing a verdict binding the parties.

The most popular typology of ADR forms was presented by Sander at the beginning of the 1980s (Sander 1985). Sander called them peaceful forms of dispute resolution, among which he distinguished adjudication, mediation and negotiation. These are the basic forms. Besides these, various hybrid forms have been distinguished, constituting combinations of these basic elements regarding real environmental conditions and needs.

Forms of Peaceful Dispute Resolution (Adjudication, Mediation) and Hybrid Methods.

Criteria	**Model**			
	Amicable		**Adjudicatory**	
	Contractual (negotiations)	**Conciliatory (mediations)**	**Arbitral**	**Judicial**
Participation of the third party	–	+	+	+
Parties decide who will be the third party	Not applicable	+	+	–
Parties decide on the course and organisation of proceedings	+	+	+/–	–
Parties decide on the result of proceedings	+	+	–	–

Source: Michael L. Moffitt (2006), 'The Making of an ADR Pionier', *Negotiation Journal October* 2006, 437.

We must strongly point out that these ADR forms are a reaction to the existing disputes taking place between individuals or social groups, and they are the expression of an adaptation to the needs and cultural traditions of a given state. These are reactions to a conflict seeking to avoid repressive forms of resolution, allowing a chance to withdraw (escape from conflict) (Balicki 2010). As I pointed out earlier, the most distinguishable forms are negotiations, mediation and arbitration. Our attention will be focused on mediation. The term 'mediation' itself comes from Greek 'medos' (mediating, neutral, not belonging to any of the parties) and from Latin 'mediatio' (intermediation) (Jabłońska-Bonca & Zeidler 2023; Mikołajczyk 2010). According to Jan Waszkiewicz (1997), the Latin term comes from the words 'neg' and 'otium' (adequately 'not' and 'idleness'). Waszkiewicz jokingly states on the Genesis of this name:

> for Romans, idleness was basic, so natural, and its denial was time occupied by work. Thus, the word 'negotiation' primarily meant practical occupations, distant from the ideal of occupations of a free man [...]. Later, the word 'negotiator' meant a merchant [...], as it is used in Old Polish (Waszkiewicz 1997: 13).

In contemporary Polish legislation, the concept of mediation appeared for the first time in the Act of 23 May 1991, on the resolution of collective disputes. So far, there is no general legal definition of this concept, although it has become the subject of regulations of civil, administrative, court administrative and criminal law, as well as in proceedings in juvenile cases.

I have taken the liberty of presenting the statutory definition contained in the Austrian legislation, where within this definition, the legislator refers to four elements: the principle of professionalism and neutrality of the mediator, his limited role (his activities consist only in directing and systematically supporting the parties in this conflict) and the responsibility of the parties themselves for resolving the conflict.

This definition fully expresses the essence of mediation as a measure for dispute resolution and formulated in the scope of ADR basic forms in US literature and practice. These are emphasised there by:

- the presence of a neutral, impartial third party (intermediary, mediator), helping the parties to achieve a suitable arrangement acceptable for themselves: 'a win–win strategy' (looking for the best solutions for both parties); this type is defined by a mediatory–conciliatory name.

- a mediator is deprived of power to impose a binding dispute resolution on the parties (non-binding)
- the exclusive decisive power concerning the dispute, and in particular, relating to conclusion of an agreement and its contents – belongs to the parties.

This form has also other features enabling us to distinguish it from the remaining ones used in the scope of ADR and existing in various intensity in their numerous forms. This includes the voluntary character of undertaking and participation in the mediatory proceedings – voluntary mediation, the informal character of mediatory proceedings, the possibility of deciding by the parties on a choice of the third party and the proceedings procedure, the confidential character of proceedings, the preferred dispute resolution, liquidating conflicts in relation of these parties and a prospective orientation concerning dispute resolution between parties remaining in permanent ties (employees, economic, family or neighbours) giving a chance to establish principles of cooperation without conflicts in the future. Distinguished features characterising mediation are expressed in the definition of this term formulated by the Social Council for Alternative Dispute Resolutions Methods at the Ministry of Justice in the preamble to standards of carrying out mediation and conduct of a mediator[2]. In the light of the definition contained there, mediation is understood as:

- a voluntary and confidential process, in which an expertly prepared, independent and impartial person, with consent of the parties, helps them to cope with the conflict. Mediation enables its participants to state contentious issues, decrease communication barriers, work out proposals of solutions and, if such is will of the parties, to conclude a mutually satisfying arrangement.

2 Resolution of the Social Council for Alternative Dispute Resolution Methods at the Ministry of Justice of 26 June 2006, <https://www.gov.pl/web/sprawiedliwosc/spoleczna-rada-do-spraw-alternatywnych-metod-rozwiazywania-sporow-przy-ministrze-sprawiedliwosci>, accessed 3 July 2024.

In the light of this term, and it is accepted by Polish mediatory practice, one can state that competence to take a decision resolving the dispute belongs exclusively to the parties in dispute, similar to mediation. This particular decision-making process leads to resolving the dispute caused by a conflict between aims and interests of the parties and the mediator leads 'a discussion' on this subject. They try to persuade the parties in dispute to accept such solutions which would be mutually beneficial for them. Their position as the mediator differs from the position of an arbiter or a judge. They do not have the power to impose solutions to the parties. They can only convince them, referring to various argumentation: logical, axiological, psychological or economic. The character and content of the dispute influence the use of these arguments by the mediator. Specifying logical irregularities allows them to disclose irregularities in reasoning processes of the parties. The axiological interpretation enables them to disclose the essence of the dispute, because its basis includes various interests conditioned by different values. Looking for a compromise is, in this case, an expression of mutual concessions to be realised by the parties or by indicating a superior value (rightness, justice), which will allow them to acquire such compromise. Psychological argumentation is an issue of the topical–rhetorical skills of the negotiator, which enables them to effectively direct conflict resolution. The economic model allows them to define the economic effectiveness of the compromise resolution and to disclose incompetence, which constitute the basis of the parties' demands in this matter.

As Andrzej Korybski (1993: 116) rightly pointed out the task of mediation is:

> not to admit grounds of a claim of one party (thus settlement of the dispute however non-binding) but to propose such dispute resolution which will reconcile these claims (or which will at least partly satisfy them), through referring to mutual values and principles.

The mediator is here only a neutral adviser helping to find such formula of problem solving, which both parties could accept (Morawski 1999).

Summing up, one can state that the aim of mediation is reaching an agreement which each party in dispute can accept. According to Lon Luvois Fuller, the author of the internal morality of the law, the mediator should aim to inform the parties on the dependence of their claims on certain values and social norms applying to the dispute subject. This allows them to assume no commonplace manner solution, causing the effect of the 'creation of values'. Such an attitude can end the conflict, which will lead to an agreement of such a solution, which may be accepted by the parties involved (Fuller 1978).

According to Howard Raiff, this effect leads to the transfer of the parties' interest from conquering the opponent to overcoming the problem and looking for the optimal, mutually satisfying result. This 'negotiation dance' (negotaciontance), conducted by the mediator, leads to a situation that both parties in dispute will decide on a common dispute resolution (Raiff 1996).

Mediation can have various forms, they can have an institutional character, when they are carried out by a permanent mediatory centre, or an *ad hoc* mediation form, when a mediator or a mediatory team is appointed for a single case by a party.

Mediation can also have the form of direct (face-to-face mediation) or indirect (private/ separate meetings), where a mediator meets with the consent and wish of the parties privately with each of them to get to know their attitude more fully.

In the scope of mediatory proceedings, one usually distinguishes two basic mediatory styles: facilitative mediation (soft mediation) and evaluative mediation (hard mediation). In the first, a mediator avoids formulating their own opinions concerning the dispute subject and the way of resolving it. Their activity is focused on presenting various types of argumentation, which I mentioned earlier, to help the parties to articulate their standpoint. Using the second style, a mediator presents his standpoint concerning the dispute but treats it as a draft, taking into account the interests of both parties (Korybski 1993; Zienkiewicz 2005).

There is no way, undertaking the problem of mediation, to assume an attitude towards problems, which is brought by the constitutional principle of the right to sue. Mediation can be started either before instituting legal proceedings or during its course. Mediation in the scope of judicial proceedings is possible only in these states, in which the law provides such a possibility.

The right to sue was expressed in Art. 45, item 1 of the Constitution of the Republic of Poland, stating that 'everyone has the right to just and open consideration of a matter without an unjustified delay by a competent, independent and impartial court'.

It is one of the most important and, at the same time, the oldest personal entitlements of an individual. However, we must point out that the right to sue does not mean that there exists an obligation to file every dispute in a common court of law. Polish legislators have agreed to settle disputes between individuals by means other than common courts of law. Thus, it is possible to appoint agencies adjudicating on disciplinary responsibility in the frames of professional groups and to establish other *quasi*-judicial or extra-judicial agencies. The Constitutional Tribunal in verdict of 8 December1998, case no. K 42/97, in the reasons for the decision, pointed out that jurisdiction should be understood objectively and not all matters and disputes relating to the legal situation of an individual must be settled by courts from the beginning. The parties in dispute can freely choose a resolution procedure only when it is not possible to settle the dispute in a negotiation, mediation or arbitration; they are given recourse to the law. However, it is understood, which the Constitutional Tribunal also pointed out, that courts always have to be vested a superior position enabling the verification of the settlement of an extra-judicial agency.

Within the framework of judicial proceedings, depending on the subject initiating mediatory proceedings, one can distinguish: mediation initiated by court, contractual mediation and mediation on the parties' motion (Balicki 2010).

Mediation initiated by a court is a process of dispute resolution in which the parties, with the help of a neutral mediator, negotiate contentious issues to conclude an agreement initiated by a court, which can but does not have to direct the parties to mediation in proceedings, and the parties can refuse. Contractual mediation is a process of dispute resolution in which the parties negotiate contentious issues with the help of a neutral mediator to settle a matter amicably. The process itself is initiated by the parties in dispute by concluding an agreement to subject the dispute to mediation or contained in the main contract a clause of 'prospective mediation/ADR agreement'. Whereas mediation on the parties' motion is a process of dispute resolution in which the parties negotiate contentious issues with the help of a neutral mediator to settle a matter amicably, initiated by one party in dispute by filing a motion for carrying out mediation (in the light of Art. 183^{1} § 2 code of civil procedure):

> mediation is conducted based on prospective mediation/ ADR agreement or a decision of the court directing the parties to mediation. The agreement can also be concluded by stating consent for mediation by a party when the other party filed a motion, provided in art. 183^{6} § 1 code of civil procedure.) (Morek 2011: 9; Wysokińska 2006: 221–227).

In summing up our considerations, we must state that mediation as well as the remaining ADR forms do not constitute a panacea to settle all problems in the scope of legal dispute resolution. They are not an optimal way of dispute settlement. There is no such medicine; they fail in a situation of flat refusal of cooperation in dispute resolution by at least one party. They also do not constitute a good means of influence in a situation in which confidential agreement of the parties could create danger for significant interests. Mediation in the form presented here will also not be applied in a situation in which it is not possible to choose an impartial third person. Moreover, binding legal provisions create barriers for ADR application in specific kinds of legal dispute. As an example, one can give cases when mediation proceedings are excluded in the Polish legal system. This refers to cases for recognition as forbidden decisions in matters of amicable agreement in relation to a pattern of contract [Art. 479^{36} – 479^{45}code of civil procedure (CPC)], according to a norm contained in Art. 479^{41} CPC, in matters for recognition of provisions of a standardised contract as forbidden, concluding an amicable agreement between the parties is in admissible.

In the light of the statistics of the Ministry of Justice, few cases are settled by mediation. Are these over 10 years of binding force of Polish mediatory and arbitration law (on the grounds of criminal law, it is over 17 years) be recognised as ineligible for mediation? I do not think so. No doubt, the lack of tradition in this matter in Polish legal practice, the lack of adequate habits and inconsiderable social consciousness in this scope means that these ADR forms have not been recognised fully by society. However, the court should perform an essential role in directing cases for mediatory dissolution in a larger measure. Its pedagogical role in this matter would be indispensable.

Negotiation Practice – From Logic through Argumentation to Rhetoric

As we know, logic is nothing more than reasoning theory. Its main task is classification and particularization of types of argumentation. On its ground, evaluation of their rationality is performed, errors in reasoning are described and dishonest tricks in argumentation are disclosed. Logic refers to all aspects of human life from science, politics, business, right through to everyday problems, because all can be the subject of reasoning (Kwiatkowski 2008; Marciszewski 1991, 1994; Trzęsicki 1995, 1996; Wójcicki 2003).

> All our dignity rests [...] in thought. [...] Thus, we try to think well" (Pascal 1968: 118). This thought of Blaise Pascal renders best the character of logic as a science. It is to indicate as one should think.
>
> "It includes in its dignity beauty of abstract thought and victory gained by power of thought in practical life. Thought – as Witold Marciszewski (1994:3) states commenting the above statement – is best perceptible in this symptom, which consist in reasoning.

No doubt, formal logic predominates here. However, it turns out that although secular tradition (beginning from Aristoteles and Stoics) and the spectacular successes of its method (deduction) exist, they do not bring satisfactory results in many areas of human activity. Such are the grounds of ethics, law, politics or philosophy, where most applied arguments do not have the character of deductive conclusions and attempts to formalise them often lead to paradoxes, giving absurd results, inconsistent with intuition of appropriate discourses (Hilpinen 2008; Świrydowicz 1995; Ziemba 1983).

The awareness of this inadequacy of formal logic towards normative discourse and different non-inferred forms of argumentation only emerged in the twentieth century. This is evident, for example, in Stephen Edelston Toulmin's *The Uses of Argument* (1953) and in the work of researcher Chaïm Perelman, *La Nouvelle Rhetorique. Traitè de l`argumentation* (1958, co-authored with Lucie Olbrechts-Tyteca) (Kiereś-Łach 2015; Perelman & Olbrecht-Tyteca 1970; Toulmin 1958; Zarębski2005). These works prompted the formation of a new field of research called informal logic. In Polish literature, they are usually defined as practical logic, logic from a rhetorical point of view, legal logic, or – more rarely for lawyers – as the 'art' of argumentation or informal logic (Szymanek 2001; Tokarz 2006; Ziembiński 1992).

However, Aristotle not only the author of the 'Analytics', but also the author of 'Topics' and 'Sophist Evidence' and Cicero, within the rhetorical tradition, are also considered precursors of this attitude (Lichański 1992).

This new attitude was not easy. As one of these authors writes: cognitivism of positivists refusing cognitive values for estimating opinions, at the same time condemning practical philosophy, prevented him from reaching a paradoxical conclusion and made him desperate for a philosopher (Perelman 2002).

Perelman realised that 'one cannot build an opinion exclusively on the grounds of factual opinions [...] And maybe there is logic in estimating opinions? If so, how?' (2002: 5).

First, Perelman followed one of co-authors of contemporary logic, Gottlob Frege, who formulated the principles of the theory of deduction and formal logic (mathematics) and to whose opinions he dedicated his dissertation. He attempted to find an answer as to whether applying his attitude to estimating opinions could extract the logic of these statements

> Work, undertaken together with Lucie Olbrechts-Tyteca, has taken us to completely unexpected conclusions, which has become for us a kind of a revelation. Namely, we realized that there does not exist a specific logic for estimating opinions, whereas what we have looked for was developed in a very old discipline, forgotten and condemned at present – in rhetoric, in the ancient art of persuasion and convincing (Heijenoort 1967: 1–82; Kamiński 1957: 31–62).

Just as the ancients had developed 'the technique of persuasive speech, indispensable in a discussion preceding taking every ingenious decision as a technique in the literal sense'.

According to Perelman, this discovery has significant meaning for legal logic.

> If in his reasoning a judge should aim at obtaining solutions, which would be rightful, sensible and suitable to be accepted independently of their compliance with the norms of positive law, then an answer to the following question is essential:

> 'With the help of which ways of reasoning can a judge recognize a given decision as rightful, sensible and possible to be accepted, since these attitudes are contentious in a high degree' (Perelman 1984: 143).

According to him, there should be rules which steer the course of rhetorical argumentation (non-inferential, deceptive where one can at most designate only the probability of truth to a conclusion with true prerequisites)[3].

The author of 'Legal Logic' perceives here their essential relation with dialectic viewing it as the 'art of discussion appeared as an appropriate method of solving practical problems related to the aims of activity, with which certain values are connected' (Perelman 1984: 144).

In the following work, he directly states that 'the present revival and rehabilitation of rhetoric were possible only thanks to the renewed studying of relations between rhetoric and dialectic in such a way as Aristotle gave to them' (Florescu 1982; Mihai 1982; Perelman 2002).

He points out that Aristotle in 'Organon' singled out two types of reasoning: analytical and dialectical. The first investigates forms of 'correct inferential reasoning' that constitute pure formal reasoning (Aristoteles limited his considerations to syllogism), where with true prerequisites, one always comes to a true conclusion; the second does not have this property because 'its prerequisites a built of commonly accepted opinions', whereas their aim is

> inducement to accept other propositions which are or can be contentious. [...] They do not constitute correct inferences and extorting acceptance, but present stronger or weaker arguments, more or less convincing, which are never purely formal (Perelman 2002:14).

---

3 See Perelman, Chaïm (1969). 'Qu`Est-ce qua la Logiquejuridique?'. In Gumański, Leon (ed.), *Rozprawy Filozoficzne*, pp. 305–311. Toruń. Gregorowicz, Jan (1967). 'Die Koncepcje Logiki Prawniczej'. In Kotarbiński, Czezowski, et al. (ed. Committee), *Fragment Filozoficzne – Seria Trzeciak. Księga Pamiątkowa ku Czci Profesora Tadeusza Kotarbińskiego w Osiemdziesiątą Rocznicę Urodzin*. Warszawa: PWN. Woleński, Jan (1978). 'Filozoficzne Aspekty Sporu o Logikę Prawniczą'. In Stróżewski, Władysław (ed.), *Studia z Teorii Poznania i Filozofii Wartości*, pp. 35–40. Wrocław–Warszawa–Kraków–Gdańsk: Zakład Narodowy Imienia Ossolińskich.

It turns out that a dialectic conclusion does not have such weight as presented by a conclusion obtained by analytical reasoning, which derives its importance from formal logic (which forejudges on summing up of such conclusion making with assumption of true prerequisites, and they are usually axiomatic). It depends on approval of the proposed prerequisites by interlocutors. As he states, for Aristotle analytical and formal conclusions:

> are only necessary; dialectical conclusions are only probable and rational. Logic and mathematics indicate abstract structures and are timeless and ahistorical. Dialectic conclusions are based, independently of whether they are expressed in a dialogue or in statements and presumptions on common human sense, and they are always situated historically: they factually aim at obtaining approval of an auditorium by argumentation (Perelman 1975: 84).

Let us observe closer his conception of argumentation as new rhetoric. He considers that the subject of such a conception is the analysis of discursive techniques aimed at causing or intensifying support for statements presented for approval (Perelman 1984). One can say that argumentation is 'a set of activities (usually linguistic – my note) undertaken to justify a belief' (Tokarz 2006: 124), or in other words 'mental verbal activity with the object of gaining the consent of a given person or persons to a proposal presented to them' (Kwiatkowski 2008: 344).

More distinctly, this element of persuasion appropriate to argumentation was pointed out in a definition presented by Krzysztof Szymanek (2008:17), for whom argumentation is 'a certain kind of discursive communication, during which a person tries in a planned way to change the beliefs of another person or persons, presenting an appropriately chosen statement or a set of statements containing arguments'.

Thus, it is a communication process in which someone (the sender) presents an argument/arguments to someone else (the receiver), with the intention of causing a planned change in the receiver's belief.

As Tomasz Gizbert-Studnicki (1995:35) rightly noted the question 'How should one argue?', which defines the scope of the term 'argumentation', can be understood in two ways. It may refer (when limited to the normative aspect of the theory of argumentation) either to 'how should one argue in order to convince an interlocutor, i.e. to gain their acceptance for a thesis being argued for?' or 'what arguments can be used to justify the objective accuracy of the thesis, in question?'.

An answer to the first question provides knowledge only of a technical character disclosing effective measures to acquire the goal, which convinces the receiver of the sender's attitude, regardless of whether the propositions, to which he is persuaded, are right or not. 'The convincing power of arguments is thus independent of the accuracy of the thesis for which one argues' (Gizbert-Studnicki 1995:35).

An answer to the second is to indicate only these arguments, which 'objectively (...) support a thesis, for which one argues' (Gizbert-Studnicki 1995:35). A problem of the objective significance of argumentation and its rightness is essential here.

Before we pass on to the closer characteristics of Chaïma Perelman's definition of argumentation, one should pay attention to certain problems related with it. First of all, argumentation discourse has a practical and rational character and is also rightful (just) (Kleszcz 1985; Stelmach 2003); it is included in the sphere of practical philosophy, where opinions are engaged and existing conflicts (it is inevitable where many axiological systems are accepted, which are not coherent and cohesive – discussed as in what follows) should be solved. Limiting logic, as positivism did, only for the analysis of recognition of a theoretical character, prevented it from being used in practice. Thus, should settlement of these practical conflicts be left to irrational factors or power and violence? Perceiving a feature of an axio-normative discourse and the limited possibilities which formal logic gives, he referred to rhetoric allowing rational formation of practical philosophy. Many principles, techniques, tactics and strategies of convincing others were worked out on its grounds. Its revival is also the contribution of the author of Legal logic. One cannot question that rhetoric has a legal–judicial origin. We should not be surprised that he recognised judicial discourse as paradigmatic in the formulation of the conception of his argumentation (Alexy 1978; Czaja & Stelmach 1995; Wróblewski 1984).

The author of a new rhetoric specifying a definition of argumentation (Perelman 1984) points out that firstly this discourse is a method of convincing an opponent of one's own standpoint; it is possible only when one rejects all absolutism and dogmatism typical for first philosophies and to which he counters a conception of open philosophy. The aim of philosophy is working out principles of existence, thought, acting, which would be sensible in a human way, and not discovering eternal and invariable principles found by metaphysical tradition (Perelman 1964). Ryszard Kleszcz (1989) characterises this openness:

- this philosophy rejects all primary and undisputed principles, not recognising what is final, obvious and necessary;
- initial principles should be treated as the results of a factual situation;
- the process of recognition in open philosophy is subject to continuous improving, upgrading and extending;
- open philosophy allows, by exclusion, all order necessary to maintain the power of choice and judgement (Kleszcz 1989: 124).

It can be seen, in the preceding characteristics of philosophy, which Perelman accepted and promoted, an inspiration for the so-called new rationalism, presented among others by Gaston Bachelard, Ferdinand Gonseth and his master Eugene Duprèel (Kleszcz 1985). As is turns out, he did not accept unconditionally and uncritically all their propositions. 'He differs from them among others in that he points out distinctly the autonomy of philosophy in relation to science, also accepting methodological pluralism and opposing to any reductionism' (Kleszcz 1989: 124). His attitude is close to Isaiah Berlin's standpoint (Berlin 1978), though I have not noticed that he referred to his work. In the matter of pluralism, he refers to Duprèel (Kleszcz 1985) omitting the output of 'the author of pluralism of values and initiator of this trend' (Polanowska-Sygulska 2008).

The second specification refers to the proof and the relationship of formal logic to rhetoric. He realises that every deductive inference is conclusive (it justifies its conclusion) on condition of the veracity of its premises. When we take argumentation, which belongs to rhetoric, the matter also depends on this condition. We do not always have to deal with a situation in which premises are true statements. 'The subject of dispute is, however, not only the veracity of a statement, but also the value of a decision, choice of an action, which on certain grounds are considered as just, rightful, sensible or suitable' (Kleszcz 1985).

When we accept axiological pluralis, various axiological choices can be equally rational because any choice can be recognised as rightful which has some justification (Perelman 1967). However, the matter does not lie in countering evidence or suggestions. Such a dualistic attitude is a relic of closed philosophy. According to Perelman, procedures leading to consent cannot be reduced only to evidence and suggestion. Techniques which are used in the argumentation process include methods which are approximate to logic and the methodology of sciences (nowadays, we could say that they are the expression of paraphrases of formal logic on the grounds of practical discourse, legal through the application of techniques of logical or linguistic analysis (Stelmach & Brożek 2006), rhetoric (as the theory of argumentation) as well as eristic. Between formal logic and eristic (specified by him as stylistic figures) is a place for new rhetoric using a great variety (analysed by him) of techniques of argumentation).

The following note – the third one – indicates the degree of approval of any statement. A dispute takes place in a matter of values, not truth. There are many values and various hierarchisations of them. Thus, a dispute arises. Without a dialogue, and such is possible only when nobody is convinced that he has absolute and final truth, there is no way to take a rational decision in this matter and undertake adequate evaluation.

The fourth note qualifies the previous ones – the author strongly points out that rhetoric refers to beliefs, not – as logic – to truth. 'Truth is impersonal and whether it is recognised or not, it does not change its character in any way. Whereas a belief is always a belief of one or many minds to which we speak, it means: auditorium' (Perelman 1984: 147).

The notion of auditorium plays a significant role in his conception of argumentation. 'A statement can be effective only when it is adopted to an auditorium which must be persuaded or convinced' (Perelman 1984: 147).

As Jan Czaja and Jerzy Stelmach write, this notion is 'a key to understanding [his] practical theory of discourse' (Czaja & Stelmach 1995: 26). According to Tomasz Gizbert-Studnicki (1995) – it is 'a starting point of (his) theory. (...) A measure of objective significance of argumentation', which guarantees its common significance and impartiality to everyone.

Referring to Aristotle, he assumes that 'argumentation (...) can be directed to any auditorium, scientists or laymen, to one person, to a small number of persons or to the whole humanity. In internal considerations, an individual can argue even with oneself' (Perelman 1984).

He does not exclude a situation where the same statement can be directed simultaneously to several auditoriums. However, it is assumed that, from a theoretical point of view, one should assume a common auditorium (universal), understood as a set of all rational human beings (Perelman 1984). He also assumes that language should not be disregarded, and one's own statements should be formulated in language understandable for a given auditorium. Knowledge relating to allegations, which is already accepted by them and a degree (intensity) of this acceptance, is also important.

A truncated characteristic of this notion gives rise to a series of doubts. A common, universal auditorium constituting an ideal and formal category can be understood regarding single persons (individuals), some specified societies or – to a community of all arguing people (Alexy 1978). One cannot unambiguously answer which of these meanings Perelman uses. 'This category is a philosophical attempt at a defence of rationality, objectivity and universality of a specified type of argumentation, an attempt which many methodologists do not accept at all' (Czaja & Stelmach 1995:26).

Any idealisation as a method of construction of notions means 'terminal elements (...) of orderly objects in specified respects', as e.g. a set of human beings ordered regarding the rationality of their actions, is a counter-factual notion (their substantiation on grounds of social sciences is generally impossible) (Nowak 1987).

For the authors of new rhetoric, this notion has a normative character: 'L' accord d' un audutoire universel donc pas une question de fait, mais de droit'.

Gizbert-Studnicki (1995: 39) rightly notices

> a universal auditorium consists of persons, whose circle is specified by a normative criterion [...]. Empirical data of an individual are participants of a universal auditorium to such an extent they recognize beliefs on the grounds of own reason, not on the grounds of emotions, habits or superstitions. The universal auditorium is not identical with any set of humans because no individual is directed exclusively by reason while accepting beliefs. Argumentation is objectively important, if it should be accepted by every human being.

A duty of sensibility appoints a set of human beings. It is an idealist assumption; thus Perelman specifies requirements which a process of argumentation of a rational human being should fulfil. These are among others, a prohibition on presenting propositions in which a speaker does not believe, an order to admit adverse arguments, a ban on partiality, an order to adapt one's own statement to an auditorium, its level and competence. We enter here into the problems of language, in which an argumentative discourse takes place. It should be adopted to an auditorium, expressed in language appropriate for cultural, professional communities, because they must understand the contents of discourse; specialistic issues should, when they do not refer to such circle of specialists, be formulated in common language, etc. (Kleszcz 1985).

Requirements, which the author of 'Legal logic' formulates towards such discourse, specify necessary conditions but are not sufficient for the objective significance of argumentation. Thus, they are insufficient and prevent agreement from being reached, which would prejudge its objective importance.

It is worth reflecting to what degree one can adopt his idea of discourse and legal argumentation on the grounds of mediation.

No doubt taking into attention the aim of negotiation, which is finding an effective way to resolve a contentious problem. This aim can be obtained through people participating in negotiations, which in some measure will be a compromise of their often-contradictory mutual demands. We must realise that a notion of conviction can be connected with the issue of rightness or validity of an argument, whereas a notion of abetment is connected with effectiveness. Conviction in relation to a negotiation resolution is sought regarding the criterion of rightness. We obtain acceptance of these settlements referring to a differently understood auditorium, about which I wrote earlier. This constitutes a community of all well-informed and sensible humans.

Abetment serves to formulate a conciliary decision, which a specific community of negotiating persons obtains, through which it is limited to a decision of a particular auditorium. It is based on some psychological beliefs that a negotiatory resolution for which the negotiating parties declare will be effective. Such abetment is thus more a category from the domain of psychology. We abet somebody, we abet one another not to settle principal ethic issues (axiological), to obtain acceptance of a universal auditorium, in our case (negotiations), to attain assumed aims. This particular auditorium takes decisions.

Earlier accepted procedure determines what it is to be. Acceptance of a certain solution by the majority of participants of a negotiation forming a particular auditorium should be considered as fully sufficient. In this way, significant relativisation of criteria takes place which allow us to accept the results of negotiation. Negotiatory resolution (conciliation) can be accepted as final because it is a result of abetment. The essence of abetment is based on its voluntary character, without which one cannot speak about negotiations at all. Abetment, with such an understood majority (particular auditorium) means negotiatory compromise. A case of unilateral efficiency is not involved here, winning all by one of the negotiating parties. Thus, it is impossible for one party to win with the violation of interests of other participants of the negotiatory process.

An initial point of negotiation is always a particular case, some event constituting the beginning of an inductive chain of certain reasons. In this case, it is said about a bottom–up strategy (this strategy has inductive character). The whole negotiation process serves to resolve a specific case. Any *a priori* resolutions are not assumed. This model constitutes a contradiction to the strategy preferred by a model of judicial administration of the law, in conformity with a deductive top–down strategy. Admittedly, one can refer to some general solution, a principle or standard but only for the use of this case. The law stops being a permanent dimension, specified forever; there are not any universal principles and rules; all is to take place only in a particular process of negotiation (Stelmach & Brożek 2011, 2014).

Thus, topical–rhetorical argumentation refers to an initial case which is the subject of negotiation. The negotiation process itself, already discussed, is mediated in a specific event, in negotiation, which becomes an initial point for bottom–up reasoning. Before we pass on to determine the topical–rhetorical moments of negotiatory argumentation, we must realise that they defy order and structure. They are a dynamic process, during which all is subject to continuous change. It means that the process of negotiation seems to be complex and indefinite. One cannot present and unambiguously define this model. On one hand, it is said about topics, on the other hand about rhetoric, on psychological aspects of this process, and sometimes its eristic character. For many authors, it is not only indefinite but also realised too widely. For some people, it is a fault and for others it is an advantage. It turns out that many elements of this model can be used in any situation of negotiation. Thus, because of its elasticity, it has become a universal model. Jerzy Stelmach and Bartosz Brożek (2011) think that it is the most open among all models of negotiation. Persuasive reasoning (like rhetorical argumentation) characterises its deep structure, and interpretation itself and negotiation has a topical–rhetoric structure. Exhibiting efficiency is conditioned by a need to realise the aim, even with the cost of distance from ethical reasons. This means that a charge of amorality can be attributed to it. This charge can be referred only to the eristic sphere of this model (Schopenhauer 1976). It can be eliminated, because it is a technique of persuasion, which does not respect the basic topical–rhetoric requirements of rightness. A procedural criterion of understood justice upholds the ethical legitimisation of the topical–rhetoric model. What is mutually beneficial should be, in negotiation, recognised as rightful, and a certain formal minimum of justice is assured by the procedure accepted by participants of negotiation. A negotiator, as well as a court, recognises as legal this type of negotiated resolution, which fulfils a legal condition. Such resolution must also be binding from the positive point of view of just law.

Let us observe, in detail, the process which points to this topical–rhetoric model of negotiation. No doubt, as the first stage, it should be admitted this is the moment which begins negotiations and the precise designation of the subject of this negotiation. Thus, one excludes these facts from the process, which are not important, or which have been earlier recognised as unchallenged. The subsequent stages of this model undoubtedly have a situational character. One should consider the psychological situation of the participants in the negotiation process. This usually differentiates the dissimilarity of attitudes of the subjects of negotiation, and it has a basic influence on the course and results of the whole process. However, one cannot omit normative contexts from factual contexts, where the emotions and psychology of the negotiating subjects (e.g. economic factors) appear.

It is necessary to specify the aim or aims of negotiation. It allows for more precision, which should fulfil future negotiated resolutions. Pointing out this aim, the subject of the negotiation itself and negotiation contexts are made definite. Admittedly, the topical–rhetoric model, because of its nature, has a formal character; however, arrangements performed already in the pre-negotiation process, which refer to procedural rules that specify the sequence and the methods of negotiation, are highly significant. Normative and factual circumstances are excluded from the above, which could be considered unchallenged. Thus, after such clearing of the foreground, one can accede to proper negotiation. In their duration, one can use all suitable methods and tools suitable for direct use if they are consistent with earlier made procedural arrangements, and they serve to find an efficient solution. As I have mentioned earlier, by highlighting the elimination of eristic techniques, in the topical–rhetoric model, the end does not always justify the means.

> Realisation of the aim of negotiation, finding an efficient resolution – is one, and use of forbidden methods of negotiation – is the second. These methods cannot be simply used in negotiations, and negotiators should differentiate (Stelmach & Brożek 2014: 103–104).

For this reason, every resolution accepted by the parties should be justified. In principle, it involves stating compliance of the accepted negotiatory resolution with provisions of binding law. This is obviously done by the court. When we consider ethical reasoning, it is usually performed only when one of the parties participating in negotiations demands it. In the course of such reasons, it is checked whether negotiatory resolution fulfilling the requirements of efficiency is consistent with the minimal requirements of efficiency. These requirements forejudge the rightness of such decision, but not its efficiency. Effective resolution has to refer to economic efficiency.

In the light of our reasoning, till now we can say, following Perelman, that his new rhetoric is a type of discourse which tends towards convincing an opponent of his position. This is possible – as I mentioned earlier – only when one rejects all absolutism and dogmatism typical for the first philosophy, which he opposes with the conception of open philosophy. Thus, new rhetoric constitutes such discursive technique, with the object of causing or strengthening allegations presented for acceptance. Being the expression of open philosophy, it consists in working out such principles of acting which would be sensible in a human way and do not consist in discovering some eternal or invariable rules which are sought by traditional metaphysics (understood as the first philosophy).

In the light of the aforementioned arguments, it turns out that the methods of new rhetoric, being a specific discursive technique, allow the parties in conflict to jointly agree on a balanced position, which is aimed at mitigating those elements that led to the conflict. By rejecting 'wicked techniques', they implement solutions that correspond to procedural arrangements and lead to a fair settlement acceptable to both parties, which can be described as negotiation justice (Plucińska-Nowak 2021). Such negotiated settlements not only allow us to eliminate and understand what the conflict was about, but also lead to an integrated position of the 'conflicting parties'. We must remember that in mediation proceedings ended with a settlement, there is no winning and losing party. It can be said that it was the two parties who reached an agreement, which allowed the dispute to end (Zamelski 2015).

This requires the acquisition of communication, rhetorical and negotiation skills not only of mediators, but also of the parties themselves, and changes in the professional requirements of the lawyers themselves, especially judges (Michór 2015).

In Stalmach's 'Argumentative code for lawyers', general rules include:

1. argumentation should be conducted only in case of rise of vagueness justifying the origin of setting a dispute;
2. argumentation should be conducted with the conviction of its rightness;
3. argumentation should be conducted with respect for veracity;
4. argumentation should consider commonly accepted practices and principles;
5. argumentation should be conducted with respect for principles of equality and freedom;
6. argumentation should refer directly to its aim;
7. argumentation should respect basic principles of linguistic communication (Stelmach 2003; Kuczyński et al. 2010).

So-called arguments and legal topics contain more detailed rules. The following arguments are mentioned:

1. a *simili* argument (argument by similarity, by analogy)
2. a *contrario* argument (argument by contrast)

3. a *fortiori* argument (argument from stronger – has two forms, *a maiori ad minus*– from larger to smaller and *a minori ad maius* – from smaller to larger)
4. *ab exemplo* argument
5. argument by indirect evidence
6. a *rerum natura* argument
7. a *loco communi* argument
8. a *loco speciali* argument
9. a *cohaerentia* argument
10. a *completudine* argument
11. systematic argument
12. teleological argument
13. historical argument
14. economic argument
15. psychological argument (Kuczyński et al. 2010: 3–6; Stelmach 2003: 72–87).

Legal topics supplement a legal as well as a mediation discourse. I will mention only these among legal topics, which can be directly referred to negotiation:

1. *affirmanti occumbit comprobatio* (a party making an allegation must give evidence);
2. *audiatur et altera pars* (the opposing party should also be heard);
3. *contractus ab initio volontatis est, ex post facto necessitatis* (concluding a contract is voluntary but enforcement is compulsory);
4. *consensus facitlegem* (assent makes the law);
5. *ex non scripto ius venit quod usus comprobavit. nam diuturni mores consensu utentium comprabati legem imitantur* (the unwritten law is the one which was acknowledged by application, because long-term customs, acknowledged by consent of their users, take a form of the law);
6. *favor legitimatis* (the law favours what is in conformity with the law);
7. *ignorantia iuris nocet, non excusat* (ignorance of the law harms and does not constitute an excuse);
8. *impossibilium nulla obligatio est* (liability to perform an impossible obligation is invalid);

9. *in dubio pro libertate* (in case of doubt one should resolve for the benefit of freedom);
10. *in dubiislenius (mitius)* (in case of doubt more leniently);
11. *in re dubia benigniorem interpretationem sequi, non minis justius est quam tutius* (in doubtful cases following a more lenient interpretation is both more rightful as well as provident);
12. *ius publicum privatorum pactis mutari non potest* (public law cannot be changed by contracts of private persons);
13. *necessitas frangit legem* (necessity breaches the law);
14. *negativa non sunt probanta* (facts are to be proved, not their negotiations);
15. *nemo debet lucrari ex alieno damno* (nobody can be enriched through another person's harm);
16. *nemo iudex in causa sua* (nobody can be a judge in his own case);
17. *nemo plus iuris ad alium transferre potest, quam ipse habet* (nobody can transfer more rights than he has);
18. *nulla regula sine exceptione* (there is not a rule without an exception);
19. *non omne quod licet, honestum est* (not all which is lawful is just);
20. *qui licet quod est plus utique quod est minus* (the more one is allowed, the less one is allowed);
21. *quisquis praesumitur bonus* (it is presumed that everyone acts in good faith);
22. *res iudicata pro veritate accipitur* (the adjudged matter is accepted as truth);
23. *scire leges non hoc est verba earum tenere, sed vim ac potestatem* (knowledge of statutes does not consists in acquiring their words, but their contents and force of law);
24. *sententia facit ius* (a valid judgement makes the law);
25. *ubi lex, ibi poena* (where the law is, there is penalty);
26. *verba volant, scripta manent* (words are forgotten, the script remains);
27. *vim vi repellere licet* (force is allowed to force back);
28. *volenti non fit iniuria* (a willing person does not suffer wrong) (Jabłońska-Bonca & Zeidler 2016; Zajadło 2013).

As I mentioned earlier, the number of topics is significantly larger. I have limited them only exclusively to the sphere of usability towards negotiation.

It seems that this review shows what meaning they have in the course of mediational argumentation.

Summary

Because of its argumentative character, mediation is treated as an exemplification of a legal dialogue, where various attitudes clash, and, according to the aim accepted in mediation, has obtained a degree of consensus. All parties of this dialogue realise that it does not always end with a dispute resolution. Thus, it lowers a praxiological value on this dialogue and is the expression of the inefficacy of a decisive process (Kalisz 2016: 146). When the working out of a dispute resolution takes place, it always has an intersubjective dimension. It is the expression of the parties' consensus formed during discourse.

As Anna Kalisz (2016: 148) rightfully noted:

> taking a decision resolving a dispute, is based on [...] a common denominator established by the same parties of the conflict. It is a belief connected with what is just (and rightful) in a specific case, obtained in a way of argumentative discourse, in the grounds of which values and norms lie which are mutually accepted by the parties (often also commonly internalized).

It is sometimes stated that it is the specific administration of justice. Some people define it as mediatory justice. Therefore, it turns out that in a dispute, we give fair solutions as the best solution. Only such solutions serve to strengthen the autonomy https://pl.bab.la/slownik/angielski-polski/theof individuals, their groups and other subjects (Czapska 2024). This is the way to shape a civil society.

We must keep in mind that such understanding of the then notion of justice is not based on proven reasons, but on the recognition and acceptance of these, in which the parties in dispute accepted in compromise or consensus. Thus, this final decision is firstly the act of the parties, starting from an example, in which *notabene* the hero of my considerations presented. He considered a relatively simple situation. Two employees, one of whom is a bachelor and does not have anybody to provide for, and the second, the father of a large family responsible for their maintenance. Both work in the same post and have made identical contributions to a given product. If the employer treats them equally, each of them will receive identical payment for the same work, a certain contradiction (paradox) takes place between the demands of formal justice (in compliance with their formula, equal persons should be treated equally and unequal persons unequally), and material justice expressed in a formula, to everyone according to their needs. Whereas if they are treated unequally (the father of the family will receive a higher payment), then the requirement of formal justice is infringed from the point of view of the formula 'to everyone according to their labour contribution'. In this situation, Perelman points out that we must refer to integrity, while it has a servient function towards formal justice; it serves to standardise decisions taken in situations, in which this complex formula of justice (constituted by the two formulas of material justice mentioned earlier) creates a risk of far-reaching decisive divergence. Standardisation involves avoiding excessive unequal treatment of persons belonging to the same category (Perelman 1963). Thus, integrity creates compromises among criteria of material justice leading to the realisation of the principle of formal justice in a possibly high degree. It enables taking a decision in the form of compromise and consensus.

Favor legitimatis and *consensus facit legem* are to be found in the argumentation presented earlier. Because every argumentation should be carried out with belief of its rightness (general rule 2 Kodeks argumentacyjny by Jerzy Stelmach) based on *non omne quod licet, honestumest*, the parties corrected contradictions caused by formulas of material justice in such degree to give satisfaction to formal justice (according to them required in its maximal degree and accepted by them).

Bibliography

Alexy, Robert (1978). *Theorie der Juristischen Argumentation. Die Theorie des Rationalen Diskursesals der Juristischen Begründung*. Frankfurt am Main: Suhrkamp Verlag.

Arkuszewska, Aneta, and Plis, Jerzy (2014). *Zarys Metodyki Pracy Mediatora w Sprawach Cywilnych*. Warszawa: Wolters Kluwer.

Balicki, Ryszard (2010). 'Pozasądowe Procedury Rozwiązywania Sporów między Jednostkami'. In M. Jabłoński (ed.), *Realizacja i Ochrona Konstytucyjnych Wolności i Praw Jednostki w Polskim Porządku*

Prawnym. Wrocław: Ekonomiczna Biblioteka Cyfrowa. Wydział Prawa, Administracji i Ekonomii Uniwersytetu Wrocławskiego.

Berlin, Isaiah (1978). *Concepts and Categories. Philosophical Essays*. London: The Hogarth Press Ltd.

Czaja, Jacek, and Stelmach, Jerzy (1995). 'Teoria Argumentacji Prawniczej', *Krakowskie Studia Prawnicze*, annual set (XXVI–XXVII), 24–28.

Czapska, Janina (2024). 'ADR w Społeczeństwie Obywatelskim? Rozważania z Początku Trzeciej Dekady XXI Wieku'. In Czapska Janina (ed.), *Alternatywnie. Nowe Spojrzenia na Zastosowanie Alternatywnych Metod Rozwiązywania Sporów w Prawie*. Kraków: Wydawnictwo Uniwersytetu Jagiellońskiego.

Florescu, Vasile (1982). *La Rhètorique et la Nèorhètorique. Genèse – Évolution – Perspectives*, pp 152–172. Bucureşti–Paris: Les Belles Lettres.

Fuller, Lon Luvois (1978). 'The Forms and Limits of Adjudication', *Harvard Law Review Association*, 92 (2), 353–354.

Gizbert-Studnicki, Tomasz (1995). 'Podstawy Argumentacji Prawniczej'. In Kaźmierczak Stanisław (ed.), *Historia – Prawo – Państwo. Zbiór Studiów*. Wrocław: Acta Universitatis Wratislaviensis, No. 1772.

Gregorowicz, Jan (1967). 'Dwie Koncepcje Logiki Prawniczej'. In Kotarbiński, Czezowski, et al. (ed. Committee), *Fragmenty Filozoficzne – Seria Trzecia. Księga Pamiątkowa ku Czci Profesora Tadeusza Kotarbińskiego w Osiemdziesiątą Rocznicę Urodzin*. Warszawa: PWN.

Heijenoort, Jean (1967). *From Frege to Gödel. A Source Book in Mathematical Logic, 1879–1931*. London: Harvard University Press.

Hilpinen, Risto (2008). 'Deontic Logic'. In L. Goble (ed.), *The Backwell Guide to Philosophical Logic*. Oxford: Blackwell Publishers Ltd.

Jabłońska-Bonca, Jolanta & Zeidler, Kamil (2023). *Prawnika Sztuka Retoryki i Negocjacji*. Warszawa: Wolters Kluwer.

Kalisz, Anna (2016). *Mediacja Jako Forma Dialogu w Stosowaniu Prawa*. Warszawa: Difin.

Kamiński, Stanisław (1957). 'Fregego Logika Zdań', *Roczniki Filozoficzne*, V (fascicle 2/1957), Faculty of Philosophy, John Paul II Catholic University of Lublin, 31–62.

Kiereś-Łach, Joanna (2015). *Filozofia i Retoryka. Kontekst Myślowy "Nowej Retoryki" Chaïma Perelmana*. Lublin: Academicon Press.

Kleszcz, Ryszard (1989). 'Od Analizy do Argumentacji. Wprowadzenie do Perelmana'. *Studia Filozoficzne*, 6 (283), 124–127.
Kleszcz, Ryszard (1988). 'Perelman a Tradycja Racjonalizmu', *Acta Universitatis Lodziensis – Folia Philosophica*, fascicle 5, 129–145.
Kleszcz, Ryszard (1985a). 'Pluralizm Jako Warunek Dyskursu w Myśli Ch. Perelmana', *Kultura i Społeczeństwo*, annual set, XXX (3), 153–164.
Kleszcz, Ryszard (1985b). 'Teoria Argumentacji w Ujęciu Ch. Perelmana', *Acta Iniversitatis Lodziensis – Folia Philosophica*, fascicle 3, 143–167.
Korybski, Andrzej (1993). *Alternatywne Rozwiązywanie Sporów w USA*. Lublin: Wydawnictwo Uniwersytetu Marii Curie-Skłodowskiej.
Kobielska, Katarzyna (2023). 'ADR (Alternative Dispute Resolution)'. In Cetera, Magdalena and Taber Nacka, Magdalena (eds), *Leksykon Mediacji*, pp. 173–179. Warszawa: Difin.
Kuczyński, Grzegorz (2010). 'Argument'. In Rybiński, Przemysław, and Zeidler, Kamil (eds), *Leksykon Retoryki. 100 Podstawowych Pojęć*, pp. 4–9. Warszawa: Wydawnictwo C.H. Beck.
Kwiatkowski, Tadeusz (2008). *Wykłady i Szkice z Logiki Ogólnej*. Lublin: Wydawnictwo Uniwersytetu Marii Curie-Skłodowskiej.
Lewiński, Piotr. (2012). *Neosofistyka. Argumentacja Retoryczna w Komunikacji Potocznej*. Wrocław: Wydawnictwo Uniwersytetu Wrocławskiego.
Lichański, Jakub (1992). *Retoryka od Średniowiecza do Baroku*. Warszawa: Wydawnictwo Naukowe PWN.
Lusińska, Anna (2023). 'Negocjacje'. In Łukasz Wirkus and Marta Pięta-Chrystofiak (eds), *Mediacje Sądowe i Interwencja Kryzysowa w Teorii i Praktyce*, pp. 69–87. Gdańsk: Wydawnictwo Uniwersytetu Gdańskiego.
Marciszewski, Witold (1991). *Logika z Retorycznego Punktu Widzenia*. Warszawa: Zakład Semiotyki logicznej Uniwersytetu Warszawskiego.
Marciszewski, Witold (1994). *Sztuka Rozumowania w Świetle Logiki*. Warszawa: Wydawnictwo Aleph.
Meyer, Michel, Manuel Maria Carrilho, and Timmermans, Benoit (2010). *Historia Retoryki od Greków do Dziś*. Warszawa: Wydawnictwo ALETHEIA.
Michór, Andrzej (2015). 'Sędzia jako Mediator Pierwszego Kontaktu w Postępowaniu Cywilnym'. In Przemysław Malinowski, Hanna

Duszka-Jakimko, and Arleta Suchorska (eds), *Wokół Praktycznych i Teoretycznych Aspektów Mediacji*. Kraków: AT Wydawnictwo.
Mihai, Gheorghe (1982). *Elemente Constructive de Argumentarejuridica*. Bucureşti: Academiei R.S.R.
Mikołajczyk, Adam (2010). 'Negocjacje'. In Rybiński, Przemysław & Zeidler, Kamil (eds), *Leksykon Retoryki. 100 Podstawowych Pojęć*, pp. 175–184. Warszawa: Wydawnictwo C.H. Beck.
Moffitt, Michael (2006). 'The Making of an ADR Pionier', *Negotiation Journal October*, 22 (4), 437–443.
Morawski, Lech (1999). *Główne Problemy Współczesnej Filozofii Prawa. Prawo w Toku Przemian*. Warszawa: Wydawnictwo LexisNexis.
Morek, Rafał (2011). *Mediacja w Sprawach Cywilnych*. Warszawa: Oficyna Wydawnicza Ministerstwa Sprawiedliwości.
Nęcki, Zbigniew (2000). *Komunikacja Międzyludzka*. Kraków: Wydawnictwo Antykwa.
Nowak, Leszek (1987). 'Idealizacja'. In Cackowski, Zdzisław, Kmita, Jerzy, Szaniawski, Klemens, and P. J. Smoczyński (eds), *Filozofia a Nauka. Zarys Encyklopedyczny*, pp. 210–231. Wrocław-Warszawa-Kraków-Gdańsk-Łódź: Wydawnictwo Ossolineum.
Pascal, Blaise (1968). *Myśli*. Warszawa: Wydawnictwo PAX.
Perelman, Chaïm (1963). *The Idea of Justice and the Problem of Argument*. London, New York: Humanities Press.
Perelman, Chaïm (1975). 'Dialektyka i Dialog'. *Studia Filozoficzne*, 5 (114), 84–93.
Perelman, Chaïm (2002). *Imperium Retoryki. Retoryka i Argumentacja*. Warszawa: Wydawnictwo Naukowe PWN.
Perelman, Chaïm and Olbrecht-Tyteca, Lucie (1970). *Traitè de l'Argumentation. La Nouvelle Rhètorique*. Bruxelle – Paris, Presses Universitaires de France.
Perelman, Chaïm (1986). 'Logika a Teoria Argumentacji: Teoretyczne Zagadnienia Poprawności Decyzji Sądowej', *Nowe Prawo*, 7–8, 10–15.
Perelman, Chaïm (1984). *Logika Prawnicza. Nowa Retoryka*. Warszawa: Wydawnictwo PWN.

Perelman, Chaïm (1967). 'O Decyzjach Niezgodnych i Racjonalnych', *Fragmenty Filozoficzne*, Seria III, pp. 356–365. Warszawa: Wydawnictwo Academicon.

Perelman, Chaïm (1964). 'O Oczywistości w Metafizyce'. In Żarnecka, Zofia (ed.), *Szkice Filozoficzne*, pp. 159–165. Warszawa: Wydawnictwo PWN.

Perelman, Chaïm (1969). 'Qu`Est-ce qua la Logiquejuridique?'. In Gumański, Leon (ed.), *Rozprawy Filozoficzne*, pp. 305–311. Toruń: Państwowe Wydawnictwo Naukowe .

Plucińska-Nowak, Martyna (2021). *The Status and Faces of Mediation in Polish Society*. Poznań: Wydawnictwo Nauk Społecznych i Humanistycznych.

Polanowska-Sygulska, Beata (2008). *Pluralizm Wartości i Jego Implikacje w Filozofii Prawa*. Kraków: Księgarnia Akademicka.

Raiff, Howard (1996). *The Art and Science of Negotiation*. Cambridge: Harvard University Press.

Resolution of the Social Council for Alternative Dispute Resolution Methods at the Ministry of Justice of 26 June 2006, <https://www.gov.pl/web/sprawiedliwosc/spoleczna-rada-do-spraw-alternatywnych-metod-rozwiazywania-sporow-przy-ministrze-sprawiedliwosci>, accessed 3 July 2024.

Sander, Frank (1985). *Dispute Resolution*. Boston. West Academic Press.

Schopenhauer, Artur (1976). *Erystyka, czyli Sztuka Prowadzenia Sporów*. Kraków: Wydawnictwo SBM.

Sołtysiak, Patrycja (2012). 'Mediacja jako Alternatywna Metoda Rozwiązywania Sporów', *Zeszyty Naukowe Instytutu Administracji AJD w Częstochowie*, 2 (6), 14–20.

Stelmach, Jerzy (2003). *Kodeks Argumentacyjny dla Prawników*. Kraków: Zakamycze.

Stelmach, Jerzy, and Brożek, Bartosz (2006). *Metody Prawnicze. Logika – Analiza – Argumentacja – Hermeneutyka*. Warszawa: Wolters Kluwer.

Stelmach, Jerzy and Brożek, Bartosz (2014). *Negocjacje*. Kraków: Copernicus Center Press.

Stelmach, Jerzy, and Brożek, Bartosz (2011). *Sztuka Negocjacji Prawniczych*. Warszawa: Wolters Kluwer.

Szymanek, Krzysztof (2008). *Argument z Podobieństwa*. Katowice: Wydawnictwo Uniwersytetu Śląskiego.

Szymanek, Krzysztof (2001). *Sztuka Argumentacji*. Warszawa: Wydawnictwo Naukowe PWN.

Świrydowicz, Kazimierz (1995). *Logiczne Teorie Obowiązku Warunkowego*. Poznań: Wydawnictwo Naukowe UAM.

Tokarz, Marek (2006). *Argumentacja. Perswazja. Manipulacja*. Gdańsk: Gdańskie Wydawnictwo Psychologiczne.

Toulmin, Stephen (1958). *The Uses of Argument*. Cambridge University Press.

Trzęsicki, Kazimierz (1995). *Logika Nieformalna – Zagadnienia Wybrane*. Warszawa-Białystok: Wydawnictwo Temida2.

Trzęsicki, Kazimierz (1996). *Logika. Nauka i Sztuka*. Białystok: Wydawnictwo Temida2.

Waszkiewicz, Jan (1997). *Jak Polak z Polakiem? Szkice o Kulturze Negocjowania*. Warszawa – Wrocław: Wydawnictwo PWN.

Woleński, Jan (1978). 'Filozoficzne Aspekty Sporu o Logikę Prawniczą'. In Stróżewski, Władysław (ed.), *Studia z Teorii Poznania i Filozofii Wartości*, pp. 35–40. Wrocław–Warszawa–Kraków–Gdańsk: Zakład Narodowy Imienia Ossolińskich.

Wójcicki, Ryszard (2003). *Wykłady z Logiki z Elementami Teorii Wiedzy*. Warszawa: Wydawnictwo Naukowe Scholar.

Wróblewski, Jerzy (1984). 'Logika Prawnicza a Teoria Argumentacji Chaima Perelmana'. In *Chaim Perelman, Logika Prawnicza*, pp. 14–18. *Nowa Retoryka*, Warszawa: Wydawnictwo PWN.

Wysokińska, Natalia (2006). *Instytucja Mediacji w Kodeksie Postępowania Cywilnego*. Wrocław: Wydawnictwo Uniwersytetu Wrocławskiego.

Zajadło, Jerzy (2013). *Łacińska Terminologia Prawnicza*. Warszawa: Wydawnictwo Wolters Kluwer.

Zamelski, Piotr (2015). 'Filozoficzno – Prawne i Aksjologiczne Aspekty Mediacji'. In Malinowski, Przemysław, Duszka-Jakimko, Hanna, and Suchorska Arleta (eds), *Wokół Praktycznych i Teoretycznych Aspektów Mediacji*, pp. 37–47. Kraków: Wydawnictwo AT.

Zarębski, Tomasz (2005). *Od Paradygmatu do Kosmopolis. Filozofia Stephena E. Toulmina*. Wrocław: Wydawnictwo Oświatowe Atut.

Ziemba, Zdzisław (1983). *Analityczna Teoria Obowiązku. Studium z Logiki Deontycznej*. Warszawa: Wydawnictwo Naukowe PWN.

Ziembiński, Zygmunt (1992). *Logika Praktyczna*. Warszawa: Wydawnictwo Naukowe PWN.

Zienkiewicz, Adam (2005). 'Alternatywne Rozwiązywanie i Rozstrzyganie Sporów Prawnych', *Studia Prawnoustrojowe*, 5, 33–50.

Zirk-Sadowski, Marek (2012). 'Wstęp'. In Łukowski, Piotr (ed.), *Logika Praktyczna z Elementami Wiedzy o Manipulacji*, pp. 18–19. Warszawa: Wolters Kluwer Polska.

CHAPTER 5

The Balkans Powder Keg Reloaded

Hungary and the Western Balkan Region at the Crossroads of European Integration

Viktor Glied[1] and Andrea Schmidt[2]

Introduction

Since the onset of the global financial crisis in 2008, the European Union (EU) has been confronted with a succession of escalating challenges. These include the migration and integration crisis, increasing political fragmentation, Brexit, the ongoing war in Ukraine, the widening conflicts in the Middle East, the economic and social impacts of COVID-19 and the issues arising from climate change. Each of these has posed increasingly severe challenges to the EU. As discussions continue about the future of integration – particularly regarding the depth and scope of its advancement – the question of enlargement remains prominent, especially with respect to the Balkan countries.

In July 2024, Hungary assumed the rotating presidency of the European Union. In May, Péter Szijjártó, the Minister of Foreign Affairs and Trade, outlined the areas in which the Hungarian presidency seeks to make progress. He emphasised Hungary's commitment to contributing to the stability, peace and development of the Western Balkans. Szijjártó acknowledged the complexity of the Western Balkans but asserted that a common ground must be identified, which could be the process of European integration. Hungary has significant political, economic and security interests in the accession of the Western Balkan states. Szijjártó argued that the delay in the accession of these countries undermines the EU's credibility and, therefore, it is in Budapest's interest to advocate for a pro-peace, sovereigntist European shift. He noted that the EU has a greater need for the Balkan countries than they have for

1 Dr Habil University of Pécs, email: <glied.viktor@pte.hu>
2 Dr Habil, University of Pécs, email: <schmidt.andrea@pte.hu>

the EU, citing three NATO Member States in the Balkans – Albania, North Macedonia and Montenegro – that have yet to join the European community[3].

Right after Hungary took over the rotating EU presidency, Prime Minister of Hungary Viktor Orbán – one of the last EU leaders to do so – visited President of Ukraine Volodymyr Zelenskiy in Kyiv. Three days later, he left for Moscow, where he met the President of Russia Vladimir Putin. Questions have been raised about the purpose of the visit series, the entity on behalf of which the Hungarian Prime Minister was acting, whether he had the authorisation to act on behalf of the European Union, or whether it could be considered an autonomous action by the government of Hungary. This is because 'Peace' was the core message and slogan of the government in the 2024 European Parliamentary elections in Hungary. Although this catchy phrase overrode all other political and economic challenges in the government's communication, the unexpected visits extraordinarily surprised the EU decision-makers. The usual narrative that called these trips as peace missions were shattered when – after Viktor Orbán visited Moscow – the Ukrainian capital came under greater attack than ever before, the largest children's hospital was hit by a heavy rocket attack and the 'peace mission' had the opposite effect. This is one of the reasons why Viktor Orbán's visits were considered a failure by both Ukraine and the European Union. Apparently, Hungary intended to use the rotating presidency to act as a mediator between Kyiv and Moscow, as well as in other conflicts (between Iran and Israel, or the conflicts of the Balkans).

The venue and date of the Council of Foreign Ministers were set against the Hungarian proposal, and further sanctions were imposed in a spirit of disagreement. Shortly after the peace mission, Ukraine announced that it would not allow Russian Lukoil's oil to be transported through its territory to Hungary and Slovakia, even though the sanctions imposed did not apply to Russian supply to these two countries via the pipeline (Hovet & Komuves 2024). The Hungarian government's response was not to retreat into its

3 Hungary Today (2024). Peace and Development in the Western Balkans will be of Focus During EU Presidency. MTI-Hungary Today, <https://hungarytoday.hu/peace-and-development-in-the-western-balkans-will-be-in-focus-during-eu-presidency/>, accessed 27 May 2024.

mediation role, but to take a 180-degree turn and start blackmailing Brussels politicians with the prospect of the usual Hungarian veto[4], this time blocking financial support to countries providing arms supplies to the Ukrainian belligerent. Hungary, however, introduced mediation into its own narrative of its mission, emphasising the importance of peace-building efforts.

Chapter V shall analyse the role of mediation in Hungarian–Balkan relations. Hungary's geographical location at the border of East and West set the mission of Hungarian politicians and statesmen in the past to act as a bridge, or to serve as a Bastion of Christianity. Both its geopolitical and cultural landscapes are all factors that have deeply determined Hungarian political orientation. We would like to focus on the Balkans as a multilayer phenomenon, a geographical and cultural landscape. The Balkan Peninsula which is described as a 'powder keg' (Gallagher 1997; Jelavich 1996; Makkai 2014) and the crossroads of cultural and geopolitical conflicts, has been standing in the forefront of interest of the neighbouring countries. We will also analyse the Balkans as the target of geopolitical and geostrategic interest starting from the presence of empires, such as the Ottoman, the Russian and the Habsburg Empires, the consequences of the dissolution of empires and the birth of new successor states on their ruins, the consequences of Peace Treaty of Trianon from the point of view of Hungary and the position of the Balkans as a 'defence wall'. Owing to its geographical location, Hungary is situated on the border of two direct conflict zones, which in principle allows it to play the role of mediator. Although it is Hungary's ambition to perform this role, Hungarian foreign policy focuses not only on its neighbourhood but also on the Balkans in a wider focus. It also appears to be a bridge towards the South-East dimension. As economics is also a specific layer of international relations, the intensity, scale and direction of Hungarian investments are also characteristic elements of Hungarian foreign policy.

4 The hysteria over oil supply has been denied by the parties involved, the Slovak and Hungarian refinery owner MOL, and the EU; and even European Commission Vice President for Trade Valdis Dombrovskis said that according to information received from Hungary's MOL, no complaints about the continuity of supply have been received because of sanctions against Lukoil, while the Croatian partner has at the same time offered to increase the amount of oil coming through the Adriatic pipeline. However, the Hungarian Foreign Minister has not stopped making accusations.

Hungary's Position in the Light of the Current Balkan Conflicts

Analysing the role of Hungary as the mediator in the conflict within the fragmented Balkan Peninsula, it is also the task of Chapter V to describe whether such an approach can be successful. We would like to point out the Hungarian standpoint regarding the caching-up after the dissolution of Yugoslavia, South Slavic unity, both political and economic perspectives, while also focusing on the role of international organisations and consultative platforms, such as NATO, EU, CEFTA and the Visegrad Group. Hungarian presence has been visible since 2019, when the European Commission appointed a Hungarian expert, Olivér Várhelyi as the Commissioner for Neighbourhood and Enlargement whose task was to facilitate the integration of the Western Balkan countries into the EU[5].

Péter Szijjártó delivered a speech in April 2024 at the joint press conference with the Montenegrin minister responsible for European affairs, Maida Gorčević and confirmed this complex position, which is strongly driven by political motives[6]. The continuous prioritisation of economic interests sheds some light on political goals, since the Chinese communist regime – which maintains good relations with the Hungarian government, as well as Turkey, Russia and other Asian and Middle Eastern countries – is interested in establishing closer relations with the countries of the Western Balkans. As soon as these countries join the EU, it may become more difficult for non-EU economic actors to enter the market, which in turn may benefit Hungary.

Szijjártó highlighted another aspect that has been on the political agenda in the EU and its Member States with varying intensity since the migration crisis in 2015: conflicts arising from illegal/irregular migration to the EU

5 About Hungary (2020). Commissioner Várhelyi on EU Enlargement: We Need to Speed Up Accession for the Western Balkans, <https://abouthungary.hu/blog/commissioner-varhelyi-on-eu-enlargement-we-need-to-speed-up-accession-for-the-western-balkans>, accessed 21 March 2024.

6 Government of Hungary (2024a). A Nyugat-Balkáni EU-csatlakozási folyamat lassúsága az egész bővítéspolitika hitelét aláássa (The slowness of the EU accession process in the Western Balkans undermines the credibility of the whole enlargement policy), <https://kormany.hu/hirek/a-nyugat-balkani-eu-csatlakozasi-folyamat-lassusaga-az-egesz-bovitespolitika-hitelet-alaassa>, accessed 3 June 2024.

and non-uniform migration regulations. One of the sharpest criticisms of the Hungarian government against EU decision-makers stems from the lack of effective regulations on migration. This is answered by the statement that 'it is in the interest of the entire Western Balkans and Hungary, which serves as the gateway to the EU, to keep these migration processes as far away from us as possible; therefore, we will develop our anti-migration cooperation, just as we develop our administrative cooperation too'[7]. If the Western Balkan states were admitted to the Union, it would result in a completely new geopolitical/geostrategic situation. In this case, the gateway to the EU through the Eastern Mediterranean (Balkan) migration corridor running from the Middle East and North Africa would not only be Greece and Bulgaria, but also Albania and Montenegro in some respects. At the same time, Serbia and Bosnia–Herzegovina would remain present as inclusions wedged into the already-joined states. This constellation would also pose a security risk, because the two states border Hungary, Romania and Croatia, i.e. the countries which currently constitute the external borders of the EU.

Characteristics of Hungarian Foreign Policy and Mediation

Hungary has a deep and long-lasting connection with the Balkans from political, economic and cultural perspectives, stretching back centuries. This region, which served as a bridge between Asia and Central Europe, has often been where Hungary's southern borders met powerful empires such as Byzantium and the Ottoman Empire. The Balkans have always been what might be called 'a transition and a buffer zone', where the influence of past empires can still be felt. It is a place where political and cultural elements mingled, where different religions, ethnic groups and nationalities have lived together, where states have both come together and fallen apart and where patterns of state integration and disintegration could be found.

7 Government of Hungary (2024b). Magyarország mindent megtesz a Nyugat-Balkán békéje és fejlődése érdekében (Hungary helps peace and development processes of the Western Balkans), <https://kormany.hu/hirek/magyarorszag-mindent-megtesz-a-nyugat-balkan-bekeje-es-fejlodese-erdekeben>, accessed 29 May 2024.

Given this complex history, it is impossible to view Hungary's foreign policy in a vacuum. The decisions made by Hungarian leaders are shaped by rapidly changing political and economic realities. Various theories are employed to assess Hungary's role in Balkan affairs. Critical geopolitics, for instance, helps interpret the ever-shifting political–geopolitical landscape, considering not just the nation–state as a standalone entity, but also the factors influencing policymakers, such as civil society, soft power, transnational corporations and the growing influence of media. The balance of power in the world is changing, and this is very much felt in the Balkans too. The region used to be under the influence of empires such as the Turks, Russians, Italians and British. Today, though, these old powers find themselves competing with new actors, e.g. China and Saudi Arabia. In this challenging environment, full of crises and security threats including migration, terrorism, radicalism, armed conflicts and even genocide, Hungary needs to find ways to connect with the Balkans. These connections go back to the days of the Kingdom of Hungary and the Austro–Hungarian Empire, and they still offer opportunities for cooperation today (Bumman 2023; Simurdic 2016).

The Balkans are characterised by continuous conflicts, which is why this region is still called a powder keg. After 2015, Hungarian foreign policy assumed an increasingly active role in international affairs, and after 2022 it became extremely proactive in this field (Tarrósy & Vörös 2020). The Orbán administration appeared in international processes partly as a generator of disputes and partly as an actor trying to reconcile parties in conflict with each other. Mediation in foreign policy involves the use of diplomatic strategies by a third party to facilitate the resolution of conflicts between two or more states or international actors. It aims to achieve peaceful settlements and prevent escalations that could lead to war or prolonged disputes. Mediation is almost as old as various conflicts itself. The best mediators can resolve disputes discreetly, effectively and most importantly, with fairness to both parties. With mediation, the involved parties usually reach a suitable compromise, and this tool can be significant in conflict resolution where the mediator makes it possible for everyone to benefit.

Generally, mediation can cover various layers; however, one of the most significant spheres where mediation can fulfil its role is the legal issues and diplomacy. The formalisation of mediation and its incorporation into the legal system clearly stems from recognising that law cannot fully address all interpersonal conflicts. Also, it cannot formalise interpersonal situations in which problems arise (Németh 2022). The cooperative negotiation technique was first demonstrated by Roger Fisher and William Ury (1991) in their book 'Getting to Yes'. The authors divide the process into four main phases, the first of which is the exploration of interests separating the problem from the individual. In the second stage, the focus is on the realisation of interests and the achievement of goals. The third phase is to identify the opportunities that can be used to increase the common good, the distributive good. The fourth phase is the distribution of goods, using objective criteria. It is important to mention the term 'BATNA' (Best Alternative To a Negotiated Agreement) which refers to the best negotiated outcome. The outcome to be achieved is defined by the parties in cooperative negotiation, and with this in mind, they can shape their room for manoeuvre. As the mediation approach is spread in Europe, it has also been adopted by Western European countries fora few decades. As it began to gain ground as a problem-solving protocol, it became increasingly broadened, along with the field of use of mediation. It began to be used to not only settle workplace and financial disputes, but also disputes in family, community, school-related matters, including peer mediation, health mediation and intercultural mediation; moreover, it has also been introduced to criminal proceedings (Dawson 1999).

On the other hand, various factors that influence Hungarian foreign policy decision-making blend elements of strategic choices with pragmatic considerations that prioritise Hungary's national interests. As with any international decision, multiple aspects come into play in Hungary's foreign policy (Kacziba 2024). Some of these are shaped by rational thought, while others remain speculative due to the unknown factors and motivations behind the decisions. Hungary's mediation approach is often pragmatic, focusing on fostering dialogue and keeping communication channels open, even in complex or contentious situations. Recently, Hungary has increasingly positioned itself as a mediator in various diplomatic contexts, particularly within Central and Eastern Europe and the broader international arena. This role aligns with Hungary's strategic interests in enhancing its influence and promoting stability in neighbouring regions through effective, or at least promising, diplomatic manoeuvres. Key areas of Hungary's diplomatic mediation are the Western Balkans, especially the Serbia–Kosovo conflict where Budapest leveraged its good relations with both Belgrade and Pristina. As was also mentioned, Hungary has also pursued a somewhat independent foreign policy, emphasising the need for dialogue and often calling for a balanced approach to sanctions. Hungary has positioned itself as a voice advocating for peace and dialogue, although its close ties with Russia have sometimes led to tensions with its Western allies. Hungary has also shown an interest in playing a role in the Middle East, particularly in the context of Israel and Palestine. Hungary's government has maintained strong relations with Israel and has occasionally offered to facilitate dialogue in the region, promoting itself as a bridge between Europe and the Middle East. Hungary's approach to mediation is often characterised by pragmatism, focusing on fostering dialogue and maintaining open channels of communication, even in complex or contentious situations[8].

Hungarian foreign policy is frequently recognised as pragmatic, with the national interest standing behind the government's decisions. The pragmatic foreign policy is not only an idea that must be contradicted and criticised, but also an alternative, the principled pragmatism which is a foreign policy approach that combines realism and idealism when a country acts in its national interests and for its national security while at the same time upholding its values and principles. In other words, principled pragmatism is a flexible, adaptable approach to foreign policy that varies depending on the challenges and the context (Ralph 2023). According to the modern concept, pragmatic foreign policy fundamentally amounts to decision-making void of moral and ethical considerations, wherein only short-term political and economic interests play a role. Reference to national interests overrides all other interests. International cooperation (military, economic, political), as well as simple economic interests (trade, energy policy, military procurement), are driven by those pragmatic national interests that can be suited to long-term strategic plans. Hungarian foreign policy employs this flexible decision-making system to provide increasing room for government

8 About Hungary (2024). FM: Hungarian Diplomacy Gave the Right Responses During Recent Challenges, <https://abouthungary.hu/news-in-brief/fm-hungarian-diplomacy-gave-the-right-responses-during-recent-challenges>, accessed 22 May 2024.

movements. In its history, Hungary was often defined as a ship, a ferry or a bridge in related scholarly literature and by politicians, referring to the fact that the Carpathian Basin was a pivot between East and West. For years, the Hungarian Prime Minister has been balancing between the EU and NATO and the Eastern partners, openly befriending the Russian President despite the European Union's reproaches. The Hungarian stance is clear: when scrutinising Hungary's foreign policy, the strategic complexity of connectivity determines Budapest's position, which means that Hungary seeks to maintain a balanced and pragmatic approach in its diplomatic relations (Orbán 2023). The Hungarian government claims that energy security is a primary concern for Budapest, i.e. it rejects any steps that might threaten it to refer to the protection of national sovereignty.

The Balkans and Its Challenges

For a long time, the Balkans represented the external border of Central Europe, Western civilisation, and Christianity up to the eighteenth century. Eastern European scholars have used post-colonial studies to explore representations of the region as Western Europe's 'other'. They have also used post-colonial studies to understand the political, social, military and economic interference and domination by Russia, Western countries, or entities such as the European Union. Whether the entire region of Eastern Europe was truly colonised by Soviet Russia during the socialist period is open to debate, and the tremendous diversity in the socialist experience among different countries cautions against broad generalisations (Owczarzak 2009; Schmidt 2023).

The southern border region of Hungary is a multidimensional entity. If the Western Balkans could be identified with the former Yugoslavia and Albania and focus our investigation on this region, a complex, yet internally fragmented region can be drawn, where cultural, religious and civilisational fault lines are stretching (Reményi 2020). In addition, the borders of its countries have changed frequently and continue to do so in the twenty-first century, as do the names of countries, which foreshadows challenges in preserving national identity.

In terms of colonial theories, Hungary was in a special and unique geographical position. It was both a subordinate entity within the imperial structure of the region and a multi-ethnic construct. The ethnic groups and the Hungarian ruling nation were in an asymmetrical position in terms of different political rights, the existence of interest groups and the inequality of collective rights. The Austro–Hungarian 'Dual Monarchy' was thus an asymmetrical and unbalanced federation (Pelinka 2015).

The image of the Balkans as 'half-other' plays a particular role in the fact that while some European countries have been successful in EU integration, others are still in that process. The Western Balkans are perceived as part of Europe in geographical, historical and civilisational terms (as European and local politicians are keen to emphasise), but they still have a long way to go before becoming European. Or, on the other hand, it is an ambiguous place 'where some countries have a European identity, while others have to work for it' (Schmidt 2022). The Balkan Peninsula remained a buffer zone up until the early twentieth century marking the collapse of empires. However, on the ruins of those collapsed empires, a new integration started to develop, the unity of Southern Slavic nations, Yugoslavia. That model did not survive the beginning of the Second World War; however, after 1945, Yugoslavia with its charismatic leader, Josip Broz Tito managed to create an individual path in the bipolar system becoming one of the leaders of the non-aligned states.

The concept of *Antemurale Christianitatis* (Latin for 'bulwark of Christianity') has a long and complex history, deeply rooted in the political, cultural and religious landscape of Central and Eastern Europe (Martín-Arroyo 2013). It refers to the role certain countries and regions have historically assumed — or been assigned — as defenders of Christian Europe against non-Christian forces, particularly the Ottoman Empire. This idea has significantly influenced national identities and historical narratives across the region.

The notion of *Antemurale Christianitatis* has experienced a revival in recent decades, particularly in the context of contemporary political and social issues, such as the European migrant crisis that began in 2015. In this modern context, the term has been reinterpreted and repurposed by some political leaders, especially in Central and Eastern Europe, to emphasise a defensive posture against the perceived threat posed by non-European, non-Christian immigrants, particularly from Muslim-majority countries.

Hungary, under the leadership of Viktor Orbán, is a prominent example of this revival. Orbán has frequently invoked the idea of Hungary as a 'bastion of Christian Europe', framing the influx of predominantly Muslim refugees and migrants as a direct threat to European civilisation and Christian values (Glied & Pap 2016). In his rhetoric, Orbán presents Hungary not just as a nation with its own borders to protect, but as a guardian of Europe's cultural and religious heritage. Orbán's reference to the *Antemurale Christianitatis* concept reflects a broader trend in which historical myths and symbols are repurposed to address modern political issues. The emphasis on 'keeping Europe Christian' taps into deep-seated fears and cultural anxieties about the future of European identity in an increasingly globalised and multicultural world.

According to their historical narrative, Austrians, Croats, Hungarians and Poles of the nineteenth century claimed that their ancestors saved Europe from Islam, while Bulgars, Greeks, Montenegrins, Romanians and Serbs, still under Ottoman overlordship in the romantic period, framed their respective bids for independence as fighting for the Christian world.

For centuries, the Balkan Peninsula served as a bridge between Asia (Middle East, Turkey) and the inner parts of Europe, both in terms of cultural and population flows (Kitanics & Pap 2016). Trans-Balkan roads were stretching primarily a North–South connection for the transport of goods. In the second half of the twentieth century, the limited open markets of Tito's Yugoslavia and the import of Western goods led to an increasingly serious smuggling activity at the border of Yugoslavia. The regime changes in the 1990s also brought freedom to the Balkan countries, Bulgaria, Romania and Albania, and the former Yugoslav Member States entered the stage of the international community as sovereign players because of a political–economic transition. Meanwhile, the so-called Eastern Mediterranean (Balkan) route has become an increasingly popular transit route for illegal trade operated by organised crime groups, traffickers (trafficking humans, drugs, weapons, cigarettes) and irregular migrants (United Nations Office on Drugs and Crime 2008).

Starting in 2014, mass migration to Europe appeared on the Balkan route beside the traditional Western and Central Mediterranean one. As a result of the bloody conflicts that broke out in Afghanistan and the Middle East, Turkey became a junction for migrants/refugees. More than 1 million people departed from Turkey through Greece, Bulgaria, North Macedonia and Serbia, across Croatia and Hungary, to continue their trip to a Western European country (Kallius 2017). States affected by mass migration attempted to maintain their border protection with different intensities. In 2015, it turned out that all this was not possible, so all the Balkan countries started erecting security fences. Greece started constructing a fence in 2012 along its land border with Turkey in the Evros River region (40 km long), North Macedonia erected a security fence along its border with Greece. Bulgaria began building a security fence along its border with Turkey as early as 2013, before the peak of the migration crisis. The fence has been designed to prevent illegal crossings and manage migration from Turkey. Hungary constructed its security border fence in 2015 alongside the entire Serbian–Hungarian border and a smaller part between Hungary and Croatia. As a result, tens of thousands of irregular migrants were stuck in Serbia which established temporary refugee camps. Hungary and Serbia have engaged in joint border patrols and enhanced security cooperation to manage their shared border. This collaboration has been crucial in controlling the flow of migrants attempting to cross from Serbia into Hungary, which is an external border of the EU. As a help to Serbia, Hungary has provided technical assistance, equipment and training to strengthen Serbia's border management capabilities (Tošić 2017). This has included sharing best practices on border security and migration management.

The phrase 'protection zone' appeared in the Hungarian narrative about refugees from the Middle East. Reflecting on the migrant crisis in 2015, the Hungarian Prime Minister recalled the topos of bastion. He has been particularly fond of the Christian theme and remains steadfast in his commitment to 'keeping Europe Christian' because, reportedly, 'European identity (has been) rooted in Christianity'. Muslims became explicitly unwelcome and were treated as a threat to security as well as civilisation (Schmidt 2022).

The Ukrainian crisis is a similar instability in the Eastern borderland 'Non-paper on Bosnia and Herzegovina', and the attempt to divide the territorial integration of Bosnia–Herzegovina guaranteed by the Dayton Accords[9] from 1995. With the initiative to separate the Croatian and Serbian populated regions, there is a threat that a new territorial arrangement would allow

9 Dayton Accords, a peace agreement reached on 21 November 1995, by the presidents of Bosnia, Croatia and Serbia, ending the war in Bosnia and outlining a General Framework Agreement for Peace in Bosnia and Herzegovina. It preserved Bosnia as a single state made up of two parts, the Bosniak–Croat Federation and the Bosnian Serb Republic, with Sarajevo remaining as the undivided capital city.

Greater Albania, Greater Croatia and Greater Serbia to 'right-size' and 'right-people' their respective states all at the same time, as noted by Emir Suljagić, the Director of the Srebrenica Memorial Centre. According to Austrian and Slovenian resources, it was probably Hungary that was the initiator (Latal 2021; Mujanovic 2022).

In 2019, Olivér Várhelyi from Hungary was appointed Commissioner for Neighbourhood and Enlargement. While sceptics and critics acknowledge his controversial record, particularly his concessionary stance on the absence of the rule of law in Serbia and Hungary's contentious relationship with controversial former political leaders in the Western Balkans, his position places particular emphasis on the relationship between the V4 and its neighbours. This Hungarian action was widely criticised by Bosnian politicians, who suggested the cancellation of the Hungarian Prime Minister's planned visit to Sarajevo, but the United States has introduced sanctions against the Bosnian Serb leader, Milorad Dodik (Jávor 2019). In July 2023 Bosnia's state court has upheld a ruling sentencing Bosnian Serb leader Milorad Dodik to one year in prison and banning him from serving as president of the Republika Srpska entity for six years. Dodik's first trip was to Hungary, where he emphasized that the attacks against him were politically motivated. Prime Minister Viktor Orbán has reframed the connotation of the Dodik case, writing, this attempt by the EU to remove Milorad Dodik happened because the Bosnian politician opposed the globalist agenda.

After 2020, the new geopolitical situations have rapidly brought the issues of the EU enlargement back into the focus of discussions. Ukraine, Moldova and the Western Balkan countries are heading towards the EU, but the integration became critical due to the increasing influence of Russia and China and the permanent tensions cause destabilisation in the region (Marku & Allushi Teqja 2024). The six countries that wish to join the EU must implement radical institutional reforms and achieve massive economic development to be eligible for EU membership. Border disputes in the region and the state of Kosovo, which are a constant source of tension between Albania and Serbia, are also problematic. The already existing agreements and political–economic initiatives such as the Open Balkans (2021) and the Berlin Process (2014) have not been able to achieve radical changes, leaders of states realised that help and contribution of external players might be inevitable (Kamberi 2021).

Visegrad and the Western Balkans Region

'The Balkans are likely to present the next big opportunity for the EU, and the region could become the bloc's next economic engine' – these were the words of Viktor Orbán's in September 2021, addressing the Conference of Speakers of Parliaments of the Visegrad Group and South-Eastern Europe[10]. He also added that the V4 and Balkan countries may end up building together the most significant economic area of the entire European continent.

From the Hungarian viewpoint, the Western Balkans should also join the EU soon, otherwise they will remain a conflict zone and a buffer zone. In September 2019, during the Czech presidency of the V4 Group, the prime ministers of the Visegrad countries met in Prague with partners from the Western Balkans. They issued a joint declaration on the support of the European integration of the West Balkan countries based on security, including energy security, and infrastructural issues. They also emphasised the necessity of the harmonisation of their initiative with the EU's Balkan Strategy accepted in 2018[11].

The establishment of the Visegrad group (V4) in 1991 symbolised the fact that the founding members, Poland and (at that time still) Czechoslovakia, were engaged in a common goal, the Euro-Atlantic integration. A year later, in 1992 an additional cooperation was declared, called CEFTA (Central European Free Trade Agreement). This agreement, signed in Kraków in 1992, entered into force in 1994 and, although institutionally a separate entity, gave visibility and practical substance to regional cooperation. Although the Visegrad group states were determined about the Euro-Atlantic integration, this latter agreement focused on cooperation on trade and made them more visible in the international environment. Later, more countries joined this

10 Hungary Today (2021). PM Orbán: Balkans 'Next Big Opportunity' for EU, <https://hungarytoday.hu/pm-orban-balkans-next-opportunity-eu-economy-kover-varhelyi/>, accessed 8 June 2024.

11 They reiterated their unequivocal support for the EU accession of the Western Balkans and their firm belief that reunification of Europe cannot be complete without them joining the EU. They underlined that the EU enlargement policy provides an invaluable tool for achieving security, stability and prosperity in the Western Balkans; consequently, a credible enlargement policy represents a strategic investment in the security, stability and prosperity of the EU as well, <https://www.visegradgroup.eu/documents/official-statements/v4-statement-on-the-190912>, accessed 16 April 2024.

group, however, with the EU accession the four Visegrad group Member States – Romania, Bulgaria, Slovenia and Croatia – left the CEFTA. Nowadays, Moldova and the Western Balkan states remain partners in this cooperation that is strongly cooperating with the EU, their central office is also located in Brussels. The V4 is characterised by three clearly declared goals that are incorporated into V4 policy:

1. the support of the Eastern and South-Eastern directions of the EU enlargement;
2. the support of the Eastern dimension of the European neighbourhood policy;
3. a shared vision of regional energy policy (Schmidt 2022).

The V4 Group, thanks to its centre position, can thus support the EU neighbourhood policy from two directions; while Poland is mostly engaged in the Eastern dimension, Hungary mostly focuses on the Balkan peninsula. The joint involvement was emphasised during the Polish Presidency of the Visegrad Group. On 28th June 2021 in Rogalin, the Polish hosts organised an annual meeting of the Ministers of Foreign Affairs of the Visegrad Group with the participation of the Western Balkan representatives that ended with a joint declaration[12]. A similar declaration was composed in 2023 in Prague

12 This joint document focused, among others, on the following questions: that EU enlargement is a joint strategic goal of the EU and the Western Balkans, and that the future of the whole region lies in the Union. The V4 ministers of foreign affairs underscored the assistance provided by the EU and its member states to the Western Balkans in the context of the COVID-19 pandemic, expressed their commitment to supporting the green and digital transformation of the region and emphasised the role of the EU's Economic and Investment Plan for the Western Balkans from the perspective of the post-pandemic recovery. The V4 ministers expressed their support for including the Western Balkan partners in the framework of the conference on the future of Europe. They underlined the need for effective communication on the benefits of the enlargement process for the candidate countries and their citizens as well as for countering disinformation. The V4 ministers welcomed the briefings by the Executive Directors of the International Visegrad Fund and the Western Balkans Fund (WBF) on the cooperation between the two institutions during the past year and on projects carried out in the Western Balkans as well as the signing in Rogaland of a memorandum of understanding on further technical assistance to the WBF,

during the Czech presidency with the participation of the Hungarian and Czech Ministers of Defence[13].

Hungary's involvement in the Balkan region is understandable, since in addition to geographic proximity and historical relations, economic interests also require that the stability of the region be maintained, and its economy strengthened (Pokrócos 2018).

One of the first activities of the Orbán government in the international arena was the signing of the document in March 1999 that resulted in a determining step in the Hungarian Euro-Atlantic orientation as Hungary, together with Czechia and Poland as the first formal Warsaw Pact Member States, joined the NATO[14]. Roughly two weeks later, the war broke out in Serbia and Hungary's role has been strengthened as the only NATO Member State sharing a common border with Yugoslavian Federation. Because until 1999 Hungary had been a neutral state, it was an unexpected challenge to have to react to NATO's initiatives, while in the 1999 Kosovo crisis, when Russia sent a humanitarian convoy to Serbia, the government banned their entry into Hungary (Schnabel & Thakur 2000). Although in the first years of NATO membership Hungary seemed to be making good progress, the NATO bombing in Serbia was considered a controversial military operation by the Hungarian people. The Vojvodina region (a formal autonomous territory of Yugoslavia) was an ethnically mixed region with a relatively large Hungarian ethnic population. The nationalistic Serbian policy has been criticised by the

---

<https://www.visegradgroup.eu/calendar/2021/joint-statement-of-the-210629>, accessed 27 March 2024.

13 The Hungarian presidency starting in January will build on the results of the Czech presidency and will continue the ongoing initiatives. The security of Central Europe is inseparable from the security of the Western Balkan; therefore, the program of the Hungarian CEDC presidency lays significant emphasis on the further extension of the high-level dialogue and practical cooperation between the two groups of countries… 'The stability of the Western Balkan is especially important to us as it affects the security of Europe, especially Central Europe, <https://defence.hu/news/hungary-is-committed-to-the-v4-countries.html>, accessed 23 March 2024..

14 As a matter of fact, the first NATO enlargement in the direction of the post-Warsaw Pact region happened in October 1990 with the German unification when East Germany formally merged into West Germany.

Hungarian government time after time; however, the developing political and economic relations smoothly cover tensions beneath the surface.

In 2008 Hungary was among the first dozen countries that officially recognised Kosovo as an independent state; however, the recognition was not unanimous even among the EU Member States. Obviously, those countries that had troubles with their significant share of ethnic minorities were faced with the fear that the Kosovo case could serve as an example of secession for Spain, Slovakia, Romania, Cyprus and Greece, furthermore Russia, which traditionally has a special relationship with Serbian politicians. Sharing the views of the majority of EU and NATO Member States, the government concluded that internationally controlled independence for Kosovo was the way out of the crisis. Based on the document, Hungary also declared that 'Hungary will continue to actively contribute to strengthening stability and security in the region, including through its participation in KFOR (NATO Kosovo Force) and EULEX (European Union Law Mission in Kosovo) missions'[15].

From the 2010s, Hungary's standpoint has gradually been changing; however, Orbán always emphasised the importance of the EU accession of the Western Balkan states. Based on this particular interest, the Hungarian government feels empowered to influence relations in the Southern Slav countries. Recognition of Kosovo inevitably harmed Serbian interests but was also in line with the views of the majority of EU Member States. The flight of the Prime Minister of North Macedonia, Nikola Gruevski, to Hungary, or the tacit support for Milorad Dodik's plans for a Serbian state in Bosnia, all indicate that the Hungarian government feels entitled to conduct its own policy in the Balkans, even in contrast to EU interests.

Orbán, likewise, showcases versatility in his relations with the countries of the Western Balkans, whose EU accession prospects he has systematically

15 The EULEX (European Union Law Mission in Kosovo) rule of law monitoring mission was decided by the European Council on 28 January 2007. The mission was launched in 2008 and reached full capacity in 2009. In its first 2 years of operation, it took over almost all tasks of the United Nations Interim Administration Mission in Kosovo. On 26 November 2008, the United Nations Security Council gave the green light to the deployment of the EULEX mission in Kosovo. The EU mission is to assume police, justice and customs duties from the UN, while operating under the United Nations Security Council Resolution, 1244.

supported. Among the six EU hopefuls, however, Serbia stands out as Budapest's preferred partner. Considering this privileged partnership, several concerns emerge in relation to Hungary's relations with other countries in the region, nevertheless the most critical case seems to be Kosovo.

Hungary found itself at a crucial juncture between Serbia and Kosovo, where it benefits from carefully nurtured ties with the former and holds cordial diplomatic relations with the latter. However, the balance is set to tilt in favour of Belgrade, as Hungary will follow a policy supportive of Serbia's domestic and international goals, even if this jeopardises Kosovo's national interests and calls Hungary's recognition of it into question.

Budapest's vested interests in the Western Balkans span:

1. trade and investment,
2. the protection of national minority rights,
3. energy security.

Changes in Political Orientation of Hungary

Hungary will always prioritise its shared goals with Serbia over any interest it has in maintaining relations with Kosovo (Pérez 2024). When mentioning the Western Balkans, Hungarian government communication consistently refers to peace and stability. These concepts have become synonymous with development, and a set of normative comparative conceptual frameworks that are used to blame the war for every problem that arises. However, the communication and political actions of the government seem to be contradictory in many cases, as was the case with the introduction of the Memorial Day of the massacre in Srebrenica in 1995. By 2024, the internal political tension in Bosnia–Herzegovina had deepened to such an extent that the leader of the Republic of Serbia in Bosnia and Herzegovina (Republika Srpska), Milorad Dodik, threatened that if the UN accepted the proposal on the international Memorial Day for the Srebrenica genocide, the Republic of Serbia would secede from Bosnia–Herzegovina. The interpretation given to the question by Serbian leaders, Dodik and Aleksandar Vučić, was that the decision would make the Serbian people collectively guilty. According to the Hungarian point of view, any international step that changes the status quo in the Balkans would generate additional tension in the region;

so European integration could be the only solution to clarify the political disputes. Péter Szijjártó emphasised that 'unnecessary' external attempts at intervention lead to the emergence of new crises, which is why these are tension-inducing decisions (Fődi 2024). The denial of Hungarian acceptance of the Srebrenica massacre, where Hungary, as the only EU member voted against the decision in the UN, opened a new confrontation with another Western Balkans region.

From the 2010s, however, a slight shift was recognisable in the direction of Serbia; as it appeared from symbolic visits, Kosovo remained on the agenda of Hungarian diplomacy. The Hungarian reaction in favour of Serbian claims and in denying the support of Kosovo was a good example of this change. In the spring of 2023, the Parliamentary Assembly of the Council of Europe (PACE) took an extraordinary decision, recommending that Kosovo be invited to become a member of the Council of Europe. This action seemed to be unusual because Kosovo's independence is recognised by only 53% of the UN Member States, and several countries of the 46-member Council of Europe—besides Serbia, five EU states (Romania, Spain, Cyprus, Slovakia and Greece) have not recognised Kosovo as an independent state. Hungary has recognised Kosovo, but the Orbán government, which has established a close friendship with Serbia under Aleksandar Vučić, in line with Belgrade, refuses to accept membership of the EU (Ozturk 2023).

The assembly, in view of the unprecedented situation, called for 'diplomatic action, dialogue and compromise' and asked the Committee of Ministers to find a solution so that Kosovo's membership 'does not prejudice the position of individual Member States on Kosovo's statehood' while, obviously, it faces reactions from Serbia[16].

Katalin Novák, Head of the State of Hungary, visited Pristina in 2023. Her trip was a symbolic event, as she, as officially the Head of the Hungarian

16 'Tuesday was a day of shame, when the Parliamentary Assembly of the Council of Europe voted in favour of the report on Kosovo's admission to the Council of Europe', Serbian Foreign Minister Ivica Dacic said in a statement issued after the vote. President of the Republic of Kosovo, Vjosa Osmani said: 'The voice of Europeans has finally been heard'. VG/MTI: The Balkans' powder keg might be exploded, <https://www.vg.hu/kozelet/2024/04/robbanhat-a-balkan-puskaporos-hordoja>, accessed 3 May 2024.

Army, also paid a visit to the Hungarian base in Kosovo. She even had a run together with the soldiers. Meanwhile, she also met her colleague, Vjosa Osmani, the President of Kosovo. They agreed on the Hungarian support towards Kosovo's EU candidacy and visa facilitation. Although Novák strove to find the balance in Hungarian position, her more frequent meetings with the Serbian President epitomised the gradual shift in Hungarian relations with Serbia and Kosovo. In Hungarian foreign policy, a double game is recognisable, where Prime Minister Orbán and Foreign Minister Szijjártó often stand at the crossroads of criticism, experience the increasing isolation of Hungary within the EU and NATO, with the President acting the role of the 'good cop'. From March 2022 until her resignation, Katalin Novák posed as a goodwill ambassador and a mediator of Hungary. She visited the Hungarian–Serbian border with Vučić (and the Czech candidate for president, Andrej Babiš), where they (once again) made a joint statement on the Hungarian mission—to protect the Christian Europe against migrants. There she again emphasised that Hungary should remain an island of peace and confirmed Hungary's assistance by accepting more than one million refugees from Ukraine (accurate number was between 60,000 and 65,000 in 2024) (UNHCR 2024).

Hungary has been participating in peacekeeping tasks in Kosovo since the beginning. The foundations of the peacekeeping mission were already laid in 1999, during the Rambouillet Agreement[17]. Like with Bosnia, the planners divided Kosovo into 'national' sectors, placing each under the command of a country with a dominant-sized contingent. The Hungarian contingent performed its security duties in the area of Pristina and Mitrovica, built the first camp in Pristina, and contributed to the maintenance of public safety. The operation of KFOR has been subject to a lot of criticism, mainly due to its slow reaction time and passivity. Starting from the 2010s, the presence of KFOR meant protection and security guarantees for the Kosovo Serbs, which is why Belgrade began to support the mission's work. It is no coincidence that the Hungarian government, which is maintaining increasingly good political and economic relations with the Serbian leadership, increased its contribution

17 Interim Agreement for Peace and Self-Government in Kosovo, 1999. United Nations Security Council.

to KFOR after 2017. Partly because of this, in 2021, Major General Ferenc Kajári took over the command of the international peacekeeping mission, and by 2022, the 3,600-strong KFOR mission became NATO's largest campaign (Márkusz 2022). In 2024, the KFOR mission was the largest Hungarian military engagement abroad, with 411 soldiers serving in Kosovo emphasising the commitment of Hungary to the peacekeeping processes in the Balkans.

How quickly the fragile Balkan structures can become controversial is highlighted by the riots in northern Kosovo in April and May 2023. Special municipal elections were held in three mixed-ethnicity settlements in northern Kosovo after the leaders of the settlements resigned for political reasons. The local Serbian population boycotted the elections; thus, the participation rate was only 3.5%. The protests of Serbian residents prevented the elected Albanian mayors from taking their offices. A serious clash broke out between the Hungarian KFOR forces deployed to maintain order and the Serbian protesters, in which twenty-five Hungarian soldiers were injured (Bytyci 2023). An interesting scene of the riots was when, referring to the Hungarian government's pro-Serbian stance, the Serbian protesters chanted *'Let's go, Orbán!'*, after recognising the Hungarian flag on the soldiers' shields. In the meantime, the complete confusion was underpinned by the fact that the Serbian army lined up along the Kosovo–Serbia border, because, according to Belgrade, representatives of the international community, including KFOR soldiers, were protecting the Albanian 'troublemakers'.

Another gesture in favour of the Serbian nation was Hungary's opposing vote in the UN National Assembly[18]. On 24 May 2024, the UN General Assembly adopted a draft resolution on the commemoration of the Srebrenica Genocide Day in memory of the massacre that claimed more than 8,000 lives in 1995. At the assembly, eighty-four countries voted in favour of the proposal, and nineteen against it, including Hungary. In January 2024, the leader of the Bosnian Serbs, Milorad Dodik, who is also on the US sanctions list, awarded Viktor Orbán the same medal that he had previously awarded to Russian President Putin, which he presented on 9 January marking a Bosnian Serb national holiday, when they celebrated the Bosnian Serbs' separation and

18 United Nations (2024). UN establishes International Day of Reflection for Srebrenica genocide.

proclamation of the Serbian People's Republic of Bosnia and Herzegovina in 1992. The celebrations are banned in the Bosnian and Croatian regions. In any case, standing up for the Serbs was quite a significant shift from the time of the outbreak of the South Slavic war, when Hungary sent 10,000 machine guns and some 3 million rounds of ammunition from the former workers' guards in October 1990. The announcement of the deal caused a major scandal in Belgrade. The Hungarian government first denied the fact of the shipment and then said that a Hungarian foreign trade company had shipped machine guns to Yugoslavia in October 1990 on the order of a third-country trading company. On 4 February 1991, the Yugoslav Federal Government even sent a note of protest to the Hungarian government. Eight years later, in 1999, the Hungarian Prime Minister, Viktor Orbán, was among the few statesmen—together with the Turkish president and the heads of that time already independent states of former Yugoslavia—who participated in the funeral of the Croatian President Franjo Tuđman.

While in 2022 alone, the Bosnian Serb Republic received €110 million in aid from the Hungarian government, which in no small way attempted to influence the elections of that year, €6.4 million were contributed in 2020 by pro-government media circles in North Macedonia and Slovenia through partners including former Slovenian Prime Minister, Janez Janša, and Nikola Gruevski, Prime Minister of North Macedonia, and the Serbian media agency involved in the 2017 Serbian presidential election campaign also received significant Hungarian contracts (Bozzay & Horváth Kávai 2023). The Hungarian National Trading Houses, originally run by the Hungarian government to support businesses, also received significant support and were headed by people close to the government.

'Opening to Serbia'

Strong cooperation prevails also in the energy sector, reinforced by Russia's war in Ukraine and by the decision of most EU Member States to shift away from Moscow's energy supplies. Both Serbia and Hungary systematically reject such sanctions on pragmatic grounds. 'The origin of gas and oil is not relevant to Serbia and—I believe—Hungary. It is only important for us to have them. Our citizens cannot live and heat on promises', said the Serbian Foreign Minister Ivica Dacic (Pérez 2024).

Serbian–Hungarian relations began to improve spectacularly in the early 2010s. This was partly for economic reasons since – MOL, OTP, KÉSZ, Waberer's and other firms, more than forty Hungarian companies expanded their operations to Serbia, and – Hungary doubled its exports to the Western Balkans. On the other hand, Serbia is also an important partner of Hungary in terms of energy supply. From Serbia, 9–15 million cubic metres of natural gas per day is supplied via the Turkish Stream, but according to the plans, the gas coming from Azerbaijan will also pass through Serbia. In 2023, Hungary also undertook to store 500 million cubic meters of natural gas for Serbia in Hungarian storage facilities as part of a framework agreement, and the Hungarian MVM (Hungarian Electrical Works Company) and Srinagar will jointly distribute gas on the Central European market. The two countries have also begun cooperation on the construction of a crude oil pipeline and the development of the transmission capacity of electricity lines (Stojanovic & Inotai 2023).

There is another project that has been sharply criticised over transparency, financing and geopolitical concerns. The Budapest–Belgrade railway, a 350-km high-speed rail line project is also a part of the planned Budapest–Belgrade–Skopje–Athens railway international connection in Central and Southeast Europe, a Chinese-CEE hallmark project of Beijing's Belt and Road initiative (BRI), connecting the China-owned Piraeus port in Greece with Central Europe (Peragovics & Szunomár 2024). Critics argue that the loans from China could increase the debt burden of Hungary and Serbia, and there are concerns about China's growing influence in Europe through such infrastructure projects. For Hungary and Serbia, the railway is expected to enhance trade and economic cooperation with China and other European countries. For China, it is a strategic investment that strengthens its influence in Europe, especially in the Balkans and Central Europe. Currently, this construction is projected to cost HUF 949 billion ($3.6 billion) with interest. In Hungary, the project is carried out by Chinese–Hungarian Railway Nonprofit Ltd., a Hungarian Chinese joint venture of Hungarian State Railways Zrt.

In 2023, the bilateral relations between Serbia and Hungary reached a new level with the establishment of the Hungarian–Serbian Cooperation Council. At this time, twelve agreements have been signed on border control, European integration, information exchange, infrastructure, economy, security issues and tariffs. Former President of Hungary, Katalin Novák, stated that Serbia has 'demonstrated repeatedly that it belongs to Europe' since applying for EU membership in 2009 and starting accession talks in 2014. Until Serbia joins the EU's passport-free Schengen zone, Hungary plans to make it easier to cross the border between the two countries. Viktor Orbán made some crucial points in his speech when he said that relations between Hungary and Serbia began to improve when both countries realised that they could not be hostages of history. 'Freedom, sovereignty and independence are in the DNA of the Serbs, just as they are in that of the Hungarians' – he added. Orbán used the concept of strategic cooperation to describe the development of relations between the two countries, which he believes unleashes tremendous energy that both nations can benefit from[19]. In international relations, strategic cooperation usually refers to a long-term partnership between countries that is designed to achieve shared goals and mutual benefits, particularly in areas of crucial significance such as security, economic development and political interests. This type of cooperation often goes beyond simple agreements or alliances; it involves deep, institutionalised collaboration that is strategically aligned with the partners' broader national interests.

Regarding the relationship between the Serbian President and the Hungarian Prime Minister, a range of similarities can be pointed out. Both have been in power since the early 2010s, they both share right-wing populist, Eurosceptic, and nativist approaches to politics, and both of them admire illiberal solutions, they are not admirers of media freedom or the rule of law. However, there is a significant difference, as while Vučić can act as a leader of a non-EU Member State, Orbán's hands are tied within the EU membership and his liberty is controlled and reduced by the EU's institutions. Their fraternal behaviour (and Orbán's suspicious relationship with suspicious statesmen in the Balkan Peninsula) can be explained as one of the reasons why there is a deeply stuck disbelief in the EU towards the integration of the Western Balkan region. 'Brussels' does not really want to invite disruptive politicians as it is enough to concentrate on the 'deepening' of the EU integration.

19 MTI – Econews (2023). Hungarian–Serbian Strategic Cooperation Council Formed, <https://bbj.hu/politics/foreign-affairs/intl-relations/hungarian-serbian-strategic-co-operation-council-formed/>, accessed 14 May 2024.

Like so many other times in the last 100 years of history, Hungary has tried to pursue a balanced policy and a kind of seesaw policy towards both powers in conflict with each other, but experience has shown that this has never worked. In the case of Kosovo and Serbia, the interesting fact is that when the conflict broke out, Orbán sided with Kosovo in line with international trends. Now the same politician, contrary to the position of the allies, is trying to commit himself to the other side. One of the blemishes of the case is the neglect of dozens of Hungarian peacekeepers, along with the whole international environment in which Hungary is becoming increasingly isolated and distrusted.

Summary

The Hungarian Prime Minister was invited to an event commemorating the 50th anniversary of the Hungarian Institute of Foreign Affairs where he delivered a speech about the vision of Hungarian foreign policy. He stressed that a national interest-based foreign policy combines the best elements of idealism and realism. In this context, the word 'national' refers to the idealist element as the nation is primarily an ideal. He explained that at the same time, the word 'interest' is an embodiment of realism, a collective term for all things necessary, useful and practical. He also emphasised the importance of expression of national interest-based foreign policy that has 'intellectual content, conveys both principles and values, but continuously compels the policymakers to engage in flexible adaptation'[20]. As the Prime Minister also perceives that the most common accusation concerning this foreign policy is isolationism, he wants to emphasise in words and deeds that this is not the case, as 'the system of relations with the West is intensive, and the opening to the East and South is booming. All of this is combined with speed, agility, trade, investment and connectivity, according to the Hungarian perception. Hungary's foreign policy, which has developed from being a follower to a leader in Europe, is often accused of attempting to exploit the opportunity of being a member of the EU and NATO to benefit from the safety net of Western organisations, while at the same time engage in dilemmatic deals in

20 See more: <https://miniszterelnok.hu/en/hungarian-foreign-policy-is-national-interest-based/>, accessed 24 September 2024.

both the East and the South. Since the 1910s, the Balkans have been described as a powder keg of unresolved conflicts. The Hungarian foreign policy, which has been successful at various levels, prefers to invoke historical, geographic and geopolitical arguments when it turns to the region, while often proving an unreceptive promoter or troublemaker. As the past two world wars and the current conflicts indicate, in the changing world order, Hungary is increasingly seeking to play the role of an intermediary, which is often criticised by those who question their preparedness behind the Hungarian actions. Historical experience has shown that, although Hungary has so far been keen to act as a bridge between East and West, it has rarely succeeded in this mission without an international presence. The Balkan adventure, however, raises several questions as to whose interests are ultimately represented by Hungary in its increased involvement in such a heterogeneous, politically and economically conflict-ridden area, and to what extent Hungary can play its role as a mediator, especially when it has to argue for contradicting interests.

Bibliography

Bozzay, Balázs – Horváth Kávai Andrea. (2023) 'Hungarian government has financed several foreign politicians, but they consider the same a violation of sovereignty at home'. *Telex*., https://telex.hu/english/2023/12/11/the-hungarian-government-has-financed-several-foreign-politicians-but-they-consider-it-a-violation-of-sovereignty-at-home (Accessed: 1 June 2024).

Bullock, Stephen G., and Gallagher, Linda Rose (1997). 'Surveying the State of the Mediative Art: A Guide to Institutionalizing Mediation in Louisiana', *Louisiana Law Review*, 57(3) Rev.

Bumman, Paul. (2023) 'The Geopolitical Dynamics in the Balkans: Unraveling Complexities and Shifting Alliances', *The Diplomatic Affairs*, <https://www.thediplomaticaffairs.com/2023/07/12/the-geopolitical-dynamics-in-the-balkans-unraveling-complexities-and-shifting-alliances/>, accessed 28 May 2024.

Bytyci, Fatos (2023). 'NATO Soldiers Injured in Kosovo Clashes with Serb Protesters', *Reuters*, <https://www.reuters.com/world/europe/nato-soldiers-deploy-around-kosovo-town-halls-standoff-with-serb-protesters-2023-05-29/>, accessed 6 June 2024.

Dalby, Simon (1996). 'The Critical Geopolitics Constellation: Problematizing Fusions of geographical Knowledge and Power', *Political Geography*, 15 (6/70, 451–456.

Dawson, Roger (1999). *Secrets of Power Negotiating. Inside Secrets from a Master Negotiator.* Franklin Lakes, NJ: Career Press.

Fisher, Roger, and Ury, William (1991). *Getting to Yes: Negotiating Agreement Without Giving.* Houghton Mifflin: Random House Business Books.

Fődi, Kitti (2024). 'A Magyar kormány nem fogja megszavazni a srebrenciai népirtásról szóló ENSZ-Határozat tervezetet', <https://444.hu/2024/05/15/a-magyar-kormany-nem-fogja-megszavazni-a-srebrenciai-nepirtasrol-szolo-ensz-hatarozattervezetet>, accessed 31 May 2024.

Glied, Viktor, and Pap, Norbert (2016). 'The Christian Fortress of Hungary: The Anatomy of the Migration Crisis in Hungary'. In ed. Bogdan Góralczyk (ed.), *Yearbook of Polish European Studies*, pp. 133–151. Warsaw: Centre for European Regional and Local Studies, University of Warsaw.

Hovet, Jason, and Komuves, Anita (2024). 'Slovakia, Hungary say Ukraine has Halted Lukoil's Russian Oil Transit', *Reuters*, <https://www.reuters.com/business/energy/slovakia-hungary-say-ukraine-has-halted-lukoils-russian-oil-transit-2024-07-18/>, accessed 30 July 2024.

Jávor, Benedek (2019). 'The Wrong Man in the Wrong Place. Heinrich Böll Stiftung', *Brussels: EU*, <https://eu.boell.org/en/2019/10/08/wrong-man-wrong-place>, accessed 18 May 2024.

Jelavich, Barbara (1996). *A Balkántörténete.* Budapest: Osiris.

Kacziba, Péter (2024). 'Applying Negative Soft Power? Examining Hungary's Digital Criticism of the European Union', *STUDIA EUROPEJSKIE*, 28(2), 135–155.

Kallius, Annastiina (2017). 'The East-South Axis: Legitimizing the "Hungarian Solution to Migration"', *Revue Européenne des Migrations Internationales*, 33 (2/3), <http://journals.openedition.org/remi/8761>, accessed 27 May 2024.

Kamberi, Donika (2021). 'Open Balkan vs. Berlin Process – Same, Same but Different?', *Freedom Journal for Peacebuilding and Transcultural Communication*, 2 (3/4), 60–71, <https://eprints.unite.edu.mk/886/1/60-71.pdf>, accessed 15 May 2024.

Kitanics, Máté, and Pap, Norbert (2016). 'Ázsiaés Európa szorításában – Migráció a Balkánon. In István Tarrósy, Viktor Glied and Zoltán Vörös (eds), *Migration in the 21st Century*, pp. 295–310. Pécs: Publikon Publishers.

Latal, Srecko (2021). 'Disputed Non-Paper is Stirring Dangerous Dreams in the Balkans', *Balkan Insight*, <https://balkaninsight.com/2021/04/21/disputed-non-paper-is-stirring-dangerous-dreams-in-the-balkans/>, accessed 11 June 2024.

Makkai, Béla (2014). 'A Balkáni "Lőporoshordó" Izzókanóca. Bosznia-Hercegovinaikonfliktus-Leltár a Világháború előestéjén'. *Közép Európa Közlemények*, 7 (3/4), 7–16.

Marku, Alketa, and Allushi Teqja, Eva (2024). 'The European Integration Process of Western Balkans, Time for a New Approach', *Journal of Educational and Social Research*, 14 (1), 137–148.

Márkusz, László (2022). 'A koszovói háborúés a KFOR békefenntartó misszió *Nemzetés Biztonság*, 15 (3), 89–104.

Martín-Arroyo, Pedro Correa (2013). *Histoeuropeanisation: Challenges and Implications of (Re)writing the History of Europe "Europeanly", 1989–2015*. Warsaw: College of Europe in Natolin Campus.

Mujanovic, Jasmin (2022). 'Bosnia's HDZ Doesn't Want Election Reform but Gerrymandering', *Balkan Insight*, <https://balkaninsight.com/2022/02/02/bosnias-hdz-doesnt-want-election-reform-but-gerrymandering/>, accessed 11 June 2024.

Németh, Viktor (2022). 'A mediáció szabályozásának története *BelügyiSzemle: A BelügyminisztériumSzakmai, Tudományos Folyóirata*, 70 (12), 2631–2643.

Ó Tuathail, Gearóid (1996). *Critical Geopolitics: The Politics of Writing Global Space*. Minneapolis: University of Minnesota Press.

Orbán, Balázs (2023). *Connectivity: A Hungarian Globalisation Strategy. European Council on Foreign Relations*, <https://ecfr.eu/article/connectivity-a-hungarian-globalisation-strategy/>, accessed 26 May 2024.

Owczarzak, Jill (2009). 'Introduction: Postcolonial Studies and Postsocialism in Eastern Europe', *Focaal – European Journal of Anthropology* , 2009 (53), 3–19.

Ozturk, Talha (2023). *Hungary to Veto Kosovo's Applications to EU Bodies: Foreign Minister*, <https://www.aa.com.tr/en/europe/hungary-to-veto-kosovos-applications-to-eu-bodies-foreign-minister/2784438>, accessed 3 June 2024.

Pap, Norbert (2020). *Kapcsolati Terek Éshelyek. Magyarországés a Balkán*. Pécs: PTE TTK Földrajzi Intézet Kelet-Mediterránés Balkán Tanulmányok Központja.

Pelinka, Anton (2015). 'From Habsburg to Communism to Democracy: Reflections on (Non)Federalism in Central Europe'. In G. Bischof, Ferdinand and Karlhofer, Günther (eds), *Austrian Federalism in Comparative Perspective*, vol. 24, pp. 1–10. Innsbruck University: UNO Press.

Peragovics, Tamás and Szunomár, Ágnes (2024). 'The Great Connection – The Budapest-Belgrade Railway Project and Its Significance for Hungary's Foreign Policy Identity', *Asian Perspective*, Johns Hopkins University Press, 48 (2), 253–275.

Pérez, Alejandro Esteso Pérez (2024). 'Orbán Will Sacrifice Kosovo to Keep Serbian Ally Sweet', *Balkan Insight*, <https://balkaninsight.com/2024/05/16/orban-will-sacrifice-kosovo-to-keep-serbian-ally-sweet/>, accessed 23 May 2024.

Pokrócos György (2018). 'Gondolatokaz EULEX-misszióról, *Magyar Rendészet*, 18 (1), 185–192.

Ralph, Jason (2023). *On Global Learning: Pragmatic Constructivism, International Practice and the Challenge of Global Governance*. Cambridge: Cambridge University Press. Cambridge Studies in International Relations.

Reuters (2025). Hungary's Orban meets Russian-backed, Bosnian Serb leader, <https://www.reuters.com/world/hungarys-orban-meets-russian-backed-bosnian-serb-leader-2025-08-05/>, accessed 7 August 2025.

Reményi, Péter (2020). 'Border Disputes and Water Conflicts in the Western Balkans'. In Glied, Viktor, and Kacziba, Péter (eds), *Water Stress: Emerging Challenges of Global Water Scarcity*, pp. 107–121. Pécs: PTE BTK.

Schmidt, Andrea (2022). 'Borders Connecting and Dividing – East Meets West and the Borders of the European Union', *Eastern Journal of European Studies*, 13 (SP), 9–32.

Schmidt, Andrea (2023). 'Visegrad Group – Real Entity or Mirage'. In Zięba, Ryszard (ed.), *Politics and Security of Central and Eastern Europe*. Warsaw: Springer, Cham. <https://doi.org/10.1007/978-3-031-16419-4_12>.

Schnabel, Albrecht, and Thakur, Ramesh (2000), *Kosovo and the Challenge of Humanitarian Intervention: Selective Indignation, Collective Action, and International Citizenship*. Tokyo: UNU Press.

Simurdic, Milan (2016). 'Western Balkans Between Geography and Geopolitics', *Foreign Policy Papers 2016 No. 1*, pp. 3–6. Belgrade: Friedrich Ebert Stiftung.

Stojanovic, Milica, and Inotai, Edit (2023). 'News Serbia and Hungary Set Up Joint Natural Gas Company', *Balkan Insight*, <https://balkaninsight.com/2023/06/20/serbia-and-hungary-set-up-joint-natural-gas-company/>, accessed 31 May 2024.

Tarrósy, István, and Vörös, Zoltán (2020). 'Hungary's Pragmatic Foreign Policy in a Post-American World', *Politics in Central Europe*, 16 (1S), 113–134.

Tošić, Jelena (2017). 'From a Transit Route to the "backyard of Europe"? Tracing the Past, Present and Future of the Balkan Route'. In Gebhard Fartacek and Susanne Binder (eds), *Facetten von Flucht aus dem Nahen und Mittleren Osten*, pp. 150–166. Wien: Facultas Universität's verlag.

UNHCR Operational Data Portal (2024). *Ukraine Refugee Situation*, <https://data.unhcr.org/en/situations/ukraine/location/10783>, accessed 30 August 2024.

United Nations Office on Drugs and Crime (2008). *Impact on the Balkans and Affected Countries*. Hungary–Poland.

United Nations (2024). *UN Establishes International Day of Reflection for Srebrenica Genocide*, <https://news.un.org/en/story/2024/05/1150156>, accessed 3 June 2024.

Internet Sources

Hungary Today (2024). Peace and Development in the Western Balkans will be of Focus During EU Presidency. MTI-Hungary Today, <https://

hungarytoday.hu/peace-and-development-in-the-western-balkans-will-be-in-focus-during-eu-presidency/>, accessed 27 May 2024.

About Hungary (2020). Commissioner Várhelyi on EU Enlargement: We Need to Speed Up Accession for the Western Balkans, <https://abouthungary.hu/blog/commissioner-varhelyi-on-eu-enlargement-we-need-to-speed-up-accession-for-the-western-balkans>, accessed 3 August 2024.

Government of Hungary (2024a). A Nyugat-Balkáni EU-csatlakozási folyamat lassúsága az egész bővítéspolitika hitelét aláássa, <https://kormany.hu/hirek/a-nyugat-balkani-eu-csatlakozasi-folyamat-lassusaga-az-egesz-bovitespolitika-hitelet-alaassa>, accessed 3 June 2024.

Government of Hungary (2024b). Magyarország mindent megtesz a Nyugat-Balkán békéje és fejlődése érdekében, <https://kormany.hu/hirek/magyarorszag-mindent-megtesz-a-nyugat-balkan-bekeje-es-fejlodese-erdekeben>, accessed 29 May 2024.

About Hungary (2024). FM: Hungarian Diplomacy Gave the Right Responses During Recent Challenges, <https://abouthungary.hu/news-in-brief/fm-hungarian-diplomacy-gave-the-right-responses-during-recent-challenges>, accessed 22 May 2024.

Hungary Today (2021). PM Orbán: Balkans 'Next Big Opportunity' for EU, <https://hungarytoday.hu/pm-orban-balkans-next-opportunity-eu-economy-kover-varhelyi/>, accessed 6 August 2024.

MTI – Econews (2023). Hungarian–Serbian Strategic Cooperation Council Formed, <https://bbj.hu/politics/foreign-affairs/intl-relations/hungarian-serbian-strategic-cooperation-council-formed/>, accessed 14 May 2024.

PART II

Comparative Mediation in the Light of National Law

Mediation for Sustainable Resolution of Commercial Disputes within the Polish Legal Framework: A Path to Sustainable Development

Małgorzata Skawińska[1]

Introduction

In today's dynamically evolving global economy, businesses are confronted with myriad challenges impacting their operations. A notable challenge for European, including Polish, entrepreneurs is the imperative to adapt to a paradigm where business activities must conform to the principles of sustainable development[2]. Despite opposition from proponents of a purely profit-driven approach, legal norms are progressively shaping business operations with a focus on environmental, social and governance (ESG) criteria[3]. Conversely,

1 PhD, WSPIA Rzeszowska Szkoła Wyższa; Emba, DBA; advocate (Poland), mediator; Kancelaria Prawna LEXALIS; email: m.skawinska@lexalis.eu

2 See Verbatim Report of Proceedings, Debate in European Parliament on 31 May, <https://www.europarl.europa.eu/doceo/document/CRE-9-2023-05-31_EN.pdf>, accessed 3 July 2024.

3 Among the key ESG regulations at the European level are: European Parliament and Council (2022/2464), 'Directive (EU) 2022/2464 of the European Parliament and of the Council of 14 December 2022 amending Regulation (EU) No 537/2014, Directive 2004/109/EC, Directive 2006/43/EC and Directive 2013/34/EU, as regards corporate sustainability reporting', <https://eur-lex.europa.eu/eli/dir/2022/2464/oj>, accessed 3 July 2024; Commission (2023/2772), 'Commission Delegated Regulation (EU) 2023/2772 of 31 July 2023 supplementing Directive 2013/34/EU of the European Parliament and of the Council as regards sustainability reporting standards', <https://eur-lex.europa.eu/legal-content/EN/TXT/?uri=OJ:L_202302772>, accessed 3 July 2024; European Parliament and Council (2022/2381), 'Directive (EU) 2022/2381 of the European Parliament and of the Council of 23 November 2022 on improving the gender balance among directors of listed companies and related measures', <https://eur-lex.europa.eu/eli/dir/2022/2381/oj>, accessed 3 July 2024; European Parliament and Council (2023/970), 'Directive (EU) 2023/970 of the European Parliament and of the Council of 10 May 2023 to strengthen the application of the principle of equal pay for equal work or work of equal value between men and women through pay transparency and enforcement mechanisms', <https://eur-lex.europa.eu/eli/dir/2023/970/oj>, accessed 3 July 2024; European Parliament and Council (2020/852), 'Regulation (EU) 2020/852 of the European Parliament and of the Council of 18 June 2020 on

for those recognising the necessity to balance economic, social and ecological aspects, this requirement has catalysed a shift towards long-term strategic actions rather than short-term profit maximisation (Hart & Zingales 2017).

Within this framework, there exists an opportunity to re-evaluate the approach to commercial and corporate disputes, traditionally perceived as inherently destructive in the business environment. Through appropriate mechanisms, disputes between business partners, ranging from boardroom battles to labour strikes involving employees, can be transformed into opportunities for fostering constructive dialogue and collaborative problem-solving. Mediation, as a method of appropriate dispute resolution[4], can play an important role in facilitating the transformation of conflicts into processes that enhance mutual understanding between parties. It is a voluntary and collaborative process that empowers conflicting parties to actively participate in devising mutually acceptable solutions (Zienkiewicz 2007). With the assistance of an impartial and neutral mediator, parties can concentrate on comprehending each other's needs and interests, striving to reach agreements that are advantageous to both the parties and the broader business milieu.

In the pertinent literature, a set of principles is consistently identified as integral to the concept of mediation (Kalisz 2020). The principles of voluntariness, confidentiality, impartiality and neutrality, flexibility, expediency of proceedings, autonomy, satisfaction of both parties and low costs are

---

the establishment of a framework to facilitate sustainable investment and amending Regulation (EU) 2019/2088', <https://eur-lex.europa.eu/eli/reg/2020/852/oj>, accessed 3 July 2024; European Parliament and Council (2019/904), 'Directive (EU) 2019/904 of the European Parliament and of the Council of 5 June 2019 on the reduction of the impact of certain plastic products on the environment', <https://eur-lex.europa.eu/eli/dir/2019/904/oj>, accessed 3 July 2024.

4 The author joins the appeal to stop using the phrase 'alternative dispute resolution', as it implies a secondary status, and proposes to replace them with the phrases 'amicable' or 'appropriate' dispute resolution (Antony & Njuguna 2024; McGregor 2015). ADR methods could actually serve as the primary means of resolving conflicts and should be seen as an integral part of the judicial system. See also: Alternative Dispute Resolution Report: Mediation and Conciliation (LRC 98-2010), Law Reform Commission, 2010, <https://www.lawreform.ie/_fileupload/Reports/r98ADR.pdf>, accessed 3 July 2024.

fundamental to the mediation process[5]. These principles are enshrined, either directly or indirectly, in legal provisions, particularly in codes and regulations governing mediation in different countries (De Palo & Trevor 2012). It is impracticable to draw rigid boundaries between the various principles of mediation proceedings. Thus, inclusivity and sustainability permeate other principles, necessitating their consideration in every mediation proceeding. This raises the issue of whether it is appropriate to revise this set of principles to explicitly include inclusivity and sustainability. Each principle will be analysed individually to examine the manifestations of inclusivity and sustainability within the main principles of mediation. This thesis will have theoretical significance not only by supplementing the definition with additional features, but also by raising awareness about mediation as an inclusive and sustainable method of dispute resolution; companies that are committed to sustainability will be more inclined to incorporate mediation into their business strategies.

In this scenario, mediation can play a pivotal role in constructing a new model of a sustainable enterprise[6]. The proliferation of mediation and other ADR methods can not only transform the approach to resolving commercial disputes, but also expedite the implementation of changes in alignment with ESG principles. By integrating mediation and other appropriate dispute resolution mechanisms, enterprises can leverage an additional tool that aids in managing change within the specific entity and contributes to creating a resilient, equitable and progressive business environment. This aligns with the broader objectives of sustainable development, ensuring that businesses not only prosper in the present but also contribute positively to

5 The concept of mediation and the principles of mediation have been the subject of numerous studies. See Spencer, David, and Brogan, Michael (2007). *Mediation Law and Practice*, pp. 263–264. Cambridge: Cambridge University Press; Esplugues, Carlos, Mediation in the EU after the Transposition of the Directive 2008/52/EC on Mediation in Civil and Commercial Matters (2014). 'Civil and Commercial Mediation in the EU after the Transposition of the Directive 2008/52/EC'. In Carlos Esplugues (ed.), *Civil and Commercial Mediation in Europe. Cross-Border Mediation Vol II.*, pp. 485–771. Cambridge: Intersentia.

6 More about the concept of sustainable enterprise, see *Sustainable Enterprises of the Future*, edited by Irena K. Hejduk and Wiesław M. Grudzewski (2012).

future generations. Consequently, mediation can become instrumental in cultivating a business culture that values long-term relationships, ethical practices and sustainable growth.

The Concept of Inclusivity and Sustainability in Mediation

In the literature, sustainable development is described as a normative concept, representing a vision for how humanity should progress. It is also noted to be an ambiguous concept, allowing for a wide range of interpretations and understandings of its principles (Drosik et al. 2022). The concept of sustainability, as articulated by the United Nations Brundtland Commission in 1987, refers to 'meeting the needs of the present without compromising the ability of future generations to meet their own needs'[7]. According to the Cambridge English Dictionary, sustainability refers to 'the quality of being able to continue over a period of time'[8]. The sustainability of mediation is reflected in its capacity to mitigate the adverse impacts of conflicts. This can be considered on two fundamental levels: human and material. On the human level, mediation mitigates the negative effects of conflicts on the participants, safeguarding interpersonal relationships and promoting long-term cooperation. On the material level, it enables efficient management of business resources, reducing costs and losses associated with protracted disputes. Sustainability undeniably relates to a sustainable outcome understood as the result of mediation but should also be emphasised during all phases of the mediation process. This entails incorporating sustainable practices from the initial discussions through to the final agreements. Such practices include fostering an environment conducive to open communication, mutual respect, active listening and understanding among the parties involved. Furthermore, sustainable mediation necessitates the employment

7 Our Common Future, Report of the World Commission on Environment and Development, United Nations, A/42/427, 1987, <http://www.un-documents.net/ocf-09.htm>, accessed 5 July 2024. See also <https://www.un.org/en/academic-impact/sustainability>, accessed 5 July 2024.

8 <https://dictionary.cambridge.org/dictionary/english/sustainability>, accessed 5 July 2024.

of strategies and techniques that ensure the longevity and durability of the agreements reached. By prioritising sustainability throughout the mediation process, the likelihood of achieving resolutions that are effective in the short term and resilient and beneficial in the long term is significantly enhanced. This comprehensive approach ensures that the positive impacts of mediation extend beyond the immediate resolution of conflict, contributing to a peaceful environment, stability and efficient use of resources.

In a business context, sustainable mediation practices can yield several advantageous outcomes. Organisations that adopt these practices are likely to experience improved employee morale and retention due to the respectful resolution of conflicts. Furthermore, efficient resource management during disputes can lead to substantial cost savings, enhanced financial performance, reduced staff turnover and less sick leave in workplaces (Bohm & Laurell 2014). By cultivating a culture of cooperation and mutual respect, businesses can enhance their reputations and strengthen relationships with clients, partners, employees and other stakeholders. Additionally, mediation can sometimes prevent the termination of a business, a common consequence of unresolved conflicts. Ultimately, sustainable mediation can drive long-term business success and resilience in a dynamic market environment.

According to the Cambridge English Dictionary, inclusivity refers to 'the fact of including all types of people, things or ideas and treating them all fairly and equally'[9]. The inclusive nature of mediation ensures that all perspectives are acknowledged, thereby supporting the integration of diverse viewpoints and fostering a more just and equitable business environment. Inclusivity can be viewed from multiple perspectives and cannot be solely equated with the principle of autonomy, although it is most strongly associated with this principle.

This inclusivity is crucial in creating a fair and balanced process where diverse needs and interests are considered. Different legal systems have provisions that support this inclusive approach by emphasising the voluntary nature of the process and granting parties broad decision-making powers at every stage of the mediation process. This is a main principle of mediation,

9 <https://dictionary.cambridge.org/dictionary/english/inclusivity>, accessed 5 July 2024.

and traditionally the principle of voluntariness applies to every stage of the mediation, i.e. the initiation of mediation, its conduct and the conclusion of a settlement[10].

The principle of confidentiality ensures that all communications within the mediation process are protected from disclosure. This confidentiality is essential for creating a safe environment where parties can freely express their concerns and perspectives without fear of repercussions. By safeguarding the privacy of the discussions, mediation encourages honest dialogue and trust among participants, which is crucial for achieving inclusive and sustainable outcomes. In commercial mediation confidentiality allows entrepreneurs to discuss sensitive business information and potential solutions openly, facilitating a resolution that is in the best interest of all parties without risking competitive disadvantage. Importantly, the disclosure of certain information can sometimes be more damaging than the conflict itself, underscoring the critical importance of confidentiality in the mediation process.

The principle of impartiality and neutrality mandates that mediators conduct the process without bias and disclose any circumstances that might affect their impartiality. This principle is crucial as it guarantees that the mediator treats all parties equally, without favouring any side. An impartial mediator fosters a balanced environment where all voices are heard and respected, which is vital for a fair resolution. Inclusivity is naturally embedded in this process, as it ensures that all parties, regardless of their size or power, have an equal opportunity to present their case and be heard. In commercial disputes, this approach provides that both small businesses and large

10 However, there are systems that are deviated from the principle of voluntariness at the initial stage. In Italy, the latest reform 'Cartabbia' introduced new areas of mandatory mediation (for more information, see Chapter VII). This deviation, although seemingly counter to voluntariness, can be structured in an appropriate way to ensure that all potential benefits of mediation, such as inclusivity and sustainability, are explored before parties proceed to more adversarial methods of dispute resolution. Even if business partners are initially reluctant to meet together in mediation, there is a possibility of separate preliminary meetings with each party, as provided for within the Polish legal framework. These separate meetings, known as caucuses, during the mediation process allow the mediator to understand the concerns and interests of each party individually, thereby laying a foundation for a more inclusive and constructive dialogue when joint sessions occur.

corporations, employees and employers, franchisors and franchisees receive equal consideration, promoting equitable outcomes. By upholding impartiality and neutrality, mediation aligns with the broader goal of inclusivity. This approach not only levels the playing field but also reinforces trust in the mediation process. Therefore, establishing inclusivity as a core principle in mediation further legitimises the process, aligning it with new standards of sustainable business development.

The principle of flexibility allows mediation to adapt to the specific needs and circumstances of the parties involved. This adaptability is a cornerstone of inclusivity, ensuring that the mediation process can accommodate diverse perspectives and interests. Flexibility in mediation also contributes to sustainability by enabling the process to evolve in ways that meet the current and future needs of the parties, leading to durable and practical solutions. For instance, a flexible approach in business mediation could involve exploring various settlement options that preserve ongoing commercial relationships and adapt to market changes. Additionally, flexibility in scheduling mediation meetings – such as accommodating different locations, hours and formats – ensures that all parties can participate fully, thereby enhancing the process's effectiveness and accessibility. This adaptability is particularly important in a business environment, where time constraints and logistical challenges can otherwise impede conflict resolution.

The principle of expediency in mediation emphasises resolving disputes promptly and efficiently. This principle supports sustainability by reducing the time and resources spent on conflict resolution, which is particularly beneficial in commercial disputes where prolonged conflicts can be detrimental to business operations. Expedient proceedings ensure that the focus remains on achieving a timely and effective resolution, thereby supporting the long-term interests of all parties. For businesses, this means quicker resolution of disputes, minimising disruption and enhancing overall operational efficiency. Lengthy court processes not only incur costs but also require the presence of employees at hearings and the allocation of human resources to prepare evidence, which is not necessary in mediation due to the absence of an evidence phase. By streamlining conflict resolution processes, companies can allocate their resources more effectively, maintain productivity and focus on growth and strategic initiatives.

The principle of autonomy of the conflict is based on the assumption that parties are actively included in the justice process. In this assertion, the concept of inclusivity is actualised. The greater the readiness within a legal system to adopt inclusive methods of dispute resolution, the greater the chances for party autonomy. Parties are empowered to retain control over the resolution of their dispute[11]. Inclusivity thus serves as a foundational element that enables and ensures that the parties are the primary decision-makers in the process. By maintaining control over the outcome, the parties can craft agreements that are tailored to their specific needs and circumstances, thereby enhancing the sustainability of the resolution. In a commercial context, this autonomy allows businesses to negotiate terms that align with their strategic goals and operational realities. Business leaders, who are accustomed to making autonomous decisions, find this aspect particularly advantageous, as it enables them to integrate dispute resolution seamlessly into their broader strategic framework. By negotiating terms that reflect their business priorities and operational constraints, companies can ensure that resolutions are not only fair but also practically viable. Thus, autonomy in mediation is a reflection of the inclusivity concept, facilitating resolutions that are both sustainable and aligned with the dynamic needs of the business environment.

The principle of mutual satisfaction underscores the goal of mediation to achieve solutions that are acceptable to both parties. This principle aligns with inclusivity by striving to meet the interests and needs of all involved. A critical distinction exists between the parties' interests and positions. As Roger Fisher and William Ury explain, 'Your position is something you have decided upon. Your interests are what caused you to so decide' (Fisher et al. 2011). Finding a solution is possible once parties focus on their needs and interests instead of remaining fixed in their positions. A resolution that satisfies both parties is more likely to be sustainable, as it reflects a balanced agreement that all participants are willing to uphold. It makes no sense to conclude agreements that will create a new conflict on the scene

11 There is no autonomy in adjudicative methods of dispute resolution, where the focus is on obtaining a judgement and not on solving the problem. It is worth recommending the thesis of Nils Christie, who on the basis of criminal matters proved how we were deprived of the property of our own conflicts. See Christie 1977.

of the old conflict (Ertel & Gordon 2008). In business disputes, this mutual satisfaction can lead to the preservation of business relationships and foster a cooperative spirit for future interactions.

The principle of low costs in mediation highlights the affordability of the process compared to traditional litigation or arbitration. By minimising the financial burden on the parties, mediation makes dispute resolution more accessible and inclusive. Lower costs also contribute to sustainability by allowing parties to allocate their resources more efficiently, supporting the long-term viability of their business operations. For entrepreneurs, the cost-effectiveness of mediation can make the difference between resolving a dispute and facing financial strain from prolonged litigation.

In some cases, the high cost of litigation or arbitration can prevent smaller businesses from defending their interests effectively. Mediation becomes a viable solution in these scenarios, offering an affordable alternative that levels the playing field. However, it is crucial for parties to consider mediation well before a dispute arises, ideally by including a mediation clause in their contracts. This proactive approach ensures that mediation is a pre-agreed method for resolving conflicts, making the process more streamlined and predictable when disputes do occur. By integrating mediation clauses into agreements, businesses can further enhance their commitment to cost-effective and sustainable dispute resolution practices.

In conclusion, the principles of voluntariness, confidentiality, impartiality and neutrality, flexibility, expediency of proceedings, autonomy of the conflict, satisfaction of both parties and low costs are deeply intertwined with the concepts of inclusivity and sustainability in mediation. These principles collectively ensure that mediation is a fair, equitable and effective method for resolving commercial disputes, fostering a business environment where relationships are preserved and sustainable outcomes are achieved. These principles are integral to the practice of mediation within commercial disputes, emphasising the preservation of business relationships and the attainment of equitable outcomes. By promoting inclusivity and sustainability, mediation aligns with the overarching goals of modern business practices that prioritise long-term, equitable solutions over short-term gains. The inclusive and sustainable nature of mediation is one of its defining characteristics.

Inclusivity and Sustainability within the Polish Regulatory Framework

In the Polish legal system, there is no statutory definition of mediation (Głodowski 2020). However, a legal definition can be found in Article 3(a) of Directive 2008/52/Ec of The European Parliament and of The Council of 21st May 2008 on certain aspects of mediation in civil and commercial matters. According to this directive:

> Mediation means a structured process, however named or referred to, whereby two or more parties to a dispute attempt by themselves, on a voluntary basis, to reach an agreement on the settlement of their dispute with the assistance of a mediator. This process may be initiated by the parties or suggested or ordered by a court or prescribed by the law of a Member State[12].

The primary legal provisions concerning commercial mediation in Poland are found in the Code of Civil Procedure (CPC)[13]. These provisions will be analysed to identify elements of inclusivity and sustainability within the Polish regulatory framework. The analysis will be conducted chronologically, from the initiation of mediation, through its course, to its conclusion, focusing on specific legal provisions that illustrate these characteristics in practice.

---

12 European Parliament and Council (2008/52). Directive 2008/52/EC of the European Parliament and of the Council of 21 May 2008 on certain aspects of mediation in civil and commercial matters, <https://eur-lex.europa.eu/legal-content/EN/TXT/?uri=CELEX%3A32008L0052&qid=1720201337436>, accessed 5 July 2024 .

13 The legal framework for mediation in Poland is detailed in the ACT of 17 November 1964 – Code of Civil Procedure, SECTION II – Proceeding Before the Court of the First Instance, Chapter 1 – Mediation and Conciliation, Subchapter 1 – Mediation (Art. 183^1–183^{15}). Key provisions include the voluntary nature of mediation (Article 183^1), the impartiality of mediators (Article 183^3), confidentiality (Article 183^4) and the formal requirements for mediation agreements and proceedings (Articles 183^2–183^{14}), <https://isap.sejm.gov.pl/isap.nsf/download.xsp/WDU19640430296/U/D19640296Lj.pdf>

Opening Mediation. Inclusivity and Sustainability during the Proceedings

The mediation process in Poland can be initiated either by a mediation agreement or a court decision to refer parties to mediation, as stipulated by Article 183^1 §2of the CPC:

> Meditation shall be conducted on the basis of a mediation agreement or the court decision to refer parties to mediation. An agreement may also be concluded if a party consents to mediation in the event that the other party files a petition as referred to in Article 183^6 § 1.

In Poland, there is no mandatory mediation in commercial cases. Even when directed by the court, according to Article 183^8 § 2 CPC, a mediation shall not be conducted if a party did not agree to mediation within one week from the date on which a decision referring the parties to mediation is published or served to that party. This provision ensures that parties retain the autonomy to oppose court-directed mediation within 1 week of receiving the court's order, reinforcing their control over entering the mediation process. In the case of private mediation, if one party submits a mediation request, the counterpart must consent for the process to proceed. These provisions ensure that all parties involved have a say in whether mediation should take place and if they agree to the choice of mediator.

Inclusivity during the mediation process is critical, ensuring all parties involved in a dispute are given equal consideration and the opportunity to voice their concerns. This principle aligns with broader sustainable development goals, emphasising processes that are efficient, equitable and inclusive. According to Article 183^1§1 of the CPC, mediation is a fundamentally voluntary process. This voluntary nature ensures that all parties engage willingly, creating an inclusive environment where all voices can be heard. The principle of voluntariness remains relevant throughout the proceedings, as the process cannot proceed without the consent of all involved parties, thereby ensuring no party is coerced into participation.

The impartiality and neutrality of mediators are fundamental aspects of ensuring inclusivity in the mediation process, also within the context of commercial disputes in Poland. According to Article 183^3§1 and §2 of the

CPC, mediators are mandated to maintain impartiality and disclose any circumstances that could potentially raise doubts about their impartiality. This disclosure requirement ensures that all parties can trust the mediator to facilitate the process fairly, without bias, creating an environment where all participants feel their perspectives are valued equally. When mediators are seen as neutral facilitators, all participants are more likely to engage openly, knowing that their concerns will be addressed without prejudice.

Confidentiality in mediation, as mandated by Article 183[4] of the CPC, further enhances inclusivity by creating a safe space for open dialogue. The article stipulates: 'Mediation shall not be open to the public. A mediator, the parties and other persons participating in mediation proceedings shall keep confidential any facts disclosed to them in connection with the mediation'. This assurance encourages parties to share their true concerns and interests without fear of external judgement or repercussions. Confidentiality ensures that the discussions remain private, fostering a sense of security and trust among the parties, which is crucial for a genuinely inclusive mediation process. As mentioned earlier, this principle is particularly significant in corporate and commercial disputes, where the disclosure of certain information may cause reputational damage and loss of company value.

Mediators play a crucial role in commercial disputes, by using various methods to facilitate the amicable settlement of conflicts. According to Article 183[3a] of the CPC:

> A mediator shall conduct mediation using various methods with the aim of an amicable settlement of dispute, including the provision of support to the parties in the elaboration of settlement proposals. At a common request of the parties, the mediator may also indicate manners for settling the dispute which shall not be binding for the parties.

This legal provision highlights the flexibility and adaptability of mediation, emphasising that it is a process driven by the consent of the parties involved. In the context of commercial disputes, this consent-based approach is particularly advantageous. Businesses often face complex issues that require nuanced and bespoke solutions. The ability of mediators to use a variety of methods ensures that the mediation process can be tailored to the specific needs and dynamics of the parties involved. This flexibility is essential for creating solutions that are not only effective but also acceptable to all parties. The provision of support in the elaboration of settlement proposals, as mandated by Article 183^{3a}, underscores the mediator's role in guiding parties towards mutually beneficial outcomes. In commercial settings, where disputes can significantly impact business operations and relationships, this supportive role is vital. Mediators help parties articulate their interests and needs, facilitating a deeper understanding and fostering a collaborative environment. This process ensures that the solutions derived are practical and sustainable, reflecting the true intent and agreement of the parties. Furthermore, the ability of mediators to suggest non-binding settlement options, upon the parties' common request, adds an additional layer of inclusivity to the mediation process. In commercial disputes, where innovative and unconventional solutions might be necessary, this provision allows mediators to propose potential resolutions that parties may not have initially considered. While these suggestions are non-binding, they can serve as valuable starting points for negotiation, helping parties explore a wider range of possibilities. Since there is no person who has indicated to the parties how to find an appropriate space, they remain unable to reconsider their situation and, as a result, continue to hold on to their old beliefs[14].

The consent-based nature of mediation, reinforced by Article 183^{3a}, ensures that the parties retain control over the process and the outcomes. This is a critical aspect of inclusivity, as it empowers all involved parties to actively participate and shape the resolution of their dispute. In commercial disputes, where the stakes are high, this empowerment fosters a sense of ownership and commitment to the agreed-upon solutions, enhancing their likelihood of success and implementation.

Outcomes in Mediation

The inclusivity and sustainability of the mediation process are particularly evident in its outcomes. Legal provisions ensure that settlements accepted by the parties are also legally binding. Article 183^{12} of the CPC mandates that

14 See The Arbinger Institute (2018). *The Anatomy of Peace*, Polish edition, p. 314. Warsaw: MT Business.

the mediation report includes details of the agreement reached, specifying: 'A mediation report shall be drawn specifying the place and time of mediation as well as the names and addresses of the respective parties, name and surname of the mediator and the outcome of mediation'. This requirement underscores the formal nature of mediation outcomes and ensures transparency and accountability.

Moreover, recent amendments to Polish legislation, specifically Article 183^{14}§2^{1} of the CPC, permit the inclusion of claims in the settlement that were not originally covered by the lawsuit. This provision underscores the comprehensive and flexible nature of mediation, allowing parties to address and resolve all related issues. By accommodating additional claims, mediation ensures that the concerns of all parties are considered and resolved in a holistic manner, further enhancing the sustainability of the agreements reached.

A critical provision within the Polish legal framework is Article 183^{14}§3 of the CPC, which delineates the limited circumstances under which a court can refuse to declare a settlement enforceable or validate a settlement reached before a mediator. Specifically, the court shall refuse validation only if the settlement is contrary to the law or social norms, intends to circumvent the law, or is incomprehensible or contradictory. This provision is vital as it ensures that judicial intervention in mediation outcomes is minimal and only occurs to maintain legal and social integrity. The restriction of judicial review to these three specific conditions underscores the autonomy and finality of mediated agreements, provided they adhere to these essential standards.

Finally, Article 183^{15} of the CPC states that a settlement validated by the court has the binding effect of a court judgement, noting: 'A settlement reached before a mediator once validated by the court has the binding effect of a settlement reached before the court'. This legal backing ensures that the efforts of the mediation process are respected and upheld, providing all parties with a sense of legal certainty. The enforceability of mediated settlements reinforces the finality and reliability of the agreements, promoting confidence in the mediation process.

Summary

The legal framework governing mediation in Poland, as articulated in the Polish CPC, emphasises the principles of voluntariness, impartiality, confidentiality, autonomy and impartiality of the mediator. These principles collectively contribute to an inclusive mediation process, ensuring that all parties can participate equally and openly. The robust legal structure facilitates resolutions that are legally binding, equitable and satisfactory to all involved. The inclusive nature of mediation, reinforced by these legal guarantees, supports the integration of diverse perspectives and fosters the creation of a more just and equitable business environment.

Advocating for the inclusion of sustainability and inclusivity as core principles of mediation is essential for several reasons. Firstly, these principles align with the broader goals of sustainable development, promoting long-term, resilient business practices. Secondly, they encourage a cooperative and collaborative problem-solving culture, which is crucial for addressing complex challenges in the modern business environment.

Within the European legislative framework, ESG factors will remain a key priority despite recent moves to reduce reporting burdens. For Polish entrepreneurs, navigating this evolving regulatory landscape continues to present a significant challenge. It is essential to not only determine the scope of the obligations but also to understand that compliance will require organizational changes, particularly in communication and conflict resolution. Mediation can serve as an effective tool in this regard. Incorporating ESG factors into business operations demands a shift in conflict resolution approaches. Mediation supports this transition by providing a framework for inclusively and sustainably addressing challenges, ensuring that all parties involved have a voice in the resolution process. This leads to outcomes that are fair, balanced and reflective of the diverse interests. Mediation, with its emphasis on voluntariness and neutrality, is well-suited to help businesses meet their ESG obligations. It facilitates open dialogue and mutual understanding, which are critical in aligning with sustainable development goals. By integrating these principles into the mediation process, businesses can enhance their capacity to manage disputes effectively while fostering a culture of ethical practices, long-term relationships and sustainable growth.

In conclusion, the principles of inclusivity and sustainability should be explicitly recognised as core values of mediation. This recognition not only enhances the efficacy of mediation in resolving commercial disputes, but also is congruent with evolving regulatory requirements and expectations in the European business environment. Mediation aligns seamlessly with the ESG framework, offering a rapid, adaptable, consensual and mutually advantageous solution centred on the parties' agreed interests. This approach provides a practical and workable resolution, promoting a more sustainable and inclusive economic landscape. By embracing these principles, businesses can navigate the complexities of ESG regulations more effectively and contribute to a more sustainable and inclusive economic landscape.

De lege ferenda, it is recommended that future legislative efforts introduce mandatory mediation in commercial disputes in Poland and develop a simple, electronic system for filing mediation requests. Additionally, tax incentives for companies that utilise mediation should be implemented. This would align the mediation instrument with a business-oriented approach, making it more accessible and efficient for companies.

Furthermore, it is crucial to enhance the promotion of mediation and the education of judges to ensure they are more inclined to refer cases to mediation. Increasing awareness and understanding of mediation among businesses and the public can significantly boost its utilisation. Providing targeted education and training for judges on the benefits and processes of mediation is essential. Judges who are well-informed about mediation are more likely to recommend it as a viable option for dispute resolution. This education can include workshops, seminars and continuous professional development programmes that highlight the advantages of mediation in achieving fair and efficient outcomes. By integrating these promotional and educational initiatives, alongside mandatory mediation and an electronic filing system, the legal framework can more effectively support businesses in resolving disputes sustainably and inclusively, ultimately fostering a more resilient and progressive economic environment.

It is crucial to implement comprehensive conflict resolution policies within workplaces. Such policies should be embedded in the organisational culture and consistently reinforced through training and clear communication. By establishing a proactive approach to conflict resolution, businesses can address potential disputes before they escalate, ensuring that conflicts are managed in a way that preserves relationships and promotes collaboration.

This comprehensive approach not only addresses immediate conflicts, but also aligns with long-term business strategies focused on resilience and sustainability. By fostering an environment where conflicts are resolved constructively, businesses can reduce the potential for costly litigation, minimise disruption and create a more harmonious workplace. Ultimately, these measures would contribute to a more stable and progressive economic landscape, benefiting businesses and society as a whole.

Bibliography

Antony, Murithi, and Njuguna, James (2024). 'Harnessing Appropriate Dispute Resolution (ADR) for Achieving Environmental Justice: A Path to Sustainable Development', *Journal of Appropriate Dispute Resolution (ADR) & Sustainability*, 2, 57–82.

Bohm Fredric, and Laurell Stefan (2014). *Rozwiązywanie Konfliktów. Praktyczny Poradnik dla Pracodawców i Menedżerów*. Warszawa: BL Info Polska.

Christie, Nils (1977). 'Conflicts as property', *The British Journal of Criminology*, 17 (1), Oxford University Press, 1–15.

De Palo, Giuseppe, and Trevor, Mary B. (2012). *EU Mediation Law and Practice, 1st Ed*. Oxford: Oxford University Press.

Drosik, Adam, Heidrich Dorota, and Ratajczak Magdalena (2022). *Wprowadzenie do Zrównoważonego Rozwoju: Podręcznik Akademicki*. Warszawa: Wydawnictwo Naukowe Scholar.

Ertel Danny, and Gordon Mark (2008). *Negocjacje Fair Play. Budowanie Zdrowego Partnerstwa Zamiast Wymuszania 'Tak'. Czyste Praktyki Najlepszych Negocjatorów*. Warszawa: MT Biznes.

Esplugues, Carlos A. (ed.) (2014). 'Civil and Commercial Mediation in the EU after the Transposition of the Directive 2008/52/EC'. *Civil and Commercial Mediation in Europe. Cross-Border Mediation Vol II.*, pp. 485–771. Cambridge: Intersentia.

Fisher, Roger, Ury, William, **and Patton, Bruce** (2011). *Getting to Yes: Negotiating Agreement Without Giving In*, 3rd edition. New York, NY: Penguin Books.

Głodowski, Włodzimierz (2020). 'Arbitraż i Mediacja jako wiodące alternatywne metody.' In Włodzimierz Głodowski (ed.), *Alternatywne Metody Rozwiązywania Sporów w Polskim Systemie Prawnym*. Poznań: Wydawnictwo Naukowe UAM.

Hart, Oliver, and Zingales Luigi (2017). 'Companies Should Maximize Shareholder Welfare Not Market Value', *Journal of Law, Finance, and Accounting*, 2, 247–274.

Hejduk Irena K., and Grudzewski Wiesław M. (2012). 'Sustainable Enterprise – Enterprise of the Future – As the Response to the Economic Crisis'. In Irena K. Hejduk and Wiesław M. Grudzewski (eds), *Sustainable Enterprises of the Future*. Pittsburgh – Warsaw: Wyższa Szkoła Zarządzania i Prawa im. Heleny Chodkowskiej w Warszawie.

Kalisz Anna (2020). 'Mediacja cywilna (Gospodarcza) w Sporach Prawnych, w Tym Sądowych'. In Anna Kalisz & Adam Zienkiewicz (eds), *Mediacja w Sprawach Gospodarczych Jako Narzędzie w Spierające Sukces w Biznesie*, pp. 152–160. Warszawa: Difin.

McGregor Lorna. (2015). 'Alternative Dispute Resolution and Human Rights: Developing a Rights-Based Approach through the ECHR', *European Journal of International Law*, 26 (3), 607–634, <https://doi.org/10.1093/ejil/chv039>, accessed 30 July 2024.

Spencer, David, and Brogan, Michael (2007). *Mediation Law and Practice*. Cambridge: Cambridge University Press.

The Arbinger Institute (2018). *The Anatomy of Peace*, Polish edition. Warsaw: MT Business.

Zienkiewicz, Adam (2007). *Studium Mediacji. od Teorii ku Praktyce*, pp. 44–45. Warszawa: Difin.

Legal sources

ACT of 17 November 1964 – Code of Civil Procedure, <https://isap.sejm.gov.pl/isap.nsf/download.xsp/WDU19640430296/U/D19640296Lj.pdf>, accessed 29 September 2024.

Directive 2008/52/EC of the European Parliament and of the Council of 21 May 2008 on certain aspects of mediation in civil and commercial matters, <https://eur-lex.europa.eu/legal-content/EN/TXT/?uri=CELEX%3A32008L0052&qid=1720201337436>, accessed 5 July 2024.

CHAPTER 7

Civil and Commercial Mediation in Italy – Part One: Origins and Functioning for a Comparative View

Isidoro Barbagallo[1]

Introduction

A study comparing the rules of various national systems regarding Alternative Dispute Resolution (ADR) and mediation, in particular, with those in force in Italy implies an in-depth study of the latter and of the historical and cultural background in which they developed, together with considering the experiences carried out so far in the matter.

Procedures for the pre-litigation settlement of disputes have been known in the Western world since ancient times. Even in the law of the XII Tables (Lex Duodecim Tabularum, 451–449 BC) we find it written (Tabula I):

> Rem ubi pacunt, orato. Ni pacunt, in comitioaut in foro ante meridiem causam coiciunto (If the parties reach an agreement, in this case the magistrate issues the sentence. If the parties do not reach an agreement, the parties themselves must explain the essential aspects of the case in the Forum in a meeting before midday (Picione 2010: 11).

Personal presence was, therefore, required and the attempt at conciliation between the parties was, in that phase of ancient Roman Law, a sort of condition of admissibility that continues and even today it is in Italian law for many matters. Other references to private solutions to disputes can also be found in earlier times, even in the Books of the Holy Bible (Carrese 2010: 19).

The modern concept of ADR initially originated in the common law systems, in particular, in the United States in the mid-1970s, and was developed considerably from the 1990s onwards with the primary aim of reducing the burden of ordinary jurisdiction.

---

1 PhD and Postdoc, Attorney at Law in Catania (Italy), expert in Comparative Public Law at the "Kore" University of Enna (Italy), email: studioibarbagallo@gmail.com

Section 3 of the US *Alternative Dispute Act* of 1998 defines ADR as 'any process or procedure, other than an adjudication by a presiding judge, in which a neutral third party participates to assist in the resolution of issues in controversy, through processes such as early neutral evaluation, mediation, minitrial and arbitration' (Falco & Spina 2014: 7). Mediation is, therefore, expressly included in this.

In Europe, the first countries to go in this direction were the United Kingdom, in the early 1990s, and France in 1993 (De Luca 2012: 1–10), where rules were introduced as 'Réglerautrement les conflits'.

The European Union (EU), acting on the basis of Article 263 of the *Treaty on the Functioning of the European Union* (TFEU), Article 6 of the **European Convention on Human Rights** (ECHR) and Article 47 of the Charter of Fundamental Rights of the EU, has intervened on several occasions in ADR matters. It started from the conciliation system for cross-border disputes introduced with the 'Solvit' Network in 1997 (Stefanizzi 2012: 28) and, then in Recommendations 98/257/EC and 2001/310/EC (Pacelli 2012: 13–21), from in the European Commission's Green Paper of 2002, and again in Directive 2008/52/EC, relating to certain profiles of mediation in civil and commercial matters, up to the Report of the European Commission of 26 August 2016 on the application of Directive 2008/52/EC and the Resolution of the European Parliament of 12 September 2017 on the implementation of Directive 2008/52/EC, etc.

In Italy, conciliation systems had traditionally existed for a long time, both within the civil process and externally (with the former 'Conciliator Judge' who only dealt with disputes of modest value, and then with the justice of the peace, in addition to conciliation in labour disputes, in arbitration, in consumer law, in banking law, ombudsman, etc.). However, it is with the introduction of civil and commercial mediation that ADR in Italy made a further truly important leap in quality, in the wake of a 'dejurisdictionalisation', moving from a sustainable and inclusive vision of the management of private and commercial conflicts (see as in what follows) and which, as some observed, suggests a sort of 'forensic jurisdiction' (Danovi 2016: 23–37)[2].

2 For further information on the concepts of 'inclusion' and 'sustainability', see Chapter VI.

Preliminary mediation, namely coming prior to ordinary litigation, is often mandatory as a condition of admissibility (Barbagallo 2012: 29–30). Another thing is voluntary mediation: it is a different situation, but one that is often applied.

Today in Italy, as in many other parts of Europe and the world, it is possible to resolve a dispute without going through judicial bodies but alternatively mediating the dispute through qualified bodies and individuals. It has been observed (De Luca 2012: 1) that in Italian, ADR could also take on the meaning of 'Systems alternative to jurisdiction' (Sistemi alternativi alla giurisdizione).

The updated text of Article 1, letter a) of Legislative Decree No 28 of 4 March 2010 implementing Article 60 of Law No 69 of 18 June 2009 on mediation for the purposes of conciliation in civil and commercial litigation offers a definition of civil and commercial 'mediation' pursuant to the current law, indicating it as:

> the activity, however named, carried out by an impartial third party and aimed at assisting two or more subjects in the search for an amicable agreement for the settlement of a dispute, also with the formulation of a proposal for its resolution.

The formulation of a proposal by the mediator is not mandatory: it can (optionally) be formulated when no agreement has been reached between the parties. However, the parties may make a mutual request at any time, in which case the mediator is required to formulate a proposal, after warning the parties about the possible consequences referred to in the all-too-severe Article 13 of Legislative Decree No 28/2010 regarding the reimbursement of procedural costs, which states:

1. When the provision that defines the judgement corresponds entirely to the content of the proposal, the judge excludes the reimbursement of the expenses incurred by the winning party who rejected the proposal, referable to the period following its formulation, and orders the reimbursement of the expenses incurred by the party losing the case relating to the same period, as well as the payment to the State budget of a further sum corresponding to the unified contribution

due. The applicability of Articles 92 and 96 of the civil procedure code remains valid. The provisions referred to in this paragraph also apply to the expenses for the compensation paid to the mediator and for the compensation due to the expert referred to in Article 8, paragraph 4.

2. When the provision that defines the judgement does not entirely correspond to the content of the proposal, the judge, if serious and exceptional reasons exist, may nevertheless exclude the reimbursement of the expenses incurred by the winning party for the indemnity paid to the mediator and for the compensation due to the expert referred to in Article 8, paragraph 4. The judge must explicitly indicate, in the motivation, the reasons for the provision on costs referred to in the previous period.
3. Unless otherwise agreed, the provisions of paragraphs 1 and 2 do not apply to proceedings before arbitrators (Article 13, Legislative Decree No 28/2010).

The figure of the 'mediator' is thus defined by letter b) of Article 1 of Legislative Decree No 28, which indicates that this is a 'natural person or persons who, individually or collectively, carry out mediation without, in any case, the power to make judgements or decisions binding on the recipients of the service itself'.

Legislative Decree No 28/2010 then defines 'conciliation' as the settlement of a dispute following mediation. Mediation is carried out at an 'organisation', which is a 'public or private body where the mediation process can take place'.

All civil and commercial mediation bodies are entered in a 'Register of Bodies' (Registro degli organismi), established by decree of the Minister of Justice pursuant to Article 16 of Legislative Decree No. 28/2010 (until this decree is issued, they are entered in the Register of Bodies established by decree of the Minister of Justice of 23 July 2004, No. 222).

To better understand the reasons for these choices by the Italian legislator (in the wake of what also happened in many other parts of the world), it is necessary to bear in mind that Justice in Italy has long been afflicted by an exhausting slowness of court cases and trials[3], coming at significant cost also

3 For a synthetic overview of the problems and attempts to reform the Italian Justice system, also in light of the 'comparatistic turn' of *de iure condendo* scientific studies, see Taruffo 2015: 450–453.

to the economy, in addition to the understandable inconvenience of those seeking justice.

In recent years, following the reforms, something has changed for the better regarding the timing of justice, though the number of incorrect sentences at first instance, and sometimes even on appeal, remains very high, to the point of 'flooding' the Court of Cassation (which in Italy does not judge on the merits of a case, but only in respect of the legitimacy of the proceedings).

The 2023 Report of the Italian National Institute of Statistics (ISTAT) highlighted that, for each level of judgement, only 28% of civil cases in Italy are closed within 1 year of their start. However, 33.4% of cases take between 2 and 5 years to close, with 16.9% of cases, many of which concern inheritance and property rights ('Rem Rights', in Italian *'Diritti Reali'*) taking more than 5 years to reach a conclusion (ISTAT 2024: 8).

The percentage rates of the objects of cases that are appealed in the main matters are as follows: 65% of special proceedings cases are appealed; 40% industrial and corporate law; 25% *'Diritti Reali'*; 24% contracts, non-contractual liability and labour disputes; 19% real estate leases and other matters, including inheritance; 15% social security; 11% bankruptcy and other insolvency proceedings and 8% families and minors. On average, 36% of cases are completely or partially overturned on appeal[4]. These uninspiring statistics clearly justifies the growing development of ADR tools, though their use for settling civil disputes still remains a rarity. However, things are improving significantly: in 2023, 7.1% of citizens (8.5% of men and 5.8% of women) used ADR to reach a settlement, which is a vast improvement on the 2015 figure of 3.6%[5].

Citizens and their defence lawyers are evidently coming to understand more and more that civil and commercial mediation, along with other ADR tools, represent extrajudicial procedures that are important for the sustainability of the litigation activity management system, significantly speeding up the time needed to settle disputes, increasing satisfaction with the final outcome and easing the burden on the court system.

4 Italian Ministry of Justice – Dg Stat, 2024: 12, 21.
5 ISTAT 2024: 12.

In this context, civil and commercial mediation shines in both actual and potential terms as a tool for the better sustainability of litigation, as well as inclusiveness, due to its lower costs (see as in what follows). If conducted well, it also produces a high level of mutual satisfaction between the parties.

The Origins of Civil and Commercial Mediation in Italy; the Figure of the Mediator

Civil and commercial mediation was developed in Italy, as well as in other states around the world, primarily to ease the burden on judicial litigation and to speed up the time required to settle disputes, as this is fundamental not only for citizen satisfaction, but also for the growth of the economy of any state. We have already seen earlier the disheartening picture of proceedings heard before the bodies of the ordinary jurisdiction, which gave rise to the need to find new, different and more effective tools – in addition to the ordinary jurisdiction, but independent from it – in order to speed up proceedings and, given the significant expense of hearing cases before courts, reduce costs. Overall, mediation is certainly more sustainable than taking cases to court, and so it also fulfils a support function (compulsory preliminary mediation) in deflating court litigation.

It was Legislative Decree No. 28/2010, issued in implementation of Article 60 of Law No. 69 of 18 June 2009, that introduced the rules on civil and commercial mediation into Italian law.

After an initial ruling of unconstitutionality in 2012 (C. Cost., No. 272/2012), the institute was relaunched with changes included in Legislative Decree No. 69 of 21 June 2013 and converted into Law No. 98 of 9 August 2013.

This was not the first form of ADR in Italy, as the regulation of corporate conciliation had previously been introduced with Legislative Decree No. 5/2003. Other forms of dispute conciliation had also already been known in the judicial field for a long time, while from an extrajudicial point of view, conciliation through a non-judicial commission, even before the institution of civil and commercial mediation, was already present, for example, in labour disputes[6].

6 The same is true in other European member states, as has been highlighted, even in scientific works from non-EU countries, including, for example and *ex multis*, Kaplan 2014: 67–68 (which also has an interesting definition of voluntary mediation, taken from public regulatory studies).

Civil and commercial mediation in Italy, like in most other states where it is used, is carried out through 'mediation bodies' that are independent of the judicial apparatus. Many of these are established at bar associations and at chambers of commerce, while others are operated by specially established private companies.

The Register of Mediation Bodies is kept in Italy at the Ministry of Justice, in the Department for Justice Affairs. The Director General of Civil Justice is responsible for it, and it is managed electronically.

For their foundation, and throughout their existence, private mediation bodies must satisfy certain minimum requirements in compliance with the principles of professionalism and efficiency, organisational and financial capacity (Isoni & Pasquale 2018: 8–11). Those of public bodies (lawyers' associations, chambers of commerce, etc.) require less stringent, but still present, requirements.

There is no difference between public and private bodies in terms of mediation powers. The difference is that public bodies require fewer bureaucratic formalities, as the State provides greater initial confidence, including in their impartiality.

Both public and private entities must file an application for registration before they can start their mediation activity. In that application, they must prove that they meet the requirements referred to in Article 4 Ministerial Decree [Decreto Ministeriale (D.M.)] No. 180/2010.

The application must be accompanied by the applicant's regulations code of ethics, in addition to tables indicating the compensation requested for the service provided. Each mediation body can have multiple offices in the country and must have offices in at least two different provinces or regions. Mediations must be carried out by qualified mediators, who are required to attend refresher courses to maintain their qualifications.

We have already seen in Chapter VI, to which we refer, the definition of 'mediator': the profession of lawyer is compatible with that of mediator. In this regard, the National Forensic Council (Consiglio Nazionale Forense – CNF), in its Circular No. 6/C/2014, specified that, in order to practice the profession of civil mediator, lawyers are obliged to follow a training course lasting a minimum of 15 hours and then carry out an internship of two entire mediation proceedings that have gone beyond the first meeting.

Pursuant to Articles 54 and 55-*bis* of the Italian Forensic Code of Conduct (CNF), there are certain specific cases linked to a lawyer's competence, or to their current, previous or future activity (and its type) in favour of one of the parties, etc., which may make the lawyer incompatible with the role of mediator in a specific deal, or in the presence of a certain party (Barbagallo 2012: 31–34). This incompatibility can extend to the lawyer's collaborators and to other professionals who are associated with them. Concerning mediators, they do not necessarily have to be lawyers (even though in Italy most mediators are). They must have obtained at least a secondary school diploma, have attended a training course of at least 50 hours run by bodies accredited by the Ministry of Justice and have passed a direct exam to ascertain their aptitude and professional capacity in relation to the chosen branch of mediation.

The personal qualities of the mediator are extremely important for the success of their activity: a mediator with an inflexible mentality – and unfortunately, there are some – will find it much harder to help the parties to reach a satisfactory mediation agreement. In this respect, it is up to the mediation bodies to ensure that public authorities are not co-opted into their own structures. The limited number of hours of training does not in itself constitute a guarantee of the quality of the human and personal qualities of the aspiring mediator. Passing the course for mediators only certifies knowledge of the legal rules of mediation and some other technical–behavioural notions. The personal and innate ability to mediate cannot be acquired with a course, but belongs to the character heritage of each person, to a different extent from one person to another: and here, the course for mediators does not allow for adequate study of this important aspect.

Neither a mediator nor any assistants can assume any rights or obligations directly or indirectly connected with the business handled, except for those that are strictly inherent to the provision of the work or service. They are paid by the mediation body and are prohibited from receiving any form of compensation directly from the parties. In addition, mediators have to sign, from time to time and for each matter they mediate, a declaration of their independence and impartiality according to the templates provided for in the applicable procedural regulations, as well as any further commitments provided for there.

If, before or during the procedure, the mediator detects any elements capable of affecting their independence and impartiality, they must immediately, and in detail, communicate this to the person in charge of the mediation body and to the parties, to arrange a possible replacement (which can also take place at the request of a party).

Furthermore, when formulating conciliation proposals, the mediator must do so in accordance with the spirit of the rules on mediation, always respecting the limits of public order and without violating the law.

The Growth of the 'Dejurisdictionalisation' of Justice: Assisted Negotiation

A more incisive path towards the dejurisdictionalisation of Justice, one that started with the launch of civil and commercial mediation procedures for cases, was made during the Renzi Government with the birth of 'Assisted Negotiation', an activity of dispute resolution that is conducted by the parties with the help and assistance of their lawyers. This step was taken as part of the Justice Reform implemented with Legislative Decree No. 132/2014, which was converted, with amendments, into Law No. 162/2014. This had three main purposes: the rapid recovery of the economy, the simplification of civil justice and other measures aimed at closing the existing civil backlog with the issuance of sentences (Giorgetti 2015: 5).

'Assisted Negotiation' is procedure whereby the parties, assisted by one or more lawyers, collaborate in good faith and with loyalty to resolve a dispute amicably.

It is mandatory by law and must be attempted as a pre-trial condition in cases of compensation for damage caused by the use of vehicles and boats, or for the payment of sums of any kind that do not exceed €50,000.

Assisted Negotiation differs from mediation, in that it is the lawyers who assist the parties and lead the procedure, while in civil mediation the leadership role is taken by the mediators (lawyers or other professionals impartial, in a third party position), who must be registered in a specific national register and periodically attend refresher courses. It also differs from voluntary mediation, where the presence of a lawyer as party defenders is optional, whereas in Assisted Negotiation and in mandatory mediation it is fundamental.

The Italian legal experience in the field of mediation is very important, because from Legislative Decree (D. Lgs.) 4 March 2010, No. 28 onwards, continuous corrections have been made to its rules, until very recently. These have aimed to capitalise on the experience, both positive and negative, to improve and make the use of civil and commercial mediation tools more effective and sustainable.

The last modification it has been prepared on 17 September 2024, when the Council of Ministers approved, in preliminary examination, a Legislative Decree that introduces supplementary and corrective provisions to Legislative Decree 10 October 2022, No. 149. It is in the process of being promulgated by the president of the Republic, after which it can come into force.

Civil Mediation and Civil Trial: Main Differences and Inclusiveness

Civil and commercial mediation revolves around the principle of the centrality of the parties in the dispute (Isoni & Pasquale 2018: 2–4), as well as the availability of the right which is the subject of the dispute and the willingness of the parties to meet. In fact, while in civil trials the case is dealt with solely on the basis of the rules of law, in mediation the definition of the dispute aim is to resolve the dispute above all through the identification of the real and concrete and specific interests at stake, regardless of identifying the wrongs under the applicable law and upholding the rights that everyone deserves.

This is the main difference between mediation and an ordinary trial, in addition to various other differences regarding procedural rules.

To obtain mutual satisfaction between the parties, it is, therefore, frequently necessary to overcome their respective initial positions, working within the framework of the logic of full, or at least acceptable, mutual satisfaction, looking as closely as possible at the specific grievances of the parties and their particular and concrete interests. For the purposes of settling the dispute, these may also be unrelated to the topic of the issue to be resolved.

The civil and commercial mediation system, thanks to its lower costs and tax benefits, contributes not only to making the resolution of disputes more sustainable for citizens, but also to them being able to access these tools more easily, given the high costs involved in recourse to the courts in Italy.

The tax cost of bringing a matter before the courts in Italy can be very high, even several thousand euros (depending on the value of the case, the subject matter and the degree of complexity). Mediation costs, on the other hand, tend to be considerably lower, especially at the start (and when reaching a resolution of the dispute). This makes the management of the conflict through mediation much more inclusive, given lower costs, much faster times, tax benefits and the search for a resolution to the dispute that is not necessarily anchored to legal rules, but to the interests of the parties. As a result, even those who are wrong from a legal point of view may find it convenient to seek an amicable resolution of the conflict.

Overall, civil and commercial mediation is more inclusive and more sustainable than ordinary jurisdiction.

The Civil Mediation Process

In order to give it even greater effectiveness and participation, the mediation procedure was recently reformed by Ministerial Decree No. 150/2023 (Marinaro 2024: 21–29), in the framework as a further part of the 'Cartabia Reform' (Legislative Decree of 10 October 2022, No. 149), which modified and sometimes completely redrafted many articles of the previous Legislative Decree No. 28/2010, while also repealing the previous Ministerial Decree No. 180/2010. It came into force on 15 November 2023 and also reformed the criteria for training and updating mediators, the requirements for carrying out the related mediation training and establishing the content of the training courses[7].

Some important changes to the 'Cartabia Reform' could come into force soon, after the subsequent corrections to it introduced by the Legislative Decree approved on 17 September 2024 by the Italian Council of Ministers, which at the date of writing has not yet been promulgated by the President of the Republic, but could be soon[8].

During the mediation sessions, the mediator must make the conflicting parties talk to explain their problems and their particular interests in the matter, to understand the other party's problems and work out how to find a resolution.

7 *Ex multis*, for a synthetic look, Matteucci 2024: 5–8.

8 In this chapter, we make some references to the most important new developments foreseen.

It is very important, then, that the mediator also enters individual dialogue with each of them.

Civil mediation can be: (a) voluntary (with or without legal assistance); (b) mandatory, where the party must be assisted by a lawyer, in matters expressly indicated, where it is a condition for the legal action to proceed; (c) requested by the judge (known as 'delegated', in Italian: demandata), in matters where mediation is not mandatory or was not mandatory at the start of the process. Here, the assistance of a lawyer is necessary, and it can also be ordered on appeal and (d) ordered by the judge if the mandatory mediation, prior to the start of the trial, has not been carried out.

As provided by Art. 5-quater, D. Lgs., preliminarily approved by the Italian Council of Ministers on 17 September 2024 (but not yet promulgated by the President of the Italian Republic at the date of this writing), the judge, up until the time he will sets the hearing for referral of the case to a decision, having assessed the nature of the case, the state of the investigation, the behaviour of the parties and any other circumstances, may order, with a reasoned order, the implementation of a mediation procedure. With the same order he sets the next hearing after the expiry of the term.

The parties, therefore, can always voluntarily choose to rely on civil mediation as a way of resolving a conflict, as long as the dispute does not concern what are known as 'unavailable rights'.

Mediation is only mandatory in a series of cases provided for by law; if it is not performed, this must be raised at the first hearing (or *ex officio* by the judge). If the judge finds that mediation has not been carried out, they will assign the parties a period of 15 days within which to submit a request for mediation to an authorised mediation body.

Mandatory mediation is a 'condition of admissibility' for civil cases and is established for condominium cases, real rights, divisions, hereditary successions, family agreements, leases, mortgages, business rentals, compensation for damages deriving from medical-healthcare liability and for defamation in the press, or through other means of advertising, in insurance, banking and financial contracts. From 2023, following the 'Cartabia Reform', it is also mandatory for cases relating to joint ventures, consortia, franchising, manual or intellectual work contracts, networks, administration, partnerships and subcontracts. Further innovations are provided for by Art. 5-sexies of the Legislative Decree of 2024, not yet promulgated by the President of the Republic at the date of drafting of this document: when the contract, the statute or the articles of association of the public or private entity include a mediation clause, the mediation experiment is a condition for the admissibility of the legal claim. This decree, approved in a preliminary stage, also introduces mandatory mediation for cases concerning condominiums, real rights, divisions and inheritance.

The United Sections of the Italian Civil Court of Cassation, in its judgement of 7 February 2024, No. 3452[9], specified that the condition of admissibility exists only for the document initiating proceedings and not for counterclaims (Giuridico 2024).

Mediation can also be ordered by the judge during the case, even during an appeal, based on the assessments of opportunity, in which case it becomes a condition for the further continuation of the trial (called 'delegated mediation'). It must be completed within 3 months, though this period can be extended (Avvisati 2024); this terms until today, but within 6 months, extendable too, as provided for by the aforementioned D. Lgs. 2024, in the process of being promulgated (Avvisati 2024).

Delegated mediation can be ordered by the judge for matters where mediation is not mandatory. This was already provided for in Article 5, paragraph 2, of Legislative Decree No. 28/2010, which stated that during the trial, the judge can invite the parties to proceed with mediation but is not binding on the parties.

Legislative Decree No 69/2013, modified Article 5 that gives the judge the power to order the start of the mediation procedure, 'having assessed the nature of the case, the state of the investigation and the behaviour of the parties'. It is no longer simply an 'invitation', therefore, but an 'order', with mediation constituting a condition for the admissibility of the judicial request.

However, this rule has rarely been applied and so is not considered very successful. However, the Cartabia Reform did manage to make judge-delegated mediation more effective, by introducing into Legislative Decree No. 28/2010 Article 5 quater (mediation delegated by the judge). Delegated mediation,

9 Parties: Bo.Ge.Im. s.r.l. adv. A.A.

therefore, obeys the rules of the new Article 5 quater, with its autonomous placement in the regulatory framework.

It should be noted that the judge's power to refer the parties to mediation can be exercised at first and second instance, indeed up until the moment of clarifying the conclusions in the case. The law also specifies that the order for delegated mediation must be justified ('justified order').

Article 4 of Legislative Decree No. 28/2010 provides that a request for mediation is made by one or both of the parties filing an application with a mediation body in the relevant jurisdiction for the dispute, based on the territory where the dispute arises, which could soon be derogable if the parties agree, as expected in the mentioned draft of Legislative Decree approved from the Council of Ministers on 17 September 2024 (art. 4, first paragraph), in the process of being promulgated at the time of writing. The request must indicate the mediation body, the parties, the object and the reasons for the claim[10]. When a lawyer is assigned to the defendant, they are required to inform the client of the possibility of making use of the mediation procedure referred to in Legislative Decree No. 28/2010 and the tax benefits referred to in its Articles 17 and 20. The lawyer must also inform their client of cases in which the mediation procedure is a condition for the admissibility of the judicial request. This must be clear and in written form; it must be countersigned by the client and attached to the document initiating the proceedings. If these information obligations are not performed, the contract between the lawyer and the client becomes invalid. If the judge finds that the document has not been attached, they can take action pursuant to Article 5, paragraph 1-*bis* (setting a new hearing and granting a period of 15

10 According to the Court of Rome, Section V, Sentence 8 February 2024, no. 2345 (Parties: Ma.Ga. c. Co.), the mediation procedure is correctly introduced when the relevant request indicates, with sufficient clarity, the subject of the dispute and the summary reasons for the claim: Article 4 of Legislative Decree no. 28/2010, which provides 'reasons for the claim' among the essential contents of the mediation request, does not oblige it to be presented with the equivalent in-depth analysis formally necessary for a complete judicial act, nor does it require the precise indication of the 'legal elements' (One Legale 2024, database, Milan: Wolters and Kluwer Ed., editorial maximum).

days to file a mediation request)[11] or will inform the party of the power to request mediation. If mediation has been proposed but not yet concluded and the legal action is already underway, then the judge sets a new hearing after the deadline expires.

Once a request has been received, the mediation body will designate a mediator and set the first meeting between the parties, which will take place no later than 30 days from the filing of the request. Howver, the D. Lgs. approved on 17 September 2024, not yet promulgated by the President of the Republic, will provide that the mediation body sets the first meeting between the parties, which must be held no earlier than 20 days and no later than 40 days after the filing of the application, unless otherwise agreed by the parties.

If the first mediation meeting ends without the parties agreeing to join it, the admissibility condition is considered fulfilled, just as when an agreement is not reached. The procedure, which takes place according to the rules established by the individual mediation bodies in accordance with the laws in force, lasts no more than 3 months (but 6 months from the date of promulgation of the Legislative Decree approved on 17 September 2024, if there are no changes) from the date of filing of the mediation request, or from the expiry of the deadline set by the judge for filing the application.

The deadline, however, can be extended by a further 3 months (which will become 6 months from the date of promulgation of the new Legislative Decree mentioned earlier) if the parties so wish, after the start of mediation and before the expiry date.

The meetings take place in an informal atmosphere. During the first meeting, the mediator clarifies to the parties the function and methods of carrying out the mediation, then invites the parties and their lawyers to express their opinion on the possibility of continuing the mediation procedure, to see whether it will proceed.

11 The Italian Civil Court of Cassation, Section III, with Order of 14 February 2024, no. 4133, clarified that the 15-day deadline for starting delegated mediation is not to be considered peremptory, provided that at least the first meeting before the mediator has taken place before the referral hearing set by the judge (One Legale 2024, database, Milan: Wolters and Kluwer Ed., editorial maximum).

In disputes that require specific technical skills, the mediation body can appoint one or more technical auxiliary mediators.

In the case of a failure to participate in the mediation procedure without justified reason, the judge may deduce evidentiary arguments in the subsequent trial and may order the party who did not participate in the procedure in the cases provided for in Article 5 without justified reason to pay a fine corresponding to the total court fee due for the judgement (Article 4-*bis*). The mediator will draw up a conciliation proposal in the event that an agreement is not reached or at the parties' mutual request at any time during the proceedings (Article 11, Legislative Decree No. 28/2010).

The proposal only has to be accepted if there was a mutual request from the parties to the mediator to draw up a proposal.

However, any unjustified refusal of a conciliation proposal drawn up during the mediation can lead to a court order to pay court costs not exceeding that of the possible conciliation proposal [Article 91, first paragraph, second sentence, Code of Civil Procedure (CPC)].

The definitive mediation agreement, if reached, is attached to the minutes of the final mediation session, with the formal legal requirements and is enforceable.

The Technique of Civil and Commercial Mediation

The first objective of a civil and commercial mediation session is ensuring that the parties meet and get closer, rediscovering a mutual trust between them, with loyal, open and good faith collaboration. This relates to the famous sociological theory on the 'behaviour of law', known as the 'theory of Donald Black' (Black 1976: 38–42) whereby:

> The theory of Donald Black explains that "the relationship between law and relational distance is curvilinear." With the expression "relational distance", he refers to the intensity of the bond between two individuals: as the extremes, we find, on the one side, close relatives, while, on the other, complete strangers. According to Black, the closer is the relationship between the parties, the less likely they are to find the solution of their dispute through the law and the judicial system; rather,

> they look for a more friendly and private settlement. This theory can be applied also to lawyers: the more intimate is their relationship, the more they will look for an out-of-court-solution between their clients. On the contrary, strangers are more eager to use legal tools to solve dispute (Cominelli & Jacqmin 2020: 13–14).

Bearing in mind as this principle suggests, it is often very difficult to find an agreement between parties in bitter conflict with each other, which is why it is worth taking a closer look at some of the techniques used most often in mediation to reach an agreement.

Once the parties meet in mediation, the mediator must induce them to find a mutually satisfactory solution, which could also be one that is very different from what they initially imagined or hoped for when the dispute arose.

The first mediation meeting takes place at the headquarters of the mediation body, or in a place indicated by the body's procedural regulations (Article 8, paragraph 3 of Legislative Decree No. 28/2010). The procedural regulations must provide for the indication of the location of the mediation to be communicated to the parties. However, the venue can be changed with the consent of all the parties, the mediator and the person in charge of the mediation body (Article 22, first paragraph, letter a of Ministerial Decree No. 150/2023). The meeting takes place in an appropriate and welcoming room, preferably around a meeting table where the parties sit assisted by their lawyers, if present, and with the mediator seated in a position where they can visually check the entire venue of the ongoing mediation. The tones must be as friendly and conversational as possible, thereby reducing the conflict between the parties from the very beginning.

Mediation can also take place totally or partially remotely, with one or more of the participants attending the meeting through audiovisual means (Marinaro 2024: 26–27), although in both cases, this may involve some difficulties in coordination and confidential dialogue between individual parties and their lawyers, if the latter is not physically present in the same location.

As provided for by Art. 8-bis of the Legislative Decree approved on 17 September 2024, currently being promulgated, when mediation, with the consent of the parties, takes place in electronic mode, the documents of the procedure are drawn up by the mediator and signed in accordance with this decree in compliance with the provisions of the Italian Digital Administration Code[12].

At the conclusion of the procedure, the mediator will draw up an electronic document containing the minutes and any agreement for the signature by the parties required to do so. The document is immediately signed and returned to the mediator.

The latter, having received the document and verified the affixing, validity and integrity of the signatures, affixes his or her signature, ensuring that it is deposited with the secretariat of the Mediation Body, which sends it to the parties and their lawyers, if appointed. The preservation and display of documents of the mediation procedure carried out electronically are carried out by the mediation body in accordance with Art. 43, Legislative Decree No. 82/2005. Art. 8-*ter* of the Legislative Decree approved on 17 September 2024 provides for new provisions regarding mediation meetings with remote audiovisual methods.

Each party may always ask the person in charge of the mediation body to participate in meetings with remote audiovisual connection. The audiovisual connection systems used for these meetings ensure the simultaneous, effective and reciprocal audibility and visibility of the persons connected.

When the mediator is required to acquire the signatures of the participants for the documents drawn up during a meeting in which one or more parties participate in the manner provided for in this article, all signatures are affixed in compliance with the provisions of the Italian *Digital Administration Code* (D. Lgs. No. 82/2005).

This provision, in our opinion, could create difficulties in signing documents by very elderly people or in any case not very versed in computer habits, still very widespread in Italy as in the rest of the world.

Furthermore, where the person who must sign digitally is a foreign person, even if provided with a device for digital signature, problems could arise if it does not meet the technical standards required by Italian and/or European laws.

---

12 See Legislative Decree 7 March 2005, no. 82.

Only when the mediation is not carried out using telematic methods can the parties agree to establish, by way of derogation, that the signatures of all participants be affixed in analogue mode before the mediator.

The new provision also requires that the parties cooperate in good faith and loyally so that the documents drawn up during a meeting in which one or more parties participate in the manner provided in this article are signed without delay.

In any case, it is the mediator who must guide the meeting using the techniques of mediation, psychology (including non-verbal communication techniques) and verbal diplomacy.

To reach an agreement, the mediator can also operate in some way using a 'maieutic method', whereby the agreement to resolve the conflict is drawn from the reasoning and concrete interests of the parties.

The lawyers of the parties will also have to do the same, albeit in partially different terms and ways, and this in order to arrive at a creative solution to the conflict, through 'brainstorming' from which the various possible proposals aimed at settling the dispute emerge by looking at the interests of the parties. They will then identify the proposal of greatest mutual interest among those raised by the discussion.

The concept of a 'search for concrete and specific interests' is, therefore, absolutely central in the resolution of the dispute through mediation. As mentioned, the solution can also be 'creative', obtained abstracting both from the rules of law and from notions of right and by a Solomonic division of the stakes.

The identification of the concrete and specific interests of the parties and reaching a resolution through 'free-wheeling' conversations, directed by the mediator, who stimulates the parties to see things in a 'creative' perspective different from what was initially envisaged and identifying the respective concrete and specific interests to be brought into play – even if completely unrelated to the subject of the dispute will be useful for resolving the dispute, ideally according to the 'win–win' logic.

Joint and Separate Mediation Sessions

To resolve a dispute, especially when the mediator comes to realise that it can best be resolved only through a creative solution, one method is the organisation of both joint and separate confidential sessions of dialogue and discussion with the parties to the mediation. This can be very important and offers a friendly and non-judgemental atmosphere.

(a) Joint sessions: Mediation sessions usually begin and end with joint sessions in which all the parties are present before the mediator, together with their lawyers. During the mediation, it is also possible to appoint technical consultants to analyse and resolve any technical issues that may arise before the matter under discussion.

A party may decide not to be personally present only in exceptional cases, which must be properly documented (e.g. excessive distance to the headquarters of the mediation body, proven serious health reasons, etc.). In such cases, it is possible to act by delegating another subject through a special power of attorney, even called 'substantial'[13].

However, the participation of a party remotely, via videoconference, is admissible, as established by the recent reform referred to in the Ministerial Decree No 150/2023, which amended Article 8, paragraph 2 of Legislative Decree No 28/2010:

> Meetings can be held with remote audiovisual connection. The audiovisual connection systems used for the mediation proceedings meetings ensure the contextual, effective and mutual audibility and visibility of the connected people. Each party may ask the head of the mediation body to participate remotely or in person.

The first meeting must take place, according to the draft Legislative Decree approved on 17 September 2024, currently being promulgated, within 20 and 40 days from the submission of the application, unless otherwise agreed by the parties. In delegated mediation, there is no start deadline and the deadline for the conclusion of the entire procedure is 3 months (to date), extendable (Avvisati 2024)[14].

In the first joint session, the mediator explains to the parties his role and the methods of carrying out the mediation, indicating a series of rules of

13 On its meaning, see, among others, Zanussi 2022.

14 The deadline, when the decree approved on 17 September 2024 is promulgated, will be 6 months, extendable for once.

conduct and providing any other information in this regard. The parties present their requests already anticipated in the introductory documents to the mediation specifying them better and going into more detail, at the first meeting.

(b) Separate sessions (caucus): Though it unfortunately does not always happen, one or more separate sessions after the first joint session take place can be a very important and absolutely advisable move. During such sessions, the parties meet with the mediator individually without the presence of the other party, which allows them to reveal what they would not necessarily say in the presence of the opponent, even about their own concrete and specific interests. Naturally, this is done in full reliance on the mediator's obligation of confidentiality.

These separate sessions are also known as a 'caucus' (Leigh 2018: 1), with a term that originated around the mid-eighteenth century in political language and was later transferred, with a slight mutation of meaning, to that of the mediation of civil and commercial affairs. Each caucus is:

> as a private, confidential meeting of members of one side of a dispute, often with the mediator, to discuss options with the intent to find a resolution. This meeting is separate and distinct from the joint session. The parties can meet in caucus without the mediator and consult in private with their advisor (Leigh 2018: 1).

The mediator thus invites each party to reflect on the opportunity to define the dispute, tries to identify the conceptual interests that can be used to come up with possible feasible solutions, whether they are anchored in law or totally or partially creative.

Mediation sessions are not always actually implemented in Italy: if one of the two parties does not show up at the mediation, the mediator draws up minutes of the session that, in the case of compulsory mediation, allows the party who promoted the mediation to start the proceedings directly in court, given that the admissibility condition has now been met. The failure by the duly invited party to participate without a justified reason results in unfavourable effects (Article 12-*bis* of Legislative Decree No. 28/10, as amended by Ministerial Decree No. 150/2023, which aggravated the consequences of this conduct).

Some examples of creative mediation solutions:

(1) Mandatory mediation and delegated mediation

Turning now to explore a specific case that actually occurred in Italian mediation – involving compulsory mediation, i.e. prior to the start of a civil trial – in this case a lawsuit for adverse possession and its condition of legal admissibility:

A man had been cultivating farmland for over 20 years. He proposed compulsory mediation against the landowner to obtain recognition of adverse possession.

However, the elderly and sick owner of the land contested in mediation that he had declared to the tax authorities every year the ownership of the land, on which he had paid taxes, adding that, until 2006, the farmer had paid him rent. All this confirmed not only that the farmer did not have possession *uti dominus* of the land for over 20 years, but also that the owner had uninterrupted possession *animo domini*.

However, the elderly owner had no real interest in maintaining the land, because it was 80 km away from his residence and his age did not allow him to make frequent long journeys. Furthermore, part of the land had been expropriated for the construction of a railway and negotiations were underway between the owner and the expropriating company.

During the mediation, the owner and the farmer agreed on the sale of part of the land for a symbolic price (about one-third of its value), which the owner had already effectively lost as the farmer would continue to cultivate it and he, who lived far from that property, could not have checked to prevent it. To prevent this, the owner would have had to start a long lawsuit (and at the age of 83 years, he would have no guarantee of seeing the end of the case). Subsequently, the elderly man received compensation for the expropriated part of the land that had not been sold, so recovered a further good sum that he would not have obtained if he had lost the land through adverse possession.

In this way, not only did the parties avoid the expense and time-consuming nature of a court trial, with all the uncertainty that this entails regarding the final victory, but they also achieved their respective specific interests in the best possible way, which allowed them to close the dispute in just 3 months with mutual satisfaction, in a 'win–win' resolution.

This rapid resolution of the dispute is also advantageous for the economic system, because it allows for the faster circulation of available rights and, consequently, also a more efficient and rapid circulation of earnings and investments.

(2) Voluntary mediation

Another example of a creative solution can be found involving voluntary mediation.

A co-heir, ordered by court to pay €160,000 for the integration and rebalancing of a cousin's share in the inheritance, did not have the entire sum. To avoid a legal action for debt collection, which the co-heir cousin had already expressed the intention of enforcing, the man invited his cousin to voluntary mediation to prevent the risk of one of his properties being auctioned to compensate for the difference in share declared by the judge.

The co-heirs owned five properties in undivided co-ownership. The man proposed to his cousin the dissolution of the joint inheritance and the division of the assets, but with the donation of his share of a house by the sea, worth €165,000, without asking for the difference in value, with the aim of rebalancing the values of the altered shares in the inheritance.

The man knew that his cousin was very fond of that beautiful house, where she had spent holidays with her parents during her childhood and youth. So, thanks to the cousin's interest in acquiring a share in the beach house, the proposed agreement was reached. The entire house was attributed to the cousin and the rest was then divided without difficulty between the two. This was settled in a short time, without delays and without incurring the increased costs of a civil case, while also enjoying the tax benefits provided for mediation.

The two examples mentioned earlier demonstrate how, by leveraging concrete and specific interests, identified with thorough research, it is possible to reach an agreement even without following the indications of the sentence (or of the law, in other cases).

Questions of Evidence and Professional Secrecy

Anyone who participates in the mediation process in any role in the organisation is bound by the obligation of confidentiality with respect to any statements made and any information acquired during the process itself.

In particular, the mediator is required to maintain confidentiality towards the parties regarding the content of declarations made and any information acquired during the separate sessions, except with the express consent of the declaring party from whom the information comes (Article 9, D. Lgs. No. 28/2010).

A peculiarity of the mediation procedure is given by the regime whereby certain elements of evidence and means of proof cannot be used in a subsequent possible trial, as well as by the obligations arising from the duty of professional secrecy.

The first paragraph of Article 10 of Legislative Decree No. 28/2010 provides that:

> the declarations made or the information acquired during the mediation procedure cannot be used in proceedings having the same object, even if partial, begun, summarized or continued after the failure of the mediation, without consent of the declaring party or from whom the information comes. Testimonial evidence is not permitted on the content of the same declarations and information and a decision-making oath cannot be taken.

Not even the mediator, therefore, can be required to testify about the content of the statements made and the information acquired in the mediation procedure,

> neither before the judicial authority nor before any other authority. The provisions of Article 200 of the Criminal Procedure Code apply to the mediator and the guarantees provided for the defender by the provisions of Article 103 of the Criminal Procedure Code are extended insofar as they are applicable.

Conciliation

'Conciliation' is the result of mediation when an agreement is reached between the parties. Article 1, letter (f) of Ministerial Decree No. 150/2023 and Article 1, letter (c) of Legislative Decree No. 28/2010 define it as 'the settlement of a dispute following mediation.'

Anyone can access mediation with the aim of reaching the conciliation of a civil and commercial dispute, as long as it concerns available rights.

Pursuant to Article 11 of Legislative Decree No. 28/2020, if an amicable agreement is reached between the parties, the mediator makes a report, to which the text of the agreement itself is attached. If no agreement is reached, the mediator can formulate a conciliation proposal[15]. The mediator also draws up a conciliation proposal if the parties mutually request it at any time during the proceedings. Before drafting the proposal, the mediator informs the parties of the possible procedural consequences referred to in Article 13.

The mediator communicates the draft proposal to the parties in writing, and they then have 7 days in which to send the mediator their written acceptance or rejection of the proposal. In the absence of a response within the deadline, the proposal is considered rejected.

Unless agreed otherwise by the parties, the text of the proposal cannot contain references of any kind to the declarations made or information acquired during the procedure.

If the amicable agreement referred to in the first paragraph is reached, or if all the parties agree to the mediator's proposal, a report is drawn up and signed by the parties and the mediator, who also certifies the parties' signatures, or their inability to sign.

If the agreement involves the parties concluding one of the contracts or carrying out one of the acts provided for by Article 2643 of the Civil Code (deeds subject to entry in the public real estate registers), the report must be authenticated by an authorised public official (usually a notary, but the authentication costs are far lower than for a notarial deed on the transfer of rights, which makes it more inclusive and sustainable, even economically, than the path of civil mediation for many cases of transfers of real rights,

15 On the difference between the mediator's conciliation proposal and the judge's conciliation proposal at the first hearing, see Avvisati 2024.

declaration of adverse possession, etc.) before the entry can be made. The agreement reached may also provide for the imposition of constraints whose non-observance is punishable by the payment of sums of money as 'astreintes', for each violation or failure to comply with the established obligations, or for a delay in fulfilling them.

However, if conciliation fails, the mediator draws up a report indicating the proposal, which is signed by the parties and by the mediator, who certifies the signatures of the parties, or their inability to sign and also acknowledges, if applicable, the non-participation of one of the parties in the mediation process.

Finally, and in any case, the final report is filed with the secretariat of the mediation body and a copy is issued to the parties upon request.

The Executive Efficacy and Execution of the Settlement Agreement

Article 12 of Legislative Decree No. 28/2010 deals with the executive effectiveness and execution of the conciliation report containing the agreement reached.

If all the parties participating in the mediation have been assisted by a lawyer, the final report on the agreement, signed by the parties and by the lawyers, directly constitutes an enforceable title for the forced expropriation, for execution by delivery and release, for the execution of obligations to do and not to do something and, therefore, for execution in a specific form (when the creditor's right consists in the delivery of an asset or in the performance of an activity that constitutes a specific object), as well as for the registration of a judicial mortgage.

Lawyers attest and certify the compliance of the agreement with mandatory regulations and public order. If a writ of injunction is subsequently issued pursuant to Article 480, second paragraph, of the CPC, the agreement must be fully reported and transcribed there.

If the agreement attached to the report was reached without all the parties being assisted by a lawyer, it is approved – as in the case of voluntary mediation – at the request of a party, by decree of the president of the court, subject to verification of the formal regularity and compliance with the mandatory rules and the principles of public order. Both the court approval and the enforceability of the agreement reached between parties assisted by lawyers guarantee the future compliance with the agreement reached during mediation, in the event that one of the parties does not respect it.

Even in cross-border disputes, as referred to in Article 2 of Directive 2008/52/EC of the European Parliament and of the Council of 21 May 2008, the conciliation report is approved by the president of the court in whose district the agreement is to be enforced.

These forms of approval do not have a decision-making nature, but are merely executive, limiting themselves to certifying the regularity of the procedure and of the agreement with the mandatory rules and principles of public order (Battaglia 2010: 198).

The Mediation Allowance

The reform of the rules on mediation, brought about by the recent Ministerial Decree No. 150/2023, also affected the mediation 'indemnity', i.e. the expenses in favour of the mediation body that the parties must pay, which were the subject of an important review.

The payment of a (modest) compensation is set out for holding the first mediation meeting, but it is possible to apply for legal aid, with which even the mediator and the attorneys for the parties will be paid by the state in the event of reaching a conciliatory agreement in a mandatory mediation.

There are also appreciable tax benefits, especially in case of agreement reached, in civil and commercial mediation, though these are not explored further here, as they form the topic of Chapter VIII in this volume, containing the second part of the study on mediation in Italy (Botti 2024).

Upon submitting a request for mediation, or subsequent adhesion to it the parties are required to pay the mediation body a fee covering the start-up costs and the mediation costs for holding the first meeting. Where several subjects constitute a single 'centre of interest', for the purposes of the envisaged fee, they must be considered by the mediation body 'as a single part' (Article 34, paragraph 4 of Ministerial Decree No. 150/23). This means that several people who have the same interest (e.g. opposing the same part) are considered a single centre of interest and therefore pay as if they were one person and no longer as many individual people.

There is a single centre of interests when two or more parties cannot have – abstractly – conflicting legal interests in a dispute having the same object of the mediation procedure. For example, the co-owners who sue a neighbour who violates their property rights constitute a single centre of interests; on the other hand, the co-heirs in the division of the inheritance are not a single centre of interests, where conflicts may arise between them on the distribution of the assets.

If the mediation ends without agreement at the first meeting, the parties are not required to pay further amounts (Article 17, paragraph 3 of Legislative Decree No. 28/2010). For meetings subsequent to the first, and in the case of reaching an agreement, there are further mediation costs set by the mediation body[16].

If conciliation is reached in subsequent meetings, the table of fees of the mediation body may provide that the maximum amounts may be increased by up to 20%, in the presence of at least one of the following criteria: (a) the experience and competence of the mediator designated upon mutual agreement of the parties; (b) the complexity of the issues covered by the procedure, such as the commitment required of the mediator, which can additionally be assessed based on the number of meetings (Article 32, paragraph 3 of Ministerial Decree No. 150/23).

It should be noted that the 'parties are jointly obliged to pay the body further mediation costs in the event of conciliation or continuation of the proceedings with meetings subsequent to the first' (Article 34, paragraph 3 of Ministerial Decree No. 150/23).

Tax Benefits (Reference)

The sustainability of mediation and its spirit of inclusiveness arise not only from the lower costs and greater speed of conciliations in relation to what happens in ordinary jurisdiction, but also from the tax benefits that the Italian legislator has conferred on the institution of civil and commercial mediation, in particular through Articles 17 and 20 of Legislative Decree No. 28/2010, already in its original form and even more so with the recent reform referred to in Ministerial Decree No. 150/2023[17].

---

16 For further information, also in light of the recent reform, see Marinaro 2024: 27–29.

17 More on this point, in the next chapter of this volume (see Chapter VIII), where a detailed analysis, both theoretical and practical, is carried out of the tax legislation that benefits those who participate in the mediation.

In favour of the parties and the mediation bodies, it is envisaged that in the event of an agreement, the parties are granted a 'tax credit' equal to the compensation paid up to €600 per mediation. The documents of the mediation procedure are exempt from stamp duty and any other expense. Other significant tax advantages are foreseen for the registration tax for those who reach and formalise the conciliation agreement, with a significant exemption.

In the draft legislative decree approved on 17 September 2024 (not yet promulgated as of this writing), Article 20 provides important new rules and provisions on tax benefits arising from mediation, including tax credits in favour of the parties and mediation bodies.

Mediation as a Tool for Resolving International Commercial Disputes

At an international level, the ADR tool most often used, almost exclusively, has traditionally not been mediation, but rather arbitration. Very widespread in East Asia, it has been a little less so in the West, in part not only because of the high costs involved, but also because of a sort of barely veiled distrust towards a 'jurisdiction' external to the ordinary one. In recent years, efforts have been made, especially with input from the United States, to better develop the instrument of mediation in private international relations, especially as it offers greater flexibility, greater speed, lower costs and good tax benefits compared to arbitration.

The 'Singapore Convention on Commercial Mediation' is moving in this direction, opened for signature within the United Nations Commission on International Commercial Law (UNCITRAL), in Singapore on 7 August 2019 and in force since 12 December 2020. This gives executive effect to agreements reached through a mediation procedure on international commercial disputes in the adhering states: as of 18 June 2024, there are 57 states. Signatories include the United States, China and India, but neither EU Member States have yet joined, nor the EU itself; only 14 states have formally ratified it: Saudi Arabia, Belarus, Ecuador, Fiji, Honduras, Qatar, Singapore, Japan, Turkey, Georgia, Kazakhstan, Uruguay, Nigeria and Sri Lanka.

The preamble of the Convention highlights the advantages of mediation and the reasons that led the UN to approve the Convention back in 2018:

> Recognizing the value for international trade of mediation as a method for settling commercial disputes in which the parties in dispute request a third person or persons to assist them in their attempt to settle the dispute amicably – Noting that mediation is increasingly used in international and domestic commercial practice as an alternative to litigation – Considering that the use of mediation results in significant benefits, such as reducing the instances where a dispute leads to the termination of a commercial relationship, facilitating the administration of international transactions by commercial parties and producing savings in the administration of justice by States – Convinced that the establishment of a framework for international settlement agreements resulting from mediation that is acceptable to States with different legal, social and economic systems would contribute to the development of harmonious international economic relations.

While there are many appreciable considerations contained in the text, there are other parts that can certainly still be improved, as the Convention contains certain critical points[18] which have led to resistance even in within the EU and its individual Member States, which have not yet ratified.

The Singapore Convention allows mediation agreements to be concluded directly in the state's parties to this instrument. However, its application does not require reciprocity, unlike the New York Convention.

Article 1 of the Singapore Convention limits its scope of applicability to commercial mediation agreements of an international nature, excluding disputes relating to consumers, inheritance law, labour law, family law and agreements settled within the ordinary jurisdiction, which limits its general scope of application, but increases its specialty.

The courts of the state where the agreement will be enforced will be required to enforce it if the state is a party to the Singapore Convention. The same obligation also applies if the parties to the mediation agreement are citizens of a state that is not a party to the Singapore Convention.

Many of the objectives pursued by the Singapore Convention coincide with those that the EU has undertaken itself in terms developing the spread of mediation during its normative production, already indicated by here (§ 1.).

18 See, in summary, Cabanes Alanon et al. 2022.

However, there are some significant differences, as mentioned, which, as long as they are properly smoothed out over in the years to come, will be able to attenuate or eliminate the mistrust of the EU Member States and the EU. To this end, Article 12 of the Singapore Convention also includes the possibility of membership by a 'regional economic integration organisation', in addition to the formal membership of its Member States. It seems that the EU will wait for more states to sign and ratify the Singapore Convention before taking significant steps towards joining (perhaps also waiting for some corrections to the text, as suggested by some, to give it a more formal look and stronger guarantees on the quality of mediators and mediation bodies).

Summary

Chapter VII has illustrated and commented on the regulations in force in Italy on civil and commercial mediation, broadening the topic also to cover the mediation of international civil and commercial disputes and to the Singapore Convention (which Italy has not yet joined), in the hope that it may also be useful in a comparative vision between foreign systems on this matter, which is one of the main purposes of this volume.

What makes the Italian regulatory framework more current and interesting, also in terms of sustainability and inclusiveness of the mediation tool for civil and commercial disputes, are the recently introduced rules referred to in Ministerial Decree No. 150/2023 (further to the 'Cartabia Reform') which – issued after 13 years of experience in mediation, since the time of Legislative Decree No. 28/2010 – has brought important changes to the previous legislation, making it more incisive, attractive, inclusive and therefore participatory, thereby giving greater importance to mediation as a method of resolving civil and commercial conflicts.

Other corrections may be supported by the legislation when the Legislative Decree approved by the Council of Ministers on 17 September 2024 is promulgated, which has identified some practical critical issues identified over time and will try to remedy them.

From this perspective, a study of the Italian ADR system, particularly civil and commercial mediation, is certainly of great interest, both *de iure condita* and *de iurecondendo*. It draws attention on the recent reform from past experiences, some of which have identified knots and weak points in the previous regulatory structure, while also offering relevant corrective measures.

It remains to be seen what the concrete and specific outcomes will be, but it is encouraging to observe how the statistics highlight the growing use of ADR in Italy, as well as in other states, along with growth in the civil and commercial mediation sector. In this regard, the Italian bar has come to believe more and more in this tool, which, if well applied – and in this sense the cultural and human qualities of the mediators is very important – can provide an excellent service to users, acting as an alternative valid, free and serious to ordinary jurisdiction, which, as pointed out in Chapter VII, does not always constitute an ideal solution in terms of speed, cost-effectiveness and user satisfaction.

It also appears evident that the speed and flexibility of civil and commercial mediation – even superior to that of other ADR means – makes the resolution of the dispute more sustainable, on the one hand, easing the workload of the courts which to be sustainable must reduce the number of cases to be treated, and on the other hand, returning the resolution of the dispute directly to the parties, through an impartial third party – the mediator.

It also appears evident that the speed and flexibility of civil and commercial mediation – even superior to that of other ADR means – make the resolution of the dispute more sustainable in an alternative way to the jurisdiction of the courts, thus reducing the amount of legal litigation sustained by judges: to be sustainable, it must reduce the number of cases filed. Civil and commercial mediation, on the other hand, returns the solution directly to the parties, through an impartial third party – the mediator, with faster times and reduced costs.

Mediation is certainly an important tool for speeding up the time needed to resolve disputes and for reducing the judicial burden, which in Italy is very heavy. As of 30 June 2022, there were 2,881,886 pending civil trials and almost every other judgement is amended on appeal, with many appeal sentences then amended again in the Supreme Court.

The errors and the resulting failures of the first instance of the courts in Italy is one of the main causes of congestion in courtrooms.

The lower costs and greater tax breaks of civil and commercial mediation in Italy have also further raised the specific inclusiveness of mediation, which today, after the 2023 reform, is even more inclusive than before. This is enhanced further as access to state-funded legal aid (at state expense) has been allowed for the less well-off, for both mandatory and delegated mediation, through which, as regards the expenses of the party admitted to legal aid, the lawyer and the mediator are paid by the State in the event of a positive outcome of the mediation, when the agreement avoids starting a legal dispute in court[19].

It is still necessary to work towards the formation of a new legal culture that sees the lawyer not only as a defender in ordinary jurisdiction, but also as a professional in out-of-court conflict resolution. Even the universities, within the framework of their teaching autonomy, must offer students appropriate training that considers the mediation of civil and commercial conflicts and the use of ADR in general.

Although civil and commercial mediation, as an alternative to ordinary jurisdiction, offers the possibility of satisfying the concrete and specific interests of the parties in a few months rather than years, while also offering important tax advantages, in Italy it has long been viewed with little favour by lawyers and users of justice. This is due both to a (changing) mentality marked by distrust towards non-ordinary jurisdiction, and because not all mediators have always demonstrated the requisite ability to carry out the task effectively. However, as has been the case for international issues for some time, the use of civil and commercial mediation is destined to grow also in Italy and the rest of Europe, given that it is an increasingly strong tool for out-of-court dispute resolution and a driving force for growth for the economy of individual states.

As also demonstrated by the growing accession to the Singapore Convention – opened for signature in 2019 and with a much narrower scope than civil and commercial mediation in Italy and many other European Member States – the resolution of disputes through the mediation of an external body and a conciliation agreement between the parties seems destined to become an instrument of ever greater application, both nationally and internationally. With this will come changes in mentality and a more open mind among

19 Italian Civil Court of Cassation, Section II, Ordinance of 25 March 2024, no. 7974 (rev. 670573-01). In *CED Cassazione* (2024).

users and operators of justice and the business world. Being a justice operator does not necessarily mean operating through ordinary jurisdiction, but also outside of it, in a framework of alternativeness or compulsory preliminaries (mandatory mediation) or complementarity (delegated mediation) or even voluntary (voluntary mediation).

The latter can also be provided for in the clauses of contracts, both national and international, as a preferential or sole instrument for resolving conflicts that could arise from the execution of the contract itself.

Furthermore, it is conceivable that the mediation of civil and commercial disputes will remain for some time removed from the dynamics, predictive algorithms and the domain of artificial intelligence (AI),[20] even though there are already those who look with optimism at the potential applications of this phenomenon (Niola 2024), which seems to want to make its way also within the world of justice, despite all the legitimate doubts, including bioethical ones, that this implies. On these issues, it is always necessary to proceed with great caution, keeping the needs of true justice in the foreground, without a merely bureaucratic vision.

20 On this topic, consider also Regulation (EU) 2024/1689/Regulation on artificial intelligence (AI), ID 22235 of the European Parliament and of the Council of 13 June 2024, which establishes harmonised rules on AI, amending the regulations (CE) no. 300/2008, (EU) no. 167/2013, (EU) no. 168/2013, (EU) 2018/858, (EU) 2018/1139 and (EU) 2019/2144 and Directives 2014/90/EU, (EU) 2016/797 and (EU) 2020/1828 (regulation on AI), published on 12 July 2024, which entered into force on 1 August 2024 and whose chapters will be applicable from 2 August 2025, with the exception of some of its chapters, which will come into force already in different periods of 2025. The European Parliament, in its session on 13 March 2024, voted on its amendments to the proposal for a European Regulation presented by the European Commission on 21 April 2021, containing a legal framework on artificial intelligence, containing harmonised rules between Member States on the matter. The definition of AI system formulated in the Regulation is that of 'a machine-based system designed to function with different levels of autonomy and which can show adaptivity after implementation and which, for explicit or implicit objectives, deduces, from the input it receives, how to generate outputs such as predictions, content, recommendations or decisions that can influence physical or virtual environments'. The European Commission will have to adopt guidelines on the application of this definition of AI system (Camera dei Deputati, Italy: 2; our translation into English from the Italian text).

Think, among other things, of what is written in the Book of Deuteronomy (12–18) of the Holy Bible, where Moses from Mount Horeb tells the people that 'Judgement belongs to God' and must emanate from wise men, chosen by the people themselves and capable of judging impartially: people were chosen, therefore, not machines without conscience and with rigid thinking.

Humans, thanks to their conscience and their heart, are more capable of thinking and judging with balance and wisdom in such circumstances than machines, which, although trained by humans through predictive algorithms, have impartiality but little elasticity 'of thought' and, therefore, their judgements may be difficult for ordinary citizens to understand and accept.

While a conciliation agreement is not a judgement in the strict sense, it is still the outcome of the parties' evaluations 'guided' by the mediator. In this sense, the activity of mediating might look vaguely like a sort of judgement, at least in a broad and non-procedural sense, because the mediator's activity implies his ability to 'judge' and, above all, to evaluate, even if only to identify the concrete and specific interests of the parties and propose these to them as a possible solution to the dispute. The conciliation agreement contains the solution to the case that the parties themselves have found with the help of the mediator, or their acceptance of the mediator's conciliation proposal, which, as we have highlighted, is more aimed at resolving the concrete and specific interests of the parties, rather than worrying only about the legal rules in force.

The mediator, therefore, evaluates the points of view of the parties and then proposes or arouses from themselves an agreement which, from a technical point of view, is not a judicial decision.

The intervention of a human mediator, with their thought, conscience and eclecticism, currently remains central and irreplaceable. The future, with the constant acceleration of technology and progressive growth, might see innovations in this field, and jurists will have to be prepared to understand problematic issues and potential applications, always aiming to maintain the control and dominion of man over machines. In fact, it is man who has the right to make judgements and choices, even in terms of a conciliatory agreement, and it is the man who is subjected to judgements and who must have the last word in the (not judging) mediation of civil and commercial disputes.

The intervention of a human mediator, with his thought, his conscience, his eclecticism and his wisdom, remains central and irreplaceable today, even by machines equipped with AI. The identification of the specific and concrete interests of the parties presupposes the search in each of them for often internal and hidden elements of their personality, their desires, their past and their purposes.

This can only be achieved – at least until now – through free and frank conversation between the parties, even individually, and the mediator who will then use his balance, wisdom and intuition to suggest a fair, balanced and acceptable solution to the dispute or to maieutically stimulate its identification directly by the parties.

Bibliography

Avvisati, Pier Giorgio (2024). 'Proposta Conciliativa del Giudice e Mediazione Demandata'. CFnews.it, Roma: Cassa di Previdenza e Assistenza Forense, <https://www.cfnews.it/diritto/proposta-conciliativa-del-giudice-e-mediazione-demandata/>, accessed 27 June 2024.

Barbagallo, Isidoro (2012). 'Le Modifiche al Codice Deontologico Forense in Materia di A.D.R.', *Vita Forense No. 1*, pp. 29–34. Catania: Ordine Avvocati di Catania. Also online: <https://ordineavvocaticatania.it/vita-forense/documenti/vita-forense-2012-n1.pdf>, accessed 19 May 2024.

Battaglia, Giuseppe (2010). 'Art. 12. Efficacia esecutiva ed Esecuzione'. In Angelo Castagnola and Francesco Delfini (eds), *La Mediazione nelle controversie civili e Commerciali*, pp. 191–202. Padova: Cedam.

Black, Donald (1976). *The Behavior of Law*. New York and London: Academic Press.

Camera dei Deputati, 'Il Regolamento UE in Materia di Intelligenzaartificiale', XIX Legislatura, Documentazione per le Commissioni Attività dell'Unione Europea, Roma: Ufficio Rapporti con l'Unione Europea (curatore), No. 26, <http://documenti.camera.it/leg19/dossier/pdf/AT026.pdf>, accessed 18 July 2024.

Castagnola, Angelo, and Delfini, Francesco (eds) (2012). *La Mediazione Nelle Controversie Civili e Commerciali*, II edizione. Padova: Cedam.

Cominelli, Luigi, and Jacqmin, Arianna (2020). 'Civil and Commercial Mediation in Italy: Lights and Shadow', *Revista da Emerj*,

January–March, Rio de Janeiro: Escola da Magistratura do Estado do Rio de Janeiro Ed., vol. 22, no. 1, pp. 11–26.

Corradino, Michele, & Sticchi Damiani, Saverio (eds) (2012). *ADR e Mediazione*. Torino: Giappichelli.

Cabanes Alanon, Jaime, Carmona Sanchez, Antonio, Chevalier, Anne Lise, Sanz-Pastore Gonzalez-Fierro, Cristina, and Tordesillas Rodriguez, Javier Manuel (2022). 'Situación Actual de la Convención de Singapur: Entrevista a Ana Fernández-Tresguerrespor Alvaro López de Argumedo Piñeiro'. Foundation for Research in Law and Business (FIDE), <https://thinkfide.com/it/situacion-actual-de-la-convencion-de-singapur-entrevista-a-ana-fernandez-tresguerres-por-alvaro-lopez-de-argumedo-pineiro/>, accessed 18 June 2024.

Carrese, Carlo (2010). 'Storia Della mediazione'. In *Temi Romana*, Roma: Ed. Ordinedegli Avvocati di Roma, Special Issue No. 1–3, pp. 19–21.

Danovi, Remo (2016). 'Una "Giustizia Senza Processo": la Giurisdizione forense'. *Giustizia Senza Processo? La Funzione dell'Avvocatura*, *Quaderni dell'Ordine di Milano*, Special Issue for the XXXIII Congresso Nazionale Forense, Rimini: Ordinedegli Avvocati di Milano, pp. 23–37.

De Luca, Ugo (2012). 'La Nozione Europea di ADR'. In Michele Corradino and Saverio Stucchi Damiani (eds), *ADR e Mediazione*, pp. 1–10. Torino: Giappichelli.

De Luca Picione, Mario (2010). 'Cenni Storicisulle ADR'. *Temi Romana*, Roma: Ed. Ordinedegli Avvocati di Roma, Special Issue No. 1–3, pp. 9–18.

Falco, Gianluca, and Spina, Giulio (eds) (2014). *La Nuova Mediazione*. Milano: Giuffré.

Fragomeni, Tiziana (2010). *Mediazione e Conciliazione*. Piacenza: Celt – Casa Editrice La Tribuna.

Giorgetti, Mariacarla (2015). *Negoziazione Assistita, Coll. Officina del Diritto*. Milano: Giuffrè.

Isoni, Corinne, and Pasquale, Fabrizio (eds) (2018). *Mediazione e Conciliazione Delle Controversie*. Milano: Wolters Kluwer.

ISTAT (2024). 'Statistiche Report', Roma: Istituto Nazionale di Statistica (National Institute of Statistics), issue 22 May 2024, <https://www.istat.it/it/files//2024/05/REPORT-GIUSTIZIA-CIVILE-1.pdf>, accessed 31 May 2024.

Kaplan, Fatih Halil (2014). '2012 Irland Arabuluculuk Kanunu Taslaği Genel Şemasi'. In Türkiye Adalet Akademisi (Justice Academy of Türkiye) (eds), *Küresel Bakiş – Çeviri Hukuk Dergisi*, pp. 65–82. Çankaya-Ankara, Edition of 14 July 2014.

Leigh, Steven (2018). 'Caucus: An Aid in Mediation', <https://mediate.com/caucus-an-aid-in-mediation/>, accessed 27 July 2024.

Lucarelli, Paola (2019). *Mediazionedeiconflitti. Una Scelta condivisa*. Torino: UTET.

Marinaro, Marco (2024). 'Il Nuovo Regolamento Ministeriale per la Mediazione Civile e Commerciale: Profili Rilevanti del "Primo Incontro"', *Foro Italiano*, No. 1, pp. 21–29. Milano: Società Editrice Il Foro Italiano.

Matteucci, Giovanni (2024). 'Civil and Commercial Mediation 4.0 in Italy After the Riforma Cartabia', <https://mediate.com/civil-and-commercial-mediation-4-0-in-italy-after-the-riforma-cartabia/>, accessed: 27 July 2024.

Niola, Francesca (2024). 'Algoritmi Predittivi per le ADR: Come Cambia la Giustizia Civile', *Network Digital 360*, <https://www.agendadigitale.eu/documenti/giustizia-digitale/algoritmi-predittivi-per-le-adr-come-cambia-la-giustizia-civile/>, accessed 21 June 2024.

Miccolis, Giuseppe (2023). *Le Nuove Norme in Tema di Mediazione e Negoziazione Assistita*. *Rivista di Diritto Processuale*, No. 3, 1 July, pp. 1058–1079. Milano: Wolters Kluwer.

Ministero della Giustizia – DG Stat. (2024). 'Tassi di Appello e di Riforma dei Procedimenti Civili-Anni 2016–2020', <https://webstat.giustizia.it/Analisi e ricerche/Tassi di appello e di riforma 2016-2020.pdf>, accessed: 1 June 2024.

Pacelli, Giacomo (2012). 'Le ADR Aggiudicative e le ADR Consensuali'. In Michele Corradino, & Saverio Sticchi Damiani (eds), *ADR e Mediazione*, pp. 11–21. Torino: Giappichelli.

Quotidiano Giuridico (2024). 'Cass. Civ., Sez. Unite, 07/02/2024, n. 3452', editorial maxim: <https://onelegale.wolterskluwer.it/document/cass-civ-sez-unite-07-02-2024-n-3452/44MA0002939162?searchId=2365120920&pathId=e9bd4d73429a98&offset=24&contentModuleContext=all>, accessed 25 June 2024.

Stefanizzi, Camilla (2012). 'La Rete Solvit'. In Michele Corradino and Saverio Sticchi Damiani (eds), *ADR e Mediazione*, pp. 23–37. Torino: Giappichelli.

Taruffo, Michele (2015). 'La Giustizia civile', *Il Pensiero Giuridico Italiano*, pp. 446–453. Roma: Treccani.

Unione Europea (2024). 'Mediation in EU countries', *European Justice*, <https://e-justice.europa.eu/content_mediation_in_member_states-64-it-en.do?member=1>, accessed 14 June 2023.

Zanussi, Manuela (2022). 'Necessità di Procura Notarile in Mediazione? Sì, no, Dipende', in CFnews.it, Roma: Cassa di Previdenza e Assistenza Forense, <https://www.cfnews.it/diritto/necessit%C3%A0-di-procura-notarile-in-mediazione-s%C3%AC-no-dipende/>, accessed: 23 July 2024.

Zanussi, Manuela (2024). 'La Mediazione Non va in Ferie: La Difficile Gestione dei Rinvii Degli Incontri'. CFnews.it, Roma: Cassa di Previdenza e Assistenza Forense, <https://www.cfnews.it/diritto/la-mediazione-non-va-in-ferie-la-difficile-gestione-dei-rinvii-degli-incontri/>.

CHAPTER 8

Mediation of Civil Affairs in Italy – Second Part: Tax Benefits in the Fiscal Approach to Supporting Sustainability

Valeria Botti[1]

Introduction: Legislative Framework

The regulation of mediation aimed at resolving civil and commercial disputes is contained in Legislative Decree No. 28 dated 4th March 2010 whose approval derived from Directive 2008/52/EC of the European Parliament and of the Council, dated 21st May 2008, which in Article 1 set the objective 'to facilitate access to alternative dispute resolution (ADR) and to promote the amicable settlement of disputes by encouraging the use of mediation and ensuring a balanced relationship between mediation and judicial proceedings'[2]. The Italian Parliament, with Law No. 69, dated 19th June 2009, delegated the government to mediate and conciliate civil and commercial disputes, the result of which was the issuing of the aforementioned legislative decree.

The mediation procedure, introduced by Legislative Decree No. 28/2010, and consisting of the activities of an impartial third party assisting two or more parties in the search for an amicable agreement for the settlement of a dispute, has been significantly modified with the so-called Cartabia Reform introduced by Legislative Decree No. 149, dated 10th October 2022, which was followed by a series of implementing measures, namely the respective decrees of 1st August 2023 on tax incentives and legal aid.

With the provision of the mediation procedure, the legislator wanted to reduce the workload of judicial offices, with an undoubted deflationary purpose, by providing a series of tax breaks. The first issue to be discussed

1 Attorney at law, economics graduate and mediator, Studio Legale Avv. Valeria Botti, email: valeriabotti@studiovaleriabotti.it

2 Directive 2008/52/EC of the European Parliament and the Council of 21 May 2008 on certain aspects of mediation in civil and commercial matters, OJ L 136/3 on 24 May 2008, <https://eur-lex.europa.eu/legal-content/en/ALL/?uri=CELEX:32008L0052#:~:text=DIRECTIVE%202008/52/EC%20OF%20THE%20EUROPEAN%20PARLIAMENT>, accessed: 25 August 2024.

in Chapter VIII are tax breaks which will be analysed in their current form, with an evaluation of their tax impact and then, the evolution of tax breaks shall be traced from 2010 until the present day to draw conclusions in terms of sustainability and tax impact.

Mediation Tax Regime: Different Treatment Compared to Judicial Decisions

The tax regime of mediation is contained in Article 17 of Legislative Decree No. 28/2010, which in the first paragraph states that

> All acts, documents and measures relating to the mediation procedure are exempt from stamp duty and from any expense, tax or right of any kind and nature. The minutes containing the conciliation agreement are exempt from registration tax within the value limit of one hundred thousand euros, otherwise, the tax is due for the excess part[3].

It follows that all acts and documents generated during the mediation are available to the entity and the parties cannot be subject to any type of taxation, contrary to documents drawn up during judicial proceedings.

In addition, the mediation instruments issued by the mediator – including the conciliation proposal, the conciliation report and any copies thereof – as well as the appointment and acceptance of the assignment conferred upon the mediator by the conciliation body, are exempt from taxes and duties, as mentioned earlier, unlike judicial instruments which are subject to registration tax. Moreover, an allowance of €100,000 has been set so that all mediations below this value can be totally exempt.

This last assumption, in particular, constitutes a real competitive advantage of mediation over the judicial litigation tools: to understand the innovative scope and advantage envisaged in this sense for mediation, it is necessary to briefly discuss the taxation of judicial documents.

---

3 <https://def.finanze.it/DocTribFrontend/getAttoNormativoDetail.do?ACTION=getArticolo&id=%7B6AA17826-33CD-4B33-B047-A240424BC1E4%7D&codiceOrdinamento=200001700000000&articolo=Articolo%2017>

Through the registration tax, the Italian legislator also subjects the instruments issued by the judicial authority to indirect taxation. To define what are the prerequisites for the registration of a judicial act, as well as the methods of liquidation and collection of the tax, is the Presidential Decree No. 131/86, Consolidated Law on Registration Tax, in Art. 37 states that they are subject to tax: 'the acts of the judicial authority in the field of civil disputes that settle the judgement, even partially, the executive injunctions, the measures declaring the arbitral awards enforceable and the judgements declaring foreign judgements effective in the State'[4]. Objectively, the tax in question does not concern all acts of the judicial authority as defined earlier, but only those that intervene 'in the field of civil disputes', meaning – according to the best doctrine – 'those in which judicial protection is invoked against an alleged violation of a subjective right and which, therefore, pertain to the existence, implementation, modification and extinction of a subjective right' (Busani 2018: 378–380)[5].

It is envisaged that the registration tax applies to measures 'that define the judgement even partially': what matters, in fact, is that on a given issue the judicial authority has ruled definitively[6], exhausting its jurisdictional power

4 Presidential Decree No. 131 of 26 April 1986, *Testo unico delle disposizioni concernenti l'imposta di registro*(Consolidated Law on Registration Tax), Gazzetta Ufficiale No. 99 of 30 April 1986 <https://www.agenziaentrate.gov.it/portale/documents/20143/267689/Decreto+Presidente+della+Repubblica+26+aprile+1986_T.U.+registro.pdf/177b81ab-6cff-af9a-be03-3d15dd588770>, accessed 30 September 2024.

5 'La Tassazione Degli Atti Dell'Autorità Giudiziaria', Diritto e Pratica Tributaria, 4, 1768–1771, which in turn refers to Uricchio, Antonio F. (2006). 'Attività Giudiziaria e Imposizione Tributaria tra Imposta di Registro e Contributo Unificato per L'iscrizione a Ruolo,' Bollettino Tributario d'Informazioni, 5, 378–380.

6 On the other hand, the enforceability of the judicial measure (except for injunctions) is not a prerequisite for taxation: in this sense, cf. Cass. Civ., sec. VI–V, ord. No. 12480/2018, according to which 'the measure suspending the provisional execution of the first instance judgment does not remove the prerequisite of the tax, constituted, pursuant to Art. 37 of Presidential Decree No. 131 of 1986, not by the enforceability, but by the existence of a judicial title subject to registration'.

on the point and issuing a decision that may possibly be the subject of other future proceedings at the merits stage or other stages[7].

To determine the taxable amount of a judicial act, reference must be made to the effects that it actually determines: Art. 43, paragraph 4, T.U.R. – through a reference *per relationem* – in fact sets out the same criteria for calculating the taxable base applicable to judicial measures as for other types of (public and private) acts that produce similar legal effects.

The applicable rates are established by Art. 8, Tariff, Part I in relation to homogeneous categories of judicial acts: (a) instruments concerning the transfer or establishment of rights in rem over real estate or pleasure crafts or other assets and rights (the same rates provided in the Tariff for the corresponding public or private acts; in particular, the rate of 9% for buildings and 15% for land); (b) instruments ordering payment of sums or valuables, for other services or for the delivery of goods of any kind (rate of 3%); (c) instruments for the assessment of rights with a patrimonial content (rate of 1%).

By way of example, let us examine the case of the first stage of a civil lawsuit concerning chattels worth €50,000, whether it is an injunction, a sentence or a precautionary measure: the registration tax due is €1,500. A dispute of the same value resolved by a mediation agreement does not result in the payment of any *sic et simpliciter* tax; even if one of the two parties deems it necessary to register the mediation agreement for the purpose of its subsequent use, also in this case no registration tax is due since its value is included within the allowance of €100,000 pursuant to the aforementioned Article 17, paragraph 2 of the Legislative Decree No. 28/2010 mentioned earlier.

With respect to the mandatory taxation of the judicial acts already described, the payment of which is borne jointly and *in solid* by all parties, without prejudice to the possibility for the winning party to recover what has been paid in accordance with the losing party principle; therefore, the total exemption of the mediation agreement up to a value of €100,000 is

7 For an application of the principle of the ability to pay also to the taxation of judicial acts, reference is made to Cassazione Civile, Sec. V, sentence no. 11149/2006, which – ruling in the matter of optional joining of several cases connected by commonality of object – has, i.a., stated that 'the tax does not affect the judgment as such, but the relationship contained in it, as an index of ability to pay'.

excluded. It is reiterated that, regarding the value indicated in the agreement, no tax (not even registration tax) is due within the threshold of €100,000, while it is due only for excess if it exists. Once again, however, the regime in favour of mediation provides that the mediation agreement is subject to registration tax for excess only if one of the parties requests its registration since it falls within the category of deeds that can be voluntarily submitted to the Revenue Agency for registration, as there is no obligation to register.

The favourable climate given by the Italian legislator to mediation is best illustrated if one examines the mediation agreements that have real estate rights as their object; to understand this, it is necessary to premise the taxation regime of real estate dispositions, which must be drawn up by a notary who not only prepares the deed and verifies that the property can be bought and sold, but also pays tax on behalf of the parties.

In fact, 'Where advertising formalities are required to be entered with the public registers (Register of Companies, Land Office – Real Estate Advertising Service), the signatures of the conciliation agreement must be authenticated by an authorised public official (Article 11, paragraph 7, Legislative Decree No. 28/2010), since a mediator cannot issue suitable instruments to carry out the formalities in public offices (Smaniotto & Fochi 2023)[8].

Let us assume that two private individuals have to carry out a purchase and sale of real estate worth €95,000. By making the purchase in an ordinary manner, they will hire a notary who, in addition to collecting a fee to draw up the deed, will ask the buyer (who is usually the one required to pay for the transfer) to pay the taxes due, consisting of the registration tax at 9% as well as the mortgage and cadastral tax in a fixed amount of €50.00 each. The buyer will, therefore, pay a total of €8,650 to the treasury and will also pay the notary's fee.

The same real estate transfer of €95,000 carried out within the mediation procedure, on the other hand, will result in the total fiscal neutrality of the transaction since the agreement will have an object included within the aforementioned exemption of €100,000: the party will have saved €8,500 for the sole fact of having carried out the sale as a final act of the mediation,

8 See also Judgment No. 10792 of 21 June 2021, issued by the Court of Rome.

paying only a fee to the notary, who will draw up the deed of sale which will consist of the actual final agreement of the mediation.

Let us now assume that the property being sold has a value of €150,000. If the sale takes place outside the mediation, it will involve payment of taxes amounting to €13,600. If the sale is conducted under a mediation agreement, the taxes will be reduced to €4,600, as they are payable only on the excess of the allowance, i.e. €50,000.

It would be interesting to point out a situation, occurring frequently before the ruling of the Supreme Court that shall be described later, in which the parties, after concluding the agreement at the end of the mediation procedure, chose to draw up a separate notarial deed of real estate sale. The deed was the real source of the final effect with which the parties, after mediation, arranged for the transfer of the property and, therefore, the described facilitated regime could not apply to it. In this sense, the Supreme Court passed judgement No. 11617/2020, which stated that:

> The application of the preferential tax regime must be limited to acts concerning the mediation procedure strictly understood, also in consideration of the fact that a preferential tax treatment, having an exceptional nature, is to be considered of rigid interpretation and not susceptible to analogous application[9].

Therefore, according to the jurisprudence of legitimacy, a mediation agreement which has already been signed before the mediation entity should not be referred to a subsequent notarial deed in the form of a public deed that has the same content, under penalty of loss of the tax benefit. This confirms the substantial irrelevance of the transposition of the provisions of the relevant mediation report into the notarial deed, since in this case the mediation agreement would act as a preliminary contract, postponing the effect of transfer to a notarial deed external to the mediation[10].

9 <https://www.gazzettanotarile.com/wp-content/uploads/2020/07/Cass.-n.-11617-del-2020.pdf>, accessed 30 September 2024.

10 See also Judgment No. 94 of 17 May 2023, issued by the Tax Court of First Instance of Reggio Emilia; <https://www.fiscooggi.it/rubrica/giurisprudenza/articolo/solo-primo-verbale-mediazione-e-esente-dallimposta-registro>, accessed 30 September 2024.

The exemption, therefore, pursuant to the cited Art. 17 must be reserved only and exclusively for the mediation agreement signed before a notary. Therefore, the deemed mere transposition of the provisions of the mediation agreement in the deed subject to taxation does not meet the essential prerequisites of the institution and the related advantageous tax regime.[11]

The tax advantage in favour of the parties in mediation is, therefore, evident and constitutes the main means by which the legislator exercises their favour in the practical use of this ADR tool.

Tax Credits in Favour of Parties to Mediation

A further tax advantage for the parties of mediation is the possibility of benefiting from a tax credit that can be used to offset any debts to the treasury in the annual tax return process[12].

The regulation is contained in Article 20, paragraphs 1–4, Legislative Decree No. 28/2010, which provides that:

> The parties are granted, when the conciliation agreement is reached, a tax credit commensurate with the indemnity paid pursuant to Article 17, paragraphs 3 and 4, up to a maximum of six hundred euros. In the cases referred to in Article 5, paragraph 1, and when mediation is entrusted by the judge, the parties are also granted a tax credit commensurate with the fee paid to their respective lawyers for assistance in the mediation procedure, within the limits provided for by the forensic parameters and up to a maximum of six hundred euros. The tax credits provided for in paragraph 1 may be used by the party within the overall limit of six hundred euros per procedure and up to a maximum annual amount of two thousand four hundred euros for natural persons and twenty-four thousand euros for legal persons. In the event of unsuccessful mediation, the tax credits are reduced by half. An additional tax credit is recognised commensurate with the

11 See also Judgment No. 5016 of 4 September 2023, issued by the Second Instance Tax Court of Lazio – Rome, Section 3.

12 "The tax credits recognised do not give rise to a refund but can be used as compensation, within the amount communicated by the ministry, under penalty of rejection of the payment transaction. Lastly, natural persons who do not earn income from business or self-employment can use the credit entitlement to reduce the taxes payable based on tax return" (Smaniotto & Fochi 2023).

> unified contribution paid by the party to the proceedings discontinued following the conclusion of a conciliation agreement, within the limit of the amount paid and up to a maximum of five hundred and eighteen euros.[13]

The legislator thus intends to reward the parties who reach an agreement in mediation, while those who participate in the mediation benefit from the facilitation reduced by half.

The tax credit that is granted to them is commensurate with the sums paid to the mediation entity for start-up costs, the first and subsequent meetings and the agreement since it is common for a success fee to be paid to the mediation entity. These fees are known in advance to the parties from the moment the request for mediation is made since each entity publishes its own tariffs for the various stages of the procedure.

Generally, the parties who have reconciled will be able to benefit from a tax credit equal to all the indemnities paid to the mediation body up to a maximum of €600, and up to €300 for those who have not reached an agreement.

On the other hand, when mediation is delegated by the judge who obliges the parties to initiate the conciliation procedure, or it is mandatory (because it concerns one of the matters for which it must be carried out before the introduction of the judgement as a condition of admissibility – a case mentioned in Part I by Adv. Isidoro Barbagallo and to which reference is made), the parties will be able to benefit from an additional tax credit up to a maximum of €600 (or €300 in the event of unsuccessful mediation) corresponding to the fee payable to the lawyer for assistance in the mediation procedure and within the limits of the forensic parameters established by the ministerial decree.

For each mediation procedure it will be possible to take advantage of a credit of €600, and the maximum limit is revised on an annual basis and amounts to €2,400 for natural persons and €24,000 for legal persons.

Finally, of no small importance is the attention paid to the different cases in which the conclusion of the conciliation agreement puts an end to an

13 Legislative Decree No. 28 of 4 March 2010, *Attuazione dell'articolo 60 della legge 18 giugno 2009, n. 69, in materia di mediazione finalizzata alla conciliazione delle controversie civili e commerciali* (Implementation of Article 60 of Law No. 69 of 18 June 2009, on mediation for civil and commercial disputes), Art. 20, available at https://www.normattiva.it/uri-res/N2Ls?urn:nir:stato:decreto.legislativo:2010-03-04;28, accessed 30 September 2024.

ongoing legal dispute, which will consequently be resolved. In this case, the party who paid the unified fee to introduce the judgement is granted a tax credit up to a maximum of €518.00. It should be noted that, for example, for civil cases of the first stage up to a value of €52,000, the unified contribution can be fully reimbursed in the form of a tax credit.

Wishing to express an opinion based on the author's experience as a mediator and lawyer assisting parties in mediation, it is argued that these sums may in many cases consist only of a partial reimbursement of the indemnities paid to the entity. However, it can be assumed that the entire costs for mediations worth approximately €20,000–25,000 can be recouped. Regarding legal costs, it is unlikely that they will be fully reimbursed except for very modest values of the dispute up to approximately €1,000. In any case, taking into consideration that no amounts are reimbursed to the parties involved in the lawsuit, and indeed they bear all the registration and stamp duties as mentioned in the previous paragraph, it is certainly an advantage of no small importance to be able to obtain up to € 1,200 in the form of a tax credit.

Recently, the Revenue Agency with its resolution No. 23/E dated 14th May 2024 published the tax codes enabling parties to benefit from mediation using an F24 form (Tarabusi 2024)[14].

It is not obvious that the parties entering the mediation process are aware of the tax benefits referred to in Articles 17 and 20 of the legislative decree in question and one might wonder who is responsible for informing them about these benefits. Nonetheless, in practice, it is usual for the mediator to emphasise in their introductory speech the tax advantages while describing the competitive characteristics of mediation. However, they are not required by law to provide complete information to the parties. In fact, it is at the discretion of the lawyer assisting the party in mediation to inform them of the tax advantages deriving from it, as provided for in Article 4 of Legislative Decree 28/2010.

14 'I passaggi per scalare i crediti di imposta per la mediazione nelle tasse', https://ntplusdiritto.ilsole24ore.com/art/i-passaggi-scalare-crediti-imposta-la-mediazione-tasse-AG5i8nC?uuid=i-passaggi-scalare-crediti-imposta-la-mediazione-tasse-AG5i8nC, accessed 27 May 2024.

Article 20 of Legislative Decree 28/2010 provides for another facilitation, this time in favour of the mediation entity which is granted a tax credit corresponding to the indemnity not payable by the party benefitting from legal aid, up to a maximum annual amount of €24,000.

Historical Evolution of Tax Breaks in Mediation

Since the date on which Legislative Decree No. 28/2010 came into effect, the tax benefits of mediation have undergone an evolution aimed at expanding their use.

While the text referred to in Art. 17 of Legislative Decree No. 28/2010, relating to the total exemption from any tax, has remained unchanged, Art. 20, dedicated to tax credits, has undergone some subtle changes: in its original version, the parties were granted a tax credit commensurate with the remuneration paid to the mediation entity in the event of its success up to a maximum of €500 and of half of that amount in the event of failure.

It was envisaged by a decree of the Ministry of Justice that, starting from 2011, the amount of funds allocated to cover the loss of revenue deriving from the granting of the concluded mediations tax credit would be determined by 30th April of each year.

The same decree identified the tax credit actually due for each mediation, calculated in proportion to the allocated resources and, in any case, within the range from €250 to €500, as mentioned earlier. The Ministry of Justice then communicated the amount of tax credit payable to the interested party and electronically transmitted the list of beneficiaries and the related amounts to the Revenue Agencies.

The tax credit had to be indicated, under penalty of forfeiture, in the tax return and could be used from the date of receipt of the ministerial communication about compensation pursuant to Article 17 of Legislative Decree No. 241, dated 9th July 1997, also by natural persons who do not earn income from business or self-employment making it possible for them to make income tax deductions.

Under the then-current wording, the tax credit did not give entitlement to refunds, nor did it contribute to the amount of income subject to income tax or to the value of net production for the purposes of regional tax on production activities. Additionally, it was not relevant for the purposes of the *ratio* referred to in Articles 61 and 109, paragraph 5, Consolidated Law on Income Taxes, referred to in Presidential Decree No. 917, dated 22 December 1986.

However, the mechanism described earlier in practice has given poor results in terms of recognition of tax credits: it has only been possible to obtain the certification of the credit for the purpose of its use only after many years and for very few subjects.

It would seem, however, that with the methodology introduced by the so-called 'Cartabia Reform', such recognition will be easier and more streamlined and the use of the same will depend on the sole will of the party without the need to wait for the intervention of the ministry.

Summary

Subject to an onerousness test, the possibility to rely on tax relief measures and the current certainty of the exemptions illustrated in Chapter VIII, the institution of mediation is strengthened in its fiscal sustainability with the recent so-called 'Cartabia Reform' from 2022. The effort made to increase the incentives available to the parties, in order to encourage the spread of this out-of-court instrument as much as possible, is significant.

It should be noted that the convenience of this particular form of ADR had already been certified by the European Parliament with its Resolution of 13th September 2011, on the implementation of Directive 2008/52/EC, by virtue of which the 'made in Italy' mediation had received approval precisely because of the assumed role of a pioneer among the countries of the European Union (EU), in the field of tax incentives.

The practical experience of this tool demonstrates its convenience and versatility and, where there are lawyers who know the institution well, the probability that tax incentives will be used by clients increases exponentially. In fact, since coming into effect, mediation has progressively changed the way in which law firms approach dispute resolution. In the advice that is given to the client, it is possible to include the impact of tax incentives in the general economic structure of the dispute, comparing it with what would happen outside mediation.

Mediation, therefore, is not only a tool for integrated social sustainability, as it transforms conflict into an opportunity for innovation and community integration, but also a means for economic sustainability both on an individual and on collective basis. Through a favourable economic impact on the individual, tax incentives aspire to produce an advantage for the national economic system, which benefits from reducing the use of the judicial system and its time burden and costs. In fact, the EU frequently invokes the expeditiousness of Italian justice.

In conclusion, the tax breaks provided for mediation can be translated into an indirect tool capable of increasing the collective sustainability of the entire dispute resolution system.

Bibliography

Busani, Angelo (2018). 'La Tassazione degli atti dell'autorità giudiziaria', *Diritto e Pratica Tributaria*, 4, 1768–1771.

Smaniotto Elisabetta, and Fochi Federica (2023). 'Mediazione civile al restyling con nuove Agevolazioni', *Norme & Tributi Plus Fisco*, <https://ntplusfisco.ilsole24ore.com/art/mediazione-civile-restyling-nuove-agevolazioni-AFM5IqXB>, accessed 30 June 2024.

Tarabusi Marcello (2024). 'I passaggi per scalare i crediti di imposta per la mediazione nelle tasse', <https://ntplusdiritto.ilsole24ore.com/art/i-passaggi-scalare-crediti-imposta-la-mediazione-tasse-AG5i8nC?uuid=i-passaggi-scalare-crediti-imposta-la-mediazione-tasse-AG5i8nC>, accessed 27 May 2024.

Uricchio, Antonio F. (2006). 'Attività giudiziaria e imposizione tributaria tra imposta di registro e contributo unificato per l'iscrizione a ruolo,' *Bollettino Tributario d'Informazioni*, 5, 378–380.

Legal sources

Directive 2008/52/EC of the European Parliament and the Council of 21 May 2008 on certain aspects of mediation in civil and commercial matters, OJ L 136/3 on 24 May 2008, <https://eur-lex.europa.eu/legal-content/en/ALL/?uri=CELEX:32008L0052#:~:text=DIRECTIVE%202008/52/EC%20OF%20THE%20EUROPEAN%20PARLIAMENT>, accessed 25 August 2024.

Legislative Decree No. 28 of 4 March 2010, <https://def.finanze.it/DocTribFrontend/getAttoNormativoDetail.do?ACTION=getArticolo

&id=%7B6AA17826-33CD-4B33-B047-A240424BC1E4%7D&codiceOrdinamento=200001700000000&articolo=Articolo%2017>, accessed 30 June 2024.
Presidential Decree 131/86, Consolidated Law on Registration Tax, <https://www.agenziaentrate.gov.it/portale/documents/20143/267689/Decreto+Presidente+della+Repubblica+26+aprile+1986_T.U.+registro.pdf/177b81ab-6cff-af9a-be03-3d15dd588770>.

CHAPTER 9

Mediation in Switzerland: A Comprehensive Overview

Lara Pair[1] *and Małgorzata Skawińska*[2]

Introduction

Mediation has become an essential element of dispute resolution within the Swiss legal system. Recognised for its potential to resolve conflicts amicably and efficiently, mediation offers an alternative to the often lengthy and adversarial nature of traditional litigation. This article explores how the Swiss Code of Procedure incorporates mediation, detailing the legal framework, practical applications and the role of federal offices in promoting and supporting mediation processes.

Historical Context and Development

The evolution of mediation in Switzerland has been characterised by a gradual but significant shift towards recognising and formalising alternative dispute resolution (ADR) mechanisms within the legal framework. This section will delve into the key historical developments that have shaped mediation in Switzerland, highlighting important legislative milestones, the influence of international trends and the growing acceptance of mediation as a viable alternative to traditional litigation.

In the early stages, mediation in Switzerland was largely an informal practice, often utilised in community and family disputes where parties sought amicable resolutions without resorting to court proceedings. These informal mediations were typically facilitated by respected community members or elders who acted as neutral intermediaries. The success of these early mediation efforts demonstrated the potential of mediation to resolve conflicts efficiently and amicably.

1 Dr iur. HSG, J.D., LL.M., FCIArb.; Lawyer in CH, D, GA (USA); pair.fact.legal AG, email: lara.pair@pairfactlegal.com

2 PhD, WSPiA Rzeszowska Szkoła Wyższa; Emba, DBA; advocate (Poland), mediator; Kancelaria Prawna LEXALIS, email: m.skawińska@lexalis.eu

The concept became established in Switzerland around 20 years ago, starting in French-speaking Switzerland. In 1989, the 'Group romand pour la médiation familiale' was founded followed by the founding of the Swiss Association for Family Mediation, now known as the Swiss Association for Mediation, in 1992 (Meier 2002). These organisations played a pivotal role in promoting and formalising mediation practices.

The development of mediation in Switzerland was significantly influenced by international trends and the growing global acceptance of ADR mechanisms. One key was the United Nations and the United Nations Commission on International Commercial Law (UNCITRAL) Model Law on International Commercial Conciliation (2002), which provided a framework for countries to develop their own mediation and conciliation laws, promoting uniformity and encouraging the use of mediation in international commercial disputes[3]. Switzerland adopted principles from this model law, integrating them into its national legislation to facilitate cross-border mediation.

Another major influence was the European Union Directive on Mediation (2008/52/EC)[4]. Although Switzerland is not a member of the European Union (EU), the EU Mediation Directive influenced Swiss mediation practices by setting standards for the mediation process, mediator training and the enforceability of mediation agreements. The directive aimed to promote mediation as a cost-effective and efficient means of resolving disputes across the EU, providing a model that Switzerland adapted to fit its legal system.

A significant turning point in the formal recognition of mediation was the introduction of specific provisions within the civil justice system by the Swiss Civil Procedure Code (CPC or ZPO – *Zivilprozessordnung*)[5]. The code not only acknowledged mediation as a legitimate form of dispute resolution

---

3 <https://uncitral.un.org/sites/uncitral.un.org/files/media-documents/uncitral/en/03-90953_ebook.pdf>, accessed 30 July 2024.

4 Directive 2008/52/EC of the European Parliament and the Council of 21 May 2008 on certain aspects of mediation in civil and commercial matters, OJ L 136/3 on 24 May 2008, <https://eur-lex.europa.eu/legal-content/en/ALL/?uri=CELEX:32008L0052#:~:text=DIRECTIVE%202008/52/EC%20OF%20THE%20EUROPEAN%20PARLIAMENT>, accessed 30 July 2024.

5 Swiss Parliament (2008). Swiss Civil Procedure Code of 19 December 2008, <https://www.fedlex.admin.ch/eli/cc/2010/262/en>, accessed 30 July 2024.

but also integrated it into the civil procedure, encouraging courts to propose mediation to parties and providing a clear legal framework for its implementation. Articles 213 to 218 CPC outline various aspects of mediation. Article 213 CPC encourages courts to propose mediation to parties at any stage of the proceedings, highlighting the judiciary's role in promoting mediation as an alternative to litigation. This provision highlights the judiciary's commitment to facilitating amicable dispute resolution processes. Furthermore, Article 214 CPC allows parties to request mediation before initiating formal litigation, underscoring the voluntary nature of the process. This article reinforces the principle that parties can choose mediation to resolve their disputes without the necessity of engaging in formal court proceedings. Article 215 CPC details the suspension of court proceedings during mediation, ensuring that parties could resolve their disputes without the pressure of ongoing litigation. Moreover, Article 216 CPC ensures the confidentiality of mediation discussions, a critical aspect that encourages open and honest dialogue between parties. Article 217 CPC provides for the enforceability of mediation agreements within the scope of the chapter upon approval by the court, giving mediated settlements the same legal standing as court judgements under such limited circumstances. Finally, Article 218 CPC outlines the allocation of costs associated with mediation. This article provides clarity on the financial responsibilities related to the mediation process, ensuring transparency and fairness in the allocation of mediation costs.

The gradual formalisation of mediation in Switzerland was accompanied by increasing acceptance and support from legal institutions, professional organisations and the general public. Several mediation centres and institutes were established to provide training, resources and support for mediators. Organisations, such as the Swiss Association for Mediation (SDM-FSM), played a crucial role in promoting mediation, offering certification programmes and advocating for its integration into the legal system.

Swiss courts increasingly embraced mediation, recognising its potential to reduce case backlogs and provide more satisfactory outcomes for parties. Judicial training programmes incorporated mediation principles, ensuring that judges were equipped to identify cases suitable for mediation and encourage parties to consider this alternative. Public awareness campaigns and educational initiatives helped to increase acceptance of mediation among the general population. These efforts highlighted the benefits of mediation, such as cost savings, quicker resolution times and the preservation of relationships, encouraging more people to consider mediation as a first step in resolving disputes.

Another milestone was the integration of mediation into legal education. Law schools and continuing legal education programmes began to include mediation courses, ensuring that future lawyers and legal professionals were familiar with mediation processes and techniques. This educational emphasis helped to create a new generation of lawyers who viewed mediation as an integral part of their practice, rather than a peripheral or secondary option.

Federal offices and non-governmental organisations in Switzerland play a significant role in supporting and promoting mediation. These offices provide resources, training and oversight to ensure the effective implementation of mediation processes. Key federal offices involved in mediation include the Federal Office of Justice (FOJ)[6] and the Federal Department of Foreign Affairs[7]. The FOJ provides guidance on mediation practices, develops training programmes for mediators and supports research and policy development related to mediation. By offering these resources, the office ensures that mediation is conducted professionally and in accordance with legal standards. The office also collaborates with cantonal authorities to promote consistent and effective mediation practices across Switzerland.

The Federal Department of Foreign Affairs (FDFA) plays a crucial role in promoting Swiss mediation efforts on the international stage. The department facilitates international mediation initiatives, supports the training of mediators and collaborates with international organisations to promote peaceful conflict resolution. The FDFA's involvement underscores Switzerland's commitment to mediation as a tool for both domestic and international dispute resolution.

---

6 <https://www.bj.admin.ch/bj/en/home.html>, accessed 30 July 2024.

7 <https://www.eda.admin.ch/eda/en/fdfa/foreign-policy/human-rights/peace/switzerland-s-good-offices/facilitation-and-mediation.html>, accessed 30 July 2024.

The Swiss Association for Mediation (SDM-FSM) exemplifies one of the key organisations that set standards for mediator training and certification. It also provides a comprehensive code of ethics that mediators are required to follow, thereby ensuring professionalism and integrity in mediation practice[8].

Standards and Regulations for Mediator Training and Practice

The professionalisation of mediation is critical for maintaining high standards and ensuring the effectiveness of mediation processes. Switzerland has established rigorous training and certification requirements for mediators, which are outlined in various regulations and professional guidelines.

In Switzerland, mediators must meet specific educational and professional criteria to become certified. Certification typically requires completion of an accredited training programme, practical experience in mediation and adherence to a code of ethics. Accredited organisations, such as the Swiss Chamber of Commercial Mediation (SCCM)[9], oversee the certification process and ensure that mediators maintain high professional standards.

Ethical guidelines form a crucial component of the legal framework for mediation. These guidelines ensure that mediators conduct themselves with integrity, impartiality and respect for the parties involved. Mediators are expected to maintain confidentiality, avoid conflicts of interest and facilitate fair and balanced negotiations. Adherence to ethical guidelines is essential for building trust in the mediation process.

Legal Framework for Mediation in Switzerland

In Switzerland, one cannot discuss mediation without another form of ADR. Two primary forms of ADR, aside from arbitration, are accepted and utilised: meditation and conciliation.

Mediation is a voluntary and confidential conflict resolution process led and supported by a knowledgeable and independent third party who has

8 FSM Federation Swiss Mediation, Ethical Guidelines for Mediators, <https://www.mediation-ch.org/cms3/fileadmin/doc/Regulative/2024/fr/FSM_LDF_Edition_2024.pdf>, accessed 30 July 2024.

9 <https://skwm.ch/?lang=en>, accessed 30 July 2024.

no decision-making or sanctioning powers. The primarily responsibility for determining the subject matter of the negotiation and developing solutions rests with the parties involved, while the mediator is solely responsible for organizing the process. It is then typical of mediation that, as far as possible, the aim is not to negotiate positions. Rather, in line with the Harvard Negotiation concept, the interests in the legal positions and their significance for the parties should be uncovered, thus creating a basis for mutually agreeable solutions that represent a gain for both parties, commonly known as win–win solutions (Fisher et al. 2011).

Conciliation, on the other hand, refers to proceedings in which the parties to a dispute reach an amicable solution with the assistance of a third party, but without the aforementioned requirements. Accordingly, this includes proceedings in which the third party itself assesses the conflict and the behaviour of the parties and then proposes a solution. The standard for the assessment is basically the law. The interests of the parties are generally not relevant.

Additionally, there are numerous 'ombudsman's' offices in the public and private law sectors. It is typical of Swiss civil proceedings that every civil case begins with a conciliation procedure, i.e. a settlement hearing before the justice of the peace. In most cantons, conciliation proceedings are generally mandatory. For landlord–tenant disputes, special arbitration boards made up of equal numbers of tenant and landlord representatives are also prescribed by federal law[10].

These dispute resolution procedures have proven to be highly successful. In addition to the justices of the peace, the numerous public and private 'ombudsman' offices in Switzerland play an essential role in dispute resolution. The procedure before the 'ombudsman's' offices can be simplified as follows: a person who feels that they have been treated unfairly by the public administration or a company submits a written or verbal request to the competent ombudsman's office. The 'ombudsman' then investigates the facts of the case by questioning both the complainant and the other party involved. If the 'ombudsman's' office concludes that the complainant has been treated unfairly, it proposes a solution to the other party. This process is essentially a

10 See Art. 200, para. 1 of the CPC.

'single-track' form of mediation dominated by the 'ombudsman's' office, with direct negotiation between the complainant and the other party occurring rarely. This form of dispute resolution is also considered highly successful in Switzerland. Almost every civil case begins with conciliation proceedings before a justice of the peace. The court then regularly conducts conciliation hearings during the trial.

Finally, but not in the same category as such arbitration should be mentioned in passing, as it also includes proceedings in which the parties do not negotiate with each other themselves, but rather through a third party, as is typically the case in proceedings before arbitration boards. However, arbitration is more to be equated with litigation than with the two primary negotiated methods of dispute resolution mentioned here.

Integration into Civil Procedure

The integration of mediation into the Swiss civil procedure is a key aspect of the country's approach to dispute resolution. This integration ensures that mediation is not just an alternative but a complementary and integral process within the formal legal system, providing parties with multiple avenues for resolving conflicts. This section delves deeper into how mediation is embedded within the civil procedure, examining the procedural steps, judicial support and practical implications for litigants.

Mediation serves the same fundamental purpose as the conciliation procedure, which is to resolve disputes through the involvement of a neutral third party. However, unlike state-led conciliation, mediation is characterised by voluntary participation and party autonomy. The mediator does not hold any decision-making power and is in a horizontal relationship with the parties. This ensures that the mediator cannot exert pressure, and any decisions made reflect the genuine will of the parties.

The principle of voluntariness means that mediation usually only occurs if all parties request it, and it can be terminated at any time. In particular cases, such as those involving child law, court-ordered mediation might be permissible[11].

11 See Art. 297, Abs. 2 of the CPC; <https://www.fedlex.admin.ch/eli/cc/2010/262/en>, accessed 30 July 2024.

Under the Swiss CPC, the term 'mediation' is broadly defined to include any form of private dispute resolution involving a neutral third party without decision-making authority (Möhler 2023a: 616). This excludes negotiations, expert opinions and arbitration.

Mediation must be independent of the court and confidential. Therefore, some argue that so-called internal court mediation, where a judge conducts the mediation, does not constitute mediation within the meaning of the Code (Gelzer & Ruggle 2017: 8).

The Code provides for mediation as both an alternative to the state-led conciliation attempt (Article 213 CPC) and as an interim procedure during an ongoing process (Article 214 CPC). Parties can also conduct mediation entirely outside of any conciliation or court proceedings, although this does not affect the pendency and time limits (Möhler 2023a: 623).

As mentioned earlier, the procedural and substantive differences between mediation and conciliation are significant. Unlike the informal conciliation hearing, mediation is structured and follows a specific pattern, with clear roles for the parties and the mediator (Möhler 2023a: 624; The Swiss Federal Council 2006: 7335). Mediation focuses on the parties' wishes and interests, aiming for a solution that meets their legitimate demands.

In mediation, the parties are central to the process, crafting solutions through a series of discussions facilitated by the mediator, who acts as a moderator. Unlike the conciliator, the mediator does not propose solutions and has no decision-making power.

In Swiss CPC, there are instances where the courts might encourage or even mandate mediation, especially when it is deemed a suitable means for dispute resolution. Article 213 of the CPC allows for mediation instead of conciliation procedures, giving parties the option to choose mediation as an alternative at any stage of the legal process (Möhler 2023b: 622).

A particularly interesting feature of mediation in Switzerland is that, despite its voluntary nature, it can be mandated, particularly in matters concerning child law. Article 297 Abs. 2 CPC states that the court can 'urge' the parties to undergo mediation[12].

---

12 See Art. 297, Abs. 2 of the CPC; <https://www.fedlex.admin.ch/eli/cc/2010/262/en>, accessed 30 July 2024.

Article 213 CPC, the first article concerning mediation, proscribes the initiation and conclusion of mediation should there be no agreement found. According to the principle of voluntariness, mediation only takes place if it is requested by all parties; it can also be terminated at any time (Möhler 2023a: 616).

The parties are also at liberty to conduct mediation entirely outside of arbitration or court proceedings. However, in this case, the effects of *lis pendens* and compliance with time limits do not apply (Möhler 2023a: 623). The CPC does not contain any comprehensive regulation of mediation. Rather, it only clarifies its relationship to state proceedings (conciliation and court proceedings) so that mediation can fulfil its task (The Swiss Federal Council 2006: 7335). In particular, the CPC does not contain any provisions on the organisation and implementation of mediation. This is a matter for the parties[13].

Article 213 CPC concerns the relationship between mediation and state arbitration proceedings (Article 197 CPC). Mediation can replace conciliation proceedings if all parties so request. This option is intended to allow the parties themselves to determine the most suitable procedure for resolving their dispute and the mediators entrusted with it (Ruggle 2017a:1154).

Contractually agreed mediation clauses do not alter this codified scheme. The implementation of mediation is not a procedural requirement, so that the action can be filed with the conciliation authority despite the mediation clause – the conciliation authority must accept the application[14]. However, the clause is not entirely irrelevant for the conciliation authority: Each party can request the suspension of the proceedings (but not a decision not to enter

13 See Art. 215 of the CPC; <https://www.fedlex.admin.ch/eli/cc/2010/262/en>, accessed 30 July 2024.

14 Swiss Federal Tribunal (2020). *Judgment of 5 May 2020*, No. 4A_132/2019, First Civil Law Court; <https://www.bger.ch/ext/eurospider/live/fr/php/aza/http/index.php?lang=fr&type=show_document&highlight_docid=aza://05-05-2020-4A_132-2019&print=yes>, accessed: 7 October 2024; Zurich Commercial Court (2019). *Judgment of 12 June 2019*, No. HG170120-O12; <https://www.gerichte-zh.ch/fileadmin/user_upload/entscheide/oeffentlich/HG170120-O12.pdf>, accessed 6 October 2024.

into the proceedings) with reference to the mediation clause[15]. A mediation clause is irrelevant if it is invoked contrary to good faith, for example, if the defendant has unconditionally accepted the court proceedings[16].

In accordance with the principle of voluntariness, mediation can be terminated at any time and by either party. It is sufficient for the conciliation authority to be informed accordingly. If a party informs the conciliation authority of the failure of the mediation, the authorisation to sue is granted (213 para. 3 CPC). This authorisation is granted directly, without the need for conciliation proceedings. In this respect, the failure of mediation is comparable to a failed attempt at conciliation (The Swiss Federal Council 2006: 7336). The conciliation authority must issue an authorisation to sue.

Article 214 CPC outlines the integration of mediation into ongoing legal proceedings. It permits courts to recommend mediation at any stage of judicial proceedings. While the court can suggest mediation, this recommendation is non-binding, preserving the voluntary nature of the process. The judicial recommendation is intended to serve as an entry point to mediation without imposing any obligation on the parties. If the parties agree, the judicial proceedings are stayed pending the outcome of the mediation (Möhler 2023b: 623).

The principle of voluntary mediation does not preclude the possibility of court-ordered mediation in specific contexts. For instance, in family law disputes, particularly those involving child custody or visitation rights, courts may mandate mediation to safeguard the best interests of the child. In such cases, the court's role extends to facilitating a mediated agreement, reflecting a blend of voluntary and mandatory elements (Möhler 2023b: 622).

If mediation occurs, the ongoing court proceedings must be suspended (Art. 214 para. 3 of the CPC). In principle, the court has no discretion in

15 See Swiss Federal Tribunal (2016). *Judgment of 16 March 2016*, No. 4A_628/2015, First Civil Law Court; <http://relevancy.bger.ch/php/clir/http/index.php?highlight_docid=atf%3A%2F%2F142-III-296%3Ade&lang=de&type=show_document>, accessed 7 October 2024.

16 Swiss Federal Tribunal (2007). *Judgment of 6 June 2007*, No. 4A_18/2007, First Civil Law Court; <https://www.bger.ch/ext/eurospider/live/de/php/aza/http/index.php?highlight_docid=aza%3A%2F%2F06-06-2007-4A_18-2007&lang=de&type=show_document&zoom=YES&>, accessed 7 October 2024.

this regard (Ruggle 2017b: 1160). The suspension remains valid, until a party revokes its request for mediation or until the court is notified of the termination of the mediation[17]. In these cases, the court must lift the suspension and continue the proceedings. In principle, the revocation of the application can be declared at any time, even if mediation has not even taken place (Ruggle 2017b: 1163). Unlike the conciliation authority, the court does not verify whether mediation has taken place, as mediation merely suspends the court proceedings rather than replacing them (Gloor & Umbricht Lukas 2021: 9).

Article 215 CPC is straightforward and declares the actual method of mediation to be a matter solely for the parties to decide on without interference from the court or conciliation authority, unless it was court-ordered mediation.

Article 216 CPC establishes two essential principles that govern the relationship between mediation and state jurisdiction, namely independence and confidentiality (Möhler 2023c: 625; Ruggle 2017d: 1167).

Independence means independence from the judiciary branch (Art. 216, para. 1 CPC; The Swiss Federal Council 2006: 7337). Neither the court nor the conciliation authority shall issue instructions, and mediators are not accountable to either (The Swiss Federal Council 2006: 7337). Mandated mediation as a child protection measure under the Art. 297, Abs. 2 of the CPC remains the exception[18].

It is further noteworthy that acting as a mediator precludes subsequent involvement in conciliation or court proceedings: According to Art. 47, para. Ib CPC, the mediator must withdraw[19].

Confidentiality seeks to ensure that the content of the communication and the events of the mediation are not available for the subsequent proceedings, regardless of their legal significance (The Swiss Federal Council 2006: 7337; Möhler 2023c: 625–626; Ruggle 2017d: 1168). However, neither beginning nor ending of the mediation are confidential (Ruggle 2017d: 1168). A waiver of the confidentiality of the mediation is possible with the agreement of both parties (Möhler 2023c: 625–626; Ruggle 2017d: 1168).

---

17 Art. 214, para. 3 of the CPC; <https://www.fedlex.admin.ch/eli/cc/2010/262/en>, accessed 30 July 2024.

18 See 214 N 2 of the CPC and for details ZPO 297 N 6 f; Sutter-Somm, N 1003.

19 So-called formal relationship (The Swiss Federal Council 2006, 7337; Ruggle 2017).

Article 217 CPC stipulates that if the mediation procedure ends with an agreement, the parties can have this approved by the court (The Swiss Federal Council 2006: 7337). The approval of the mediation agreement gives the private law contracts a procedural component. The mediation agreement to be approved must clearly and specifically describe the services owed and state the legal basis on which these services are based. Only in this way can the mediation agreement be reviewed and the approved agreement be given the effect of a legally binding decision (Gelzer 2017: 1173; Möhler 2023d: 628). Usually, the agreement also contains a provision regarding the mediation and litigation costs; otherwise, these are to be distributed in accordance with Art. 218 CPC. Agreements on issues outside the subject matter of the dispute are also eligible for approval, provided they can be made the subject of a legal obligation.

The ratified agreement obtains the effect of a legally binding decision. Through the so-called 'homologation', the mediation agreement is equated with a court settlement and thus becomes an enforceable title. At the same time, the approved agreement has the effect of a *res iudicata* within the meaning of Article 59 para. 2, lit. e.

Article 218 of the CPC finally refers to costs. It states:

1. The parties shall bear the costs of mediation.
2. In matters of child law, the parties are entitled to cost-free mediation if:
   a. they do not have the necessary financial resources; and
   b. the court recommends mediation.
3. Cantonal law may provide for further exemptions from costs[20].

The parties must, therefore, reach an agreement on the distribution of costs; it is usually agreed that the costs are to be borne in equal shares (Möhler 2023d: 630). A lack of agreement can result in the matter not being completely resolved and thus not terminated in its entirety as mandated for a closing of a court or conciliation authority case. The exception again applies to court mandated cases.

20 See Swiss Civil Procedure Code of 19 December 2008; <https://www.fedlex.admin.ch/eli/cc/2010/262/en>, accessed 30 July 2024.

Judicial Support for Mediation

Judicial support for mediation is evident in the procedural framework allowing for its recommendation and integration into formal proceedings. The courts' ability to stay proceedings for mediation underscores the institutional support for ADR methods. However, it is crucial to note that judicial recommendations are not coercive. While the primary responsibility lies with the parties, judicial support can manifest in providing information to facilitate the mediation process. Courts and conciliation authorities can offer practical information, such as providing lists of recognised mediators, to assist the parties (Möhler 2023d: 630).

In cases where the parties cannot agree on a mediator or the organisation of the mediation, the conciliation authority may summon the parties to a conciliation hearing or the court may resume the judicial proceedings. Judicial interference is limited to ensuring that mediated agreements do not violate mandatory legal provisions. The courts do not assess the fairness of the agreement terms unless they involve mandatory legal standards. This respect for party autonomy underscores the principle that mediation is a voluntary and self-determined process.

Mediation in Swiss civil procedure offers a structured yet flexible approach to dispute resolution, supported by judicial mechanisms that ensure the enforceability of agreements. The Swiss CPC provides a clear framework for the approval of mediation agreements and delineates the supportive role of courts, enhancing the effectiveness and reliability of mediation as an ADR method. Swiss courts play a pivotal role in integrating mediation into civil procedure by actively supporting and encouraging its use. Judges are trained to recognise cases that may benefit from mediation and to facilitate the process where appropriate.

Judicial training and awareness are crucial for the success of mediation within the legal system. Judges in Switzerland receive training on mediation principles and techniques. This training equips them with the skills to identify suitable cases for mediation and to guide parties towards considering mediation as a viable option. Judicial support for mediation is crucial for its acceptance and success within the legal system.

Some courts have appointed mediation officers or coordinators who assist judges and parties in managing the mediation process. These officers provide information about mediation, help select qualified mediators and coordinate the scheduling of mediation sessions. Their involvement ensures that the mediation process is streamlined and accessible.

Effective case management by judges includes early identification of disputes that are amenable to mediation. By intervening early in the litigation process, judges can suggest mediation before conflicts escalate, increasing the likelihood of a successful resolution. Early intervention also helps reduce court backlogs and the overall time and cost of litigation.

Federal Offices and Mediation

Federal offices in Switzerland play a crucial role in the development, promotion and implementation of mediation as an ADR mechanism. These offices provide essential resources, training, policy guidance and oversight to ensure that mediation is effective, professional and accessible to all parties involved. This section explores the involvement of key federal offices in supporting mediation, their initiatives and the impact of their work on the mediation landscape in Switzerland.

The FOJ is a central player in the promotion and regulation of mediation in Switzerland. The FOJ is responsible for developing legal frameworks, providing training resources and supporting research and policy initiatives related to mediation. The FOJ oversees the accreditation of mediator training programmes, ensuring that they meet high standards of quality and rigor. Accredited programmes cover essential topics such as mediation principles, legal aspects, communication skills, and ethical considerations. By setting these standards, the FOJ ensures that mediators are well-trained and capable of facilitating effective dispute resolution.

The FOJ supports research initiatives aimed at evaluating and improving mediation practices. By collecting and analysing data on mediation outcomes, the FOJ can identify best practices, areas for improvement and emerging trends. This research informs policy decisions and helps to promote evidence-based approaches to mediation. Additionally, the FOJ conducts public awareness campaigns to inform citizens about the benefits of mediation and how to access mediation services. These campaigns include informational materials, workshops and partnerships with community organisations. By raising awareness, the FOJ encourages more people to consider mediation as a viable option for resolving disputes.

The FDFA is actively involved in promoting mediation on an international scale. The FDFA's work in mediation is part of Switzerland's broader commitment to peacebuilding, conflict prevention and the promotion of international law. The FDFA facilitates international mediation efforts by providing expertise, resources and support to mediation processes in conflict-affected regions. Swiss mediators, often supported by the FDFA, are involved in mediating complex international disputes, ranging from political conflicts to trade disagreements. These efforts underscore Switzerland's reputation as a neutral and skilled mediator on the global stage.

The FDFA organises training programmes for international mediators and conflict resolution practitioners. These programmes cover a wide range of topics, including negotiation techniques, cultural sensitivity and the legal aspects of international mediation. By building the capacity of mediators worldwide, the FDFA contributes to the global promotion of peaceful conflict resolution. The FDFA collaborates with international organisations such as the United Nations (UN), the European Union, and various non-governmental organisations to promote mediation. These collaborations involve joint projects, funding initiatives and the sharing of best practices. The FDFA's partnerships enhance the effectiveness and reach of mediation efforts globally.

In its diplomatic engagements, the FDFA advocates for the use of mediation as a tool for resolving disputes between states and within regions. Swiss diplomats often emphasise the importance of mediation in their dialogues with other countries, promoting it as a constructive and non-violent means of addressing conflicts.

The Swiss Federal Institute of Intellectual Property (IPI) plays a specific role in promoting mediation within the context of intellectual property (IP) disputes. The IPI provides services and support tailored to the needs of IP holders and disputants. The IPI offers specialised mediation services for resolving IP disputes, such as trademark conflicts, patent infringements and copyright issues. These services are designed to provide a faster, more cost-effective and confidential alternative to litigation.

The IPI provides training programmes and resources for mediators specialising in IP disputes. These programmes cover the technical and legal aspects of IP mediation, ensuring that mediators have the necessary expertise to handle complex IP cases. The IPI conducts outreach and education initiatives to inform IP holders about the benefits of mediation. By raising awareness, the IPI encourages more IP disputes to be resolved through mediation rather than through lengthy and costly litigation processes.

In addition to these federal efforts, private organisations also play a significant role in maintaining professional standards in mediation.

International Influence and Switzerland's Role

Switzerland's commitment to mediation extends beyond its borders, positioning the country as a leader in international dispute resolution. Through its diplomatic efforts, legal frameworks and active participation in global mediation initiatives, Switzerland has significantly influenced the adoption and practice of mediation worldwide. This section explores Switzerland's role in promoting mediation on the international stage, highlighting key initiatives, partnerships and case studies that demonstrate its global impact.

Switzerland's long-standing tradition of neutrality and its reputation for impartiality make it an ideal mediator in international disputes. The Swiss government leverages these attributes to facilitate dialogue and negotiate peaceful resolutions to conflicts. Switzerland's neutrality, established in the early nineteenth century and reaffirmed in the Treaty of Paris (1815), has enabled it to act as a neutral ground for diplomatic negotiations. This historical context underpins Switzerland's role as a trusted mediator in contemporary international disputes.

Swiss diplomats are trained in mediation and conflict resolution, equipping them with the skills to manage complex negotiations. The Swiss FDFA plays a crucial role in deploying these diplomats to mediate international conflicts.

Switzerland's involvement in international mediation encompasses various initiatives and partnerships aimed at promoting peaceful conflict resolution globally. Switzerland collaborates with the UN in supporting mediation efforts worldwide. The FDFA works closely with the UN's Department of Political and Peacebuilding Affairs (DPPA)[21] to provide mediation expertise and resources. Additionally, Switzerland contributes financially to the UN's mediation support activities, including funding for the Mediation Support

21 <https://dppa.un.org/en>, accessed 30 July 2024.

Unit (MSU)[22] and the Standby Team of Senior Mediation Advisers[23], enhancing the UN's capacity to mediate conflicts effectively.

The Geneva Peace Talks, organised annually by the United Nations Office at Geneva (UNOG)[24] and the Geneva Peacebuilding Platform[25], provide a forum for discussing innovative approaches to peace and conflict resolution. Switzerland's support for this event highlights its commitment to promoting dialogue and sharing best practices in mediation. The Peace Talks feature success stories of mediation and peacebuilding from around the world, inspiring other countries and organisations to adopt similar approaches. Swiss mediators and experts often present their experiences, contributing to the global discourse on mediation.

Switzerland supports the International Committee of the Red Cross (ICRC)[26] in its humanitarian mediation efforts. The ICRC's work in conflict zones, facilitated by Swiss funding and diplomatic support, includes mediating access to humanitarian aid and negotiating ceasefires. The ICRC's mediation efforts focus on protecting civilians in armed conflicts, ensuring that humanitarian principles are upheld. Switzerland's backing reinforces the importance of neutral and impartial mediation in saving lives and alleviating suffering.

Case Studies of International Mediation

Switzerland's role in mediating international disputes is exemplified by several high-profile cases. These case studies illustrate the effectiveness of Swiss mediation in resolving complex conflicts.

---

22 <https://peacemaker.un.org/mediation-support-unit/mediation-support-unit>, accessed 30 July 2024.

23 <https://peacemaker.un.org/mediation-support-unit/standby-team-of-senior-mediation-advisers, accessed 30 July 2024.

24 <https://www.ungeneva.org/en>, accessed 30 July 2024.

25 <https://gpplatform.ch/en>, accessed 30 July 2024.

26 <https://www.icrc.org/en>, accessed 30 July 2024.

Case Study 1: Colombian Peace Process

The Colombian government and the Revolutionary Armed Forces of Colombia (FARC) engaged in a protracted civil conflict lasting over five decades. Efforts to negotiate peace faced numerous challenges, including deep-seated mistrust and ongoing violence. Switzerland played a supportive role in the Colombian peace process, providing technical assistance and mediation expertise. Swiss diplomats facilitated dialogues and offered training in mediation techniques to Colombian negotiators. The peace agreement signed in 2016 between the Colombian government and FARC marked a significant milestone in ending the conflict. Switzerland's contributions helped build trust between the parties and supported the implementation of the peace accords.

Case Study 2: Sudanese Comprehensive Peace Agreement

The Second Sudanese Civil War, which began in 1983, resulted in widespread devastation and loss of life. Efforts to negotiate peace were complicated by ethnic divisions, economic interests and external influences. Switzerland, in collaboration with other international partners, facilitated peace negotiations between the Sudanese government and the Sudan People's Liberation Movement (SPLM). Swiss mediators provided logistical support and technical expertise. The Comprehensive Peace Agreement (CPA) signed in 2005 ended the civil war and paved the way for South Sudan's independence in 2011. Switzerland's mediation efforts contributed to the successful negotiation and implementation of the CPA, highlighting its role in resolving one of Africa's longest-running conflicts.

Case Study 3: Iran Nuclear Deal

Tensions over Iran's nuclear programmes led to international sanctions and heightened the risk of military conflict. Negotiations between Iran and the P5+1 (China, France, Russia, the United Kingdom, the United States and Germany) sought to reach a diplomatic solution. Switzerland facilitated several rounds of negotiations in Geneva, providing a neutral venue and logistical support. Swiss diplomats also played a behind-the-scenes role in bridging gaps between the parties. The Joint Comprehensive Plan of Action (JCPOA) was signed in 2015, limiting Iran's nuclear programme in exchange for the lifting of economic sanctions. Switzerland's neutral facilitation was crucial in maintaining dialogue and achieving a historic agreement.

Switzerland's contributions to international mediation extend beyond specific cases, influencing global mediation practices and policies. Switzerland's role in international mediation reflects its commitment to promoting peace, stability and the rule of law. Through its neutral stance, diplomatic expertise and support for global mediation initiatives, Switzerland has significantly influenced the practice and acceptance of mediation worldwide. The country's involvement in high-profile mediation cases, support for international organizations and promotion of mediation standards underscore its leadership in the field. As global conflicts continue to evolve, Switzerland's contributions to mediation will remain essential in fostering peaceful resolutions and advancing the cause of international diplomacy.

Summary

Mediation is firmly established within the Swiss legal system as a valuable tool for resolving disputes. Its integration into civil procedures, supported by a robust legal framework and professional training standards, underscores its potential to transform conflict resolution. Switzerland's role in international mediation further highlights the importance of skilled mediators in promoting global peace and stability. As mediation practices continue to evolve, ongoing efforts towards professionalisation and adherence to legal standards will be essential in ensuring its sustained success and credibility.

Switzerland stands as an exceptional example of a country conducive to mediation, demonstrating how the role and example of a state become pivotal in shaping the behaviour and choices of its citizens. The Swiss model shows that with proper institutional support and a commitment to neutrality and impartiality, mediation can become an integral part of both domestic and international dispute resolution frameworks. This environment not only fosters trust in mediation processes but also encourages individuals and entities to choose mediation over litigation, ultimately contributing to a more peaceful and cooperative society.

Bibliography

Fisher, Roger, Ury, William, **and Patton, Bruce** (2011). *Getting to Yes: Negotiating Agreement Without Giving*, 3rd edn. New York: Penguin Books.

Gelzer, Philipp S. (2017). 'Art. 217'. In Karl Spühler, Luca Tenchio and Dominik Infanger (eds), *Basler Kommentar ZPO*, 3rd edn, pp. 1169–1177. Basel: Helbing Lichtenhahn.

Gelzer, Philipp S. and Ruggle, Peter (2017). 'Vor Art. 213–218'. In Karl Spühler, Luca Tenchio and Dominik Infanger (eds), *Basler Kommentar ZPO. 3rd edn*, pp. 1145–1151. Basel: Helbing Lichtenhahn.

Gloor, André, Umbricht, Stefan, and Lukas, Martin. (2021). 'Preface to Art. 213–218 ZPO'. In Paul Oberhammer, Tonja Domej and Ulrich Haas (eds.), *Kurzkommentar zur Schweizerischen Zivilprozessordnung* (ZPO), 3rd edn. Basel: Helbing Lichtenhahn

Kägi, Adrian (2020). 'Bundesämter und Mediation', *Zeitschrift für Juristic Weiterbildung und Praxis*, 4 (2020), 275–293.

Meier, Isaak (2002). *Mediation und Schlichtung in der Schweiz: Unterbesonderer Berücksichtigung der Gesetzlichen Rahmenbedingungen für Mediation.* Swiss Institute of Comparative Law, <https://www.175jahre.uzh.ch/fakultaeten/recht/fachbereiche/zprschkg/Dokumente/report_mediation_deu_EZPO.pdf>, accessed 7 October 2024.

Möhler, Christine (2023a). 'Art. 213 Mediation Statt Schlichtungs Verfahren'. In Myriam A. Gehri, Ingrid Jent-Sørensen and Martin Sarbach (eds), *Kommentarzur Schweizerischen Zivilprozessordnung*, pp. 616–621. Zürich: Orell Füssli Verlag AG.

Möhler, Christine (2023b) 'Art. 214 Mediation im Entscheidverfahren'. In Myriam A. Gehri, Ingrid Jent-Sørensen and Martin Sarbach (eds), *Kommentarzur Schweizerischen Zivilprozessordnung*, pp. 622–623. Zürich: Orell Fossil Verlag AG.

Mohler, Christine (2023c). 'Art. 216 Verhältniszumgerichtlichen Verfahren'. In Myriam A. Gehri, Ingrid Jent-Sørensen and Martin Sarbach (eds), *Kommentarzur Schweizerischen Zivilprozessordnung*, pp. 625–627. Zürich: Orell Füssli Verlag AG.

Mohler, Christine (2023d). 'Art. 217 Genehmigungeiner Vereinbarung'. In Myriam A. Gehri, Ingrid Jent-Sørensen and Martin Sarbach (eds), *Kommentarzur Schweizerischen Zivilprozessordnung*, pp. 627–629. Zürich: Orell Füssli Verlag AG.

Obergericht des Kantons Zürich (2022) *Merkblattzur Mediation – Kurzversion*, <https://www.gerichte-zh.ch/fileadmin/user_upload/dokumente/Themen/Zivilprozess/Kurzversion_Merkblatt_zur_Mediation.pdf>, accessed 7 October 2024.

Robert, Florence Michèle (2017). 'Spielregeln für das Recht in der Mediation', *Anwaltsrevue: Das Praxismagazin des schweizerischen Anwaltsverbandes*,NR 6/7/2017, 271–274.

Ruggle, Peter (2017a). 'Art. 213'. In Karl Spühler, Luca Tenchio and Dominik Infanger (eds), *Basler Kommentar ZPO, 3rd edn*, pp. 1151–1159. Basel: Helbing Lichtenhahn.

Ruggle, Peter (2017b). 'Art. 214'. In Karl Spühler, Luca Tenchio and Dominik Infanger (eds), *Basler Kommentar ZPO, 3rd ed.*, pp. 1160–1163. Basel: Helbing Lichtenhahn.

Ruggle, Peter (2017c). 'Art. 215'. In Karl Spühler, Luca Tenchio and Dominik Infanger (eds), *Basler Kommentar ZPO, 3rd ed.*, pp. 1164–1165. Basel: Helbing Lichtenhahn.

Ruggle, Peter (2017d). 'Art. 216'. In Karl Spühler, Luca Tenchio and Dominik Infanger (eds), *Basler Kommentar ZPO, 3rd ed.*, pp. 1166–1169. Basel: Helbing Lichtenhahn.

Ruggle, Peter (2017e). 'Art. 218'. In Spühler, Karl, Tenchio, Luca, and Infanger, Dominik (eds), *Basler Kommentar ZPO, 3rd ed.*, pp. 1177–1180. Basel: Helbing Lichtenhahn.

Sutter-Somm, Thomas, and Seiler, Benedikt (2021a). 'Art. 215'. In Thomas Sutter-Somm and Benedikt Seiler (eds), *Handkommentarzur Schweizerischen Zivilprozessordnung (ZPO)*, pp. 854–856. Zürich: Schulthess Verlag.

Sutter-Somm, Thomas, and Seiler, Benedikt (2021b). 'Art. 216'. In Thomas Sutter-Somm and Benedikt Seiler (eds), *Handkommentarzur Schweizerischen Zivilprozessordnung (ZPO)*, pp. 856–858. Zürich: Schulthess Verlag.

Sutter-Somm, Thomas, and Seiler, Benedikt (2021c). 'Art. 217'. In Thomas Sutter-Somm and Benedikt Seiler (eds), *Handkommentarzur Schweizerischen Zivilprozessordnung (ZPO)*, pp. 859–862. Zürich: Schulthess Verlag.

Sutter-Somm, Thomas, and Seiler, Benedikt (2021d). 'Art. 218'. In Thomas Sutter-Somm and Benedikt Seiler (eds), *Handkommentarzur Schweizerischen Zivilprozessordnung (ZPO)*, pp. 862–865. Zürich: Schulthess Verlag.

Legal sources

Directive 2008/52/EC of the European Parliament and the Council of 21 May 2008 on certain aspects of mediation in civil and commercial matters, OJ L 136/3 on 24 May 2008, <https://eur-lex.europa.eu/legal-content/en/ALL/?uri=CELEX:32008L0052#:~:text=DIRECTIVE%202008/52/EC%20OF%20THE%20EUROPEAN%20PARLIAMENT>.

Swiss Parliament (2008). Swiss Civil Procedure Code of 19 December 2008, <https://www.fedlex.admin.ch/eli/cc/2010/262/en>, accessed 30 July 2024.

Swiss Federal Council, Botschaft zur Schweizerischen Zivilprozessordnung (ZPO), 19 September 2006, Federal Department of Justice and Police, Official Reference: BBl 2006 7221, Parliamentary Number: 06.062, adopted 28 June 2006.

The Latest Amendments of the Law on Mediation in Lithuania: A Robust Framework for the Continuing Development of the Profession of Mediator

Indrė Korsakovienė[1] and Agnė Tvaronavičienė[2]

Introduction

Mediation is a sustainable dispute resolution method making it possible to resolve disputes efficiently while avoiding costly litigation, promoting transparency, accountability and social responsibility through open dialogue and direct stakeholder engagement (Maia 2024). Sustainability aspects in mediation are manifested through privacy and confidentiality of the process, the ability to preserve a relationship between parties to a dispute and deal with the emotional part of the conflict, providing individual approaches to possible solutions as well as efficiency, convenience and accessibility of dispute resolution procedures (Kaminskienė et al. 2014: 71). As a flexible and culturally agile process (Alexander 2020: 1), mediation is increasingly becoming a more intensively regulated field in Europe (Steffek 2012: 13). The regulation of mediation can, among others, support the development and recognition of the profession of mediator by establishing standards for credentialing mediators and other quality assurance measures for mediation practice (Alexander 2020: 8). Thus, without a solid framework for the emergence and development of the profession of mediator and its recognition, the expansion of mediation becomes inconceivable.

Lithuania is one of the European countries that have been actively searching for ways to establish this relatively new social institution within the society and to promote the use of mediation in resolving legal disputes for almost two

1 Mykolas Romeris University (Vilnius, Lithuania), email: i.korsakoviene@mruni.eu
2 Prof. Dr, Mykolas Romeris University (Vilnius, Lithuania), email: a.tvaronaviciene@mruni.eu

decades. The last-mentioned initiatives are aimed not only towards fostering mediation but also towards strengthening the credibility of the profession of mediator and creating a robust framework for the development of this activity. This chapter aims to present the development of mediation in Lithuania through the lenses of the formation and development of the profession of mediator, in order to answer the question of whether the recent legislative initiatives are a credible and sufficient basis for the development of this profession and the development of the mediator's activities in the country, and whether they can be considered as an example for other countries that are facing similar challenges.

The first section provides a brief overview of the impetus for the emergence of mediation in Lithuania and the efforts to establish this peaceful dispute resolution method in the country, as well as a short review of the development of mediation until the recent legislative initiatives. The second section is devoted to outlining the particularities of this profession in Lithuania. It aims to reveal what model of regulating mediators' activities was chosen in Lithuania and how it has evolved over the years. It also uses the criteria proposed by scholars for determining the profession to assess whether the current legal and social environment in Lithuania favours the practice of mediation and if this practice is currently recognised as a separate profession. The third section offers a more detailed overview of the latest legislative initiatives, which were mainly aimed at strengthening the mediator's profession by vesting the right of self-governance in the hands of the Lithuanian Chamber of Mediators, thus increasing the recognition and credibility of the profession and the quality of the services provided. Finally, the fourth section provides some insights into the potential challenges to the implementation of self-governance of mediators, which Lithuania is likely to encounter, and which are worth paying attention to for other countries that are planning to take measures towards strengthening this profession.

The research was carried out using the methods of scientific literature review, comparative analyses and document analyses.

The Development of Mediation in Lithuania

Mediation in Lithuania has been an integral part of the legal system of dispute resolution for almost two decades. However, it is only since 2017, as a result of amendments to the Law on Mediation (2017), that it has become an established and relatively well-developed institution, which has required a series of legislative initiatives, governmental support, the active involvement of the mediation community and the engagement of the society to achieve this result.

After the restoration of independence of Lithuania in 1991, society was facing a series of political, economic and, naturally, social transformations. While Lithuania has managed to avoid deep, long-lasting political or ethnical clashes as it is immersed into transformations, it has nevertheless struggled to develop an environment favourable to a distinctive dispute resolution culture, typical for Western European or North American countries (Lakis 2008: 38). Targeted efforts were necessary to ensure that the culture of conflict resolution adapted to the new socio-cultural and socio-political dimensions in Lithuania and litigation-oriented society would be ready to employ alternative dispute resolution (ADR) methods.

The new Lithuanian Code of Civil Procedure (CPC) (2002) entered into force in 2003 and introduced a number of reforms in the field of civil procedure with one of the main objectives – the restoration of legal peace between the disputants as quickly as possible. In order to ensure the genuine possibility of restoring legal peace in civil proceedings, the mandatory requirement was introduced for the court to undertake a conciliation procedure at the pre-litigation stage and to invite the parties to work towards a mutually agreed settlement by mutual concessions and to conclude a settlement agreement. This legislative initiative gave impetus to and created preconditions for the emergence of an ADR culture in Lithuania. It was later followed by a pilot project of judicial mediation in Lithuanian courts, which enabled judges hearing civil cases also to mediate them, and is now considered to be the starting point of the mediation movement in Lithuania (Tvaronavičienė et al. 2022: 73) and the launch of court-connected mediation.

A pilot project of mediation, based on the experience of Quebec, Canada, launched in 2005 in the Vilnius City District Court, became a genuine precursor for the emergence of judicial mediation in Lithuania. Initially involving one court, it expanded to all Lithuanian courts by 2014, despite early criticism of over-regulation by the Council of Judges, which was addressed by the 2011 amendments to the CPC. A model of court regulation began to emerge alongside judicial mediation initiatives, which was followed by the creation of the Judicial Mediation Rules (2014) and the adoption of the court mediator statute and the rules of procedure for granting the status of mediator to individuals and revoking it (2014). Thus, the judges were the first mediators who gained an actual opportunity to practice in Lithuania due to the court regulatory model. The volume of judicial mediation in Lithuania has been gradually increasing, until recent years when a stagnation of the of judicial mediation was observed (Kaminskienė et al. 2023: 217). Nevertheless, judges are still highly desired mediators in judicial mediations and in most cases, 95% of cases already pending in court in 2023, 94% in 2022 and 96% in 2021 (Lithuanian courts 2024: 3), the mediation was conducted by mediator judges. According to the Report of the Judicial Mediation Commission, at the end of 2023, 130 judges had the status of mediator, and 20% more cases (740) were referred to court-connected mediation in 2023 compared to 2022 (597) (Lithuanian courts 2024: 58). Most of them, 47% (345), are disputes arising from family law, while the rest are disputes arising from rights in rem, law of obligations, legal entities or disputes with an international element. Therefore, today, judicial mediation in Lithuania is functioning alongside out-of-court mediation and is an integral part of the mediation system.

However, the adoption of legal provisions providing for the possibility of a peaceful settlement has only created the conditions for it to occur but has not facilitated it in practice. Lithuanian society continued to perceive the courts as the main, and often the only, means of dispute resolution (Korsakovienė & Tvaronavičienė 2023). It was clear that in order to increase the number of cases settled amicably, it was necessary to take effective legislative and non-legislative measures to promote peaceful dispute resolution methods. Following the above-mentioned initiatives in Lithuania, under the auspices of Directive 2008/52/EC of the European Parliament and of the Council on Certain Aspects of Mediation in Civil and Commercial Matters (2008) ('Mediation Directive'), a Law on Conciliatory Mediation in Civil Disputes was adopted in 2008. Historically, this was supposed to become an important momentum and a starting point for institutionalising mediation in Lithuania; however, it did not create a real impetus for the development of mediation and mediator's profession in the country.

Like in many EU countries that have implemented the provisions of the Mediation Directive in their national legislation during that period, the confidentiality of mediation, the issues of the suspension of limitation periods and the matters relating to the formalisation and enforcement of agreements concluded during mediation were established with the adoption of a Law on Conciliatory Mediation. In addition, a fundamental principle of mediation – voluntariness – has been enshrined in it, covering the parties' involvement in the mediation, the possibility to choose the mediator, to control the course of the mediation and to withdraw from it at any time, as well as the definitions of mediation and mediator. However, a major drawback of the Law on Conciliatory Mediation was that it literally transposed the provisions of the Mediation Directive into national legislation, without envisaging any additional measures to consolidate and promote the use of this relatively new dispute resolution method in the national context.

The provisions of the Mediation Directive vary in their regulatory approach due to the diverse practices of Member States and the evolving nature of mediation, ensuring that some articles mandate strict rules for national laws, while others are left as aspirational, eventually leaving some aspects outside the scope of regulation (Steffek 2012: 8). Unlike the binding nature of the provisions of the Mediation Directive on the enforceability of agreements, confidentiality and suspension of limitation periods, the regulation of mediators' training and quality control mechanisms has been left exclusively to the discretion of Member States. As a consequence, the procedure for the accreditation of mediators' qualifications in Lithuania has remained undefined, no provisions have been made to regulate the mediator's liability, and no procedural incentives or sanctions have been introduced to increase the use of mediation. Moreover, there was a lack of commitment and political will to integrate mediation as an equivalent institution in the national law, as well as support from the state, including financial support, or efforts to educate the public and the legal community about this alternative to the traditional litigation.

Therefore, it is natural that the formal transposition of the Mediation Directive without extending its scope, for example, by enshrining in law some effective quality control mechanisms for mediators as well as a requirement for initial and continued training in mediation, or by providing additional procedural measures to promote the use of mediation, has been insufficient for the successful introduction of mediation in Lithuania. Thus, although the steps to institutionalise mediation have been formally implemented, the mediation has not flourished on itself, except in occasional cases, and has not contributed to the development of the profession of mediator.

Acknowledging that the development of mediation within a certain jurisdiction is, among other things, based on institutional and governmental support, one of the most significant activities in this regard was the Concept on Mediation Development in Lithuania adopted on 17 September 2015. It was aimed to provide a more detailed regulation of mediation in civil, administrative and criminal disputes as well as establishing a list of mediators and their qualification requirements thus strengthening the trust in this profession, while also envisaging procedural measures to promote mediation, such as mandatory mediation provisions for family disputes. The clearly established political will to strengthen the institution of mediation in Lithuania reflected the shift from a purely formal to a more responsible and explicit regulatory approach (Tvaronavičienė et al. 2022: 74).

The reform institutionalising mediation in Lithuania, launched in 2017, has resulted in mediation in civil justice in Lithuania being well-structured and explicitly regulated and it has become a strong basis for the further development of respected professional mediators (Tvaronavičienė et al. 2022: 75). The amendments to the Law on Conciliatory Mediation adopted on 29 June 2017 are considered to be a substantial landmark in the process of development of mediation in Lithuania, replacing the existing law and renaming it as the 'Law on Mediation' (2017). The fundamental changes have been shaped throughout the institutionalisation of mediation at the highest level, by clarifying the institutional roles in mediation administration, paving the way for mandatory family mediation, establishing the profession of mediator, laying down requirements for individuals seeking to provide mediation services, as well as the creation of an official list of mediators and outlining their disciplinary liability. For the first time, mediation was recognised as a profession, except for mediation activities conducted by judges, thus distinguishing between court mediation and out-of-court mediation.

Most of the amendments entered into force as of 1 January 2019, except the mandatory mediation provisions, which entered into force as of 1 January 2020. Starting from the latter date, out-of-court mediation became a mandatory pre-litigation step for family disputes. According to what scholars consider to be a rather liberal model of mandatory mediation (Tvaronavičienė et al. 2022: 75) in Lithuania, the plaintiff must invite the opposing party to resolve the issue through mediation before initiating court proceedings. During the next 14 days, the counterparty has the right to accept or refuse this invitation. In other words, the parties are not compelled to mediate, but to propose to each other to resolve the arising family dispute through mediation. One of the parties, or all parties jointly by mutual agreement, can choose a mediator from the List of Mediators at their own expense or have an option to apply to the State Guaranteed Legal Aid Service (SGLAS) for state-funded mandatory mediation. The State enables all Lithuanian citizens to obtain four hours of mediation by subsidising the costs of mandatory mediation in family matters.

Thus, in Lithuania, the development of mediation was supported by amendments to the Civil Procedure Code, which introduced the possibility for judges to use conciliatory methods. The first initiatives to introduce mediation in practice originated in the courts. Although they were not followed by a large number of mediations, mediation became, for the first time, an integral part of the Lithuanian legal system. Subsequent efforts to institutionalise mediation have not resulted in major changes but have served as a basis for consolidating the authorities and establishing the development of mediation as one of the strategic goals of the state. As a result, the Law on Mediation was adopted, which became a landmark for the establishment of mediation in Lithuania. Alongside it, the profession of mediator was officially recognised and qualification requirements were set for individuals willing to become mediators. Nowadays, in Lithuania, judicial mediation coexists with non-judicial mediation forming a sustainable and unified mediation system.

The Formation of the Profession of Mediator in Lithuania

Lithuanian Approach towards the Regulation of Mediators' Activities

Amidst the debate on regulating the practice of mediation (Carrel & Adrian 2017: 24), two main lines of reasoning can be distinguished as to why the profession needs to be regulated. One of them is to protect consumers by creating certain standards for the profession, while the other relates to the intention to promote the use of mediation by providing it legitimacy, credibility and internal resilience (Caser & Ramos 2019: 526). Paragraph 7 of the Mediation Directive also stipulates that the development of a legal framework addressing the main aspects of civil procedure is aimed to 'promote further the use of mediation and ensure that parties having recourse to mediation can rely on a predictable legal framework'. Boon et al. (2007: 34) had added one more argument typically deployed in favour of regulating mediation – the exclusion of unscrupulous, unethical and incompetent practitioners.

Academics also recognise the weaknesses of regulating mediation. Prematurely regulating it could stifle the development of this institution by aligning it too closely with the rule-bound justice system it aims to supplement (Boon et al. 2007: 35). Additionally, regulation could lead to a homogenised, 'one-size-fits-all' approach, undermining the flexibility of mediation and its adaptability to the unique needs of the parties and to the complexities of the disputes it handles (Boon et al. 2007: 35).

Observing how the practice of mediation is moving towards the formation of an autonomous profession worldwide (Kovach 2003: 277), Europe is witnessing yet another trend towards a more extensive and more intensive regulation of mediators (Steffek 2012: 13). While several decades ago the academic literature was devoted to the question of whether and why to regulate mediators, the fundamental question raised lately is what form of regulation should be used. Regulation of mediation is a vivid process rather than a result. Alexander analysed regulation of mediation not as a static and formalistic, but rather as a 'living framework', which, among other goals, allows both policymakers and practitioners to balance the necessity for rigid regulation leaving enough space for procedural flexibility and cultural agility (Alexander 2020: 1).

According to Alexander (2020: 6), four main categories of regulatory form associated with mediation can be distinguished: (1) market/contract regulation; (2) industry/institutional/court regulation; (3) regulation through jurisprudence/case law and (4) legislative regulation. Looking at how the institutionalisation of mediation evolved in Lithuania, one can exactly observe a changing and gradually intensifying regulatory process. Since 2005, when mediation was first introduced in Lithuania, a combination of the categories of market regulation and judicial regulation has prevailed. Individuals started to offer mediation services which were not regulated in any form and mostly relied on the experience of foreign countries' (Tvaronavičienė & Uscila 2021: 87). A pilot project of mediation, based on the experience of Quebec, Canada, became a genuine precursor for the emergence of judicial mediation in Lithuania. A model of court regulation began to emerge alongside judicial mediation initiatives, which was followed by the creation of the Judicial Mediation Rules (2018) and the adoption of the statute of court mediator and the Rules of Procedure for granting the status of mediator to individuals and revoking it (2014). Thus, the judges were the first mediators who gained an actual opportunity to practice in Lithuania due to the court regulatory model, and the volume of judicial mediation in Lithuania has been gradually increasing, until recent years when a stagnation of judicial mediation was observed (Kaminskienė et al. 2023: 217).

The Law on Conciliatory Mediation (2008) was the first attempt to move from a market/court regulatory model to legislative regulation. However, while this step was supposed to be the first attempt to institutionalise mediation in Lithuania, it is now viewed as the result of 'soft regulation', which has failed to inspire any significant progress in the acceptance of mediation, instead allowing mediation to develop like a neglected plant (Tvaronavičienė et al. 2022: 71). Formally, mediation became part of the legal system in Lithuania; however, an awareness has emerged that enormous efforts are needed to transform outmoded dispute resolution culture processes in practice (Tvaronavičienė et al. 2022: 69) in order to promote the development of mediation and the establishment and recognition of the profession of mediator in Lithuania.

Mediation has been institutionalised at the highest level and fully transferred to the legislative regulation model with the adoption of the new version of the Law on Mediation (2017). The necessity to shift to a higher regulatory density was driven by the need to protect consumers by creating professional standards and aimed to promote mediation by providing it with legitimacy, credibility and internal resilience, as well as by employing procedural incentivising measures. Thus, the institutionalisation of mediation in Lithuania was accompanied by the professionalisation of the profession of mediator.

The only regulatory form that has not yet been developed in Lithuania is regulation through jurisprudence or case law. Certainly, this is also because Lithuania is one of the Continental systems where jurisprudence is a source for the creation of objective law, unlike the Anglo-Saxon legal system, where judicial precedents form the principal source of law (Tella 2011: 1). However, courts are empowered to influence the development of mediation practice, for example by deviating from the standard rule on the allocation of litigation costs if a party uses mediation in bad faith or by exercising the discretion to refer the parties to mandatory judicial mediation. However, for the time being, these are rather occasional cases that are rarer than the standard practice.

Therefore, the institutionalisation of mediation in Lithuania has undergone all four stages of a gradually intensifying regulatory process. Over the past two decades, the development of mediation in Lithuania has evolved from a combined market- and court-based regulation to comprehensive legislative regulation. This shift has led to increased oversight of both mediation practices and the mediator profession, including, inter alia, emerging case law concerning mediators' activities and the evolving practice of mediation.

Mediation as a Profession in Lithuania

Mediation is becoming increasingly integrated into the legal systems of many countries (Boon et al. 2007: 36). Alongside the increasing popularity of the amicable dispute resolution method, the practice of mediation is starting to encompass more aspects of 'professionalism' and is moving towards being recognised as an independent profession (Kovach 2003: 277).

The most obvious way to define a profession would be to formally recognise it in legislation. Article 2 of the Law of Mediation stipulates that mediation, with a few exceptions, shall be considered a professional activity.

The exceptions include judicial mediation carried out by judges and out-of-court mediation carried out by the Administrative Disputes Commission of Lithuania and members of its territorial units. Judicial mediation in Lithuania may be provided both by judge mediators and by other mediators included in the List of Mediators. Meanwhile, out-of-court mediation may be conducted only by a mediator selected from the List of Mediators, but not by a judge. Thus, although judges in Lithuania are granted the right to mediate in a judicial mediation, the practice of mediation by judges is not considered a separate professional activity, but rather an integral part of the professional activity of a judge, which they may exercise voluntarily. Similarly, the activity of the members of the Administrative Disputes Commission of Lithuania is also considered one of their functions which they may provide selectively. Meanwhile, the activities of other individuals registered on the List of Mediators are recognised in Lithuania as a profession.

However, the literature provides a much broader perspective, which includes not only the formal but also the substantive features which make a particular activity a distinct profession. According to Crowe (2017: 5), an activity can be considered a profession when (1) there is institutional education and training, (2) there is a body of experts in the field, (3) professional licensing is in place, (4) the activity is independent of other professions, (5) there is a code of ethics and (6) there is peer-to-peer accountability. Blanco (2023: 1543) has outlined very similar elements concerning the definition of a profession: (1) specialist body of knowledge and practical skills; (2) professional associations; (3) regulated activity and a code of conduct; (4) professional identity; (5) permanent activity and source of remuneration and (6) recognised social function. Further assessment of whether mediation can be considered a profession in Lithuania shall be carried out using the aforementioned criteria.

Specialist body of knowledge and practical skills

The scientific literature continues to underline the lack of worldwide unified standards at a supranational level for mediators' qualifications. A fairly similar situation is observed at the level of the EU. The first attempt to introduce generalised requirements for mediators at EU level was the adoption of the European Code of Conduct of Mediators (hereinafter 'the Code') in 2004 and later, in 2008, The Mediation Directive obliging the Member States to encourage the initial and further training of mediators in order to ensure that mediation is conducted in an effective, impartial and competent way in relation to the parties. As previously mentioned, the provisions of the Mediation Directive offer different regulatory approaches, leaving the regulation of mediators' training and quality control mechanisms exclusively to the discretion of Member States in more aspirational rather than obligatory terms. Article 4 of the Mediation Directive envisages that Member States should encourage training of mediators and the introduction of effective quality control mechanisms but without specifying the means by which countries should do so. This consequently led EU Member States to employ different regulatory approaches choosing between a high regulatory density, few legislative stimuli and selective regulation (Steffek 2012: 15). In line with the revised Law on Mediation Law, Lithuania has opted for a high regulatory density providing, among other things, an establishment of the official List of Mediators, as well as qualification requirements for ongoing professional development.

Individuals willing to be entered on the List of Mediators must hold a university degree, in any field of study, complete at least 40 academic hours of training in mediation, pass a Mediators' Qualification Exam (hereinafter 'the Exam') and meet the requirements for being considered a person with a good reputation. It is true that some professions, mainly the legal ones, are eligible for exemptions to be included on the List of Mediators. For example, judges who have 3 years of judicial experience have to complete only 16 hours of initial training and are exempted from passing the Exam. Advocates, plaintiffs and notaries who have 3 years of professional experience are mandated to participate in 40 hours of initial mediation training but are exempted from passing the Exam. Finally, persons holding a doctoral degree in social sciences who have completed training in mediation lasting at least 100 academic hours, 3 years before applying for entry on the List of Mediators are exempted from both initial mediation training and the Exam.

The Exam consists of two parts: a written part, which tests a person's theoretical knowledge of mediation and conflict resolution, and an oral part, which tests a person's ability to apply their theoretical knowledge and skills in practice during a mediation simulation. The fact that the rate of success in passing the Exam is from 50% to 75% (Tvaronavičienė & Uscila 2021: 99) is a sign that the threshold for individuals wishing to enter the mediation field has become quite high, and a guarantee that individuals who do not have, or do not yet have, sufficient knowledge and skills to perform mediation will not be eligible to practice it. On the one hand, the above-mentioned exemption of some individuals was timely and necessary considering the intended impact of the Law on Mediation on promoting the use of mediation, which also implies the necessity to ensure a sufficient number of mediators to provide services. However, in the long perspective, these provisions only aroused opposition in the mediators' community and were considered to be anything but fair to mediators and non-legal professions, as it favoured some individuals to be included in the List of Mediators, regardless of whether they actually have the knowledge and competence to mediate. The requirements for completing courses under continuous professional development every 5 years were also imposed. Mediators on the List of Mediators must submit documentary evidence that they have completed at least 20 academic hours of mediation training during that period. These requirements will be made stricter as of the 1st January 2025 with the new wording of the Law on Mediation (2024), which shall be explored in detail in Chapter XI.

Thus, Lithuania has defined explicit and strict qualification requirements for individuals seeking to become mediators and has established a precise scope of knowledge and competences which are tested in the form of a two-level exam. The existing exemptions from the requirement to be included in the List of Mediators in Lithuania pose a challenge for some individuals, as they not only create unequal opportunities to become a mediator but also allow for some individuals to enter the profession of mediation without having the necessary knowledge and skills, thus risking the credibility of the profession of in the society.

Professional associations

The Law on Mediation created a comprehensive system of governance for mediation, with responsibilities divided among five different entities responsible for the proper functioning of the mediation system in Lithuania: the Ministry of Justice of the Republic of Lithuania, responsible for drafting legal acts governing mediation and supervising their implementation, the

Judicial Council, responsible for establishing the procedure for organising and conducting as well as monitoring judicial mediation, SGLAS, administering the List of Mediators and mandatory mediation services funded by the State organising a qualifying exam for mediators, the Chairperson of the Administrative Disputes Commission of Lithuania, administering out-of-court mediation in the Administrative Disputes Commission of Lithuania and its territorial divisions and Mediation Co-ordination Council, responsible for submitting proposals relating to the improvement of legal regulation and practical application as well as the development of mediation.

In addition to these institutions responsible for the efficient functioning of the mediation system in Lithuania, the Law on Mediation also envisaged an additional institution, the Commission for Mediator Performance Assessment (hereinafter 'the Commission'), which was assigned the task of handling complaints regarding the activities of mediators and assessing the performance of mediators.

Alongside the establishment of the official entities governing mediation, a voluntary association of mediators was established in Lithuania. Lithuanian Chamber of Mediators (hereinafter 'the Chamber') was established in 2017 by a group of private mediators and until the latest amendments acted as a non-governmental organisation with a judicial form of association. From 2017 to 2024, this organisation was gradually gaining the trust of Lithuanian mediators and by the 1st of August 2024 had already united more than 120 practising mediators. The activities of this organisation mostly were concentrated on community building, professional qualification development and social impact through the dissemination of mediation and its advocacy in Lithuania. One of the main strategic fields of activity of this organisation was the establishment and nurturing of strong social partnership relations with state institutions, such as the Ministry of Justice, the National Court Administration, and so on. From 2019, the delegates of the Chamber were invited to join the newly formed Mediation Coordination Council and Commissions of Assessment of Mediators and Mediators' Qualification Exam. Participation of the representatives of the organisations that bring together mediators in the activities of these inter-institutional bodies, were foreseen by the Law on Mediation edition of 13 June 2017, which entered into force on 1 January 2019. Still, regardless of the activeness of the Chamber and strong social partnership with governance, until June 2024 the Law on Mediation did not envisage any specific functions of this organisation leaving it out of the official mediation management structure, thus maintaining its importance and influence on decision making.

To conclude, Lithuania not only has a solid and important association of mediators, but also has a comprehensive system of mediation management entities responsible for the proper functioning of the mediation system. The downside of this model results from different functions delegated to separate institutions, thus creating challenges for timely and effective cooperation regarding the development of mediation and reaction to the challenges arising in practice.

Regulated activity and a code of conduct

Regulating the ethical conduct of mediators is a matter of establishing guidelines for action rather than precise instructions. Lithuania is among the countries that have mandated by statute mediators providing services within the jurisdiction to mandatorily comply with the provisions of the Code. Although code of ethics for mediators are often only of a recommendatory nature, paradoxically, some important aspects of mediation, such as the definition of mediators' impartiality and neutrality, are much better regulated in the Code than in the Law on Mediation. Among other things, the Law on Mediation established civil liability and disciplinary liability for activities that violate the provisions of the Law on Mediation or the Code. The Commission handling complaints from individuals, if it finds that a mediator has violated the provisions of the Law on Mediation or the Code, has the right to sanction the mediator with a private or public warning or to remove the mediator from the List of Mediators.

To sum up, in Lithuania, mediators' activities are regulated not only by the provisions of the Law on Mediation but also by a code of ethics, which is granted statutory power and may subject a mediator to disciplinary liability for non-compliance with it.

Permanent activity and source of remuneration

The Ex-post evaluation of the impact of the legal regulation of mandatory mediation in family disputes (2022) (hereinafter 'the *Ex-post* evaluation')

Table 1: Data on the implementation of mandatory family mediation in Lithuania in 2020–2023 according to the SGLAS*

Information about mediation	2020	2021	2022	2023
Total number of requests for mandatory mediation	6,789	6,369	7,345	8,469
Decisions taken to appoint a mediator	2,751	2,838	3,183	3,859
Completed mediations under appointments by the SGLAS	1,983	2,900	3,035	3,636
Disputes settled amicably	1,045	1,587	1,713	1,972
Settlement rate %	53	55	56	54

*State Guaranteed Legal Aid Service.

conducted in 2022 revealed that the introduction of mandatory mediation in family disputes has prompted more people to resolve disputes amicably. This has been confirmed by the statistics on mediation provided by the SGLAS for the fourth year in a row (see Table 1). The total number of requests for mandatory mediation continues to increase by 15% each year[3], with an overall increase of 25% in 4 years. The number of mediations appointed by the SGLAS has also increased up to 40% during the 4-year period, which clearly indicates that, despite the liberal legal imperative to only initiate mediation, individuals are becoming more likely to resolve their disputes with the help of a neutral mediator. The constant increase in the number of settlements reached in mediation compared to completed mediation proceedings and the continuing stable settlement rate of 55% also confirms that the determination of the legislator to apply a more explicit regulatory framework to promote the use of mediation has succeeded in Lithuania. Moreover, the introduction of mandatory family mediation has created the preconditions not just for the formal recognition of mediation as a profession in the legislation, but also for the actual emergence of a profession. Nearly 40% of mediators that participated in the *Ex-post* evaluation surveys stated that mandatory mediation

3 Except in 2021, when the number of requests for mandatory mediation to the SGLAS slightly decreased, most likely due to the limitations of the COVID-19 pandemic prevailing during that period.

is the only stable area to practice, and only due to the initiatives taken by the State aimed to create a stable demand for such services.

A systematic assessment of the data from the *Ex-post* evaluation suggests that not only the mandatory provisions but also the new wording of the Law on Mediation have encouraged the development of the mediation profession in Lithuania and created preconditions for its actual practice. The majority of individuals (641) were registered on the List of Mediators after entry into force of the Law on Mediation which stipulated that only the individuals included in the List of Mediators are allowed to provide mediation services. Currently, there are 763 mediators on the list. While some mediators were previously included in the Court's List of Mediators, a large number of the mediators surveyed confirmed that they only started to provide mediation services after the Law on Mediation came into force and that the possibility to practice mediation privately only emerged after the introduction of mandatory family mediation provisions.

Despite indicated positive tendencies towards the recognition of the profession of mediator, 94% of individuals perceive mediation as their additional and not main profession, which means that the supply of mediation services in Lithuania continues to significantly exceed the demand. In the Ex-post evaluation, only a small number of mediators indicated that mediation is their full-time activity. Thus, although the legislative initiatives to institutionalise mediation by adopting mandatory mediation provisions and to provide more detailed regulation of the profession of mediator are to be considered a success, the analysis of the current status and the challenges of the existing legal framework have highlighted the necessity to keep looking for more targeted measures to encourage the development of mediation in Lithuania, thus creating favourable conditions for the recognition of this profession.

It has already been mentioned that to promote the use of mediation, the State provides the possibility for all persons, regardless of their status and level of income, to obtain 4 hours of family mediation free of charge, by reimbursing the mediators who conclude a contract with the SGLAS the costs of 4 hours of conducted mediation and also 1 hour for mediation preparation and the formalisation of the mediation results, from the State budget. Following the entry into force of the Law on Mediation in 2019, the basic hourly rate for mediation has been increased from €13 to €25 in 2024 (Ex post evaluation 2022: 263). While there is no official data on average hourly rates for private mediation, it is clear that the fees provided by the SGLAS are considerably lower than the average in the private market. The fact that the provisions on mandatory mediation have created a real opportunity for mediators in Lithuania to practise mediation and generate income from it should be viewed positively. However, this practice has also a downside, as the willingness of individuals to pay for mediation services is decreasing, thus stifling the development of private mediation practice.

Professional Identity

Marta Blanco (2023: 1544) has stated that even if the above-mentioned elements of mediator's profession are successfully achieved, the lack of a professional identity is fairly common for this profession. This goes beyond a lack of recognition of this profession among groups of legal professionals (such as lawyers, psychologists or social workers), but also because individuals are unable to practise mediation due to a lack of demand and remuneration for such services. Due to the existing regulation of mediation in Lithuania, these challenges have at least partially been overcome for mediators interested in practising family mediation. Meanwhile, those willing to practice as mediators in other areas, such as mediating workplace, business or medical disputes, still struggle to achieve this.

Recognised social function is mainly related to the recognition of a profession as independent among other professionals and clients. On one hand, lawyers and other professions, such as psychologists and social workers, recognise the work of mediators, as they represent a significant group on the List of Mediators. On the other hand, many of these professionals practice mediation only as a secondary activity and only in rare cases become full-time mediators thus confirming that this profession is not yet considered independent. Possibly, this perception has led mediators to start raising their voices about the delegation of the mediators' self-government to the Lithuanian Chamber of Mediators hoping that this organisation would be the most interested in developing the policy of mediation and, therefore, in the mediators' profession, as well as in unifying mediators to increase the credibility of the profession.

To conclude, mediation is considered as a separate profession both formally and informally. The Law on Mediation stipulates that mediation is a professional activity, except for mediation provided by judges or members of the Administrative Disputes Commission of Lithuania. Evaluating informal elements for defining a particular profession, most of the criteria are also met in Lithuania due to the explicit regulation envisaged in the Law on Mediation setting the requirements for individuals seeking to provide mediation services, as well as the creation of the official List of Mediators, outlining mediators' disciplinary liability and compliance with the Code of Ethics, clarifying institutional roles in mediation administration and establishing the Lithuanian Chamber of Mediators. However, the issues related to professional identity and recognised social function are still challenging, as the profession of mediator is on one hand attractive for other professionals, such as lawyers or psychologists, but at the same time, the functions of mediators are still hard to distinguish from the activities of these professionals and most of them are engaging in two professions rather than choosing one. The possibility for a permanent activity and source of remuneration is implemented only partly mainly due to the implementation of the mandatory mediation requirements for future litigants. However, the field of private practice and the possibility for mediators to practice in other areas than family mediation is still unexploited and the supply of these services is significantly higher that the demand.

Latest Amendments of the Law on Mediation: Further Development of the Profession of Mediator

Despite the fact that the already mentioned *Ex post* evaluation (2022: 24) focused on the estimation of the impact of mandatory mediation in family disputes on the Lithuanian legal system, this research aimed as well to measure the effectiveness of the existing legal regulation on mediation, especially in relation to the profession mediator. No doubly, mandatory mediation in family disputes established grounds for the quick formation of the profession, thus all regulatory powers were vested in the hands of public authorities. One of the recommendations for public policymakers in the field of justice of *Ex post* evaluation was to provide the functions of the Chamber in the field of mediation management by law.

The recommendation of *Ex post* evaluation (2022: 5) provides for the Chamber certain functions in mediation management structure was based on insights that despite of high level of institutionalisation of mediation in Lithuania from 2019, the Lithuanian system of mediation services still needs to be developed. Systematic analyses of Ex-post evaluation results firstly showed the necessity to gather more statistical data in regard to out-of-court mediations which are financed by the parties to a dispute and their results, which is necessary for evaluating the real cost–benefit balance of applying mediation to compare with classical litigation in courts. Second, the results of quantitative analyses of the opinion of the parties in regard to the quality of mediator's services showed the necessity to develop the quality of mediation services. Third, the survey conducted among mediators has also revealed the high demand for further professional training for mediators. In addition to the Ex-post evaluation insights, it must be said that while mandatory mediation in family disputes increased in numbers and had a high success rate, other fields of dispute, where mediation as well can be beneficial both to the parties to the dispute and to the state, the progress was rather slow.

Above mentioned insights from the Ex-post evaluation and strong social partnership based on trust and mutual recognition between the Ministry of Justice and the Chamber created a presumption of the inclusion of the Chamber in mediation management entities and the assignment of specific functions to them by law. After long mutual discussions on the possible role of the Chamber in the management of the mediation, the draft of required amendments of the Law on Mediation was prepared and agreed inter-institutionally. This draft of the amendments to the Law inspired many discussions in the community of mediators. Even though exercising self-governance by the profession of mediators was the main strategic goal of the Chamber from the day of its establishment, upcoming changes raised doubts in regard of the abilities of the organisation to fulfil its planned functions. One of the main doubts was related to the capacity of the association to bear the costs of self-government implementation without receiving any direct financial grants from the state. In principle, the responsibility for the implementation of self-government will have to be assumed by the members of the Chamber, which means that their financial contribution, i.e. the annual membership fee will increase significantly. The implementation of new functions requires additional human resources, premises, organisational equipment, and other costs which will have to be covered by the members of this organisation. Also, part of the mediators who are practising this profession along their role as attorneys at law, notaries, psychologists etc., did not support the new functions related to self-governance because for them it meant assuming the self-management costs of two professions, which would directly reduce their income and force them to choose one, more profitable profession. Debates have also continued on the topic of balancing the functions of the Ministry of Justice and the Chamber as there were doubts about the real character of the suggested balance of powers as formal because still the main decisions in regard to the mediation system remained vested in the hands of the Ministry of Justice. Debates lasted more than half a year, but common ground has finally been found.

On 13 June 2024, the Seimas adopted the Law on the Amendment of Articles 3, 4, 5, 6, 7, 8, 9, 10, 11, 15, 17, 20, 21, 22, 23, 26, 28 and 29 of the Law on Mediation of the Republic of Lithuania and supplementing it with Article 31 (hereinafter 'the Law on Amendment'). According to the Minister of Justice of the Republic of Lithuania Ewelina Dobrowolska, 'This legislative initiative will not only make it possible to ensure a more efficient mediation process and better quality of mediation services, but also to create even better conditions for the peaceful resolution of disputes through mediation' (Ministry of Justice 2024). The Law on Amendment first establishes the Chamber as one of the subjects of mediation management by providing it with specific functions. Second, it provides for fundamental changes in the implementation of a state-funded mandatory mediation model. Third, it establishes other important changes aimed at increasing the quality of mediation services and increasing trust in this institution in society.

As this article aims to provide a brief review of the development of the profession of mediator in Lithuania, it is worth analysing in more detail the changes related to the status of the Chamber, mandatory mediation model and requirements for entering the profession of mediator as well as remaining in this profession.

Lithuanian Chamber of Mediators as One of Mediation Management Institutions

Self-governance of Lithuanian mediators was officially announced by the adoption of the Law on Amendment. Part I of the Law on Mediation of June 2024 was amended by adding the new Article 3 to it.[1] The first part of it states that 'Self-government of mediators is appointed by the Lithuanian Chamber of Mediators'. In addition to the specific new functions listed above, the legislator also establishes the mandatory membership of practising mediators in the Chamber. The fourth part of the article stipulates that 'Each mediator who is included in the List of Mediators of the Republic of Lithuania, with the exception of mediators, who are judges, is a member of the Lithuanian Chamber of Mediators'. It should be remembered that in Lithuania the development of mediation has been strongly supported by the judiciary and judges, some of whom have been working as mediators in court-connected mediation since 2005, and may be applied in all civil and administrative disputes which they are allowed to settle (Tvaronavičienė et al. 221: 635).

The Law on Amendment envisages a new mediation management structure from the beginning of 2025. The functions related to the administration of the mediators' profession, which currently are vested in the hands of SGLAS, will be transferred to the Chamber (Table 2).

Table 2: The new functions of the Lithuanian Chamber of Mediators from 2025

New functions of the Lithuanian Chamber of Mediators from 2025
Compiling and maintaining the List of Mediators of the Republic of Lithuania
Organising the qualification exam for mediators
Organising mediators' qualification improvement and its supervision, and processing data on it
Data processing of mediators' annual activity reports on completed mediations
Organising and implementing the assessment of mediators' activities
Applying measures to unify the practice of mediators
Representing and protecting the interests of mediators who are members of the Lithuanian Chamber of Mediators in state institutions, foreign states, international and other organisations
Public education on mediation issues
Other functions defined in the Law on Mediation and other legal acts

To sum up, the self-governance of Lithuanian mediators from 2025 will be implemented by the Chamber, which will be responsible for administering the List of Mediators, including organising the qualification exam and further improvement of mediators' qualifications, assessment of mediators' activities and setting up the guidelines of unified mediators' practice, collecting reports and processing data on completed mediations, representing members and protecting their interests and promoting mediation in society. All mediators who are currently in the List of Mediators will be obliged to the membership of the Chamber.

Changes in the State-Funded Mandatory Mediation Model

The Law on Amendment brings an important change in the State-funded model of mandatory mediation. Mandatory mediation in the private scheme which is paid by the parties to the dispute remains unchanged (Tvaronavičienė & Intė 2021: 62). As of 2025, state-funded mediation hours in the mandatory mediation scheme will be regulated by a government ruling rather than by the Law on Mediation. This amendment is expected to allow for more flexibility in responding to changes and faster improvements to the existing funding scheme. The Ministry of Justice plans to set 8 (instead of the 6 currently allocated) hours paid from the state budget funds for conducting mediation (2024). This increase in the number of state-funded hours as the maximum remuneration for the mediator was driven by the results of the Ex-post evaluation, which clearly noted that resolving family disputes through mediation is more time-consuming and that disputants are often reluctant to continue mediation beyond 6 hours as they would have to bear the cost on their own. Increasing the number of state-funded hours from 6 to 8 is also strongly related to the new functions of mediators, assigned to them by the Law on Amendment from 1st September 2024. These new functions relate to the earlier appointment of mediators in family mediation cases and their mandate to inform the other party of the beginning of the mandatory mediation process, to encourage them to participate in it and to counter their resistance to mediate.

The results of the Ex-post evaluation revealed that about 50% of the mandatory mediation processes which are initiated annually are finished at their initial stage because, despite the request made by one party, the other party to the dispute refuses to participate in mandatory mediation or does not respond within the prescribed time limit. It was then suggested to review the existing model of state-funded mandatory mediation as the need to search for non-formal, proximate to a disputant's methods to better inform them about the benefits of mediation and encourage them to take part in it. Parties to the dispute, attorneys at law, who were taking part in surveys and interviews declared that one of the main reasons why people refuse to take part in mandatory mediation in family disputes is a lack of information about the mediation process and a lack of courage to enter such a process which remains a social novelty in Lithuania. Official invitations provided by the SGLAS often look too formal, in some cases even cause anxiety in people, and generally rarely encourage them to seek more information on how the mediation process offered and funded by the state can benefit them.

Currently, mandatory state-funded mediation in Lithuania follows these steps:

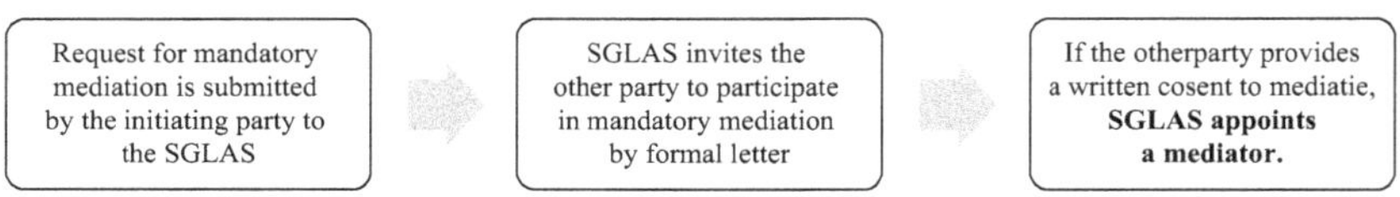

From 1st September 2024, when relevant articles of the Law on Amendment will come into force, the model will differ as a mediator will be appointed earlier:

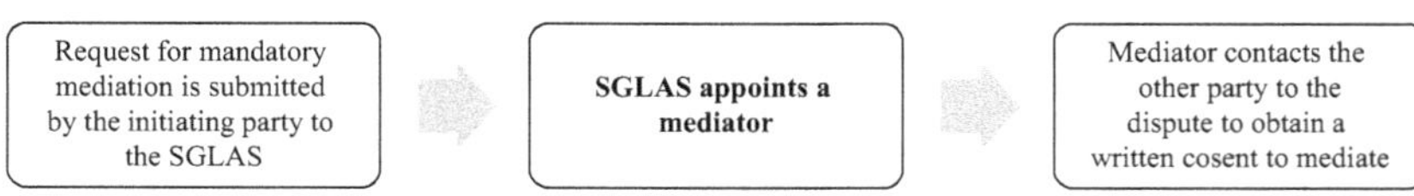

It is expected that this change (appointing a mediator earlier) will result in a less formal, more client-oriented attitude towards the disputants, which will be beneficial for the quicker and more effective establishment of trust between the parties and the mediator. The mediator meeting the parties in person will be able to introduce mediation, outline its advantages and potential benefits in a particular case, and address any questions the parties may have. It is expected that this will increase the number of people entering mediation, as mediators are believed to be more encouraging for people to engage in mandatory mediation than formal letters from state authorities. These changes will entail significant responsibilities for mediators and will increase their capacity to overcome resistance to mediation by the disputants.

Increasing the requirements for the mediators' initial training and further qualification development

The recognition of the profession of mediator as independent and entrusting the appointment of self-government of mediators to the Chamber has also raised the expectation of the Lithuanian mediators' community that the legal regulations related to the entry into the profession of mediator and presence in it will be rediscussed. Long-lasting debates with the Ministry of Justice as the main state institution in the mediation management model ended with a compromise, related to a certain increase in the required hours of mediators' basic training and qualification improvement. Currently, a person who is willing to be enrolled in the List of Mediators, beyond the fulfilment of other requirements (university degree, impeccable reputation, passing qualification exam) must attend initial mediation training of at least 40 academic hours. The Law on Amendment increases the duration of initial mediation training from 40 hours to 48 hours. Moreover, every mediator who is enrolled in the List of Mediators was obliged to participate every 5 years in further qualification improvement mediation training not shorter than 20 hours and present to the SGLAS a relevant confirmation. Law on Amendments changes this provision and establishes a requirement for every mediator (except mediator judges, as they have separate rules on further qualification development) to attend mediation training as their further qualification development for not less than 24 hours and submit proof of it (certifications) to the Chamber every 3 years. This means that the requirements for further qualification improvement of the mediator were doubled and approximately every year from 2025, each mediator is expected to have not 4, but 8 hours of mediation-related trainings (until 2025, 20 hours every 5 years, from 2025 – 24 hours every 3 years).

Several insights about the possible challenges in implementing the self-governance of mediators

The manifestation of the principle of independence of the profession and ensuring the functioning of self-government bodies is to guarantee the freedom of their activities within the law and its implementation in practice (Kovtun et al. 2022: 609). Self-governance always is related not only to rights and better opportunities to implement it but also to responsibilities and duties, which sometimes may be difficult to fulfil.

The first challenge, which the Chamber will have to overcome is operational funding. Self-governance of the mediators, just as the self-governance of other professions in Lithuania (e.g. the BAR association, Chambers of Notaries, Chamber of Bailiffs, Council of Architects, etc.), depends financially on its members' contributions and additional activities or services, rather than on public funding. Acquiring official functions and becoming an organisation which implements self-governance means the increase in the annual membership fee and the necessity to find ways to secure the financial well-being of the organisation.

Second, higher annual membership fees may result in a decreasing number of members on the one hand. On the other hand, they may serve as a tool in the cleansing of mediators' activities. Currently, most Lithuanian mediators perceive mediation only as their part-time activity and normally practise it along with another profession. Having in mind that each professional activity requires certain dedication and financial investments towards constant improvement of qualifications, there is a high risk that the current number of mediators who are enlisted in the List of Mediators will decrease. Whilst this may reduce the supply of mediation services, it may also serve to cleanse the activities of mediators and encourage qualified mediators to choose this profession as a full-time occupation (leaving other professions behind).

Third, the proposed model of self-governance of the profession is not exhaustive. There are a lot of specific safeguards vested in the hands of state bodies that require ongoing social partnership and collaboration. This can also be seen as a challenge as constant changes in political powers, their priorities and objectives for the development of the legal framework may be unconducive to mediation as has been the case so far. Mediators' self-governance body should be always ready for active advocacy of mediation and targeted publicity activities related to the development of mediation in Lithuania.

Fourth, self-governance of the profession requires unifying the mediation practice, which may also be challenging. Mediation is a flexible and agile process, which is carried out by various professionals with different educational backgrounds, following and accepting different mediation styles, trained by different mediation schools in Lithuania and abroad. Different approaches to the process will create challenges in searching for unified standards as well as in assessing the activities of mediators through the process of the investigation of complaints filed by the parties to a dispute. In addition, it should be said long-standing mediators might resist any attempts to change their practice or introduce a new standard. The management of changes requires exceptional knowledge and skills, along with an adequate level of preparation.

Fifth, as the number of hours of required initial and additional mediation training increases, the demand for high-quality mediation training is rising. Currently, there is no certification system for training centres, and the quality of the training provided in mediation and related areas is completely uncontrolled. This creates a risk that the increased number of training hours will not result in better qualification of the mediators; thus the problem will remain unsolved.

Sixth, as people are entering the mediator's profession from different educational backgrounds and mostly are closely related with other professions, there is a risk of constant conflicts of interest within the organisation. This creates a challenge for the future management bodies of the Chamber, as it will require permanent negotiations and dialogue with members who have different interests.

Finally, the profession of mediator in Lithuania (the same as in all Central Europe) is relatively new and still evolving. Self-governance in addition to all previously mentioned functions takes over the responsibility of creating the image of the mediator in society and the duty to build trust not only in self-governance but also in the whole profession as well. This duty also relates to further education of society, which is essential for the development of mediation in country. This will require not only human but also financial resources, which the Lithuanian Chamber of Mediators will have to obtain independently, without relying on state support (which is unlikely to happen), but also trying to become competitive in national and international project competitions and in collaboration with business enterprises.

These are only a few preliminary insights regarding possible challenges in the implementation of effective self-governance of mediators. Tackling these issues will require a collaborative approach and strong partnership with state institutions, judiciary, mediators and society. The effectiveness of mediators' self-governance can be achieved not only by formal changes in legislation, recognising certain bodies as an institution implementing it, but also by developing a clear strategy, allocating adequate resources, ensuring transparency and fostering a culture of constant dialogue that balances the different interests for the sake of social understanding and coexistence.

Summary

The institutionalisation of mediation in Lithuania has been a gradual and continuous process, which has not only created a solid foundation for the development of mediation, but also contributed to the actual recognition of the profession of mediator. Over two decades, significant progress has been made towards creating a solid legal framework for mediation, with an emphasis on improving access to mediation and recognition of the professional status of mediators. Thus, alongside the institutionalisation of mediation, efforts have been made to improve mediation practices and enhance the quality of services provided.

The developments in the Lithuanian legal system, in particular amendments to the Law on Mediation, reflect the commitment to create a favourable environment for mediation as an integral part of the legal system, especially in family disputes, and to strengthen public confidence in the mediation process, in particular, through establishing clear qualification requirements for individuals to become mediators and remain in the profession and creating a real opportunity to practise and generate income from this activity in the chosen area.

The Ex-post evaluation has played a crucial role in revealing key areas for improvement, inter alia, such as the importance of high-quality training for mediators, and emphasising the necessity of continuous professional development and overcoming the shortcomings of the existing model of mandatory family mediation, mainly related to the excessively formalised mediation initiation phase. These findings prompted the recent amendments to the Law on Mediation, which is likely to inspire significant evolution in the field of developing the mediation profession in Lithuania. They are mainly aimed at solidifying the role of the Lithuanian Chamber of Mediators as a central institution in the self-governance of the profession. Furthermore, the changes enhance the state-funded mandatory mediation model and raise the training and qualification requirements for mediators.

These comprehensive reforms in the institutionalisation of mediation demonstrate a gradual shift towards a more integrated and professional mediation system, aiming to enhance the quality and accessibility of mediation services across the country by strengthening the public recognition and identity of the profession. Self-governance for mediators is a positive development, laying a firm foundation for the recognition and development of the profession of mediator, yet like any change, it poses a number of challenges. These are mainly related to ensuring funding for operational activities, aligning public scrutiny and cooperation with changing political authorities, unifying the various mediation practices, ensuring that highly qualified specialists enter the profession and remain in it, and developing the profession's image and credibility in a relatively new field that will certainly require further cooperation, a clear strategy, adequate resources and continuous dialogue with all stakeholders.

Bibliography

'A report on the activity of the Judicial Mediation Commission in 2022,' *Lietuvos Teismai*, <https://www.teismai.lt/data/public/uploads/2023/04/teismines-mediacijos-komisijos-2022-m.-veiklos-ataskaita.pdf>, accessed 4 August 2024.

'The Ex post evaluation report on the impact of the current legal framework for mandatory mediation in family disputes', *STRATA*, 2022, <https://strata.gov.lt/wp-content/uploads/2024/01/Privalomosios-mediacijos-seimos-gincuose-teisinio-reguliavimo-poveikio-ex-post-vertinimas.pdf>, accessed 1 August 2024.

Alexander, Nadja Marie (2020). 'Through the Looking Glass: Exploring the Regulatory-Ethical Ecosystem for Mediation', *Singapore Management University School of Law Research Paper* No. 26/2020, pp. 2–20.

Andrea Maia (2024). 'The Importance of Mediation in ESG: Promoting Sustainability in Corporations'. Kluwer Mediation Blog, <https://mediationblog.kluwerarbitration.com/2024/03/08/the-importance-of-mediation-in-esg-promoting-sustainability-in-corporations/>, accessed 4 August 2024.

Blanco, Marta (2023). 'Is Mediation a Profession? Views of Professionals and Trainers from an International Perspective,' *International Social Work*, 66 (5), 1542–1553.

Boon, Andrew, Earle, Richard and Whyte, Avis (2007). 'Regulating Mediators?', *Legal Ethics*, 10 (1), 26–50.

Carrel, Alyson and Adrian, Lin (2017). 'Regulating Mediator Practice', *Dispute Resolution Magazine*, 24 (1), 21–25.

Caser, Ursula Sabine, and Nuno Ramos (2019). 'The Institutionalisation of Mediation: Reflections from an Expert Panel', *Oñati Socio-Legal Series*, 9 (4), 519–540.

Crowe, Jonathan (2017). 'Mediation Ethics and the Challenge of Professionalisation'. *Bond Law Review*, 29 (1), 5–14.

European Code of Conduct for Mediators (2004). <https://civilmediation.org/wp-content/uploads/2020/05/European-Code-of-Conduct-for-Mediators.pdf>.

Hinshaw, Art (2016). 'Regulating Mediators', *Harvard Negotiation Law Review*, 21 (2), 163–220.

Kaminskienė, Natalija, Tvaronavičienė, Agnė, and Žemaitaitytė, Irena (2023). 'Teisminės Mediacijos Lietuvoje Raida ir Galimos Tobulinimo Kryptys: Teisėjų požiūrio tyrimas', *Jurisprudencija*, 30 (1), 209–237.

Kaminskienė, Natalija, Žalėnienė, Inga, and Tvaronavičienė, Agnė (2014). 'Bringing Sustainability into Dispute Resolution Processes', *Journal of Security and Sustainability Issues: International Entrepreneurial Perspectives and Innovative Outcomes*, 4 (1), 69–77.

Korsakovienė, Indrė, and Tvaronavičienė, Agnė (2023). 'The Lithuanian model of mandatory mediation in family disputes: An updated scheme for overcoming the mediation paradox'. Kluwer Mediation Blog. <https://mediationblog.kluwerarbitration.com/2023/07/20/the-lithuanian-model-of-mandatory-mediation-in-family-disputes-an-updated-scheme-for-overcoming-the-mediation-paradox/>, accessed 1 August 2024.

Kovach, K. Kimberlee (2003). *Mediation in a Nutshell, Second Edition*. West Academic Publishing.

Kovtun, Svitlana, Shutak, Ilya, Denys, Solomiya, and Semchuk, Yurii (2022). 'Systems of Advocates' Self-Governance Bodies in European Union Countries', *Cuestionespolíticas*, 40 (75), 603–614.

Lakis, Juozas (2008). 'Konfliktiškumas ir Taikinimo Būdai Lietuvos Viešajame Sektoriuje – Problemos ir Gairės', *Viešoji Politika ir Administravimas*, 26, 35–44.

List of Mediators of the Republic of Lithuania, <https://teisis.lt/external/home/main>, accessed 6 August 2024.

List of members of the Lithuanian Chamber of Mediators, <https://www.lmr.lt/lmr-nariai/>, accessed 6 August 2024.

Ministry of Justice (2024). 'Self-Government of Mediators will Contribute to Better Quality Mediation Services', Ministry of Justice of Lithuania, <https://tm.lrv.lt/lt/naujienos/mediatoriu-savivalda-prisides-prie-kokybiskesniu-mediacijos-paslaugu/>, accessed 2 August 2024.

Steffek, Felix (2012). 'Mediation in the European Union: An Introduction', <https://bit.ly/4dw4lEl>, accessed: 2 August 2024.

Tella, María José Falcón (2011). *Case Law in Roman, Anglosaxon and Continental Law*, 1st edn. Boston: BRILL, Print.

Tvaronavičienė, Agnė, Kaminskienė, Natalija, Rone, Dana, and Uudeküll, Rea (2022). 'Mediation in the Baltic States: Developments and Challenges of Implementation', *Access to Justice in Eastern Europe*, 5 (4), 68–86.

Tvaronavičienė, Agnė, and Uscila, Rokas (2021). 'The System of Evaluation of Mediators' Qualifications in Lithuania: Model and Application Experience'. In *Wydział Prawa*, pp. 109–131. Wrocław: Administracji i Ekonomii Uniwersytetu Wrocławskiego.

Tvaronavičienė, Agnė, and Intė, Odeta (2021). 'Mandatory Mediation in Family Disputes in Lithuania: Model and First Year Application Experience', *Wydział Prawa, Administracji i Ekonomii Uniwersytetu Wrocławskiego*, pp. 53–69.

Tvaronavičienė, Agnė, Kaminskienė, Natalija, Žemaitaitytė Irena, and Cudowska, Maria (2021). 'Towards More Sustainable Dispute Resolution in Courts: Empirical Study on Challenges of the Court-Connected Mediation in Lithuania', *Entrepreneurship and Sustainability Issues*, 8 (3), 633–653.

Legal sources

Mediation Law of the Republic of Lithuania, and supplementing the Law by Articles 3-1, 2024, *TAR*, 11245.

The Code of Civil Procedure of the Republic of Lithuania, *Official Gazette*, 2002, 36–1340.

The Decision of the Council of Judges on the Adoption of the Rules on Judicial Mediation, *TAR*, 2018, 19675.

The Decision of the Council of Judges on the Rules of Procedure for Granting and Revoking the Status of a Court Mediator for Individuals, *TAR*, 2014, 13705.

The Decision of the Minister of Justice of the Republic of Lithuania in Regard of Adoption of the Concept on Mediation Development in Lithuania, *TAR*, 2015, 13939.

The Directive 2008/52/EC of the European Parliament and of the Council of 21 May 2008 on certain aspects of mediation in civil and commercial matters, *OJ L*, 136, 24 May 2008, <https://eur-lex.europa.eu/legal-content/en/ALL/?uri=CELEX:32008L0052>, accessed 1 August 2024.

The Law on Conciliatory Mediation in Civil Disputes, *Official Gazette*, 2008, 87–3462.

The Law on Mediation of the Republic of Lithuania, *TAR*, 2017, 12053.

CHAPTER 11

Mediations – Icelandic Model

Małgorzata Babula[1]

Introduction

The office of state mediator has played a vital role from its very inception. Its establishment was preceded by many years of preparations and was caused by social changes. The development of fishing-oriented urban settlements influenced the change in relations between business owners and employees and local communities created mainly by fishermen. From strictly partnership-based relations (fisherman-to-fisherman), communities have transitioned towards those based largely on employer–employee relationships. A natural consequence was the unification of workers, resulting in the creation of the first trade unions fighting for workers' rights, which were supported by employers' associations. There were also strikes, the first of which dates to 1916. This lively course of events motivated action to reconcile the interests of the two groups, resulting in the passage of the Act on Attempts to Settle Labour Disputes by the Parliament in 1925. Notably, the bill gained the support of all parties at that time. The Act of 1925 required the Minister of Labour to appoint a state mediator for 3 years, obliging the mediator to effectively resolve any disputes, and where no resolution was achieved, the mediator would be responsible for proposing one. In such cases, the mediator would prepare a settlement proposal and submit it to all interested parties. This proposal would then be put to a vote in all the employers' associations and employee unions concerned (Friðriksson 1976). The result of the functioning of the mediator's institution was the 1938 Act on Trade Unions and Labour Disputes, which remains in force to this day (Lög um stéttarfélög og vinnudeilur 1938; Aðalsteinsson 2003: 181)[2]. Chapter III of that Act includes provisions regulating how mediation functions. Yet, even though the above Act is crucial for mediation, amicable proceedings are also subject to

1 PhD, mediator, email: <malgorzata.babula@gmail.com>
2 Lög um stéttarfélög og vinnudeilur, No. 80/1938 (1938), <https://www.althingi.is/lagas/nuna/1938080.html>, accessed 26 July 2024.

the provisions of the Information Act[3], Administrative Law (Stjórnsýslulög 1993)[4], Public Finance Act[5] (Lög um opinberfjármál 2015) and the Act on the rights and obligations of state employees[6] (Lög um réttindi og skyldur starfsmanna ríkisins 1996).

State Mediator Under the Act of 1938

The mediator is appointed by the Minister of Social Affairs and Labour Market (Forsetaúrskurður um skiptingu stjórnarmálefna milli ráðuneyta í Stjórnarráði Íslands 2022, art. 3) for 5 years, without the possibility of re-appointment. Mediators shall report to the minister on their activities as often as necessary and, in any case, at least once a year (Lög um stéttarfélög og vinnudeilur 1938, art. 37). The seat of the state mediator is in the country's capital. The person holding the office of a state mediator must meet the following criteria: be a citizen of Iceland, have full citizenship rights, as well as have a clean criminal record (Lög 1938, art. 20). The last of these criteria was amended in 2019[7] when the requirement to have an 'impeccable reputation' was replaced by the following no-criminal-record clause: mediators may not have been convicted of an offence punishable by at least 4 months imprisonment without the possibility of parole or preventive detention, if they were at least 18 years old at the time of the offence, unless 5 years had passed since the sentence had been fully served[8].

---

3 Upplýsingalög, No. 140/2012 (2012), <https://www.althingi.is/lagas/nuna/2012140.html>, accessed 26 July 2024.

4 Stjórnsýslulög, No. 37/1993 (1993), <https://www.althingi.is/lagas/nuna/1993037.html>, accessed 26 July 2024.

5 Lög um opinber fjármál, No. 123/2015 (2015), <https://www.althingi.is/altext/lagasofn/nuna/2015123.html>, accessed 26 July 2024.

6 Lög um réttindi og skyldur starfsmanna ríkisins, No. 70/1996 (1996), <https://www.althingi.is/lagas/nuna/1996070.html>, accessed 26 July 2024.

7 Lög um breytingu á ýmsum lögum vegna brottfalls laga um kjararáð, No. 130/2016, með síðari breytingum (launafyrirkomulag), No. 79/2019 (2019), <https://www.althingi.is/altext/stjt/2019.079.html>, accessed 28 July 2024.

8 Lög um breytingu á ýmsum lögum vegna afnáms ákvæða um uppreist æru, No. 141/2018 (2018), Art. 40, <https://www.althingi.is/altext/stjt/2018.141.html>, accessed 25 July 2024.

Mediators must be impartial and may be assisted in their daily work by deputies (in case of absence or on a discretionary basis), who are subject to the same legal requirements and appointment procedure as the mediators themselves. Apart from a deputy, the state mediator may also appoint an assistant mediator, and taking on the role of an auxiliary mediator is considered a civil obligation. Where the high importance of a labour dispute is demonstrated, the government – after prior consultation with the mediator and the parties to the dispute – may appoint a special conciliation committee to work on its resolution. While performing their official duties, the deputy mediator, their assistant (auxiliary mediator) and committee members have the same rights and obligations as the mediator. The remuneration of a state mediator is determined by law and amounts to ISK 1,593,322 per month (including overtime pay and compensation for difficult working conditions of ISK 382,880)[9]. The remuneration is revised annually on 1st July. Before 1st June, Statistics Iceland calculates and publishes updates on the average regular salary of government employees for the next calendar year, and the mediator, being a public official, is subject to these provisions.

The state mediator deals with conciliation in labour disputes between employees and their unions on the one hand, and employers and their associations on the other. Under art. 22 of the Act, state mediators must monitor the business sector, the national labour market, wage issues, as well as any issues that may cause conflicts in day-to-day relations between employers' associations and trade unions. Their duties also include maintaining a register of current collective agreements (Ríkissáttasemjari 2024), and employee unions and employers' associations are obliged to send them copies of all collective agreements immediately after signing, as well as information about any amendments to existing collective agreements. The above documents must always be accompanied by the notice of termination of the collective agreement, as well as the lawsuit filed against the other party to the dispute (Lög 1938, art. 22). Moreover, mediators must prepare protocols covering such things as the places and dates of mediation meetings (1938, art. 36).

9 See Lög, 1938, Art. 20; Lög um breytingu á ýmsum lögum vegan brottfallslaga um kjararáð, 2019, Art. 15.

Where negotiations between the parties break down or one of the parties considers that there is no chance of further negotiations being successful, they may, individually or jointly with the other party, refer the dispute to a mediator. After receiving the notification, the mediator is obliged to summon the parties or their representatives to a meeting as soon as possible and then conduct the mediation proceedings. Mediators take control of the mediation in accordance with the arrangements contained in the prepared plan. However, they typically can postpone formal conciliation and instruct the parties to investigate the options for settling direct discussions among themselves if, in the mediator's opinion, this is more likely to be successful. Mediators may always take over the negotiations if they deem it appropriate. The obligation to draw up a negotiation plan for the renewal of the collective agreement rests with the employer and the unions. The negotiation plan, signed by both parties, is immediately sent to the mediator. It must be prepared no later than 10 weeks before the issuance of the current collective bargaining agreement. If the parties to the agreement have not drawn up a plan, the obligation to do so rests with the mediator, who must prepare a proposal for an agreement between the parties no later than 8 weeks before the issuance of the current collective agreement. The parties to the agreement may, at any time after publication of the negotiation plan, request the mediator's intervention or assistance, and the mediator shall immediately ensure that the mediation is conducted in accordance with the plan. The contracting parties must ensure that the mediator can freely monitor the labour dispute. Conciliation meetings, at which the parties' attendance is mandatory, are held behind closed doors. Copies of documents that have been transferred between the parties to the dispute must be submitted at the conciliation meetings unless they have already been sent to the mediator. The course of the meetings and the mediation proceedings are confidential. This means that, until the proposal to resolve the dispute is put to a vote, it cannot be disclosed to anyone other than the parties involved without the consent of the mediator. Where mediation proves unsuccessful, the mediator may provide a dispute settlement proposal to end it. This proposal is then submitted to employee unions and employers' associations, or the individual employer if the latter is involved in an employment dispute. The mediator must consult the proposals in advance with the parties' conciliation committees. If the dispute concerns only a specific company department, the mediator may decide that only this department will be included in the consultation. The parties are free to accept or reject the proposal as they see fit.

The basic assumption of the legislator is that if two or more associations or unions are involved in a dispute, the mediator, in consultation with the committees, may present one proposal to resolve the dispute with the participation of more than one party to the dispute or all parties. Voting and vote counting is then carried out jointly by all associations and unions concerned to resolve the dispute so that the total number of votes determines the acceptance or rejection of the proposal. Alternatively, the legislator provides that mediators may present more than one proposal; they are then allowed to conduct a joint vote, provided that the statutory conditions are met. First, the presentation of the proposals and the voting must take place during the same meeting. Moreover, for the mediator to be able to propose a solution, all previous attempts to reach an agreement under the negotiation plan must have proven ineffective and the time allocated for negotiations between the parties without mediation must have elapsed without reaching agreement. Parties to a labour dispute must be allowed to express their comments on the mediator's ideas, whether presented to them directly or publicly, with a view to making a joint proposal to resolve the dispute. The proposal to resolve the dispute is put to a vote by all those entitled to vote. Voting may be conducted in three ways: (i) it may take place at a mediation meeting; (ii) after consulting the parties to the labour dispute, the mediator may decide that the vote will take place outside the meeting, in specified places; (iii) alternatively, instead of voting at or outside the meeting, the mediator may, in consultation with the parties to the labour dispute, decide that the vote on the solution proposal will take place by secret universal postal vote among the members, which must be completed before a specified time. After consulting the parties to the labour dispute, the mediator gives detailed instructions regarding the voting arrangements, such as when and how it should take place. Voting takes place in writing and is secret. Vote counting takes place under the mediator's supervision, and each party's proxy may be present during its course (Lög 1938, art. 23–30).

A proposal to resolve the dispute is considered rejected if two conditions are met: (1) more than half of the votes cast are against and (2) at least one-quarter of those entitled to vote have taken part in the vote. The mediator may publish a report on such a vote, with its content to be determined by the mediator alone. The secrecy clause covers voting as well. The result of the mediation may be disclosed to the public by the mediator.

If the mediation procedure is unsuccessful, the mediator may make further attempts to reach an agreement between the parties (Association of Academics v. Iceland 2018; Sołtys 2023: 201–218)[10]. However, an attempt to resume activities must take place within 14 days of the cessation of the last negotiation attempt. If one of the parties changes its mind and wants to accept the mediator's proposal to resolve the dispute after the ineffective completion of the mediation proceedings, it shall send the mediator a declaration on this matter. The mediator is obliged to immediately notify the other party of the declaration. Where the other party also wishes to agree to the proposal to resolve the dispute, the mediator ensures that the parties reach an agreement (Lög 1938, art. 34–35).

Professional Ethics

As a government official, the mediator is subject to the provisions of the general code of ethics[11] binding on government employees (Júlíusdóttir 2013; Siedlecka-Andrychowicz 2023: 1–67), to which the Act on the Rights and Obligations of State Employees itself refers (Lög um réttindi 1996, art. 15). Complaints about a violation of ethical principles may be filed with the ombudsman. The Code of Ethics mentions the basic values in work in government positions, including (apart from honesty and impartiality) effectiveness and lists 16 principles referring to such things as promoting values based on equality and human rights; counteracting poor money management; promoting work practices that enhance trust in state institutions and the office; transparent communication in the workplace; truth, honesty and respect; freedom of opinion and expression; and avoiding conflicts of interest and cooperating in resolving problems (Júlíusdóttir 2013). The Union of State

10 Judgment of the European Court of Human Rights of 15 May 2018, case 2451/2016 (2018). <https://hudoc.echr.coe.int/fre?i=001-183375>, accessed 2 August 2024.

11 Code of Ethics for Government Employees (2013), <https://www.stjornarradid.is/media/fjarmalaraduneyti-media/media/skjal/Almennar_sidareglur_starfsmanna_rikisins2013.pdf>, accessed 28 July 2024.

Employees, the Association of Directors of State Institutions, the Institute of Ethics of the University of Iceland and the Coordinating Committee for Ethical Standards in Administration were involved in the consultation work on the creation of the code of ethics (Rikissattasemjari 2021).

Summary

Mediation proceedings in employment matters have a long tradition in Iceland; they work efficiently and fulfil their role (Rikissattasemjari, statistics, 2021). Nonetheless, mediations in other areas of the state's functioning encountered certain difficulties while adapting procedural provisions to European Union (EU) law. It is worth emphasising that although Iceland is not a Member State of the EU, it applies many EU legal acts in practice. Though part of the single market under the Agreement on the European Economic Area (EEA), it is not bound by EU law in such areas as the common agricultural and fisheries policy (the EEA Agreement does, however, contain provisions on trade in agricultural and fishery products), customs union, common commercial policy, common foreign and security policy, justice and home affairs sector [although every European Free Trade Agreement (EFTA) country is part of the Schengen area] and economic and monetary union (Ashton & Bourlon de Rouvre 2023: 1–56). Therefore, all remaining areas must be regulated considering EU legal acts. Iceland generally implements this EU law with great effectiveness, and the government's actions in this respect should be assessed positively despite occasional mistakes. One of them concerns the implementation of Directive 2013/11/EU[12] (Consumer ADR Directive 2013). Owing to the failure to implement two related acts, Regulation No. 524/2013 and Regulation No. 2015/1051, Iceland has not completed the formalities to implement the Alternative Dispute Resolution (ADR) Directive (EFTA Surveillance Authority 2023, Case No. 88725). Iceland was requested to remedy this infringement in November 2017; however, it

12 Directive 2013/11/EU of the European Parliament and the Council of 21 May 2013 on alternative dispute resolution for consumer disputes and amending Regulation (EC) No. 2006/2004 and Directive 2009/22/EC (Consumer ADR Directive) (2013). <https://eur-lex.europa.eu/legal-content/PL/TXT/PDF/?uri=CELEX:32013L0011>, accessed 1 August 2024.

responded to the above request only in January 2018, indicating that the new ADR law would be presented to Parliament in spring 2018. Owing to the ineffective expiry of the deadline, a case against Iceland was brought to the EFTA Court, which in May 2019 ruled against the republic in four proceedings, finding Iceland's government guilty (See EFTA Court 2019, Cases E-3/18[13], E-4/18[14], E-5/18[15], E-6/18[16]). As a result of the actions taken, Icelanders now have the option to resolve disputes online (in Icelandic) via the online dispute resolution (ODR) platform, and the reviewing bodies are the Housing Complaints Commission, the Consumer Complaints Commission, the Insurance Complaints Commission, the Commission for Consumer Complaints in Transactions with Financial Companies, the Motoring Commission and the Transport Authority (for services offered by airlines) (European Commission, ODR 2024).

Bibliography

Aðalsteinsson, Gylfi Dalmann (2008). Vinnulöggjöfin (lög no. 80/1938) í 70 ár. no. 2, issue 4. Stjórnmál og stjórnsýsla veftímarit Stofnun-stjórnsýslu-fræða-og-stjórnmála, <https://skemman.is/bitstream/1946/8980/1/a.2008.4.2.4.pdf>, accessed 30 July 2024.

Ashton, David, and Bourlon de Rouvre Diane (2023). *EU Mapping: Overview of International Market and Consumer Protection Related Legislation*, Luxembourg: European Parliament, <https://www.europarl.

13 Judgment of the EFTA Court in case E-3/18. (2019), https://eftacourt.int/download/3-18-judgment/?wpdmdl=6053 (Accessed: 2 August 2024). See: Case E-3/18. (2019), https://eftacourt.int/download/3-18-notification/?wpdmdl=3373 (Accessed: 2 August 2024).

14 Judgment of the EFTA Court in case E-4/18. (2019), https://eftacourt.int/download/4-18/?wpdmdl=3375 (Accessed: 2 August 2024). See: Case E-4/18. (2019), https://eftacourt.int/download/4-18/?wpdmdl=3375 (Accessed: 2 August 2024).

15 Judgment of the EFTA Court in case E-5/18. (2019), https://eftacourt.int/download/5-18-judgment/?wpdmdl=6055 (Accessed:2 August 2024). See: Case E-5/18. (2019), https://eftacourt.int/download/5-18-notification/?wpdmdl=3377 (Accessed: 2 August 2024).

16 Judgment of the EFTA Court in case E-6/18. (2019), https://eftacourt.int/download/6-18-judgment/?wpdmdl=6056 (Accessed: 2 August 2024). See: Case E-6/18. (2019), https://eftacourt.int/download/6-18-notification/?wpdmdl=3381 (Accessed: 2 August 2024).

europa.eu/RegData/etudes/STUD/2023/740062/IPOL_STU%282023 %29740062_EN.pdf>, accessed 2 August 2024.

Bartoszewicz, Jakub (2023). Obowiązkowe Mediacje z Zakresu Prawa Pracy to Krok w Dobrym Kierunku, <https://www.gazetaprawna.pl/praca/artykuly/8709302,prawo-pracy-obowiazkowe-mediacje.html>, accessed 31 July 2024.

EFTA Surveillance Authority. Case No: 72477. Document No: 1104560, <https://www.eftasurv.int/cms/sites/default/files/documents/gopro/4164-Reasoned%20opinion%20to%20Iceland%20for%20non-implementation%20of%20Directive%202013_11%20as%20regards%20consumer% 20ADR.pdf>, accessed 1 August 2024.

Friðriksson, Barði (1976). 50 Ára afmæli sattasemjara ríkisins, Tímarit lögfræðinga, <https://timarit.is/gegnir/991003692439706886>, accessed 20 July 2024.

Online Dispute Resolution (2021). <https://ec.europa.eu/consumers/odr/main/?event=main.adr.show2>, accessed: 2 August 2024.

Report of the EFTA Court (2019). Luxembourg: EFTA Court, <https://eftacourt.int/wp-content/uploads/2020/03/223792_EFTA_COURT_RA_2019.pdf?x28871>, accessed 1 August 2024.

Ríkissáttasemjari (2024a). <https://rikissattasemjari.is/embaettid/sagan/>, accessed 30 July 2024.

Ríkissáttasemjari (2024b). <https://rikissattasemjari.is/embaettid/sidareglur/>, accessed 30 July 2024.

Ríkissáttasemjari (2024c). <https://rikissattasemjari.is/en/statistics/>, accessed 9 August 2024.

Ríkissáttasemjari (2024d). <https://www.kjarasamningar.is/>, accessed 28 July 2024.

Ríkissáttasemjari (2024e). <https://www.kjarasamningar.is/unions/010801>, accessed 28 July 2024.

Siedlecka-Andrychowicz, Agnieszka (2023). *Codes of Ethics for Mediators in Poland and Selected European Countries*. Warsaw: Instytut Wymiaru Sprawiedliwości, <https://iws.gov.pl/wp-content/uploads/2023/07/IWS_Siedlecka-Andrychowicz-A._Kodeksy-etyczne-mediatorow-w-Polsce-i-wybranych-krajach-europejskich.pdf>, accessed 26 July 2024.

Sołtys, Karol (2023). 'Gloss to the Decision of the European Court of Human Rights of May 15, 2018, Case Number 2451/16, *Association of Academics v. Iceland, Hudoc.int*', *Review of European and Comparative Law*, 52 (1), 201–218, <https://doi.org/10.31743/recl.15011>, accessed 1 August 2024.

Szewczuk, Monika (2023). The Wage Dispute Went to the Courtroom, <https://icelandnews.is/informacje/z-kraju/spor-placowy-trafil-na-sale-sadowa>, accessed 28 July 2024; <https://lodz.so.gov.pl/index.php?p=new&id=302&idg=mg,141&kword=przepis%C3%B3w%20dotycz%C4%85cych%20mediacji>, accessed 31 July 2024.

Legal Sources

Case E-3/18 (2019). <https://eftacourt.int/download/3-18-notification/?wpdmdl=3373>, accessed 2 August 2024.

Case E-4/18 (2019). <https://eftacourt.int/download/4-18/?wpdmdl=3375>, accessed 2 August 2024.

Case E-5/18 (2019). <https://eftacourt.int/download/5-18-notification/?wpdmdl=3377>, accessed 2 August 2024.

Case E-6/18 (2019). <https://eftacourt.int/download/6-18-notification/?wpdmdl=3381>, accessed 2 August 2024.

Directive 2013/11/EU of the European Parliament and the Council of 21 May 2013 on alternative dispute resolution for consumer disputes and amending Regulation (EC) No. 2006/2004 and Directive 2009/22/EC (Consumer ADR Directive) (2013). <https://eur-lex.europa.eu/legal-content/PL/TXT/PDF/?uri=CELEX:32013L0011>, accessed 1 August 2024.

Forsetaúrskurður um Skiptingu stjórnarmálefna Milli Ráðuneyta í Stjórnarráði Íslands, No. 6/2022 (2022). <https://www.althingi.is/lagas/nuna/2022006.html>, accessed 25 July 2024.

Judgment of the European Court of Human Rights of 15 May 2018, case 2451/2016 (2018). <https://hudoc.echr.coe.int/fre?i=001-183375>, accessed 2 August 2024.

Judgment of the EFTA Court in case E-3/18 (2019). <https://eftacourt.int/download/3-18-judgment/?wpdmdl=6053>, accessed 2 August 2024.

Judgment of the EFTA Court in case E-4/18 (2019). <https://eftacourt.int/download/4-18/?wpdmdl=3375>, accessed 2 August 2024.
Judgment of the EFTA Court in case E-5/18 (2019). <https://eftacourt.int/download/5-18-judgment/?wpdmdl=6055>, accessed 2 August 2024.
Judgment of the EFTA Court in case E-6/18 (2019). <https://eftacourt.int/download/6-18-judgment/?wpdmdl=6056>, accessed 2 August 2024.

CHAPTER 12

Mediation: An Indian Perspective

Sayali Ganu-Dabake[1]

Introduction

Mediation is usually defined as a voluntary dispute resolution process where disputing parties take help of a neutral third party to negotiate and arrive at a mutually acceptable solution. While it is not a new concept, it has come into focus as a method of dispute resolution in recent years, especially after the Singapore Convention on Mediation[2].

Mediation, as a method of dispute resolution, is not a new concept for India. However, it lost the position as primary method for dispute resolution under colonial rule when the British introduced Court system was implemented in India. Under the various efforts to reduce the burden on Indian judiciary and pendency of cases, different alternative dispute resolution (ADR) mechanisms have been introduced in India through legislations. Mediation is the latest one of them.

Indian Parliament passed the Mediation Act in 2023[3]. This legislation aims to promote and facilitate mediation in India as a peaceful dispute resolution method. The Act focuses on dispute resolution through mediation in time bound manner and making the settlement agreement enforceable as if it is a judicial decree. The concept of mediation in present day India is completely voluntary. However, recognition of the mediation process and formalisation into a statute indicates the Government's will to promote it as an effective ADR mechanism.

---

1 Advocate, BSL LLB, LLM, MBL, PGDIPRL, LLM, email: <sayali.ganu@lexonomix.com>

2 United Nations Convention on International Settlement Agreements Resulting from Mediation (Singapore Convention on Mediation), adopted in New York on 20 December 2018, open to signature in Singapore on 7 August 2019, <https://uncitral.un.org/sites/uncitral.un.org/files/media-documents/EN/Texts/UNCITRAL/Arbitration/mediation_convention_v1900316_eng.pdf>, accessed 20 September 2024.

3 The Mediation Act enacted of 14 September 2023, <https://www.indiacode.nic.in/handle/123456789/19637?sam_handle=123456789/1362>, accessed 15 July 2024.

Chapter XII discusses the Indian perspective on Mediation. After discussing the history of mediation as a dispute resolution mechanism in India and how it has been part of the legal philosophy of India, the focus of the chapter on the Mediation Act, 2023 – its key provisions, the process of mediation under the Act, institutional mediation and the effect on and amendments to various existing statutes. After considering various challenges in ADR methods in India, the conclusion analyses the future challenges in promoting and popularising mediation as a dispute resolution method.

Benefits of Mediation

There are various benefits of mediation as discussed time to time on various fora. Ample material is available which lists the pros of mediation and also the comparative benefits as against other methods of dispute resolution including litigation, arbitration and conciliation. Some of the most important benefits of mediation can be summarised as follows:

1. It is a completely voluntary process. The parties may opt out of the mediation process at any time. As there is no compulsion on the parties to go through the whole process, in case of a successful mediation, the chances of implementation of the settlement are higher.
2. The parties involved in mediation have more control over the mediation process. Unlike arbitrator, the mediator has no authority to decide regarding any points of disputes between the parties. Therefore, the parties are not forced to accept the solutions which not acceptable to them. They can decide if they wish to settle or not and also which conditions of settlement are acceptable to them and which are not.
3. Such voluntary participation preserves the relationship between the parties. Mediator helps them to understand the issues and also sorts these issues out. Mediator encourages open communication between the parties. This helps them to understand each other's position and point of view. This further helps in maintaining the relationships between the parties. If handled rightly, in many cases, mediation also helps to restore the amicable relationships between the parties.
4. The procedure of mediation is to be decided by the parties. Thus, it is a more flexible mechanism. Meetings can be fixed as per mutual

convenience. Therefore, there is no stress on the parties to follow a rigid procedure and paperwork. Parties are not in confrontation mode whenever they meet each other. There is a better mindset. The mediation process, therefore, becomes collaborative, time-efficient and cost-effective.

5. Parties can go for more specific customised solutions, which fit their requirements, their specific needs and interests.
6. The process can be kept confidential, as the details of the disputing parties, disputes and the mediator are not part of any public records.

In addition to these benefits, some additional advantage of introduction of mediation as a dispute resolution, with respect to Indian judiciary, were also considered by the Parliamentary Standing Committee in its detailed report on the Mediation Bill, 2021[4]. The Committee observed that this will help in lessening the burden on judiciary. Faster resolution through mediation will not only save time and money for the parties, but also will reduce costs incurred by the institutions on dispute resolutions.

Mediation in India – A Historical Review

India has a long legacy and rich culture that can be traced back for 5,000 years. These ancient Indian civilisations followed the code of conduct in personal as well as social life. The Indian epics and various mythological stories refer to different codes of conduct followed in those periods, allowing us to peak into the established legal and judicial system in those periods in Indian history, including various dispute resolution mechanisms followed during the period. These epics have very clear references to mediation as a primary method for amicable resolution of disagreements between the parties.

Ramayana, the story of Ram, an ideal king, refers to an attempt of mediation between Ram and Ravan to avoid the war between them. Mahabharata is another well-known Indian epic which is a story of war of succession between

4 Department-related Parliamentary Standing Committee on Personnel, Public Grievances, Law and Justice (2022), 117th Report on the Mediation Bill, 2021, presented by the Chairman on 13th July 2022, <https://prsindia.org/files/bills_acts/bills_parliament/2021/SC%20Report_Mediation%20bill.pdf>, accessed 20 September 2024.

two sets of cousins – Kauravas and Pandavas. Mediation, as a first choice of dispute resolution can be observed in this epic tale as well. In this story, Lord Krishna attempted to mediate the disputes Kauravas and Pandavas. While the exact period of the stories narrated in both these epics is not ascertained, Ramayan is estimated to have taken place around 5000 to 7000 years ago and Mahabharata's time period is estimated to be at least 3000 to 5000 years ago.

The practice of mediation as an integral method of dispute resolution in India can be traced back from this period to the present day. Disputes were preferred to be resolved through dialogue. Community mediation was often carried out through the village councils (known as 'Panchayat' in many parts of the country). These councils consisted of 'Pancha' i.e. the mediators, who mediated the disputes and advised the parties to reach a mutually agreeable settlement.

With the development of Buddhism and Jainism in India, peaceful and harmonious society became the focus. Thus, mediation was again a preferred mechanism to settle the disputes.

Even during the Mughal Rule, the Ruler's administrative and judicial systems often attempted negotiations – especially in disputes of civil and commercial nature.

With the British Rule in India, these traditional dispute resolution methods lost their importance after introduction of the adversarial legal system in India. The dispute resolution system became more court-centric and rigid. Disputes were decided by the judges as per the codified laws and the judge's discretion as conferred by these laws. This was a result of the British attempt to control the legal system in India in order to have a better control over the huge, resource rich colony. However, mediation would still be preferred, where people did not have access to Court and also when they did not have the resources to fight a lengthy litigation or in respect of personal laws, where there was no uniform codified law applicable throughout the country. This was observed in villages and smaller towns as well as tribal communities.

Situation started changing after India gained independence from the British Rule. There have been some legislations made effective in the post-independence India, which include mediation as one of the prominent methods of settlement as part of the formal structure under the laws. Industrial Disputes Act, 1947 was one of such first laws where concept mediation was given legal recognition. The Act provides for appointment of conciliators, who have the duty of mediating and promoting the settlement of industrial disputes[5].

At later stages, various statutes have introduced mediation as the first step to resolve disputes under that legislation. Rohini Dashrath Jagtap (2022) has identified eleven different legislations on different subjects incorporated mediation as a dispute settlement mechanism. These legislations cover a wide spectrum of subjects like companies' regulations, consumer protection laws, laws regulating micro, small and medium enterprises, matrimonial laws and the real estates-related legislation.

Sahil Kanuga and Shraddha Bhosale (2021) have observed that till the decision by the Honourable Supreme Court in the case of Afcons Infrastructure Ltd. v. Cherian Varkey Construction Co. Pvt. Ltd[6], there was confusion amongst the legal fraternity, whether 'mediation' and 'conciliation' are two entirely separate dispute mechanisms or not. In this case, Court has differentiated between adjudicatory and non-adjudicatory alternative methods of dispute resolution.

There are two types of mediations observed in Indian legal system. Court-referred mediation is where a dispute is initially referred to competent court. Such court refers such matter for mediation under the provisions of the Code of Civil Procedure (CPC), 1908 – the law governing the procedures of civil courts in India[7]. However, as the mediation settlement agreements were not binding till now, not many opted for mediation as a preferred method of dispute resolution, even after it was referred by the Courts. Also, as pointed out by Deepika Kinhal and Misra Apoorva (2021), judges are not referencing matters to mediation effectively under this provision. The possible reasons are lack of awareness, ambiguity as to enforceability, comfort

5 Industrial Disputes Act (1947) enacted on 11 March 1947, Section 4, (replaced by the Industrial Relations Code 2020), <https://www.indiacode.nic.in/bitstream/123456789/15191/1/A1947-14.pdf>, accessed 15 July 2024.

6 Supreme Court of India (2010), M/s. Afcons Infra. Ltd. & Anr vs M/S Cherian Varkey Constn Co. P. Ltd. on 26 July 2010, 8 SCC 24, <https://indiankanoon.org/doc/1875345/>, accessed 20 September 2024.

7 The Code of Civil Procedure enacted on 21 March 1908, Section 89, <https://www.indiacode.nic.in/bitstream/123456789/2191/1/A1908-05.pdf>, accessed 20 July 2024.

with the adjudicatory process and lack of expert mediators with capability to handle different types of disputes, especially in case of commercial disputes.

Another significant step was the introduction of mediation as a legally recognised and preferred dispute resolution mechanism, in the new legislation governing corporates in India. The Companies Act (2013)[8] expressly introduced mediation and negation as a method of dispute resolution for corporate disputes. As observed by Rajinder Kaur (2019), intercorporate disputes impact not only the immediate parties but also the shareholders, workers, creditors and other various stakeholders. While assessing the effectiveness of mediation under the Companies Mediation and Conciliation Rules (2016)[9], Puneetish Kaur (2019) observes that mediation shall be the first choice of dispute resolution, especially in commercial disputes. However, the non-binding nature of the settlement agreements proves to be the biggest obstacle in this.

The Consumer Protection Act (2019)[10] enables the Consumer Forum to refer cases to Mediation Cell. This mediation process initiated by the Courts is also sometimes classified as 'post-litigation mediation'. The other type is where dispute is settled using services of a private mediator. This mediation is used in both pre-litigation mediation as well as in connection with disputes pending in the Court.

In 2019, India became a signatory to the United Nations Convention on International Settlement Agreements (UNISA), more commonly known as the Singapore Convention on Mediation. This convention has provided a uniform and efficient settlement framework to enforce the international settlement agreements resulting from mediation between the disputing parties. It also allows the parties to invoke such settlement agreements. The

---

8 The Companies Act on 29 August 2013, <https://www.mca.gov.in/content/mca/global/en/acts-rules/companies-act/companies-act-2013.html>, accessed 20 September 2024.

9 The Companies Mediation and Conciliation Rules on 9 September 2016, <https://ibclaw.in/the-companies-mediation-and-conciliation-rules-2016/>, accessed 20 September 2024.

10 The Consumer Protection Act of 9 August 2019, <https://www.indiacode.nic.in/bitstream/123456789/15256/1/a2019-35.pdf>, accessed 20 September 2024.

Convention grants to the Courts the discretion to refuse invoking such settlement agreements if the dispute is not capable of settlement by mediation or if the Court thinks that the enforcement would be contrary to public policy.

India has seen a rapid growth of economy in the last 20 years. Being signatory to the Singapore Convention is a significant step in promoting India in the global market. As the convention speaks about the enforcement of international mediation settlement agreements, it provides an effective and enforceable, faster alternative to litigation. This improves the ease of doing business in India and provides more stable environment for businesses and commercial ventures.

Following the commitment to mediation mechanism under the Singapore Convention on Mediation, Mediation Bill was first introduced in the Parliament in December 2021. This Bill was thoroughly reviewed by the Standing Committee of the Parliament. Based on the analysis of the Standing Committee, specific recommendations were made. After considering this recommendations, certain changes were introduced in the Bill. The revised version was re-introduced in the Parliament 2023. This revised version was passed by both the Houses and after receiving the presidential assent, became the Mediation Act (2023). This act has come in force since 9th October 2023.

The Mediation Act (2023)

As the preamble of this Act explains, Mediation Act (2023) was introduced 'to promote and facilitate mediation' in India. It is recognised in the preamble that effective dispute resolution process has a significant impact on the economy and doing business in the country. It also accepted that mediation results in amicable resolution of disputes in civil, commercial, family and matrimonial matters.

The Mediation Act establishes a framework for mediation proceedings in India

Arbitration and Conciliation Act introduced concept of mediation in India[11]. However, this legislation did not define 'mediation'. The Mediation Act

11 Arbitration and Conciliation Act (1996), <https://www.indiacode.nic.in/handle/123456789/2187?view_type=browse&sam_handle=123456789/1362>, accessed 20 September 2024.

(2023) does not only define 'mediation', but also 'mediator' and 'mediation agreement'.

'Mediation' is defined as a process by which parties attempt to reach an amicable settlement of their dispute with assistance of a third person, i.e. Mediator, who does not have the authority to impose a settlement on the parties in the dispute[12]. This definition defines the essence of the process. It also elaborates that irrespective of the terminology used, the essence of the process is to be investigated. Therefore, any mediation, pre-litigation mediation, online mediation, community mediation, conciliation or any other expression of similar import is considered as Mediation.

'Mediator' is also defined in this Act. A mediator means a person who is appointed to be a mediator, by the parties or by a mediation service provider, to undertake mediation, and includes a person registered as mediator with the Council[13].

'Mediation agreement' is an agreement in writing by and between the parties to submit to mediation certain or all disputes that may arise between the parties[14]. It may be a separate agreement or a clause in a contract. Any mediation agreement will be considered as agreement in writing if it is contained in or recorded as a document signed by the parties; in exchange of communication or letters (including in electronic format); any pleadings in any judicial proceedings and which is not denied by the other party; by way of reference in any agreement.

This law has, not only recognised various types of mediation like online mediation, pre-litigation mediation, community mediation, court-annexed mediation, institutional mediation and international mediation, but also defined and described them in depth.

---

12 Section 3(h) Mediation Act, 2023 reads as 'mediation' includes a process, whether referred to by the expression mediation, pre-litigation mediation, online mediation, community mediation, conciliation or an expression of similar import, whereby parties attempt to reach an amicable settlement of their dispute with assistance of a third person referred to as mediator, who does not have the authority to impose a settlement on the parties in the dispute.

13 Section 3(i), Mediation Act, 2023.

14 Sections 3(j) and 4, Mediation Act, 2023.

'Court-annexed mediation' is mediation including pre-litigation mediation conducted at the mediation centres established by any Court or Tribunal[15]. Pre-litigation mediation in such cases, is a process of undertaking mediation for settlement of disputes prior to the filing of a suit or proceeding of civil or commercial nature before a Court or a Tribunal[16]. Such mediation can be initiated even when there was no mediation agreement between the parties. If the dispute is of commercial nature and of specified value, then the mediation has to be according to the provisions of the Commercial Courts Act (2015).

'Institutional mediation' means any mediation conducted under the aegis of a mediation service provider[17].

'International mediation' means mediation relates to commercial dispute arising out of a legal relationship – contractual or otherwise between two parties[18]. Such mediation shall be undertaken under this law and where at least one of the parties is:

- an individual who is national of, or habitually resides in any country other than India;
- a body corporate with its place of business outside India;
- an association or body of individuals whose place of business is outside India; or
- the government of a foreign country.

For the purposes of this definition, 'place of business' includes a place from where business is ordinarily carried out, or a party maintains its books of account or a place where a party is engaged in business through an agent[19].

However, while international mediation is defined in the Act, there is no further reference to the same in the law. Also, this legislation does not have any explicit and clear provisions about or reference to enforcement of

15 Section 3(e), Mediation Act, 2023.
16 Sections 3(u) and 5, Mediation Act, 2023.
17 Section 3(f), Mediation Act, 2023.
18 Section 3(g), Mediation Act, 2023.
19 Section 3(t), Mediation Act, 2023.

international-mediated settlement agreements, where mediation has taken place out of India.

Mediation can be conducted online. 'Online mediation' means a mediation where the process at any stage is conducted using electronic format or using computer networks, secure chat rooms or conference by audio or video modes or both. For such online process, both parties need to consent in writing[20].

Key provisions in the Mediation Act

Like most of the Indian laws, the Mediation Act also has definitions of some important concepts used and referred to in the act. These terms are to be interpreted in the manner provided in these definitions, even when they may have a different primary meaning or a different definition under any other laws prevalent in India.

The Mediation Act not only defines mediation but also the mediation agreement, international mediation, mediator as well as different types of mediation processes. Pre-litigation mediation is made mandatory in case of civil and commercial disputes except for when there is urgent interim relief required. There are certain disputes for resolution of which mediation is not conducted. The detailed list of such disputes is provided in the First Schedule of the Mediation Act.

Mediation Act has clearly laid down the procedure for appointment, replacement as well as termination of any mediator. Also, there are clear guidelines as to how to avoid the conflict-of-interest situations and the mandatory disclosures by the mediators to avoid such conflicts. The role of mediator in a mediation as well as other proceedings is clearly laid down.

The act goes ahead to detail the steps in any mediation proceedings and elaborates on the procedural aspects at each of these steps. A specific time limit for completion of mediation process is defined in the act. This is to ensure a faster and timely resolution of the dispute. Such time limit is to be calculated from the date of first appearance before the mediator. The period during which mediation has been undertaken as per the provisions of the Mediation Act is to be excluded while calculating period of limitation

20 Sections 3(q) and 30 of Mediation Act, 2023.

specified under any other law. This provision ensures that mediation proceedings is not used as a method to pass time in order to deprive other party of its legally available remedies, on the grounds of expiry of limitation period to invoke such legal remedy. As it is a voluntary and mutual process, costs are to be borne equally by both the parties. Any party can opt out of it at any point in time, even if no conclusion is reached.

Mediated Settlement Agreement has been provided legal recognition and enforceability under the Act. It can be enforced like a court judgement[21]. This is a welcome step as it brings authority and authenticity to the process of mediation.

The Mediation Act emphasises on the confidentiality of the mediation process. Every stakeholder in any mediation process is under obligation to keep confidential the opinions, suggestions, acknowledgements, proposals, promises, apologies, etc., made during the process; acceptance of such promises; documents prepared solely for the mediation process and mediation communication, amongst other things. The mediation proceedings are not to be recorded in any manner. The information or communication submitted or shared during the mediation proceedings is not to be produced and used as evidence in any later proceedings before the Court or Tribunal[22].

Mediation Act establishes a Mediation Council of India. This council has been conferred with functions to ensure promotion and propagation of Mediation as a preferred method of dispute resolution for both domestic and international disputes. It also has to work for continuous education, training and certification of the mediators, the regulation of mediation service providers and other ancillary functions[23]. The law also recognises Mediation Service Providers, which shall be organisations or body incorporates providing mediation services[24]. They can accredit and empanel mediators, provide services of mediator and offer the necessary administrative support for such mediation proceedings[25].

21 Section 27, Mediation Act, 2023.
22 Section 22, Mediation Act, 2023.
23 Section 38, Mediation Act, 2023.
24 Section 40, Mediation Act, 2023.
25 Section 41, Mediation Act, 2023.

There are certain disputes, for resolution of which mediation is not conducted. The detailed list of such disputes is provided in the First Schedule of the Mediation Act[26]. These exceptions cover disputes where mediation is specifically barred in any law, disputes to be prosecuted under criminal laws, disputes initiated before a statutory authority against any practitioner or registered professional in respect of their registration, misconduct or disciplinary actions against them. Disputes against minors, persons with intellectual disabilities are also considered unfit for mediation under Mediation Act. Furthermore, disputes and proceedings to be conducted before statutory authorities established by Electricity Act (2003), Securities and Exchange Board of India Act (1992), Competition Act (2002), Telecom Regulatory Authority of India Act (1997) and National Green Tribunal Act (2010) are also excluded. A detailed list of the same can be found in the First Schedule to the Mediation Act[27].

Process of Mediation

The Mediation Act has provided in detail how the mediation proceedings are to be conducted in chapter V of the act.

It is necessary that every mediation under this law is to be undertaken within the territorial jurisdiction of the Court or Tribunal of competent jurisdiction to decide the subject matter of the dispute. Parties may mutually decide to conduct the mediation outside the territorial jurisdiction or commit to online mediation. However, in such case, the enforcement, challenge or registration of the mediated settlement agreement is to be undertaken in the Court or Tribunal of competent jurisdiction[28].

When there is an existing agreement between the parties to settle the dispute by mediation, mediation is deemed to commence on the date on which a party receives notice from the other party initiating or referring the dispute to mediation. In absence of any such agreement, when the parties agree to appoint mediator of their choice, the date of commencement of mediation shall be the date on which the mediator provides his consent. The

26 Section 6 and The First Schedule of the Mediation Act, 2023.
27 The First Schedule, Disputes or Matters Not Fit for Mediation, Mediation Act, 2023.
28 Section 13, Mediation Act, 2023.

date of appointment of mediator is considered as the date of commencement of mediation, when one of the parties applies to mediation service provider for initiating mediation process[29].

The mediation process undertaken under the Mediation Act is a time bound process. It is to be completed within a period of 120 days from the date of first appearance before the mediator. This period can be mutually extended by the parties for further period of 60 days but not beyond[30].

If any settlement is reached between the parties, then a mediation settlement agreement in writing is to be entered into and signed by the parties[31]. Such agreement is to be authenticated by the Mediator, and he shall also provide a copy to all the parties. In case of institutional mediation, such agreement is to be authenticated by the Mediator, and he shall forward it to the mediation service provider along with a covering letter. The Mediator shall also provide a copy to all the parties.

Such agreements are then to be registered with the Authority established under this Act or a body notified by the government within 180 days of receipt of authenticated copy. Such authority shall issue a unique registration number to the settlement agreements registered by it[32].

When no agreement is arrived between the parties within the prescribed time or if the mediator is of the opinion that such agreement may not be arrived at, then non-settlement report is to be prepared by the mediator and he shall also provide a signed copy to each of the parties. In case of institutional mediation, non-settlement report prepared by the mediator is to be submitted to the mediation service provider along with copies to the parties. It is very important for the mediator not to disclose the cause of non-settlement and the conduct of the parties during the mediation[33].

29 Section 14, Mediation Act, 2023.
30 Section 18, Mediation Act, 2023.
31 Section 19, Mediation Act, 2023.
32 Section 20, Mediation Act, 2023.
33 Section 21, Mediation Act, 2023.

The mediated settlement agreement once signed by parties and authenticated by the mediator shall become final and binding on the parties and is enforceable as a judgement or decree passed by the Court[34].

The mediated settlement agreement can be challenged in exceptional cases on grounds of fraud, corruption, impersonation or when the disputes resolved by mediation are disputes or matters not fit for mediation as per provisions of this law[35].

Role of Mediator

Person of any nationality can be appointed as a mediator, so long as he has the qualification, experience and the accreditation as specified. If the parties cannot mutually agree to any mediator, they can approach a mediation service provider to appoint one for them[36].

The proposed mediator, before his appointment, is required to disclose in writing potential circumstances which can constitute any conflict of interest. In the event of any conflict of interest arises during mediation, it shall be communicated to the parties in writing at such time too. Parties can waive objection and continue the mediation process with the mediator after consenting in writing[37].

The role of mediator in any mediation proceedings is very important. This importance is highlighted in the Mediation Act. Sections 16 and 17 of the Mediation Act elaborate on this role. It is mentioned that the mediator shall attempt to facilitate voluntary resolution of the dispute by the parties. The mediator shall communicate view of each party to the other, assist them in identifying the issues, clarifying priorities, exploring areas of settlement and generating options. He shall not impose any settlement. Any mediator in any particular mediation proceedings cannot later act as arbitrator in respect of the same dispute. The mediator neither can appear as a witness nor can represent any of the parties in any proceedings before any arbitration or judicial proceedings.

34 Section 27, Mediation Act, 2023.
35 Section 28, Mediation Act, 2023.
36 Section 8, Mediation Act, 2023.
37 Section 10, Mediation Act, 2023.

Impact on Other Laws

While this new legislation on mediation is newly introduced for regulating the mediation processes and system in India, mediation as a concept was already introduced in India in various other laws at different times in different manner. Therefore, this new legislation not only introduces new mediation regime in India, but also has an impact on the provisions under various legislations already in force.

Section 55 of the Mediation Act clarifies that this new legislation has an overriding effect on the provisions of existing laws in force in India, to the extent they are inconsistent with the provisions of Mediation Act, more specifically in respect of conduct of mediation and conciliation. There are nine exceptions provided to this rule in the Second Schedule to this act. These include the legislations like the Industrial Disputes Act (1947), the Industrial Relations Code (2020), the Family Courts Act (1984), the Legal Services Authorities Act (1987) and the Sexual Harassment of Women at Workplace (Prevention, Prohibition and Redressal) Act (2013).

After implementation of the Mediation Act (2023), various laws stand amended, including the Indian Contract Act (1872), the Arbitration and Conciliation Act (1996), the Micro, Small and Medium Enterprises Development Act (2006), the Companies Act (2013) and the Consumer Protection Act (2019). Also amended are the procedural laws like the CPC (1908), the Legal Service Authorities Act (1987) and the Commercial Courts Act (2015).

The Contract Act (1872) declares any agreement in restraint of legal proceedings as *void ab initio*. Thus, whenever a party restrains another from enforcing his rights under any contract or extinguishes rights of the other party then, the contract is held void to that extent[38]. Now, as mediation law is introduced in the country and mediation is to be the preferred remedy in case of any breach of contract, any mediation or arbitration agreement will not be held in restraint of legal proceedings and therefore not void[39]. This exception is applicable in respect of future disputes which the parties

38 The Indian Contract Act enacted on 25 April 1872 Section 28, <https://www.indiacode.nic.in/handle/123456789/2187?col=123456789/1362>, accessed 20 September 2024.

39 The Third Schedule, Mediation Act 2023.

agree to submit for mediation or arbitration and also the disputes that have already arisen, which the parties agree to submit to mediation or arbitration.

After introduction of this new law on mediation, pre-litigation mediation is made compulsory in case of commercial suits filed under the provisions of the Commercial Courts Act, 2015[40]. Therefore, a commercial suit cannot anymore be filed, without exhausting the remedy of pre-litigation mediation. The time limit for conclusion of the pre-litigation mediation process is 120 days, extendable up to 60 more days. Only exception to this compulsion is when there is a need for urgent interim relief. Even in case of disputes filed before the Micro and Small Enterprises Facilitation Council, the Council may refer the dispute to any mediation service provider. If the mediation is not successful, then the Council can proceed with the proceedings, as per procedure laid down by the Micro, Small and Medium Enterprises Development Act, 2006[41].

In case of consumer disputes filed or pending before the District, State or National Commission for consumer dispute redressal, the Commission may on request of the parties or on its own refer the dispute for mediation. The CPC, 1908, now authorises the courts to refer the dispute to arbitration or mediation if the Court thinks it can be settled.

Summary

A review of Indian history with specific reference to mediation shows us that mediation was a primary method of dispute resolution. This method resonated well with a society which avoided violence as far as possible and aimed at peaceful and amicable existence. It can be traced back to ancient jurisprudence as well as books reflecting the social and cultural norms. While this situation changed in the British Rule, mediation was re-embraced post-independence. However, as the British common law system set in India was not radically changed after independence, mediation became more of an alternative method of dispute resolution than a mainstream choice.

The Mediation Act (2023) is a significant and progressive step towards incorporating mediation process in the essential legal framework in India. It is a commendable effort to legislate on various small and big aspects of

40 The Ninth Schedule, Mediation Act 2023.

41 The Seventh Schedule, Mediation Act 2023.

mediation process, so that a robust environment for mutual resolution of disputes can be created. This framework, if effectively implemented, will result in availability of faster, reliable and less expensive dispute resolution system, which is necessary for certainty of legal system for any business. This will, in turn, attract more and more foreign businesses to invest in India.

Efforts will need to be taken for creating awareness about mediation as an option in the system of dispute resolution, the infrastructure to support increasing demand for mediation in physical as well as online format and also availability of trained mediators in all areas of the country – even the rural ones.

India has attempted to introduce arbitration as an ADR method. However, it has not been as successful as it was desired at the time of passing of the new law on arbitration replacing the older one in 1996. One of the biggest challenges in effective enforcement of the arbitration awards was the challenges faced by these awards in the Courts. As Mediation being a voluntary process where the mediator cannot force his decision on the parties, it is expected that the mediation settlement agreements will face lesser challenges regarding their validity in courts as compared to the arbitral awards.

Another challenge in the streamlined and effective implementation of the mediation settlement agreement. Once it is established with sufficient credibility that such agreements are enforced as court decrees, people will start believing in the sanctity of such agreements. Till then, it is going to prove a challenge, especially when, till date, mediation results were not binding on the parties.

While the Act defines international mediation, there are no specific provisions regarding implementation of the international mediation settlement agreements in India. Thus, this has a left ambiguity in respect of the judicial practices and mechanism in respect of enforcement of the international mediation settlement agreements. This may hamper the perception of the international community of India as a potential marketplace and preferred place of business. While the Act is aligned with the basic tenets of Singapore Convention on Mediation, the Act does not explicitly refer to or incorporate the provisions of the Convention. It appears that the legislation is drafted keeping in mind the needs of the Indian legal system thus focusing on the domestic need. It will be interesting to observe if such provisions are introduced by way of amendment of this legislation, at a future date, when mediation becomes a more settled way of dispute resolution in India.

Keeping with the recent trend in the legislations in India regarding the commercial transactions and topics, this legislation also segregates commercial actions of the government from that of the sovereign functions. Mediation can be initiated even with government as one of the parties. However, there are certain disputes of the private parties with the government, which may be resolved faster through mediation, which has been proved through the successful settlements at the Lok Adalats. These include both civil disputes as well as certain offences under different statutes, which are more civil in nature and where penalty or fine is a preferred mechanism. These are not at present in the scope of the legislation. Inclusion of a separate schedule listing such disputes may resolve this gap and help reduce pendency of smaller cases in the court system.

Thus, to conclude, the Mediation Act (2023) can prove to be a milestone legislation in the legal system of dispute resolution in India, success of which is going to depend on how it is implemented on ground and how mediation is integrated in the existing legal framework. There are certain gaps in this legislation which may affect the effective implementation of the Act and to achieve the objectives behind the legislation. However, no legislation is perfect at the beginning. It evolves over time after realising the gaps in the legislation and the challenges faced in implementation. The success of this framework will depend not only on how the judiciary implements the legislation in its true spirit rather than merely following the letter of the law, but also on how the legislature addresses the challenges observed during implementation and remedies the deficiencies to align with the country's ever-evolving and dynamic economy.

Bibliography

Anirban, Chakraborty (2016). *Law and Practice of Alternative Dispute Resolution in India: A Detailed Analysis*. Gurgaon: Lexis Nexis.

Astha, Tripathi (2024). *Justice Dispensation through Mediation in India*. Delhi: Sweet & Soft.

Deepika, Kinhal and Apoorva, Misra (2021). 'Mandatory Mediation in India – Resolving to Resolve'. *Indian Public Policy Review*, 2 (2), 49–69.

Department-Related Parliamentary Standing Committee on Personnel, Public Grievances, Law and Justice (2021). 'One Hundred Seventeenth Report on The Mediation Bill'.

Kanuga, Sahil and Bhosale, Shraddha (2021). 'Mediation of Commercial Disputes in India', *NLUJ Law Review*, 7 (282), <https://www.nishithdesai.com/fileadmin/user_upload/pdfs/NDA%20In%20The%20Media/News%20Articles/Mediation_of_commercial_disputes_in_India.pdf>, accessed 20 September 2024.

Kaur, Puneetish (2019a). 'Companies Mediation and Conciliation Rules, 2016 – A New Approach Towards Settlement of Corporate Governance Conflicts'. In Rajinder Kaur (ed.), *Mediation and Negotiation in Trade and Commercial Conflicts an Indian Perspective*. Thomson Reuters.

Kaur, Rajinder (2019b). 'Mediation and Negotiation in Corporate Laws with Special Reference to Companies Act, 2013'. In Rajinder Kaur (ed.), *Mediation and Negotiation in Trade and Commercial Conflicts An Indian Perspective*. Thomson Reuters.

Kaur, Rajinder (2019c). *Mediation and Negotiation in Trade and Commercial Conflicts an Indian Perspective*. Thomson Reuters.

Markanda, Parmod, Markanda, Naresh, and Markanda, Rajesh (2021). *Mediation: Step by Step*. Thomson Reuters.

Rohini, Jagtap (2022). 'Study of Mediation as a Leading Mechanism for Settlement of Disputes and its Challenges', *Pimpri Law Review Journal*, 2 (1), 1–8, <https://law.dypvp.edu.in/plr/Publication/all-publication/Rohini-Jagtap-article.pdf>, accessed 20 September 2024.

Sanyal Sanjeev and Kumar Mishra, Apurv (2023). 'Why Commercial Mediation Should be Voluntary', *EAC-PM Working Paper Series*, EAC-PM/WP/25/2023.

Legal sources

<https://www.indiacode.nic.in/handle/123456789/2013?sam_handle=...>, accessed 15 July 2024.

Industrial Disputes Act enacted on 11 March 1947, <https://www.indiacode.nic.in/bitstream/123456789/15191/1/A1947-14.pdf>, accessed 15 July 2024.

Supreme Court of India, M/S. Afcons Infra. Ltd. & Anr vs M/S Cherian Varkey Constn Co. P. Ltd. on 26 July, 2010 (2010), 8 SCC 24, <https://indiankanoon.org/doc/1875345/>, accessed 20 September 2024.

The Code of Civil Procedure enacted on 21 March 1908, Section 89, <https://www.indiacode.nic.in/bitstream/123456789/2191/1/A1908-05.pdf>, accessed 20 July 2024.

The Companies Act on 29 August 2013, <https://www.mca.gov.in/content/mca/global/en/acts-rules/companies-act/companies-act-2013.html>, accessed 20 September 2024.

The Companies Mediation and Conciliation Rules on 9 September 2016, <https://ibclaw.in/the-companies-mediation-and-conciliation-rules-2016/>, accessed 20 September 2024.

The Consumer Protection Act of 9 August 2019, <https://www.indiacode.nic.in/bitstream/123456789/15256/1/a2019-35.pdf>, accessed 20 September 2024.

The Indian Contract Act enacted on 25 April 1872 Section 28, <https://www.indiacode.nic.in/handle/123456789/2187?col=123456789/1362>, accessed 20 September 2024.

The Mediation Act enacted of 14 September 2023, <https://www.indiacode.nic.in/handle/123456789/19637?sam_handle=123456789/1362>, accessed 15 July 2024.

The Micro, Small and Medium Enterprises Development Act of 16th June 2006, United Nations Convention on International Settlement Agreements Resulting from Mediation (Singapore Convention on Mediation), adopted in New York on 20 December 2018, open to signature in Singapore on 7 August 2019, <https://uncitral.un.org/sites/uncitral.un.org/files/media-documents/EN/Texts/UNCITRAL/Arbitration/mediation_convention_v1900316_eng.pdf>, accessed 20 September 2024.

CHAPTER 13

Mediation in Australia: Development and Successful Practice in Both Aboriginal and Western Society and Their Possible Collaboration

Iwona Pruszyńska[1]

Introduction

The renowned Australian author, Tim Costello, in his book *Tips from a Travelling Soul-Searcher* reminds his readers that storytelling has profound social significance. Costello believes that through sharing life stories, one reinforces human values necessary for genuine progress.

He searches for inspiration in his Christian identity, but also in the religions and beliefs of other individuals he encounters on his travels. He swaps stories with homeless youth and CEOs, Aboriginal elders, school children and religious leaders, cattle ranchers and drug addicts.

We all live stories, either explicit or implicit. Families, clans, community groups and co-workers all have stories to tell, and these stories contain lessons, morals, insights and inspiring advice for everyday life. We, too, as practitioners, theorists and observers of mediation in Australia, have our own personal stories to tell. If Costello had asked us to share them with him, it would have been difficult to choose a leading narrative. Our story would have been a saga of expectation and hope, often of frustration and disappointment, but also triumph and satisfaction. For the beginning of our story, I would choose the year 1990, although this is just a symbolic and simply convenient date. Australian mediation movements date back decades earlier, when the first social justice programmes were introduced in the 1980s, and earlier, during

1 LLM, Solicitor Director at Cap Lawyers consultant on Australian law to Concordia Law Office in Katowice, Poland, member of The Law Society of New South Wales and Law Council of Australia; The International Law Section, email: <iwona@cap-lawyers.com.au>

the Industrial Revolution when industrial-relations systems had been introduced. However, the most important and often ignored fact is that thousands of years before Captain Cook arrived, Aboriginal people developed the rules of behaviour and the cultural imperatives aimed primarily at discouraging disruption and restoring harmony if disruption does occur. Those rules were developed in different times and for different circumstances, but they remain powerful and relevant in Aboriginal society today.

Yet, assuming that the contemporary Australian mediation was born in 1990, it was accompanied by, among others, the following events of that year in other parts of the world:

- In Africa, the release of Nelson Mandela after 27 years of incarceration.
- In Europe, Germany reunification after the fall of the Berlin Wall.
- Also in Europe, the Baltic states declaring independence from the Soviet Union.

Its beginnings coincided with the publication of 'Getting to Yes' and most early training programmes largely based on the Harvard Negotiation model, a rational and pragmatic approach that resonated with Australians' self-perception.

Dispute resolution methods develop out of the social events they are to serve. This could be in a small village, a nation-state or sometimes globally. Traditional dispute resolution systems are designed to maintain the status quo by which a given society lives and their basic function is to maintain societal order through compensation, punishment, distribution and restoration (Boulle 1999: 216–218).

The current circumstances of Australian society are dominated by economics and the ideologies used to justify many of the current social developments: privatisation, corporatisation, deregulation, outsourcing, the selling of blue-sky spectrum and the like.

Economic rationalism draws inspiration from liberal political philosophy that promotes rationality, autonomy of an individual, equality, competition, freedom from others and protection of the private sphere. It adopts a model of people who are autonomous and rational, and whose self-seeking pursuit of self-satisfaction is regulated by the market. Opposition, rivalry and struggle between individuals are essential features of this worldview.

Economic rationalism also privatises traditional functions of the state such as safeguarding peace and justice. This further results in reducing national sovereignty and shifting power from governments to financial institutions, leading to deregulated public policies and practices.

Mediation thus develops in a context where the value of social action is founded in the market structure. If some object has no economic value, it tends to be held in low regard. Relationships are interpreted in contractual terms because we become customers, not passengers, and consumers, not citizens.

Decisions in these relationships are seen as established in terms of self-interest rather than in terms of community concerns or altruistic factors.

The second significant impact on the shaping of contemporary Australia is its status as a nation of immigrants and one of the most multicultural nations on earth: only Israel has a more diverse population. After World War II, Australia set out to augment its population by 1% annually by bringing in immigrants and owes much of its post-war prosperity and growth to migration. An influx of 'boat people', Vietnamese fleeing the Communists after the fall of Saigon, followed the end of the Vietnam War, in which Australian soldiers fought alongside Americans. Suddenly Australia was forced to re-evaluate itself as part of Asia, and its geography began to rival its history as a source of self-perception.

The reality is that one cannot address a group, teach a class or attend a gathering without coming face to face with the cultural diversity of this land; nor can one expect to conduct many mediations in which cultural issues, whether acknowledged or not, are not in some way involved.

Thus, aspects of mediation do share many of the underlying values of broader social trends. They enable disputes to be individualised, encourage participants to make decisions in the light of their own interests and cultural context rather than the public interest, emphasise the private ownership of disputes and dispute resolution processes and reduce the need for judicial intervention and, therefore, the sphere of state activity.

There are many different forms of mediation and many different styles of mediators, and all mediators face a wide range of economic, social and political pressures, regardless of their individual position in life.

Mediation in Australia is practised both at the highest levels of international diplomacy and in primary schools, by traditional elders in the rural outback and by full-time officials of the Administrative Appeals Tribunals, by volunteer community mediators in draughty community halls and by unqualified luminaries through the pages of the press (Boulle 1999: 229).

This diversity, found nowhere else, is one of the reasons why it is so difficult to codify the ethical obligation and competency standard of mediators. In some sectors, the mediation procedure has become systematised and professionalised to a fairly high degree. It has educational programmes, professional organisations, codes of conduct, developing literature and international conferences. However, these factors are absent in amateur mediation systems, which are seen as a life skill focused on interpersonal techniques. Both approaches can be equally effective and reasonable.

However, whilst the past proved to be bright, there are symptoms of threats to Alternative Dispute Resolutions (ADR), including mediation, in the future. Scholars and practitioners have argued that the development of ADR in Australia will need to overcome some factors, including:

- Judicialisation of ADR;
- Institutionalisation of ADR;
- Disunity within the ADR profession;
- Lack of coordination and consistency in ADR legislation (Altobelli 2000:103).

Nevertheless, it is suggested that these challenges are fairly manageable, and that the promise of the future is far brighter than the glory of the past.

Australian Legal Framework

Some brief initial remarks on the Australian legal system may help provide a context for the Australian approach to mediation. The legal framework of Australian mediation law is an uncoordinated mixture of state regulations, court rules, case law and private regulations. Many divergent sources contribute to the body of mediation law in Australia.

Australia is a Federation and does not have a uniform legal system. The Commonwealth of Australia comprises six individual states: New South Wales, Queensland, South Australia, Tasmania, Victoria and Western Australia; two Federal territories: Australian Capital Territory and Northern Territory; and the so-called 'dependent Territories of the Commonwealth' such as the Cocos Keeling Islands, Norfolk Island and Christmas Island.

Legislative power is divided between the Federation and the individual states and territories. Jurisdiction for private and procedural law lies mainly with the individual states and territories. This generates a great variety of different legislative regulations throughout the Federation and makes generalised statements difficult. A comprehensive overview of all these is beyond the scope of this discussion, and the focus here is primarily on federal regulations and only by way of example, on the regulations of specific territories (Magnus 2013:871).

Australian civil procedure follows a traditional adversarial model, with judges acting as independent arbitrators. This system, though effective, has led to costly, lengthy and time-consuming trials. Recognising these issues, Australian courts began adopting ADR initiatives in the early 1980s, influenced by practices developed in the United States. Court actions were facilitated by the common-law tradition that the courts have rather wide discretion under their own rules to regulate themselves and their procedure. After these steps were taken by the judicature, there was a 'legislative avalanche' (Wade 1998: 61) at the federal and state level that aimed to supplement, and largely even to replace, the traditional course of procedure for ADR that was separate from the adversarial system of litigation (Magnus 2013: 871).

On 6 April 1998, Australian Attorney-General, Daryl Williams declared that 'mediation and ADR should be the norm rather than the exception' (Magnus 2013:872). Since then, ADR procedures, and especially mediation, have increased in importance in Australia. Like the USA, Australia has also developed a global role model in this field (Alexander 2013:25).

The Federal Court of Australia has been a leader in promoting mediation and developing procedural rules for its implementation. The Civil Dispute Resolution Act, 2011 (Cth) introduced a mandatory requirement to take 'genuine steps' to settle disputes before proceeding to litigation[2], making mediation or similar ADR procedures a prerequisite for federal court cases[3].

The legislation is short and simple. It invites a party in the dispute to take a 'genuine step' towards dispute resolution before commencing litigation. A party notified of a dispute must show that it has responded in a 'genuine' way. The parties can file 'genuine steps statements' if the dispute fails to be resolved, and only then can litigation commence. If a party has failed to take genuine steps and report them in a statement to the court, that failure can be considered, both in terms of how the matter is managed and its financial consequences.

The legislation has now been in place since 1st August 2011. Its role has been modest but where used, it has proved effective.

None of the predictions of harm suggested prior to the passage of the Act, including subjectiveness, has come true. This was an objection not only in relation to the Civil Dispute Resolution Bill but also in its New South Wales and Victorian equivalents, which required a 'reasonable' rather than a 'genuine' step to be taken.

Experience has shown that Courts will determine what 'genuine' or 'reasonable steps' are, as a matter of fact. Judges make such assessments within the context of a particular dispute, and the effort must appear to be 'bona fide'. There appears to be no meaningful distinction between a 'genuine step' and a 'reasonable step'[4].

---

2 See Sections 4, 6 and 7, Civil Dispute Resolution Act 2011.

3 Schedule 1 to the Access to Justice (Civil Litigation Reforms) Amendment Act 2009 had already introduced a new section 37N in the Federal Court of Australia Act 1976, which in section (1) obliged the parties to act 'in a way that is consistent with the overarching purpose' section 37N(4). The 'overarching purpose' of civil procedures is defined in section (1) of section 37M Federal Court of Australia Act 1976 as resolving disputes '(a) according to law; and (b) as quickly, inexpensively and efficiently as possible'.

4 Australian Dispute Resolution Advisory Council (ADRAC), *Submission to New South Wales Law Reform Commission on Consultation Paper* 18, pp. 8, <https://lawreform.nsw.gov.au/documents/Current-projects/ADR/Submissions/DR19.pdf>, accessed 27 July 2024.

Mediation has established itself as the most prominent form of extra-judicial dispute resolution[5]. Eventually, the legislature took a more prominent role and, finally, a broad general mediation movement came into existence combining self-regulatory, market and legislative elements, often found in common law jurisdictions.

The most important current rules on mediation, the Australian National Mediator Standards (ANMS), emerged from private organisations and have a voluntary character[6].

Operation of the Commonwealth legislation over the last 13 years has demonstrated that the predictions of harm that it would bring have not materialised. Provisions such as those of the Civil Dispute Resolution Act 2011 give Courts various tools to be used to ensure that parties act reasonably. Some legal practitioners argue that the greatest benefit of the legislation, however, is that it better enables lawyers at the beginning of a conflict to encourage 'highly invested' clients to take a step towards alternative resolution before litigating because a costs risk may result at the conclusion of litigation[7].

One of the strongest indicators of mediation's growth in Australia is the significant number of laws from the 1990s that mandate, provide for, or refer to various forms of ADR. Although some of these laws include minor references to mediation and may seem esoteric, the overall message is clear: dispute resolution is increasingly viewed in non-adversarial terms, with mediation seen as legitimate, credible and often preferred over traditional litigation.

Federal Legislation

At the federal level, the initial legislative focus was mainly on mediation in family law disputes. By modifying the Family Law Act 1975, Family Law Rules and Family Law Regulations (Cth) and the Federal Court of Australia Act

5 See Federal Court of Australia, Annual Report (2009–2010), pp. 34 (of 477 ADR referrals, 476 concerned mediation and one referral was to a conference of experts).

6 These are the Australian National Mediator Practice Standards (2007) and the Australian National Mediator Approval Standards (2008).

7 Australian Dispute Resolution Advisory Council (ADRAC), *Submission to New South Wales Law Reform Commission on Consultation Paper* 18, p. 9, <https://lawreform.nsw.gov.au/documents/Current-projects/ADR/Submissions/DR19.pdf>, accessed 27 July 2024.

1976, the Courts (Mediation and Arbitration) Act 1991 initially introduced the possibility of statutory mediation processes not only in family matters, but also in other matters.

The Family Law Act has long emphasised settlement through processes such as mediation, conciliation and counselling. The Family Law Reform Act 1995 reinforced these processes by designating them 'Primary Dispute Resolution'. The Family Law Regulations now feature one of the most comprehensive statutory mediation schemes globally, addressing critical issues of mediator accreditation, standards, duties and obligations.

The current focus is on the generalisation of pre-trial consensual procedures that, it is hoped, will reduce litigation in court. According to Subsection 53A of the Federal Court of Australia Act 1976, the Federal Court is now entitled to refer a dispute, or parts of it, to a mediator, but only with the consent of the parties.

The Federation also added mediation possibilities to administrative law (Administrative Appeals Tribunal Act 1975). The Administrative Appeals Tribunal Amendment Act 1993 (Cth) introduced section 34A, providing for mediation conferences, with 664 conferences held between 1993 and 1996.

The Native Title Act 1993 further reinforced mediation as a key process in Native Title dispute resolution.

Current efforts focus on generalising pre-trial consensual procedures to reduce court litigation. Section 53A of the Federal Court of Australia Act 1976 now allows the Federal Court to refer disputes, or parts of them, to mediation with the parties' consent.

Other examples

Commonwealth Courts (Mediation and Arbitration) Act 1991 (Cth). This act introduced voluntary mediation in the Federal Court of Australia, one of the busiest jurisdictions in Australia for the resolution of commercial and administrative disputes.

Trade Practices (Industry Codes-Franchising) Regulations 1998 (Cth) mandated a Mediation Adviser within the Franchising Code of Conduct to address high levels of dispute between franchisors and franchisees. The franchising sector was characterised by high levels of dispute generally arising out of the imbalance of power between franchisors and franchisees.

Relevant legislative frameworks include Workplace Relations Act 1996 (Cth), Aged Care Act 1997 (Cth) and Committee Principles 1997 (Cth).

State Legislation

It has been observed that in Australia hundreds of state and sector-specific legislation acts regulate mediation. Statutory regulations have been regularly enacted for specific types of disputes at both federal and state levels. By 1998, Queensland alone had around thirty different Acts and Statutory Instruments providing for ADR or mediation. Only a few examples of state regulations can be mentioned here:

Farm Debt Mediation Act 1994 (NSW). Any enforcement action under a farm mortgage to which the Act applies is subject to the farmer being given an opportunity to go to mediation.

Courts Legislation (Mediation and Evaluation) Amendment Act 1994 (NSW). This Act empowers NSW courts including the Supreme, District, Local, Compensation and Land and Environment Courts to refer matters to mediation with the consent of the parties. In 2000, the Supreme Court Amendment (Referral of Proceedings) Act 2000 (NSW) empowered the Supreme Court of NSW to order parties to attend mediation without their consent.

Strata Schemes Management Act 1996 (NSW). This legislation establishes a scheme for the mediation of disputes arising out of strata title, one of the most common forms of property ownership in NSW. This scheme extends to land under the Community Land Management Act 1989 (NSW).

Fair Trading Tribunal Act 1998 (NSW). The Fair Trading Tribunal replaces the Commercial Tribunal. It deals with and adjudicates, if necessary, consumer and commercial disputes and provides for mediation or neutral evaluation.

Domestic Relationships Act 1994 (ACT). Provides a framework for resolving financial disputes between unmarried couples in a domestic relationship, including de facto marriages. Section 8 allows the court to refer matters to mediation.

Mediation Act 1997 (ACT). The first Australian legislation explicitly addressing mediation, including mediator registration, competency standards, confidentiality and mediator immunity.

Chicken Meat Industry Committee Act 1976 (Qld) as amended. This Act establishes a committee regulating the Queensland chicken meat industry and includes the setting of guidelines and mediation of disputes between processors and growers: section 16.
Mining Act 1971 (SA) amended by the Statutes Amendment (Native Title) Act 1998. In disputes about mining licences the court having jurisdiction under this Act is required to mediate among disputing parties under section 63P.
Opal Mining Act 1995 (SA). Where one party proposes to mine opals on land subject to native title, section 58(3) provides for voluntary mediation.
Sentencing Act 1995 (WA). This Act provides for mediation between the victims of crime and offenders. The report of such mediation is relevant to sentencing.

International Treaties Incorporated into Australian Law

Australia is a party to several international treaties and conventions that provide for mediation in disputes between contracting parties. These treaties are incorporated into Australian law, either as schedules to Commonwealth Acts or through Regulations. Examples include:

- Transport and Communications Legislation Amendment Act (No. 2) 1992 (Cth) which incorporates into the Protection of the Sea (Prevention of Pollution from Ships) Act 1983, the Protocol on Environment Protection to the Antarctic Treaty.
- Fisheries Legislation Amendment Act (No 1) 1999 (Cth) which implements the Fish Stocks Agreement.
- Extradition (Narcotic Drugs) Regulations 1988 which incorporate the Convention on Narcotic Drugs 1961.
- Hazardous Waste (Regulation of Exports and Imports) (Waigani Convention) Regulations 1999, incorporating the Waigani Convention to Ban Importation of Hazardous and Radioactive Wastes of 1995.
- Ozone Protection Act 1989 (Cth), incorporating the Vienna Convention for the Protection of the Ozone Layer.

Private Regulation

In addition to state regulations, there is a robust private sector for mediation, primarily regulated by market principles, private contracts and industry standards. Most mediation, especially commercial disputes, is conducted by private mediation organisations. Notable institutions include:

- The Institute of Arbitrators and Mediators Australia (IAMA) that was founded in 1976.
- The Australian Commercial Disputes Centre (ACDC) that was established in 1986.
- Both institutions provide mediator education and training.
- Other professional associations and societies which are influential include Lawyers Engaged in Alternative Dispute Resolution (LEADR) which represents lawyers acting as mediators and advocates for their interests (Magnus 2013: 877–878).

The private mediation sector gained particular importance insofar as it has generated national standards for mediation and a (voluntary) accreditation system. The Australian National Mediator Approval Standards and the Australian National Mediator Practice Standards introduced between 2007 and 2008 regulate mediator accreditation and professional practice standards. The profession has also created a National Mediator Accreditation Committee (NMAC) for self-regulation and established a national system of Recognised Mediator Accreditation Bodies (RMABs), to which accredited mediators must belong (Magnus 2013: 878–879).

Definition of Mediation

Mediation is fundamentally defined as the assistance provided by neutral third parties to help interacting parties resolve disputes without imposing a solution. It is one of the oldest and most widespread forms of conflict resolution globally (Kressel & Pruitt 1989: 9). According to Tania Sourdin (Sourdin & Alexander 2003: 45), mediation involves a process where the parties, with the help of a mediator, identify disputed issues, explore options, consider alternatives and reach an agreement. The mediator facilitates the process but does not advise on or determine the dispute's content; in most cases, they are neutral and have no authority to impose an outcome (Wall et al. 2001: 370).

In Australian legal literature, mediation is defined as follows:

> Mediation is "a process in which the parties to a dispute, with the assistance of a dispute resolution practitioner (mediator), identify the disputed issues, develop options, consider alternatives and reach an agreement. The mediator has no advisory or determinative role regarding the content of the dispute or the outcome of its resolution but may advise on or determine the process of mediation whereby resolution is attempted. Mediation may be undertaken voluntarily, under a court order, or subject to an existing contractual agreement" (Sourdin & Alexander 2003: 45).

No Australian legislative act provides an express definition of mediation. The Civil Dispute Resolution Act 2011 does not even mention the term. Therefore, in Australian legal and mediation practice, it is suggested to use a definition of mediation provided by the National Mediator Accreditation System (NMAS):

> Mediation is a process that promotes the self-determination of participants and in which participants, with the support of a mediator:

(a) communicate with each other, exchange information and seek understanding
(b) identify, clarify and explore interests, issues and underlying needs
(c) consider their alternatives
(d) generate and evaluate options
(e) negotiate with each other; and
(f) reach and make their own decisions[8].

8 National Mediator Accreditation System (NMAS) 2015, p. 2, <https://msb.org.au/themes/msb/assets/documents/national-mediator-accreditation-system-2015.pdf>, accessed 1 August 2024.

It is important for parties to know exactly what ADR process they are entering. No party should be directed into a process the nature and function of which is either vague or misleading.

A party entering mediation is entitled to believe that the mediator will facilitate a settlement based solely on the interests of the parties and will have no professional or other agenda.

The Native Title Act 1993 describes the purpose of mediation: 'The purpose of mediation in a proceeding that does not involve a compensation application is to assist the parties to reach agreement'[9].

Types of Mediation

Despite Australia's early enthusiasm for developing a peculiar mediation model adapted to its unique circumstances and place in the world, it may be surprising that most Australian mediators use variations of a model familiar to American mediators. The model used in commercial mediation generally follows these steps:

1. Parties agree on a mediator.
2. The parties, their lawyers and the mediator meet on the day of the mediation.
3. The mediator makes an opening statement, and the parties briefly exchange greetings and introductory remarks; OR the parties, assisted by the mediator, engage in an extended opening session at which they and their lawyers set out the issues in dispute and the mediator identifies the issue.
4. The mediator shows the parties and their teams to separate rooms and conducts private sessions with each party, exchanging offers and carrying information back and forth until the parties reach a settlement.
5. The parties meet once again to discuss the terms of a settlement OR remain in their rooms until a settlement is reached. In either case, lawyers meet and draw up settlement documents.
6. Parties and lawyers sign a settlement agreement (Kalowski 2009).

9 Section 86A(1) Native Title Act 1993.

Regarding the relationship between court proceedings and mediation, three types are distinguished:

- Private mediation is completely independent of judicial proceedings. Indeed, it is often held without any subsequent court proceeding.
- Court-annexed mediation is initiated by the court but then takes place without any further involvement of the court.
- Judicial mediation is more intensely connected with the court as an institution in terms of venue and personnel. However, even judicial mediation is not performed by a judge with adjudicatory competence in the specific case.

Private mediation

Mediation has become an established private profession. Although there are no precise published figures, it can be safely assumed that most mediation procedures are conducted by private mediators who are not state servants.

For private mediation, it is necessary for both parties to agree to the mediation, and this agreement is all that is required for the mediation to take place. The agreement to mediate must specify the dispute to which it applies and the name of the mediator or the mediation organisation (which can, in turn, appoint a mediator according to its own rules). The mediation agreement has the further effect that the final agreement usually acquires the character of a binding settlement (Magnus 2013: 878).

Court-annexed mediation

Legislation prescribing compulsory pre-litigation mediation involves a delicate balance between ensuring that parties attempt to settle their disputes before litigating and retain the right of access to the Courts. The characteristics of certain disputes justify legislation deeming that good faith involves a requirement to mediate first in the context of those disputes. It is another thing entirely to assume that good faith requires disputants to mediate first in all cases.

Court-annexed mediation is highly effective. In 2010 and 2011, the Supreme Court of New South Wales referred 933 family provision disputes to court-annexed mediation, with 531 (56.9%) settled during mediation (Bergin 2012).

Since the Civil Dispute Resolution Act 2011 coming into effect, at the federal level, parties are generally obligated to undertake mediation, or at least attempt it, before they can successfully institute legal proceedings[10]. During litigation, the court may refer the dispute or parts of it to a mediator, but often only with the parties' consent[11]. The court has limited power to order mediation against the will of one or both parties if the judge is convinced that mediation is useful and may resolve the dispute[12].

The mediator may be either a specially trained registrar, a judge of the court (Dewdney 2009) or a professional external mediator. The last mentioned is the most frequently chosen. Parkinson notes that the Australian system differs from other countries by emphasising community-based services. The establishment of free or heavily subsidised Family Dispute Resolution services, such as Family Relationship Centres, resembles the Norwegian model, in contrast to the more court-centric approach found in the United States (Parkinson 2015).

Judicial mediation

Court-related mediation can be conducted by court staff, or by specially trained registrars or judges. It has been observed that court-related mediation in Australia tends to be more interventionist than private mediation procedures. Court-based mediators tend to act in a more judge-like manner; they dominate the proceedings, leaving only a limited role to the parties. They also focus on the parties' rights rather than on their interests and tend towards evaluative interventions with a view to reaching a settlement. This approach may not align with the National Mediator Standards for Australia (Magnus 2013: 879–880).

However, the more serious and important question is whether it is appropriate. It is clear from the provisions in place in those parts of Australia where judicial mediation is tolerated that the judge-mediator will not be permitted to take certain measures unless the parties give relevant approval.

10 Family Law Act 1975, for disputes over native land titles, mandatory pre-litigation mediation was already required under the Native Title Act 1993.

11 Section 53A, Federal Court of Australia Act 1975.

12 See the following decisions from New South Wales: Idoport Pty. Ltd. & Another v National Australia Bank Ltd. & 8 others [2001] NSWSC 427; Remuneration Planning Corp. Pty Ltd. v Fitton [2001] NSWSC 1208; Singh v Singh [2002] NSWSC 852; Harrison v Schipp [2002] NSWCA 27.

It is also envisaged that judge-mediators will receive information directly from the party albeit that the legal practitioner for that party will be present. In jurisdictions where judicial mediation is allowed, judge-mediators are generally prohibited from disclosing information received from a party without express authorisation. This duty of confidentiality highlights the challenges of maintaining information barriers and avoiding conflicts of interest within the judiciary[13].

Over the years, legal firms have established a 'Chinese wall' for the protection of clients' confidential information and to avoid conflicts of interest. At this stage, no debate was held in Australia as to how the judges' duty to keep the information confidential is to be accommodated. The prospect of the need to establish an information barrier between judges of a court further highlights the real difficulties with the practice (Bergin 2012).

Mediators

Accreditation of mediators

In Australia, mediator accreditation is not mandatory. However, the voluntary NMAS has been operational since early 2008 and has become the primary standard for mediators in Australia.[14] Despite the concurrent operation of multiple accreditation systems, the NMAS seems to have acquired de facto status as an endorsed accreditation system, as most providers of court-ordered mediation are accredited under the NMAS (Sourdin 2012: 115).

To obtain accreditation under NMAS, a mediator must:

- pass a 'good character' test;
- have an affiliation with an appropriate organisation that adheres to ethical standards, establish complaints and disciplinary processes and provide ongoing professional support; and

13 This is an unqualified duty to preserve the confidentiality of the information provided to the judge: Charles Hollander Q. C. & Salzedo S. (2008). *Conflicts of Interest*, par. 7-003. Thomson Sweet & Maxwell.

14 The system is provided for by two main documents known collectively as the 'Australian National Mediator Standards'. The first is 'Approval Standards for Mediators Seeking Approval under the National Mediator Accreditation System' (September 2007). The second is 'Practice Standards for Mediators Operating Under the National Mediator Accreditation System' (September 2007).

- provide evidence of competence by reference to a combination of experience, training and education[15].

If an applicant lacks sufficient mediation experience, they must complete a 38-hour workshop, which includes at least nine simulated mediation sessions[16]. Once accredited, mediators are required to conduct a minimum of 25 hours of mediation and complete 20 hours of continuing professional development every 2 years[17].

Immunity of Mediators

In Australia, mediators benefit from broad protection against civil proceedings, granted through a fragmented system of immunity primarily provided by legislation and occasionally supplemented by contractual agreements. There is no single overarching statute at the state or federal level granting immunity to all mediators. Instead, various statutes provide immunity in specific circumstances (Bergin 2012:20).

The result is a regime consisting of two different levels of immunity. Some mediators enjoy protection equal to that of a judicial officer, which is known as 'unqualified mediator immunity'. This affords mediators complete immunity from civil proceedings without the need to first establish that the impugned conduct was carried out in good faith. This form of immunity applies to, for example, mediations connected to the highest courts in New South Wales, Victoria, Queensland, Western Australia and South Australia[18].

Other mediators receive 'qualified immunity', which requires them to prove they acted in good faith, without fraud, or in alignment with the statutory purposes of the relevant legislation (Boulle 2011: 740). Such provisions apply

15 Australian National Mediator Standards (2007). 'Approval Standards for Mediators Seeking Approval Under the National Mediator Accreditation System', 3 (1).

16 Australian National Mediator Standards (2007). 'Approval Standards for Mediators Seeking Approval Under the National Mediator Accreditation System', 5 (3).

17 Australian National Mediator Standards (2007). 'Approval Standards for Mediators Seeking Approval Under the National Mediator Accreditation System', 1(3).

18 0 CPA, section 33; Supreme Court Act 1986 (Vic), p. 27A; Supreme Court of Queensland Act 1991
(Qld), section 113; Supreme Court Act 1935 (WA), p. 70; Supreme Court Act 1935 (SA), section 65.

to the highest courts in Tasmania[19] and the Australian Capital Territory[20] as well as mediators in community justice centres in New South Wales, Queensland and Victoria[21].

Parties may expressly agree that the liability of the mediator is limited or excluded.

Litigation against mediators in Australia is extremely rare. Although Australian courts have not extensively examined statutory immunity for mediators, the Queensland Court of Appeal addressed it in the case of Von Schultz v. Attorney-General[22]. That case concerned various allegations of misconduct made against a mediator, including an allegation of falsely signing a mediator's certificate to the effect that a settlement had been reached in mediation between the parties. In dismissing the application for leave to appeal, the Court of Appeal applied section 113(1) of the Supreme Court of Queensland Act 1991 (Qld), granting the mediator immunity from suit equivalent to that enjoyed by a judge.

It has also been suggested that a mediator's immunity from civil action is unnecessary because more moderate mechanisms, such as professional insurance and indemnity schemes, provide sufficient protection for mediators (Bergin 2012: 23).

Lawyers as Mediators

In Australia, lawyers have become the de facto gatekeepers of mediation. Legal expertise is highly valued, and the 'market' tends to favour lawyer-mediators with specific legal knowledge relevant to the dispute. This trend has led to a growing emphasis on evaluative mediation, which often resembles conciliation more than traditional mediation. Mediators are frequently asked to provide legal opinions on the likely outcomes of disputes if they proceed to court (Kalowski 2009).

19 Alternative Dispute Resolution Act 2001 (Tas), p. 12.

20 Mediation Act 1997 (ACT), p. 12.

21 Community Justice Centres Act 1983 (NSW), section 27(1), Dispute Resolution Centres Act 1990 (Qld), section 35(1)(c), Evidence (Miscellaneous Provisions) Act 1958 (Vic), p. 21N.

22 [2000] QCA 406.

There is also an increasing trend of former judges entering the field of mediation. Their involvement is seen to encourage reluctant parties to sit at the table and to reach agreements. As noted by Bergin (2012), some suggestions to use a well-known (facilitative) mediator were met, in one case, with mockery by a barrister, who said the matter needed someone to 'bang heads together', as he put forward the names of two former judges (Boulle 1999).

Perhaps the enthusiasm for experts and ex-judge-mediators should be attributed to Australians' authoritarianism – or at least to the belief that the parties need an authoritarian style in order to be satisfied with the dispute's outcome.

Aboriginal Mediation

Indigenous customary law

The First Peoples of Australia are the Aboriginal and Torres Strait Island peoples. According to the 2016 census, Indigenous Australians comprise 2.8% of Australia's population of nearly 25 million (about 650,000 people). Of those, 91% are of Aboriginal origin, 5% are of Torres Strait Islander origin and 4% are of both Aboriginal and Torres Strait Islander origin. There are over 150 Australian Indigenous languages still in existence today.[23]

Of the hundreds of Australian Indigenous communities, nations and societies, each has its own territories, languages, myths and laws. Relations between the communities are governed by highly organised, uncodified systems. Customary laws regulate, for example, marriage and family, distribution of property, dispute settlement and criminal justice[24].

Aboriginal customary law is recognised to varying degrees within the Australian legal system, including through legislation, judicial responses and sentencing discretion. The Native Title Act 1993 (Cth) is particularly

23 The University of Melbourne Library 'Australian Indigenous Law', <https://unimelb.libguides.com/Indigenous_Law_Australia/Australian_Indigenous_Law>, accessed 3 August 2024.

24 Australian Law Reform Commission (2010)/ 'The Definition of Aboriginal Customary Law', <https://www.alrc.gov.au/publication/recognition-of-aboriginal-customary-laws-alrc-report-31/7-the-scope-of-the-report/the-definition-of-aboriginal-customary-laws/>, accessed 17 July 2024.

significant in recognising Aboriginal customary law within the Australian legal framework.

In 1992, the landmark case of Mabo v. Queensland (No. 2) [(1992) 175 CLR 1] recognised Aboriginal land title at common law, rejecting the notion of terra nullius and acknowledging the pre-existing Indigenous legal system of native title. The Native Title Act established the National Native Title Tribunal to address native title claims and establish lawful extinguishments of title. Mediation is the only way provided in the Act to handle matters before that tribunal.

Reports arising from the Queensland Community Justice Programme (CJP) Aboriginal mediation project ('the project') that was instigated in the early 1990s have led to the perpetuation of the argument that mediation is inconsistent with, or antithetical to, Aboriginal community values, dynamics and dispute resolution needs (Ackfun 1993; Nolan 1993; O'Donnell 1995). In these reports, principles of mediation such as confidentiality, voluntariness and neutrality were seen as incompatible with Aboriginal community values and dynamics. A typical statement is made by the (then) Aboriginal project officer, Kurt Noble, that 'the hallmarks of classic mediation are severely challenged by adaptations to the Aboriginal community context' (Kelly 2002).

In contemporary Australian society, Aboriginal Australians live in two overlapping worlds, the Western and the traditional one, and neither is fully capable of dealing with disputes involving Aboriginal parties. Western dispute resolution models often conflict with Indigenous cultural practices, and European colonisation has weakened traditional dispute resolution methods. In disputes between Aboriginal and non-Aboriginal parties, Western models may further disadvantage Indigenous participants. ADR programmes need to recognise these issues and promote substantive equality for Indigenous people in ADR processes.

Justice is perceived differently in Aboriginal cultures, focusing on restoring peace and equilibrium within the community and reconciling the wrongdoer with their conscience and the affected individuals or families. This contrasts with Western approaches that emphasise punishment and deterrence. Aboriginal dispute resolution aims to maintain peace and strengthen relationships, often using holistic and flexible methods tailored to local decision-making processes.

Western European knowledge structures typically take a linear approach, with the past often representing 'primitiveness' and the present seen as the apex of achievement. Proof – whether of historical fact, scientific hypothesis, or psychological condition – is critical, and rests on the written and evidentiary record.

Aboriginal cultural values are framed differently. Whilst individuals are important, there are expectations of humility, collectivism, knowledge sharing, responsibility for nature and the environment and the interconnectedness of all aspects of life and the environment. The key differences between Anglo-Australian and Aboriginal-Australian cultures are thus identified as individual, hierarchical and competitive versus communal, egalitarian and cooperative.

The Aboriginal model recognises that mediation is not a linear path. There is no time limit set for the mediation; anyone interested in dispute-solving could be present; intake or pre-mediation sessions could be carried out by either the field officer or the mediators. In general, mediation is seen in the context of healing of both disputants and the societies they live in rather than as a legally binding contract between individuals.

Traditional Aboriginal dispute resolution:

- envisages a longer time frame;
- is more flexible;
- employs holistic approaches that many Indigenous communities seek;
- involves the building on and tailoring of processes to existing local decision-making and conflict-management processes;
- plans to keep peace and strengthen relationships;
- is linked to sustainability through 'peacekeeping' measures and
- deals with the past and allows for expressions of remorse and apologies.

Time

Traditional Aboriginal dispute resolution processes are not bound by fixed timeframes. The process is flexible and can be determined by the parties rather than the mediator. Experienced Aboriginal mediators, who are familiar with both orthodox mediation and Aboriginal cultural approaches to time, suggest allowing participants to control the choice and sequence of processes. They advocate for flexibility in mediation phases, rather than adhering to strict timelines.

Mediator Choice and Neutrality

In Anglo-European dispute resolution, the use of independent neutral third parties is central. However, in Aboriginal culture, elders are often respected and involved in resolving disputes, even if they are connected to the parties. This practice is noted in other pre-industrialised societies around the world where social hierarchy is an important element in dispute resolution (Bárrios 2020). Aboriginal practice recognises that deep cultural respect for elders will influence compliance with outcomes and result in community satisfaction. It also means that the dispute is controlled within the community.

At a practical level, given that there is a preference for Aboriginal mediators in a given dispute, it may be impossible to find a neutral mediator. Detailed and complex structures of family networks and obligations in small and close-knit communities make this difficult. Moreover, Aboriginal perceptions of the role of the mediator are more likely to value respect and moral authority than neutrality.

As Nobel rightfully noted, distinguishing the concept of neutrality from that of impartiality might help in assessing the applicability of neutrality to mediation in Aboriginal communities. Impartiality is an essential element in mediation. It refers to even-handedness, objectivity and fairness towards the parties during the mediation process. This includes matters such as time allocation, facilitation of the communication process and avoidance of any display of favouritism, bias or adversarial conduct in word or action (Noble 1995:130). In Aboriginal communities, there is a recognition that certain people are respected for their impartiality within the community and may be suitable to deal with some disputes.

Confidentiality

Western mediation emphasises privacy and confidentiality, limiting information to the mediator and the parties involved. In Aboriginal dispute resolution, however, the individual is seen as part of a larger living mechanism. The community often plays a role in resolving disputes, reflecting the importance of relatedness and consensus-building. Whilst this is the practice in many land title claims where there are multiple people interested in a claim, it is not a typical feature of the mediation process in the normal course.

Scholars argue that gossip may play an important role in maintaining social order and that a community may need to be aware of the outcomes of mediation so that the moral weight of the community can be 'brought to bear' on agreements. It is also argued that open discussion of any given dispute may be important to invoking mechanisms of advice and admonishment which help resolve conflict, and that demanding confidentiality contradicts the idea that the community maintains control of the property of the dispute (Cunneen et al. 2005).

Learning from Aboriginal Culture

One of the challenges in learning from Aboriginal practices is that many of the ideas in Aboriginal culture flow from the importance of relatedness to community and environment, from hierarchical respect for elders and from a non-competitive worldview. Euro-centric communities have ceased to share the same extent or depth of relatedness between dozens if not hundreds of kin, and the competitive perception that there is a right and a wrong outcome to any disagreement dissuades collaboration.

In the multicultural society of Australia today, there are diverse cultures, some with strong family and community connectedness. Many close-knit African communities value community adhesion above individual rights. Many Asian cultures traditionally prioritise respect, community harmony and protocols for indirect communication over confrontational direct approaches. Individuals of any culture who happen to be uneducated in the written, fact-based and chronological approach to conveying stories favoured by Western-educated professionals are not accustomed to typical Western discourse structures (Castles 2020).

Court proceedings are rigid and slow to change. ADR methods such as mediation can be more flexible and adaptive; however, they may unwittingly be informed by traditional Anglo-centric perspectives. Integrating insights from Aboriginal culture can help address the limitations of traditional Anglo-centric approaches and support the development of the mediation process and its theory in this dynamic context (Castles 2020).

It can already be said that the Aboriginal input to the mainstream mediation system has countervailed its assumptions and principles by contributing to it the ideals of collaborative aim, creative problem-solving, empowerment and relationship preservation.

Summary

Judicialisation of Mediation

When does the judicialisation of ADR become problematic? Altobelli suggests that judicialisation becomes a clear concern when it becomes intrusive, creates uncertainty, and ultimately threatens the use of ADR (Altobelli 2000: 141). This threat can manifest in two main ways.

First, ADR's central concept is that parties have the freedom to agree or disagree as they choose. A potential threat of judicialisation is that agreement may no longer be voluntary. This could occur if courts impose unreasonable obligations on parties to participate in ADR processes 'in good faith'.

Altobelli (2000: 142) is right to argue that 'the more the concept of "good faith" is unpacked, examined, refined and defined, the easier it becomes for the law to regulate whether agreement is mandatory rather than voluntary'.

The second conceivable threat of judicialisation is that it tends to both prescribe and proscribe conduct associated with ADR participation for the mediator, the parties and their representatives. For instance, if confidentiality is not maintained, all participants in mediation may become cautious about what they say and do. If courts frequently intervene to resolve uncertainties in agreements reached during ADR sessions, the focus may shift from achieving agreements to documenting them.

However, judicialisation only becomes a threat when conduct associated with participation in ADR processes becomes so regulated that the autonomy of the participants becomes illusory and that flexibility of processes and informality merely invites litigation.

The crack between intuitive understanding and systematic knowledge in mediation

We all live stories. Here is a recent mediation case that illustrates this point, as initially recounted by Boulle (1999: 229), it concludes this saga about the contemporary Australian mediation system.

The story could have happened *anywhere*, in a small village, a nation-state, or even globally. This time, it happened on the Gold Coast, in Queensland, Australia, and goes like this:

An investor, whom we shall call Bob, lent $150,000 to a developer secured by a second mortgage. The developer defaulted and returned to South Australia. The land's value only covered the first mortgage and agent's commission, leaving nothing for Bob. Bob, who had previously faced three mortgage lending failures and who was in his eighties, sued the valuer, Pat, for professional negligence. Pat's valuation had exceeded by 100% the current market value of the property and was assigned without a professional relationship between investor and valuer.

The story thus far does not sound auspicious for mediation. However, despite the challenges – no funds from the defendant, no existing relationship between parties, disputed liability and lack of professional indemnity insurance – the mediation process led to a settlement.

In pre-mediation preparation, it became apparent that the valuer Pat was prepared to reach a commercial settlement but could offer very little in the way of hard cash. He was still recovering from his second matrimonial property settlement. It was suggested in this preliminary stage that non-monetary benefits should be seriously considered. This option was accepted, and the valuer's opening statement began as follows: 'Bob, I've never met you before, and I just want to say that I'm really sorry that this has happened to you'. This was accompanied by direct eye contact, open body language and the other appropriate non-verbal messages taught in the A1 School of Mediation Training. The settlement was achieved 5 hours later.

Here is the moral of the story. Mediators need to develop an increasingly sophisticated grasp of conflict and its consequence; of what micro-skills and mini-micro skills are suitable for what disputes and what situations within disputes, in what cultural, geopolitical and religious context the dispute is situated; to avoid – using an analogy from the medical science – barber-surgeons performing procedures without a deep understanding of patients' internal anatomy.

As Boulle (1999:231) concluded in her essay:

> In the inexact human science of conflict management explanatory factors are hard to identify with precision. In the human sciences itis simply not as easy to delineate cause and effect as it is in the natural sciences. The explanatory factors could be as unscientific as ritual, timing, coincidence, the force of circumstances, serendipity, instinct and good luck. After all, even in the medical sciences we know that the red pills do actually work better than the white pills (...). Certainly life-long learning requires us to be reflective, inquiring and analytical, but none of these will provide us with scientific certainty about our craft. These are interesting issues for future speculation.

Bibliography

Ackfun, Alexander (1993). 'Aboriginal Mediation: A Personal Perspective', *1 Queensland ADR Review*, 2 (April), 13–19.

Alexander, Nadja (2013). 'Harmonisation and Diversity in Private International Law of Mediation: The Rhythms of Regulatory Reforms.' In Klaus J. Hopt and Felix Steffek (eds), *Mediation: Principles and Regulation in Comparative Perspective*, pp. 1–72. Oxford: Oxford University Press.

Altobelli, Tom (2000). 'Mediation in the Nineties: The Promise of the Past', *Macarthur Law Review*, Issue 4, 103–145.

Bárrios, Luisa B. (2020). 'Mediation in Indigenous Latin American Groups', *European Mediation and Indigenous Mediation*, vol. 115, Vilnius: Vilnius University Press, pp. 134–146.

Bergin, Patricia (2012). '*The Objectives, Scope and Focus of Mediation Legislation in Australia*', <https://classic.austlii.edu.au/au/journals/NSWJSchol/2012/24.pdf>, accessed 29 July 2024.

Boulle, Laurence (1999). 'Mining the Gaps – Reflecting on the Story of Australian Mediation', *Bond Law Review*, 11 (2), 216–229.

Boulle, Laurence (2011). *Mediation: Principles, Process, Practice*. Chatswood, Australia: LexisNexis.

Castles, M. (2020). 'Learning from Aboriginal Knowledge Systems in ADR', *The Australian Dispute Resolution Research Network*, <https://adrnetwork.blog/2020/07/10/learning-from-aboriginal-knowledge-systems-in-adr/>, accessed 17 July 2024.

Cunneen, Chris, Luff, Jocelyn, Menzies, Karen, and Ralph, Nina R., (2005). 'Indigenous Family Mediation: The New South Wales ATSIFAM Program', *Australian Indigenous Law Reporter*, 9 (1), <https://www8.austlii.edu.au/cgibin/viewdoc/au/journals/AILR/2005/1.html#fn55>, accessed 1 August 2024.

Dewdney, Micheline (2009), 'Mediation and Conciliation', *The Laws of Australia*, 13, 5–34, Pyrmont: Thomson Reuters.

Kalowski, Joanna (2009). 'Through the Cultural Prism: Mediation in Australia', <https://www.jok.com.au/publications/mediation-in-australia>, accessed 1 August 2024.

Kelly, Loretta (2002). 'Mediation in Aboriginal Communities: Familiar Dilemmas, Fresh Developments', *Indigenous Law Bulletin*, 5(14), 4, 7, <https://www8.austlii.edu.au/cgi-bin/viewdoc/au/journals/IndigLawB/2002/4.html#fn1>, accessed 7 August 2024.

Kressel, Kenneth and Pruitt, Dean G. (1989). *Mediation Research: The Process and Effectiveness of Third-Party Intervention*. San Francisco: Jossey-Bass.

Magnus, Ulrich (2013). 'Mediation in Australia: Development and Problems'. In Klaus J. Hopt, and Felix Steffek (eds), *Mediation: Principles and Regulation in Comparative Perspective*, pp. 817–907. Oxford: Oxford University Press.

Noble, Kurt (1995). *'Mediating with Aboriginal Families: Workshop Conference Paper'*. Paper presented at the 3rd National Conference on Family Mediation, Sydney, pp. 130–145.

Nolan, Christine (1993). 'Alternative Dispute Resolution in Aboriginal and Islander Communities: The Community Justice Programs Experience', *Queensland ADR Review*, 2(8), 23–28.

O'Donnell, Marg (1995). 'Mediation within Aboriginal Communities: Issues and Challenges'. In Kayleen Hazlehurst (ed.), *Popular Justice and Community Regeneration*, pp. 67–89. London, Bloomsbury Publishing.

Parkinson, Patric (2015). *Family Laws and Access to Justice. Paper for UN Experts Group*, May 2015, <http://www.un.org/esa/socdev/family/docs/egm15/PARKINSONPAPERRECOMMENDATIONS.pdf>, accessed 2 August 2024.

Sourdin, Tania (2012). 'Mediation and Conciliation'. In *The Laws of Australia*, pp. 115–130. Pyrmont: Thomson Reuters.

Sourdin, Tania, and Alexander, Nadij (2003). *Global Trends in Mediation*, pp.1–32. The Hague: Kluwer Law International.

Wade, John (1998). 'Representing Clients at Mediation and Negotiation'. *Australian Dispute Resolution Journal*, Issue 9, 61–74.

Wall, James Jr., Stark, John B., and Standifer Rhetta L. (2001). 'Mediation: A Current Review and Theory Development', *The Journal of Conflict Resolution*, 45 (3), pp. 370–391, University of Missouri – Columbia.

CHAPTER 14

Mediation as a Method of Resolving Conflicts in Singapore

Yue-En Chong[1]

Introduction

Singapore is a small island city–state located in Southeast Asia with a population of 6.04 million people[2] (Strategy Group, Prime Minister's Office 2024). It is a multiracial, multiethnic and multicultural Asian society with major religions such as Buddhism, Christianity, Islam, Taoism and Hinduism[3] (MHA 2024).

Mediation plays a crucial role in Singaporean society, particularly in maintaining social harmony and resolving conflicts among its diverse population. The government has implemented various initiatives to promote mediation as a preferred method of dispute resolution such as Community Mediation in the Community Mediation Centre (CMC), the Singapore Mediation Centre (SMC) for resolving commercial and civil disputes, Family Mediation and Workplace Mediation. Mediation techniques are also practised in Singapore's Inter-racial and Religious Confidence Circles which were formed in 2002 to address issues of extremist religious voices, weeding out deviant religious teachings and removing practices that reduce common space between the races.

The emphasis on mediation in Singapore reflects the government's commitment to maintaining social stability and harmony in a multicultural society. By encouraging open communication and peaceful conflict resolution, mediation helps preserve the delicate balance among various ethnic, religious and social groups.

---

1 Advocate, Solicitor, Managing Director at Bethel Chambers LLC, Singapore, email: <cye@bethelchambers.com>

2 Population in Brief (2024) Strategy Group, Prime Minister's Office, <https://www.strategygroup.gov.sg/media-centre/publications/population-in-brief/>, accessed 6 August 2024.

3 Maintaining Racial and Religious Harmony (2024) Ministry of Home Affairs (MHA), <https://www.mha.gov.sg/what-we-do/managing-security-threats/maintaining-racial-and-religious-harmony>, accessed 6 August 2024.

Singapore's unique demographic composition, shaped by its history as a trading hub and strategic immigration policies, has led to a diverse and multicultural society. The government's proactive approach to population management and its emphasis on mediation as a tool for conflict resolution have been instrumental in maintaining social cohesion and fostering a harmonious environment for its residents.

Singapore's mediation history and development has been marked by significant growth and institutionalisation since the 1990s, evolving into an integral part of Singapore's legal system.

Mediation is not a new concept in Singapore. It has deep roots in Singapore's multicultural society, with various Asian cultures traditionally practising informal dispute resolution through respected community elders (Dorcas 2021). However, urbanisation and industrialisation led to a decline in these practices in favour of formal litigation.

The modern mediation movement in Singapore was actively revived in the 1990s, influenced by Western mediation practices from the 1970s (Dorcas 2021; Lim & Chua 2017). This revival aimed to reintroduce alternative dispute resolution (ADR) methods alongside the existing legal system.

A major factor leading to the growth of civil mediation is the central role played by the Singapore Judiciary. Former Chief Justice Yong Pung How was a key proponent of mediation, emphasising on several occasions that mediation was a 'non-confrontational and less costly process of settling problems in terms of time, money and more importantly, relationships' (Dorcas 2021).

Concept of Mediation

Section 3 of the Mediation Act 2017 provides a very comprehensive definition of the term 'mediation'. To explain it simply, mediation is a process in which a neutral party, the mediator, assists parties in a dispute by guiding them to find a practical solution. Mediation is a voluntary and confidential process.

Depending on the parties and the matter to be decided, the mediator can adopt different mediation techniques. They range from an active involvement in the substantive outcome of the dispute using evaluative or directive approaches to a more facilitative model where the focus of the mediation process is to assist parties achieve a settlement by managing the process of negotiations between them.

Mediation can be used for an array of matters such as the settlement of disputes, management of conflicts, negotiation of contracts and conflict prevention, resolving minor criminal complaints, employment disputes, community-related and any civil or family case filed in court (Dorcas 2021).

Mediation settlement agreements are treated as a contract between parties and are enforceable in the same way as any other contract on the principles of contract law. Notwithstanding that under Singapore law, a settlement agreement need not be in writing to be enforceable, so long as it satisfies the requirements of contract formation, in practice, a mediation settlement usually stipulates that the settlement must be recorded in writing and signed by the parties to be enforceable. The mediation settlement agreement may also be recorded as an order of court pursuant to Section 12 of the Mediation Act 2017 (Lux 2022).

Benefits of Mediation

Unlike arbitration or litigation, neither party would lose as settlement agreements are reached voluntarily, and parties do not run the risk of having a judge or an arbitrator deciding against them. In terms of time and cost, mediation saves time and is significantly less expensive than adjudicatory processes. For parties that value privacy, mediators and parties are generally prohibited by contract from disclosing any information relating to the mediation. This is well stipulated in Section 9(1) of the Mediation Act 2017. In addition, should the mediation failed, the mediation communication is not allowed to be admitted as evidence in Court unless the Court or arbitration tribunal grants permission.

The Singapore Government has been very supportive towards the development of Mediation in Singapore with many political leaders promoting the merits of mediation. For example, in her Keynote Address at Singapore International Mediation Centre's (SIMC) Signature Event – MNCs for Mediation – From Disputes to Deal Making, on 30 August 2023, Second Minister for National Development of Singapore, Indranee Rajah, shared that the advantages of mediation are well-known as being cheaper and faster, relative to other modes of dispute resolution, flexible, as it enables non-legal solutions to legal problems and helps to preserve long-term relationships, as the outcome is reached and agreed willingly by parties allowing for a win–win outcome rather than a win–lose outcome.

To demonstrate the advantages of mediation and its increased prominence as a dispute resolution tool, Second Minister for National Development of Singapore, Indranee Rajah, in the same speech, shared a case study, discussed during the SIMC's SC Week event the prior year, which involved a complex multi-jurisdictional dispute between a US fuel cell manufacturer and a South Korean private energy producer and where a settlement was reached in 3.5 days with mediation. Second Minister for National Development of Singapore Indranee Rajah further shared that if the dispute had been fought out, it would have taken parties months, if not years, to reach a settlement.

It is upon this background of governmental support for the development of mediation that the development in mediation by the Singapore judiciary is further elaborated as in what follows. As it can be observed that the growth of mediation in Singapore was a combination of effective legislation being passed by the government to create a mediation infrastructure while the judiciary continued to take on a leadership role in its development on the ground.

Developments in Mediation

The history of the development of mediation in Singapore is briefly outlined in the following context:

In the early 1990s, Singapore began to formally introduce mediation as an ADR method, recognising 'justice' cannot be dispensed simpliciter. Recognising the limits of relying purely on legal jurisprudence, the courts have been applying principles akin to that of 'therapeutic jurisprudence' (elaborated in the following context) to enhance and improve the way disputes are resolved while upholding the law (Babb 1997). This move was part of a broader effort to provide more efficient and cost-effective ways to resolve conflicts outside the court system (Ng 2011; Ng et al. 2018).

The State Courts (formerly known as the Subordinate Courts till March 2014), under the leadership of the former Chief Justice Yong Pung How, piloted a mediation programme in 1994 in which selected judges mediated a range of civil disputes. Upon the successful conclusion of the pilot programme, the State Courts established the Court Mediation Centre in 1995, which was subsequently re-named the Primary Dispute Resolution Centre in 1998 and the State Courts Centre for Dispute Resolution (SCCDR) in 2015 (Kluwer Mediation Blog 2015; Mcfadden & Lim 2021).

The SMC was established in 1997 (Quek Anderson 2018), marking a significant milestone in the institutionalisation of mediation. The SMC was set up to provide private commercial mediation services and has since played a crucial role in promoting and providing mediation services for civil disputes.

The State Courts of Singapore introduced the concept of 'presumption of ADR', in which all civil cases were automatically referred to mediation or other forms of ADR unless either or both parties opted out (Lux 2022).

At the Opening of Legal Year 2013, Chief Justice Sundaresh Menon announced that an inter-agency committee, the Committee for Family Justice, would be established to study and recommend possible reforms to the Family Justice System (Menon 2013).

Subsequently, Singapore began to position itself as a hub for international commercial mediation:

2014: A Working Group recommended developing Singapore into a centre for international commercial mediation.
2014: The SIMC was established to provide mediation services for cross-border commercial disputes.
2014: The Singapore International Mediation Institute (SIMI) was established to set standards and provide accreditation for mediators.

The Mediation Act was enacted in 2017, providing a legislative framework for mediation and addressing key issues such as confidentiality and enforceability of mediated settlement agreements.

The key new feature of the Mediation Act 2017 are as follows:

> Under Section 12 of the Act, parties to a mediation agreement, where there are no prior proceedings commenced in a court, can mutually agree to apply to court to record the agreement as an order of court. This application must be within 8 weeks after the mediation settlement agreement is made unless allowed by the court for such longer periods.
>
> However, there are certain further requirements: mediation is administered by a designated mediation service provider or conducted by a certified mediator; the agreement is in writing and signed by or on behalf of all the parties to the agreement and contains the necessary information as prescribed.

> The court can still refuse to record the mediation as an order if the agreement is void or voidable because of incapacity, fraud, misrepresentation, duress, coercion, mistake or any other ground for invalidating a contract; the subject matter of the agreement is not capable of settlement; any term of the agreement is not capable of enforcement as an order of court; one or more terms of agreement is not in the best interest of the child in a child welfare or custody proceedings and the agreement is contrary to public policy.

As mentioned earlier, the enactment of the Mediation Act 2017 has allowed better enforceability by parties to a settled mediation case. Prior to the mediation act, should a party refuse to carry out the terms of agreement in a mediation settlement, the aggrieved party's sole remedy would have to sue the party in breach for breach of contract in the civil courts. However, with the option of having the mediation settlement agreement recorded quickly as an order, should a party be in breach, which would be a breach of a court order which is more serious than a mere breach of contract. For example, a breach of a court order could invoke contempt of court proceedings that would carry heavier penalties than simply monetary restitution or specific performance arising from a breach of contract. As a court order, the aggrieved party can enforce it against the party in breach straight away instead of having to go through the standard civil case of proving breach of contract.

The Mediation Act 2017 was certainly a very necessary development in buttressing the mediation system into having a firmer footing in the judicial system.

Over the years, Singapore has developed specialised mediation programmes for various types of disputes:

Family mediation in the Family Justice Courts

Family mediation plays a pivotal role especially in contested divorce matters where couples have children under 21 years of age. Mediation is made mandatory to ensure that the parents prioritise their children's well-being during the divorce process. It also reduces conflicts and promotes amicable resolution, allowing couples to communicate openly and explore options for settlement. Family mediation also helps couples resolve various aspects of divorce such as the division of matrimonial assets, spousal maintenance, child custody and care arrangements and child maintenance.

Employment mediation at the Tripartite Alliance for Dispute Management

Tripartite Alliance for Dispute Management (TADM) provides advisory and mediation services to help employees and employers manage employment disputes, including salary-related claims and wrongful dismissal cases. Mediation at TADM is a mandatory step before such claims can be escalated to the Employment Claims Tribunals (ECT) (Ministry of Manpower Singapore 2024).

Intellectual property mediation at the Intellectual Property Office of Singapore

Intellectual Property Office of Singapore (IPOS) offers mediation as an ADR option for intellectual property disputes such as trademark disputes, patent disputes, industrial design disputes, geographical indication disputes and copyright and related rights disputes. IPOS actively promotes and facilitates mediation as an effective means of resolving IP disputes, offering various programmes and collaborations to make mediation accessible and cost-effective for parties involved in IP conflicts.

In August 2019, Singapore signed the United Nations Convention on International Settlement Agreements Resulting from Mediation, also known as the Singapore Convention on Mediation, cementing the country's position as a leader in international mediation[4]. The Singapore Convention on Mediation Act 2020 came into force thereafter in September 2020. With the Act coming into force, commercial parties involved in cross-border disputes can apply directly to the courts of countries that have signed and ratified the treaty to enforce a mediated settlement agreement (Lux 2022). In order to do so, one should refer the requirement under Section 5 Singapore Convention on Mediation Act 2020.

4 United Nations Convention on International Settlement Agreements Resulting from Mediation (Singapore Convention on Mediation), adopted in New York on 20 December 2018, open to signature in Singapore on 7 August 2019, <https://uncitral.un.org/sites/uncitral.un.org/files/media-documents/EN/Texts/UNCITRAL/Arbitration/mediation_convention_v1900316_eng.pdf>, accessed 2 August 2024.

Virtual mediation has also gained traction, especially in the wake of the COVID-19 pandemic, offering new ways to conduct mediation sessions across borders.

Therapeutic Justice and Mediation

Mediation plays a major role in the Family Justice system in Singapore.

Mediation is an integral part of the Therapeutic Justice (TJ) system that had been recently introduced in the Singapore Family Justice System in 2020.

TJ and mediation are closely intertwined in Singapore's Family Justice System, working together to provide a more holistic and healing approach to resolving family disputes. The seeds of TJ were planted in the mid-1990s when mediation and counselling were incrementally introduced into the Family Justice System. This integration aimed to minimise adversarial conflicts, promote healing and ensure sustainable outcomes for families.

TJ is based on core principles such as, non-adversarial approach, where parties are encouraged to view each other not as adversaries but as participants in a process aimed at healing and restoring relationships, holistic support, a process by which support is provided to grieving parties of the loss of their marriage and to help them move forward positively and problem-solving focus, aimed to address the root cause of the dispute and provide durable solutions (Ong 2020).

In the words of Justice Debbie Ong, then-Presiding Judge of the Family Justice Courts (FJC), 'therapeutic justice is a lens of "care", a lens through which we can look at the extent to which substantive rules, laws, legal procedures and practices, as well as the roles of the legal participants, produce helpful or harmful consequences. We must build the "hardware" structure and the "software" resources that will ensure therapeutic, helpful effects' (Ong 2020).

At the Family Justice Courts Workplan 2020, Justice Debbie Ong announced that the FJC and the family justice community will be co-creating a renewed vision of family justice informed by principles of TJ.

Mediation plays a crucial role in the implementation of TJ by providing a platform for parties to resolve their disputes amicably and constructively. Mediators help with diffusing tensions between parties and encourage parties to work together to reach a mutually beneficial solution. This process transforms the family court from a place of conflict to a place of healing (SG Courts Annual Report 2021).

To provide early intervention and prevent disputes from escalating unnecessarily, Singapore's Family Justice System designed a multi-disciplinary team approach where judges, mediators, counsellors, psychologists and other specialists work together to address a family's issues holistically, ensuring that both legal and emotional needs are met (Ong 2020).

The integration of TJ and mediation has led to several positive outcomes in Singapore's Family Justice System particularly in reducing conflict, providing sustainable solutions and support for children.

TJ has been implemented in various pilot projects and ongoing projects. An example is the introduction of the triage checklist for divorce cases not filed under simplified track. This checklist helps with identifying the needs of the case early and apply appropriate resources (SG Courts 2024).

A case study of family mediation with elements of therapeutic justice

This case study is made up from several cases that the author did as a family mediator.

The author was a family mediator in this case where a father, mother and their adult child attended mediation. The mediation started out tense as the adult child was advocating for the mother for 'fairness'. Apparently, the father had also said and done things to deeply hurt the adult child as well.

One thing that the author believes is necessary for mediation is to have food on the table, lots of snacks and drinks for the comfort of the parties. During the mediation, as the adult child was pouring a drink for the mother, the adult child was observed also pouring a drink for the father. At that point, the author knew the mediation would be settled as small kindness was still shown from the 'mother's camp' to the father. The case ended with the father having to move out of the family home; however, the mediator suggested that if the adult child could assist the father with the move, to which the adult child agreed. The author believe that this helped the family to start their journey of healing.

Growth of Mediation

In a snapshot, these are the following figures in relation to the statistics on the mediation growth.

In a January 2018 news article in the Singapore Straits Times, it was reported that the SMC received 538 matters for mediation in 2017 (an 8% increase on 2016) and handled S$2.7 billion in disputed sums in 2017, a record high since it was set up more than 20 years ago (Tan 2018).

In a 2018 speech given by The Honourable Justice Belinda Ang, Judge of the Supreme Court of Singapore, it was revealed that between 2012 and 2017, 6,700 cases were mediated at the state courts annually (Ang 2018).

An August 2020 news article in the Singapore Straits Times reported that parties from Singapore and abroad have filed more than 120 cases, with a total dispute value of over $4 billion, with SIMC since its inception in November 2014 (SIMS 2020).

According to the SIMC website, the total value of disputes heard by SIMC in 2021 alone amounted to over US$3 billion. This figure was equivalent to the total dispute value of US$3 billion heard by SIMC in the previous 6 years (2014–2020) since its establishment (SIMC 2022).

The SMC website states that, to date, the SMC has mediated more than 6,300 matters worth over S$14 billion since its launch on 16 August 1997. About 67% of its cases are settled with 90% of them resolved within 1 day (SMC).

Attributing to the enactment of the Mediation Act 2017 and the Singapore Convention on Mediation Act 2020, Singapore has made significant steps to strengthen its international commercial dispute resolution framework, providing greater certainty and clarity for parties who opt to conduct their mediation in Singapore and making Singapore an attractive mediation centre.

Singapore International Mediation Institute

A significant evolution on the practice of mediation in Singapore was the set up on an official 'standard body'. Prior to this, while there were many mediation centres, each with their own 'ethical standards', there had not been a country wide standard body for mediation till the creation of the SIMI.

The SIMI was established in 2014 with the objective of upholding high mediation standards through the professionalisation of mediation; promoting understanding and inspiring the use of mediation, stimulating and facilitating the development and growth of mediation through research and innovation and fostering a strong mediation community in Asia by engaging stakeholders in discussions, events and outreach activities.

Critical functions performed by SIMI to uphold and promote professional mediation standards include administering accreditation schemes for mediators, mediation training and service providers. SIMI collaborates with accredited mediators, training/service providers and other stakeholders to co-organise thought leadership events and support publications that promote technical and professional practice issues in mediation, organises education and awareness talks about mediation, conducts outreach and teaching activities such as seminars and mediation competitions for students, works closely with educational institutes to further research in mediation and offers a credentialing scheme that recognises mediators' experience through a tiered system.

The number of SIMI accredited mediators has grown steadily over the years, standing at 561 mediators presently and spreads across 28 jurisdictions (SIMI 2024).

SIMI is a non-profit organisation supported by the Ministry of Law and is a subsidiary of the National University of Singapore. The SIMI Board of Directors comprise representatives from both mediation practitioners and corporate users of mediation, works closely with both domestic and international mediation bodies and partners with the International Mediation Institute, a non-profit public interest initiative to drive transparency and high competency standards into mediation practice across all fields worldwide. The creation of SIMI was the fruition of a recommendation by the International Commercial Mediation Working Group, which was appointed by The Honourable the Chief Justice Sundaresh Menon and Singapore's Ministry of Law and National University of Singapore.

Society of Mediation Professionals (Singapore)

Mediation in Singapore is not just lead and initiated from the 'top–down'. As more lawyers were trained in mediation, initiatives started from the 'ground–up'.

An example was the formation of the Society of Mediation Professionals (Singapore) (SMP), by a group of mediation advocates and peacemakers in 2015, with the aim of representing the interests and perspectives of mediation and mediators in Singapore. It is a social organisation for mediators in Singapore. Since its inception, the SMP has sought to build the mediation community through organising talks, workshops, social gatherings and mediation events (Society of Mediation Professionals Singapore 2022).

The SMP also provides coaching, through its Coaching Scheme, to help trainee mediators prepare for their SMC Mediation Skills Assessment (MSA). Through a simulated dispute scenario, candidates get to hone their skills, build their confidence and receive guidance and feedback from the coach. The Coaching Scheme is an excellent opportunity for coaches and role-players to hone their mediation skills, gain more mediation experience and give back to the community (Society of Mediation Professionals Singapore 2016–2022).

Unlike other mediation institutions such as the SMC, SIMC, SIMI, amongst others, the SMP is a ground-up initiative by like-minded practitioners coming together to share how mediation is practiced, developed and nurtured. Members share their concerns and find solutions as well as hone practice for each other. Presently, members are working with various stakeholders to develop a code of professional conduct and ethics to raise the practice standards of mediation in Singapore (Society of Mediation Professionals Singapore 2016–2022).

The Role of a Mediation Advocate

The importance of the SMP work is the mentoring of 'mediation advocates'. Embedded in the Singapore mediation system is the need to create as many advocates as possible (whether they are lawyer or non-lawyers) who are familiar and embraces the mediation system where they would still apply mediation techniques and have a mediation mindset and principles of therapeutic justice even outside a formal mediation setting.

A case study of two mediation advocates in a negotiation adoption therapeutic justice technique

The author was a mediation advocate in a case where he represented a father who attended mediation that was conducted by the Family Justice Court.

The dispute was over child custody. The father had the situation where the mother had taken the child away to her home country and only returned to Singapore after much persuasion by the father. In between, there was much tension in the communication between the mother and the father. What consequently happened was that the mother filed for divorce, and both were fighting over custody of the child. The father of the child was terrified that the mother would take the child away from him to a distant country again while the mother of the child was insisting that she would not do this again. The custody fight lasted for 1.5 years in total before it was settled.

Parties attended mediation at the Family Justice Court; however, there was only partial settlement and not full settlement of all issues. However, by that time, both the lawyer for the father and the lawyer for the mother had gained much trust with each other and were looking forward to trying to assist parties to come to a settlement.

While the key issue of conflict was whether the mother was a flight risk, there was no way that the father's lawyer could guarantee that this would not happen again. This constituted the impasse that was preventing the case from being settled.

However, during discussion, one of the other concerns of the father was that the wife and child would have their own apartment to stay in. He was not comfortable with them renting a room with many other tenants. Hearing that concern, and knowing that purchase of a new apartment was beyond the financial means of the wife, the suggestion that the father's lawyer made was to offer her all his Central Provision Fund monies in his ordinary account (this is part of Singapore's pension system where these funds can be used to purchase property) which was not a large sum, but would help her fund the deposit for the apartment. This was the turning point in the conflict, where goodwill was sincerely shown by the father, the mother was believed to have felt the good intentions and the atmosphere of the conflict immediately changed to being that of goodwill being continuously demonstrated to each other. The mother then agreed to reassure the father that if she brought the child back to her homeland and did not return with the child, she would allow a court order to be enforced against her to allow him to bring the child back.

Later on, the mother brought the child back to her homeland for a holiday and did bring the child back as promised. Now, the relationship between the mother and father improved to the point of friendship and congeniality. The mother continued to allow the father to spend even more time with the child than the timings stipulated in the court order. When the father's lawyer spoke to the father a year later, he had confirmed that they had returned to being friends.

Unexpectedly, a few years later, the father suddenly passed away. However, even then, the father's family did confirm that they were still in touch with the mother of the child and that relationships were good between them and her.

As a mediator, the author believes in the use of mediation and the mediation mindset to bring healing and restoration to families embroiled in conflict. He strongly believes that having parties to be able to be in the state where they can have peace with themselves, be patient with the other party, embrace self-control and not lash out to hurt the other party, be faithful to their promises made in mediation and find opportunities to show small steps of kindness and goodness to the other party, this would go towards transforming conflict into cooperation and consensus.

Summary

Referring to the Response Speech by Second Minister for Law Edwin Tong at the Committee of Supply Debate 2024, on 1st March 2024, and in line with suggestions made by Members of Parliament, a revised framework is being developed to address issues of community disputes quickly so that such disputes do not become intractable and causing irreparable rifts in society. One such revision is making mediation mandatory, in appropriate cases, to drive more cases towards an early and amicable settlement. As such, the CMC has increased the number of volunteer mediators by 15% over the past year, in anticipation of increasing cases, bringing the number close to 160 volunteer mediators and the government will continue to grow this pool. The CMC has also set up satellite mediation venues in neighbourhoods, so that residents can take part in mediation closer to their homes. In the past year, the number of satellite venues have grown from six to ten. The CMC has also started using Zoom for mediation, in the appropriate cases, to make mediation more accessible (Tong 2024).

In his welcome address at the opening of the United Nations Commission on International Commercial Law (UNCITRAL) Academy Conference and

Industry Capacity-Building Workshop, during the Singapore Convention Week (SC Week) 2023, Singapore's Minister for Culture, Community and Youth, and Second Minister for Law, Mr. Edwin Tong SC, said 'Building the world today for tomorrow has always been Singapore's philosophy since independence. We applied the same philosophy to developing Singapore into the leading international dispute resolution hub as it is today. We also developed a comprehensive suite of international commercial dispute resolution services. The Singapore Convention on Mediation is one contributing instrument that provides parties with another viable option to resolve cross-border disputes. To date, we have fifty-six signatories, and eleven parties to the Convention. I am confident more will sign and ratify soon' (Ministry of Law Singapore 2023).

'The PCA tries to offer an institutional dimension to a mediation process, which should mitigate some of the risks associated with mediation by giving it legitimacy. So, if we continue partnering with states that promote mediation such as Singapore, I think finally we will get to the point where we will have cases confirming the role of mediation and all the benefits that mediation brings to the table. But it is important to really put some trust in it and that is part of my role as Secretary-General to promote and create sufficient trust for mediation,' Dr Hab Marcin Czepelak, Secretary-General, Permanent Court of Arbitration (PCA), the oldest permanent intergovernmental institution dedicated to the settlement of international disputes, commented at the same event (Ministry of Law Singapore 2023).

As can be seen, mediation is an undeniable and integral part of the Singapore judicial system and should not be thought of as an ADR mechanism, but rather an 'appropriate' dispute resolution mechanism. It is the first port of call at the State Courts, and for matters in the Magistrates' Courts, mediation is the primary method of dispute resolution. It has also helped reduce the caseload of the courts, provide more cost-effective and efficient dispute resolution options and foster a more harmonious society.

Looking ahead, Singapore is likely to continue its efforts to strengthen its position as a global hub for mediation, particularly in the realm of international commercial disputes. The ongoing development of mediation skills among legal professionals, the integration of technology in mediation processes and the continued refinement of mediation laws and practices are expected to shape the future of mediation in Singapore, further sustaining its growth into the future.

Bibliography

Barbara A. Babb (1997). 'An Interdisciplinary Approach to Family Law Jurisprudence: Application of an Ecological and Therapeutic Perspective', *Indiana Law Journal*, 72, 775–7, 798–808; (2017), Routledge eBooks, pp. 47–60.

Dorcas, Quek A. (2021). 'The Development of Mediation for Civil Disputes'. In Danny McFadden and George Lim S.C. (eds), *Mediation in Singapore: A Practical Guide*, pp. 314–337. Singapore: Sweet & Maxwell, <https://ink.library.smu.edu.sg/cgi/viewcontent.cgi?article=5310&context=sol_research>, accessed 11 July 2024.

Lim, G. S. C., and Chua, E. (2017). 'Development of Mediation in Singapore', <https://ink.library.smu.edu.sg/sol_research/2513/#:~:text=LIM,%20George%20S.%20C.%20and%20CHUA,%20Eunice.%20Development%20of%20mediation>, accessed 11 July 2024.

Mcfadden, Danny, and Lim, George S. C. (2021). *Mediation in Singapore: A Practical Guide.* Singapore: Sweet & Maxwell.

Ng, Kevin (2011). 'Mandatory Counselling and Mediation the Child Focused Resolution Centre ("CFRC")', *Singapore Law Gazette*, 39–41, <https://imimediation.org/wp-content/uploads/2018/04/mandatory-counselling-and-mediation-the-child-focused-resolution-centre-cfrc-.pdf>, accessed 11 July 2024.

Ng, Kevin, Loi, Yarni, Ang, Sophia, and Tan, Sylvia (2018). 'Family Justice Courts – Innovations, Initiatives and Programmes, An Evolution Over Time', *Singapore Academy of Law Journal*, 1 (30), 617–646, <https://journalsonline.academypublishing.org.sg/Journals/Singapore-Academy-of-Law-Journal-Special-Issue/e-Archive/ctl/eFirstSALPDFJournalView/mid/513/ArticleId/1308/Citation/JournalsOnlinePDF#:~:text=FAMILY%20JUSTICE%20COURTS%20%E2%80%93%20INNOVATIONS,%20INITIATIVES%20AND%20PROGRAMMES%20An%20Evolution>, accessed 11 July 2024.

Legal sources

Mediation Act 2017, <https://sso.agc.gov.sg/Acts-Supp/1-2017/Published/20211231?DocDate=20170512>, accessed 11 July 2024.

United Nations Convention on International Settlement Agreements Resulting from Mediation (Singapore Convention on Mediation), adopted in New York on 20 December 2018, open to signature in Singapore on 7 August 2019.

United Nations Convention on International Settlement Agreements Resulting from Mediation (Singapore Convention on Mediation), adopted in New York on 20 December 2018, open to signature in Singapore on 7 August 2019, <https://uncitral.un.org/sites/uncitral.un.org/files/media-documents/EN/Texts/UNCITRAL/Arbitration/mediation_convention_v1900316_eng.pdf>, accessed 2 August 2024.

Other sources

Population in Brief (2024). Strategy Group, Prime Minister's Office, <https://www.strategygroup.gov.sg/media-centre/publications/population-in-brief/>, accessed 6 August 2024.

Maintaining Racial and Religious Harmony (2024). <https://www.mha.gov.sg/what-we-do/managing-security-threats/maintaining-racial-and-religious-harmony>, accessed 6 August 2024.

Lux, Jonathan (2022). Mediation Singapore Consulting Editor Lux Mediation, <https://www.rajahtannasia.com/wp-content/uploads/2022/08/rajah-tann-singapore-2022-mediation-singapore.pdf>, accessed 6 August 2024.

Mlaw.gov.sg. Keynote Address by Minister Indrani, at SIMC Signature Event – MNCs For Mediation – From Disputes to Deal-Making, <https://www.mlaw.gov.sg/news/speeches/keynote-address-min-indranee-simc-event/>, accessed 1 October 2024.

Kluwer Mediation Blog (2015). Singapore Development – Joint Launch of the State Courts Centre for Dispute Resolution and 'Mediation in Singapore: A Practical Guide' – Kluwer Mediation Blog, <https://mediationblog.kluwerarbitration.com/2015/03/14/singapore-development-joint-launch-of-the-state-courts-centre-for-dispute-resolution-and-mediation-in-singapore-a-practical-guide/>, accessed 6 August 2024.

Quek Anderson, D. (2018). Ch.03 Mediation. Singapore Law Watch, <https://www.singaporelawwatch.sg/About-Singapore-Law/Overview/ch-03-mediation>, accessed 6 August 2024.
Chief Justice Menon, S. (2013). Response by Chief Justice Sundaresh Menon Opening of the Legal Year 2013 and Welcome Reference for the Chief Justice, <https://www.sal.sg/sites/default/files/PDF%20Files/Speeches/CJ%20OLY%20Welcome%20Reference.pdf.>, accessed 6 August 2024.
Ministry of Manpower Singapore. (2024). Managing Employment Disputes, <https://www.mom.gov.sg/employment-practices/managing-employment-disputes>, accessed 6 August 2024.
Ong, Debbie (2020). 'Today is a New Day', <https://www.judiciary.gov.sg/docs/default-source/news-docs/fjc-workplan-2020.pdf?sfvrsn=8b619dc0_0>, accessed 6 August 2024.
Tong, Edwin (2024) 'Response Speech by Second Minister for Law Edwin Tong at the Committtee of Supply Debate 2024', <https://www.mlaw.gov.sg/news/parliamentary-speeches/2m-cos-2024/>, accessed 6 August 2024)
Tong, Edwin (2023) 'Welcome Address by Minister for Culture Community and Youth, and Second Minister for Law Edwin Tong SC, at the UNCITRAL Academy Conference', <https://www.mlaw.gov.sg/news/parliamentary-speeches/2m-cos-2024/>, accessed 6 August 2024)
SG Courts Annual Report (2021). Raising Awareness of Therapeutic Justice-Media Pitch to Yahoo, <https://www.judiciary.gov.sg/AnnualReport2021/theme/default/pdf/Theraputic%20Justice%20-%20Raising%20Awareness.pdf >, accessed 6 August 2024.
SG Courts (2024). Therapeutic Justice in the Family Justice Courts, <https://www.judiciary.gov.sg/who-we-are/therapeutic-justice>, accessed 6 August 2024.
Tan, Tam Mei (2018). Singapore Mediation Centre saw record number of cases and disputed sums in 2017 The Straits Times, <https://www.straitstimes.com/singapore/singapore-mediation-centre-saw-record-number-of-cases-and-disputed-sums-in-2017>, accessed 6 August 2024.
Ang, Belinda. (2018). SMU Forum – Expanding the Scope of Dispute Resolution and Access to Justice: The Use of Mediation Within the Courts – Opening Remarks by the Honourable Justice Belinda Ang

Saw Ean, Judge of the Supreme Court of Singapore, <https://www.judiciary.gov.sg/docs/default-source/news-docs/use-of-mediation-within-the-courts.pdf>, accessed: 6 August 2024).

simc.com.sg (2020). Mediation Growing in Importance as Way to Settle Business Disputes | Singapore International Mediation, <https://simc.com.sg/news/mediation-growing-importance-way-settle-business-disputes>, accessed 2 August 2024.

simc.com.sg (2022). Increase in Firms Seeking Mediation Amid the Pandemic | Singapore International Mediation Centre, <https://simc.com.sg/news/increase-firms-seeking-mediation-amid-pandemic>, accessed 2 August 2024.

mediation.com.sg (n.d.). Singapore Mediation Centre, <https://mediation.com.sg/about-us/about-smc/>, accessed 2 August 2024.

simi.org.sg (2024). About SIMI, <https://www.simi.org.sg/About-Us/Organisation-Information/About-SIMI>, accessed 2 August 2024.

National University of Singapore (NUS (2014). Singapore International Mediation Institute Launch |Newswise, <https://d.newswise.com/articles/singapore-international-mediation-institute-launched-to-set-world-class-mediation-standards>, accessed 2 August 2024.

Society of Mediation Professionals Singapore (2016–2022). Key Milestones: Our History | Society of Mediation Professionals Singapore, <https://smp.org.sg/our-history/>, accessed 2 August 2024.

Society of Mediation Professionals Singapore (2016–2022). Coaching Scheme | Society of Mediation Professionals Singapore, <https://smp.org.sg/coaching-scheme/>, accessed 2 August 2024.

Society of Mediation Professionals Singapore (2016–2022). FAQ | Society of Mediation Professionals Singapore, <https://smp.org.sg/frequently-asked-questions/>, accessed 2 August 2024.

CHAPTER 15

Frames of Regulation of the Mediator Profession: Is the Access to the Profession Inclusive?

Alina Serhieieva[1]

Introduction

The profession of a mediator, rooted in principles of negotiation and conflict resolution, has become a pivotal component of contemporary legal systems. As societies increasingly seek alternatives to adversarial court proceedings, mediation offers a path that emphasises cooperation, dialogue and mutual understanding. This shift towards mediation reflects broader changes in societal values, where the focus on restorative justice and consensual dispute resolution has gained prominence. However, the journey towards establishing mediation as a recognised and respected profession has been neither straightforward nor uniform across different jurisdictions.

Historically, mediation has been practised in various forms across cultures, often embedded within informal dispute resolution mechanisms. In many societies, community elders or respected figures would mediate disputes, relying on their wisdom and social standing rather than formal training or certification. As legal systems evolved and became more formalised, the need for structured and regulated mediation processes became apparent. This transition from informal to formal mediation practices marked the beginning of the profession's institutionalisation, with an increasing emphasis on standardisation, training and professional recognition.

In modern times, the growth of mediation as a profession has been driven by several factors. Backlog of cases in courts, high costs of litigation and the adversarial nature of traditional legal proceedings have led to a search for more efficient, cost-effective and harmonious ways to resolve disputes. Mediation, with its focus on voluntary participation, confidentiality and mutually acceptable outcomes, has emerged as an attractive alternative.

1 MA, PhD student, Law School, Mykolas Romeris University of Vilnius, email: <serhieieva.alina@mruni.eu>

However, regulation of the mediator profession is far from uniform. Various countries and regions have adopted different approaches to regulating mediation under the influence of their legal traditions, cultural contexts and policy priorities. Some jurisdictions have developed comprehensive regulatory frameworks that set clear standards for mediator training, certification and practice. Others have taken a more laissez-faire approach, leaving the profession largely unregulated or subject to minimal oversight.

This diversity in regulatory approaches has significant implications for accessibility and inclusivity of the mediation profession. In some regions, stringent regulations may create barriers to entry, limiting the diversity of individuals who can become mediators. In other areas, a lack of regulation may lead to inconsistencies in the quality of mediation services, undermining public confidence in the profession.

Chapter XV explores diverse regulatory frameworks that govern the mediator profession across various regions, highlighting the significant disparities in how these frameworks are structured and implemented. We examine implications of these regulatory differences on inclusivity and accessibility of the profession, focusing primarily on who can become a mediator and how they are trained and certified. By conducting a comprehensive analysis of the current state of mediator regulation, this study aims to contribute to the ongoing discourse on professionalisation of mediation and offer actionable insights for policymakers, professional bodies and practitioners.

As we delve into intricacies of mediator regulation, it is essential to understand that the profession's inclusivity is not merely a matter of legal standards, but is deeply intertwined with broader social, economic and cultural factors. These factors influence who has access to mediation training, who can afford to pursue certification and who ultimately enters the profession. Thus, our exploration of regulatory frameworks also considers socioeconomic contexts in which these regulations operate, providing a holistic overview of challenges and opportunities facing the mediation profession today.

Current Regulatory Frameworks

Regulatory frameworks for the mediator profession differ significantly across jurisdictions, reflecting diverse legal traditions, cultural contexts and policy priorities of each region. Some countries have well-established regulations that set clear standards for education, training and certification, while others have minimal or fragmented regulations. This section explores current regulatory frameworks in key jurisdictions, highlighting differences and commonalities that shape the accessibility and inclusivity of the mediator profession.

1. European Union

The European Union (EU) has made significant strides in harmonising mediation regulations through directives such as the EU Mediation Directive[2]. This directive aims to facilitate access to mediation and promote amicable resolution of disputes, particularly in cross-border cases. Key aspects of the directive include:

- Encouragement of Mediation: The directive encourages the use of mediation and ensures that mediated agreements can be enforced across Member States. This has been crucial in promoting mediation as a viable alternative to litigation, especially in cross-border disputes where differences in legal systems can complicate resolution.
- Quality of Mediation: The directive emphasises the importance of high-quality mediation services, requiring Member States to encourage training and accreditation of mediators. This focus on quality is intended to build public trust in mediation as a reliable and effective dispute resolution mechanism.

2 Directive 2008/52/EC of the European Parliament and the Council of 21 May 2008 on certain aspects of mediation in civil and commercial matters, OJ L 136/3 on 24 May 2008, <https://eur-lex.europa.eu/legal-content/en/ALL/?uri=CELEX:32008L0052#:~:text=DIRECTIVE%202008/52/EC%20OF%20THE%20EUROPEAN%20PARLIAMENT>, accessed 15 August 2024.

- Confidentiality: The directive stipulates that mediators must maintain confidentiality regarding information acquired during the mediation process, thereby protecting the privacy of the parties involved and fostering an environment of open communication.

Despite these efforts, Member States retain significant autonomy in implementing these regulations, resulting in varied standards and practices across the region. For instance, countries like Italy and Germany have stringent requirements for mediator training and certification, while others, such as the United Kingdom, have adopted more flexible approaches (De Palo & Trevor 2012). This divergence may lead to inconsistencies in quality and accessibility of mediation services within the EU.

In Italy, for example, the mandatory nature of mediation in certain civil and commercial disputes has led to a robust regulatory framework that includes mandatory training and certification for mediators. The Italian model has been praised for its comprehensiveness but also criticised for creating barriers to entry that may exclude individuals from diverse backgrounds.

Germany, on the other hand, has a federal system where regulation is shared between the federal government and Länder (states). This has led to a high level of regulation with mandatory qualifications for mediators, including extensive training and adherence to a code of ethics. The German approach is known for its rigour and high standards, ensuring that mediators are well-prepared for their roles. However, the stringent requirements may also act as a deterrent to some mediator candidates, particularly those from less privileged backgrounds.

In contrast, the United Kingdom has taken a more market-driven approach to mediation regulation. Absence of mandatory certification or training requirements has allowed for a more diverse pool of mediators, but it has also led to concerns about variability in the quality of services. The UK's model prioritises flexibility and accessibility, making it easier for individuals from various professional backgrounds to enter the mediation field. However, this flexibility comes with a risk of lowering standards, as there is less oversight and consistency in mediator qualifications.

The EU's efforts to harmonise mediation regulations highlight challenges of balancing quality and inclusivity. While harmonisation aims to create a level playing field across Member States, varying levels of economic development, legal traditions and social norms in these countries mean that a one-size-fits-all approach is not always feasible. The EU's experience underscores the importance of considering local contexts when designing and implementing regulatory frameworks.

2. Ukraine

Ukraine has been working towards establishing a comprehensive regulatory framework for mediation, particularly in the wake of its recent legislative reforms. In 2021, the country adopted the Law of Ukraine 'On Mediation' laying down basic principles and procedures for mediation[3]. This law represents a significant step forward in formalising mediation as a recognised profession in Ukraine. Key elements of the Law include:

- Definition and Scope: The Law clearly defines mediation and specifies types of disputes that may be resolved through mediation. This includes civil, commercial, labour and family disputes, among others. By providing a clear legal definition, the Law aims to standardise mediation practices and ensure that all parties have a shared understanding of the process.
- Requirements for Mediators: The Law sets forth qualifications required to become a mediator, including specialised training and adherence to a code of ethics. This includes a minimum number of training hours, practical experience and ongoing professional development. The Law also outlines ethical standards that mediators must uphold, including impartiality, confidentiality and integrity.
- Voluntary Participation: Mediation in Ukraine is voluntary, and parties retain the right to seek judicial or other forms of dispute resolution, if mediation is unsuccessful. This voluntary nature of mediation is crucial for ensuring that all parties are genuinely committed to the process, which increases the likelihood of a successful outcome.

3 Verkhovna Rada of Ukraine (2021). *Law of Ukraine on Mediation*, <https://zakon.rada.gov.ua/laws/show/1026-20#Text>, accessed 15 August 2024.

While the Law represents a significant step forward, challenges remain in ensuring its consistent implementation, and availability of high-quality mediation services across the country. There is also a need to promote public awareness of mediation as an effective dispute resolution mechanism. In Ukraine, mediation is still a relatively new concept, and many people are unfamiliar with its benefits. Efforts to educate the public, legal professionals and potential mediators about the advantages of mediation are essential for the Law to have its intended impact.

Moreover, the success of the Law of Ukraine on Mediation will depend on the development of a robust infrastructure to support the profession. This includes establishing training programmes, certification bodies and professional associations to oversee the implementation of the Law and to ensure that mediators are adequately trained and supported. The Ukrainian government and civil society organisations will need to work together to build this infrastructure and promote mediation as a mainstream dispute resolution option.

Ukraine's efforts to regulate mediation are part of a broader trend towards legal reform and modernisation in the country. As Ukraine continues to align its legal system with European standards, the development of a well-regulated mediation profession will be an important step in improving access to justice and reducing the burden on courts.

3. United States of America

In the United States, regulation of mediation is primarily a state-level responsibility, leading to significant variations in how the profession is regulated across different states. Some states have established comprehensive regulatory frameworks, while others have minimal or no formal regulations. Key aspects of mediation regulation in the United States include:

- State-Level Regulation: Each state has its own laws and regulations governing mediation, including requirements for mediator training, certification and practice. For example, states like California and Florida have stringent requirements for court-connected mediators, including mandatory training, certification and continuing education. These states have developed detailed guidelines to ensure that mediators are qualified and adhere to high ethical standards. (American Bar Association 2020).

- Diverse Models of Regulation: The diversity of regulatory models reflects the federal nature of the United States' legal system with states having significant autonomy in determining how mediation is regulated. This has led to a patchwork of regulations that vary widely in terms of stringency and scope. Some states have adopted voluntary certification programmes, allowing mediators to demonstrate their qualifications without mandating certification for all practitioners. Other states have more prescriptive regulations, requiring specific training and certification for mediators working in certain contexts, such as family law or court-connected mediation.
- Market-Driven Approach: In many states, mediation remains largely unregulated, with market forces playing a significant role in determining the quality and availability of mediation services. This market-driven approach not only enables flexibility and innovation but may also lead to inconsistencies in mediator qualifications and practices. Lack of uniform standards across states means that mediators may have different levels of training and experience, leading to variability in the quality of mediation services.
- Court-Connected Mediation Programmes: Many states have established court-connected mediation programmes, which often have specific requirements for mediators who wish to be included on court rosters.
- Professional Associations: Organisations such as the Association for Conflict Resolution (ACR) and the American Bar Association (ABA) provide guidelines and voluntary certification programmes for mediators, contributing to the standardisation of practice across different jurisdictions (Association for Conflict Resolution 2021).

The US approach to mediation regulation reflects the country's broader legal culture, which values flexibility, individual autonomy and role of the market in determining professional standards. However, this approach also presents challenges when it comes to ensuring consistent quality and accessibility of mediation services across the country. Decentralised nature of mediation regulation in the US means that mediators and consumers of mediation services must navigate a complex landscape of state-specific rules and practices.

One of the key challenges in the US is the lack of a unified national standard for mediator certification. While some national organisations, such as the ACR and the ABA, have developed model standards for mediators, these standards are not legally binding and vary in adoption across states. The absence of a national certification process can create barriers for mediators who wish to practice in multiple states, as they may need to meet different requirements in each jurisdiction.

Despite these challenges, the United States has seen significant growth in the use of mediation, particularly in areas such as family law, employment disputes and commercial conflicts. The flexibility of the United States regulatory approach has allowed mediation to adapt to the needs of different sectors and communities, fostering innovation and development of specialised mediation practices.

4. Australia

Australia has developed a comprehensive and well-structured regulatory framework for the mediation profession, which is considered a model for other countries. The National Mediator Accreditation System (NMAS) provides a uniform set of standards for accreditation of mediators, ensuring consistency and quality across the country. Key aspects of the Australian regulatory framework include:

- National Standards: The NMAS sets out the training, assessment and practice standards required of mediators to be accredited. This includes a minimum of 38 hours of training, ongoing professional development and adherence to a code of ethics. National standards provide a clear and consistent framework for the profession, ensuring that mediators meet high-quality standards regardless of where they practise (National Mediator Accreditation System 2020).
- Accreditation: While accreditation under the NMAS is voluntary, it is widely recognised and often required for mediators working in court-connected or government-funded programmes. This voluntary accreditation system allows for flexibility while maintaining high standards of practice. Mediators who choose to become accredited under the NMAS are

subject to rigorous training and assessment requirements, which helps to ensure that they are well-prepared to handle the challenges of mediation. Mediators must complete a specified number of hours of training and practical experience and must adhere to ongoing professional development requirements to maintain their accreditation.
- Ethical Standards: Accredited mediators are required to follow a code of conduct that emphasises impartiality, confidentiality and competence.
- Regulatory Oversight: The Australian Mediation Association and other professional bodies play a key role in overseeing the accreditation process, ensuring that mediators comply with the standards set out by the NMAS. These organisations also provide support and resources for mediators, including continuing professional development (CPD) opportunities and access to best practice guidelines.

Australia's approach to mediation regulation reflects a commitment to high standards and professionalisation, while also promoting accessibility and flexibility within the profession. The NMAS has been praised for its clarity and effectiveness, providing a strong foundation for the development of the mediation profession in Australia. The framework's emphasis on continuous professional development ensures that mediators maintain and enhance their skills throughout their careers, contributing to the overall quality and credibility of the profession.

One of the key strengths of the Australian model is its balance between regulation and flexibility. While the NMAS sets out clear standards, it also enables different pathways to accreditation, recognising the diverse backgrounds and experiences of mediators. This inclusivity is important for ensuring that the profession remains open to individuals from various professional and cultural backgrounds.

Australia's experience with mediation regulation offers valuable lessons for other countries seeking to develop or refine their regulatory frameworks. The success of the NMAS demonstrates the importance of clear standards, robust oversight and ongoing professional development in ensuring the quality and effectiveness of mediation services.

Analysis of Regulatory Frameworks

Having outlined the current regulatory frameworks in key jurisdictions, it is important to delve deeper into the impact these frameworks have on the accessibility and inclusivity of the mediation profession. This section analyses the key trends, challenges and opportunities that emerge from different approaches to regulation.

Balancing quality and accessibility

One of the central challenges in regulating the mediation profession is balancing the need for high-quality standards with the desire to make the profession accessible to a diverse range of individuals. Stringent regulatory requirements, such as mandatory training, certification and ongoing education are essential for ensuring that mediators are competent and capable of providing effective services. However, these requirements may also create barriers to entry, particularly for individuals from less-privileged backgrounds.

For example, in jurisdictions like Germany and Italy, the high cost and time commitment required for mandatory training and certification may deter individuals who cannot afford these expenses. This leads to a lack of diversity within the profession as those who are unable to meet the requirements are excluded from entering the field. In contrast, more flexible regulatory approaches, such as those in the United Kingdom and some US states, may lower entry barriers but at the risk of compromising the quality and consistency of mediation services (Boulle 2011).

The challenge, therefore, lies in finding a regulatory approach that maintains high standards without excluding individuals from diverse backgrounds. One potential solution is to offer tiered accreditation systems, where mediators may choose to pursue different levels of certification based on their experience and training. This would allow the profession to be more inclusive while still ensuring that mediators have the necessary skills and knowledge to provide effective services.

Another approach is to provide financial support or subsidies for training and certification, particularly for individuals from under-represented groups. By reducing the financial barriers to entry, governments and professional bodies can help to promote diversity and inclusion within the mediation profession (Schonewille & Schonewille 2013).

The Role of Education and Training

Education and training are critical components of any regulatory framework for the mediation profession. The quality of mediation services depends heavily on mediators' skills and knowledge developed through rigorous training and ongoing professional development. However, the accessibility of training programmes can vary widely depending on the jurisdiction and resources available.

In countries with well-established regulatory frameworks, such as Australia and Germany, robust training programmes provide comprehensive education in mediation theory and practice. These programmes are often delivered by accredited training providers and include both theoretical instruction and practical experience. In contrast, in countries with less developed regulatory frameworks, access to high-quality training may be limited, particularly in rural or underserved areas (National Mediator Accreditation System 2020).

The mode of training delivery is also an important consideration. While traditional in-person training programmes offer valuable opportunities for hands-on learning and interaction, they can be inaccessible to individuals who live in remote areas or have other commitments that make it difficult to attend in person. Online training programmes, on the other hand, offer greater flexibility and accessibility, but they may lack interactive components that are crucial for developing practical mediation skills.

To address these challenges, regulators and professional bodies should consider offering a range of training options that cater to different needs and circumstances. This could include a combination of in-person, online and hybrid training programmes, as well as opportunities for ongoing professional development through workshops, seminars and mentoring. By providing diverse and flexible training options, regulators may help to ensure that all aspiring mediators have access to the education they need to succeed in the profession (Boulle 2011).

In addition to initial training, CPD is essential for maintaining and enhancing the skills of practising mediators. CPD programmes should be an integral part of any regulatory framework, with clear requirements for the amount and type of professional development that mediators must complete. This helps to ensure that mediators remain up to date with the latest developments in the field and continue to provide high-quality services throughout their careers (Boulle 2011).

Framework for interaction with other professions

The interaction between mediators and other professionals, such as legal professionals, psychologists and social workers, is crucial for the effective functioning of the mediation process. This section examines how different regulatory frameworks facilitate or hinder such interactions, highlighting the importance of collaboration and clear delineation of roles.

Legal professionals

In many jurisdictions, legal professionals play a significant role in mediation. Regulatory frameworks often define the scope of practice for lawyers in mediation, influencing how mediators and lawyers collaborate. Key aspects include:

- Advisory Role: Lawyers frequently serve as advisors to parties in mediation, providing legal counsel and ensuring that agreements comply with relevant laws.
- Mediator–Lawyer Collaboration: In some jurisdictions, regulations encourage collaboration between mediators and lawyers, fostering a multidisciplinary approach to dispute resolution (Macfarlane 2008).
- Confidentiality and Privilege: Regulatory frameworks typically address issues of confidentiality and privilege, establishing guidelines for the information that may be shared between mediators and legal professionals.

For example, in the United States, court-connected mediation programmes often include provisions for lawyer involvement, while in the United Kingdom, the Civil Mediation Council provides guidelines for lawyer–mediator interactions (Civil Mediation Council 2020). These frameworks aim to balance the legal and facilitative aspects of mediation, ensuring that parties receive comprehensive support.

Psychologists and social workers

The involvement of psychologists and social workers in mediation may enhance the process by addressing underlying emotional and social issues.

However, regulatory frameworks must delineate roles and responsibilities to prevent overlap and ensure effective collaboration. Key considerations include:

- Complementary Roles: Psychologists and social workers may provide valuable insights into the psychological and social dynamics of disputes, contributing to more holistic resolutions.
- Interdisciplinary Training: Some jurisdictions offer interdisciplinary training programmes that prepare mediators, psychologists and social workers to work together effectively (Field 2016).
- Ethical Considerations: Regulatory frameworks often include ethical guidelines to ensure that professionals from different fields respect each other's expertise and maintain professional boundaries.

In Australia, for example, the NMAS encourages the inclusion of psychological and social perspectives in mediation training, thereby promoting a more comprehensive approach to dispute resolution (National Mediator Accreditation System 2020). Similarly, in Canada, family mediation programmes often integrate social work and psychological services to address the multifaceted nature of family disputes.

Comparing the inclusivity of regulatory frameworks

This analysis focuses on comparing the inclusivity of regulatory frameworks across different jurisdictions. Key metrics include accessibility of training and certification programmes, diversity of individuals entering the profession and barriers to entry.

Accessibility of training and certification

Availability and affordability of training programmes are crucial for inclusivity. Jurisdictions with subsidised or widely available training programmes tend to have higher diversity in the mediator profession. For instance:

- *Subsidised Programmes*: In countries like the Netherlands, government-funded training programmes make mediation education more accessible to a broader range of individuals.

- *Wide Availability*: In Canada, numerous institutions offer mediation training, ensuring that prospective mediators have access to a variety of programmes (Schonewille & Schonewille 2013).

Diversity of professionals

Diversity of individuals entering the profession, including gender, ethnicity and socioeconomic background, serves as an indicator of inclusivity. Inclusive regulatory frameworks typically correlate with higher diversity. Examples include:

- Gender Diversity: In the EU, initiatives aimed at promoting gender diversity in the mediation profession have led to a more balanced representation of men and women (European Commission 2016).
- Ethnic and Socioeconomic Diversity: In the United States, efforts to increase the participation of underrepresented groups in mediation have resulted in greater ethnic and socioeconomic diversity among mediators (American Bar Association, 2020).

Barriers to entry

Barriers such as high educational requirements, costly certification processes, and restrictive professional standards may limit access to the profession. An analysis of these barriers across jurisdictions reveals significant differences in inclusivity:

- Educational Requirements: In some jurisdictions, such as Germany, strict educational requirements may restrict entry to the profession. Conversely, countries like the United Kingdom have more flexible entry requirements, allowing a wider range of individuals to become mediators (Boulle 2011).
- Certification Costs: High certification costs may be a barrier to entry. For example, in the United States, the cost of obtaining and maintaining certification may be prohibitive for some individuals, while in Australia, government subsidies help reduce this burden (National Mediator Accreditation System 2020).

- Professional Standards: While high professional standards are essential for ensuring the quality of mediation services, overly restrictive standards may limit inclusivity. Jurisdictions that balance high standards with accessible pathways to certification tend to have more inclusive regulatory frameworks.

Policy recommendations

Based on the analysis, this chapter offers several policy recommendations to enhance the inclusivity of the mediator profession:

- Subsidised Training Programmes: Governments and professional bodies should provide subsidies for mediation training to increase accessibility, particularly for individuals from underrepresented groups.
- Flexible Certification Processes: Regulatory frameworks should offer flexible certification processes that recognise diverse educational backgrounds and professional experiences.
- Promotion of Diversity: Initiatives aimed at promoting diversity within the profession, including targeted recruitment and support programmes, can help increase the representation of underrepresented groups.
- Interdisciplinary Training: Encouraging interdisciplinary training programmes that involve mediators, legal professionals, psychologists, and social workers may enhance collaboration and improve the quality of mediation services.
- Balanced Regulatory Standards: Regulatory frameworks should balance high professional standards with accessible pathways to certification, ensuring that the profession remains inclusive without compromising quality.

5. Impact of technology on mediation

Technology is playing an ever-greater role in the mediator profession, offering new opportunities for improving access to services and enhancing the effectiveness of mediation processes. Online dispute resolution (ODR) platforms, virtual mediation services and digital tools for case management are just a few examples of how technology is transforming the field (Schonewille & Schonewille 2013).

In the context of regulatory frameworks, the rise of technology presents both opportunities and challenges. On the one hand, technology can help to make mediation services more accessible, particularly for individuals in remote or underserved areas. Online mediation platforms, for example, allow parties to participate in mediation sessions from the comfort of their own homes, reducing the need for travel and making it easier for individuals with mobility issues or other barriers to access services (National Mediator Accreditation System 2020).

On the other hand, the use of technology in mediation raises important questions about the quality and security of services. Regulators need to ensure that online mediation platforms meet the same high standards as traditional in-person services, including requirements for confidentiality, impartiality and competence. This may involve developing specific guidelines or standards for online mediation, as well as providing training for mediators on how to effectively use technology in their practice.

In addition to online mediation, digital tools for case management and communication may help to streamline the mediation process and improve efficiency. For example, case management software may help mediators keep track of case details, manage documents and communicate with parties, while digital communication tools may facilitate real-time collaboration and information sharing (National Mediator Accreditation System 2020).

However, the adoption of technology in mediation also raises concerns about access and equity. Not all individuals have equal access to technology, and there may be significant disparities in digital literacy and connectivity, particularly in rural or low-income communities. Regulators need to consider these issues when developing guidelines for the use of technology in mediation, ensuring that all individuals have equal access to services, regardless of their technological capabilities.

Summary

Regulation of the mediation profession is a multifaceted and complex issue, with significant implications for inclusivity, accessibility and quality of mediation services across different jurisdictions. Through an examination of various regulatory frameworks, this study has highlighted both advancements and challenges faced by different regions, underscoring the need for a balanced approach that upholds high standards while promoting inclusivity.

The European Union's harmonisation efforts, such as the EU Mediation Directive (2008/52/EC), represent a commendable step towards standardising practices across Member States. However, disparities in implementation, particularly among countries like Italy, Germany and the United Kingdom, reveal ongoing challenges in achieving uniformity in both quality and accessibility. Similarly, Ukraine's recent legislative efforts indicate a positive trend towards formalising mediation, though practical challenges remain.

In contrast, the United States' decentralised regulatory system fosters innovation but also results in significant variability in mediator qualifications and service quality. This highlights the need for a more coordinated approach that still respects state autonomy. Australia's NMAS offers a model for balancing stringent accreditation standards with broad accessibility, yet financial and geographic barriers to training persist.

A key component of effective dispute resolution is an interdisciplinary collaboration between mediators and other professionals, such as lawyers, psychologists and social workers. Regulatory frameworks that facilitate such collaboration, without compromising distinct roles of each profession, may lead to more holistic and satisfactory outcomes for parties involved in mediation.

To enhance the inclusivity of the mediator profession, several policy recommendations emerge. Subsidising training programmes, as practised in the Netherlands, may lower entry barriers and increase diversity within the profession. Flexible certification processes and targeted initiatives to promote gender, ethnic and socioeconomic diversity are also crucial. Additionally, interdisciplinary training may improve the quality of mediation services by integrating diverse professional insights.

Moving forward, future research should focus on the intersection of regulatory frameworks and professional inclusivity, with longitudinal studies to assess the long-term impact of regulatory changes on the mediator profession. Comparative studies between regions with varying levels of regulatory maturity may provide deeper insights into effective strategies for fostering an inclusive and high-quality mediation profession.

In conclusion, creating an inclusive and accessible mediator profession requires ongoing collaboration, innovation and a commitment to balanced regulatory frameworks. By adopting proactive policy measures and fostering interdisciplinary cooperation, a more equitable and effective dispute resolution landscape may be achieved, benefiting all stakeholders involved.

Bibliography

American Bar Association (2020). 'Model Standards of Conduct for Mediators', <https://www.americanbar.org/groups/dispute_resolution/policy_standards/>, accessed 15 August 2024.

Association for Conflict Resolution (2021). 'ACR's Standards and Ethics', <https://acrnet.org/page/standards>, accessed 15 August 2024.

Boulle, Laurence (2011). 'Mediation: Principles, Process, Practice', 3rd ed. London: Butterworths.

Civil Mediation Council (2020). 'Professional Standards and Guidance', <https://civilmediation.org/for-practitioners/professional-standards/>, accessed 15 August 2024.

De Palo, Giuseppe, and Trevor, Mary B. (2012). 'EU Mediation Law and Practice'. Oxford: Oxford University Press.

European Commission (2016). 'Gender Equality in the EU', <https://ec.europa.eu/info/policies/justice-and-fundamental-rights/gender-equality_en>, accessed 15 August 2024.

Field, Rachael (2016). *Mediation Ethics: A Practitioner's Guide*. New York: Routledge.

Macfarlane, Julie (2008). *The New Lawyer: How Settlement is Transforming the Practice of Law*. Vancouver: UBC Press.

National Mediator Accreditation System (2020). 'NMAS Standards', <https://msb.org.au/resources/documents>, accessed 15 August 2024.

Schonewille, Manon, and Schonewille, Fred (2013). *The Variegated Landscape of Mediation Regulation: A Comparative Study of Mediation Regulation and Practices in Europe and the World*. The Hague: Eleven International Publishing.

Legal sources

Directive 2008/52/EC of the European Parliament and the Council of 21 May 2008 on certain aspects of mediation in civil and commercial matters, Official Journal L 136/3 on 24 May 2008, <https://eur-lex.europa.eu/legal-content/en/ALL/?uri=CELEX:32008L0052#:~:text=DIRECTIVE%202008/52/EC%20OF%20THE%20EUROPEAN%20PARLIAMENT>, accessed 15 August 2024).

Verkhovna Rada of Ukraine (2021). Law of Ukraine on Mediation, <https://zakon.rada.gov.ua/laws/show/1026-20#Text>, accessed 15 August 2024.

Ius, Lex et Res Publica Studies in Law, Philosophy and Political Cultures

Edited by Barbara Janusz-Pohl

Vol. 1 Anna Jaron: Socio-Economic Constitutional Rights in Democratisation Processes. An Account of the Constitutional Dialogue Theory. 2012.

Vol. 2 Stanisław Filipowicz: Democracy – The Power of Illusion. 2013.

Vol. 3 Teresa Dukiet-Nagórska (ed.): The Postulates of Restorative Justice and the Continental Model of Criminal Law. As Illustrated by Polish Criminal Law 2014.

Vol. 4 Agnieszka Kupzok: Enforcement of Patents on Geographically Divisible Inventions. An Inquiry into the Standard of Substantive Patent Law Infringement in Cross-Border Constellations. 2015.

Vol. 5 Alicja Jagielska-Burduk / Wojciech Szafrański: Legal Issues in Cultural Heritage Management. A Polish Perspective. 2016.

Vol. 6 Maciej Mataczyński (ed.): The Takeover of Public Companies as a Mode of Exercising EU Treaty Freedoms. 2017.

Vol. 7 Maciej Barczewski (ed.): Value of Information. Intellectual Property, Privacy and Big Data. 2018.

Vol. 8 Pawel Smoleń, Marcin Burzec: Introduction to Polish Tax Law. 2018.

Vol. 9 Łukasz Pohl, Konrad Burdziak: Judicial Interpretation of the 1997 Criminal Code Provisions on Self-Defence. 2019.

Vol. 10 Adam Szot: Judicial Review of Administrative Discretion. The Influence of Court Decisions on Administrative Actions. 2019.

Vol. 11 Michał Peno / Konrad Burdziak (eds.): The Concept of Modern Law. Polish and Central European Tradition. 2019.

Vol. 12 Leszek Leszczyński / Bartosz Liṅewski / Adam Szot (eds.): Potential of Precedent in the Statutory Legal Order. 2019.

Vol. 13 Łukasz Bolesta: In Search of a Model for the Legal Protection of a Whistleblower in the Workplace in Poland. A legal and comparative study. 2020.

Vol. 14 Paweł Chmielnicki / Adam Sulikowski (eds.): New Perspectives on Legislation. A Comparative Approach. 2020.

Vol. 15 Marcin Burzec / Beata Kucia-Guściora / Paweł Smoleś: Agricultural Activity in Poland: A Fiscal and Legal Study. 2020.

Vol. 16 Magdalena Półtorak / Ilona Topa (eds.): Women, Children and (Other) Vulnerable Groups. Standards of Protection and Challenges for International Law. 2021.

Vol. 17 Josef Albert Fox: Die polnische Verfassung vom 3. Mai 1791. Hintergründe der Entstehung und der Außerkraftsetzung. Stellung Polens im Zeitalter der Aufklärung. 2021.

Vol. 18 Barbara Janusz-Pohl (ed.): Juvenile Justice Systems: Poland-Brazil-Portugal. 2021.

Vol. 19 Leszek Leszczyński: General Reference Clauses in the Judicial Process. Context of Legislative Intentions Interpretative Discretion. 2021.

Vol. 20 Francisco J. Campos Zamora: Das Problem der Begründung richterlicher Entscheidungen. Eine Analyse auf der Grundlage der Theorie der juristischen Argumentation. 2021.

Vol. 21 Aneta Skorupa-Wulczyńska: Language Rights of the Citizen of the European Union. 2022.

Vol. 22 Mateusz Osiecki: International Legal Aspects of Aerial Terrorism. Methods of Law Enforcement in Aviation. 2022.

Vol. 23 Vladimír Sharp / Gabriela Blahoudková / Jakub Handrlica (eds.): Law, Pandemics and Ownership Restrictions. 2022.

Vol. 24 Piotr Kasprzyk / Anna Konert: Drones – Future of Aviation Law? Interference of Public Law in Private Law. 2023.

Vol. 25 Szymon Pawelec (ed.): Consensual Mechanisms in Criminal Proceedings – Integrative and Comparative Perspective. 2023.

Vol. 26 Dorota Pudzianowska: Statelessness in Public Law. 2023.

Vol. 27 Boguslaw Przywora / Aleksander Wróbel: Formalised Access to Pre-jurisdictional Free Legal Aid. 2023.

Vol. 28 Ewa Dawidziuk / Patricia Panero / Anny Tarwacka (eds.): Family, Law, and Society: from Roman Law to the Present Day. 2024.

Vol. 29 Marian Grzybowsk / Boguslaw Przywora / Aleksandra Syryt (eds.): Free Legal Aid, Theory, Legal Basis and Practice. European Standards. 2024.

Vol. 30 Karolina Gmerek: Trial as a Social Communication Occurrence. 2024.

Vol. 31 Pawel Wiliński (ed.): Effective Legal Remedies in Criminal Justice System. European Perspective. 2024.

Vol. 32 Jakub Hanc / Olga Sitarz / Anna Jaworska-Wieloch: On the (non)existence of the right to religious freedom of persons deprived of liberty. 2024.

Vol. 33 Marian Grzybowsk / Boguslaw Przywora / Aleksandra Syryt (eds.): Free Legal Aid – A Comparative Approach. 2024.

Vol. 34 Dominik Gajewski (ed.): Functioning of Administrative Judiciary in the Context of Economic Changes. 2024.

Vol. 35 Mikołajczyk, Barbara: Older Migrants – Vulnerable and Excluded. 2024.

Vol. 36 Świder, Maciej: The Exercise of the Right to a Fair Trial in the Era of the COVID-19 Pandemic. 2024.

Vol. 37 Tomasz Barankiewicz / Boguslaw Przywora (eds.): Public and Civil Service in Poland. 2024.

Vol. 38 Daniele Vicoli (ed.): Effective Justice 1. Effective Justice. International and Comparative Approaches. 2025.

Vol. 39 Barbara Janusz-Pohl (ed.): Effective Justice 2. Effective Justice. International and Comparative Approaches. 2025.

Vol. 40 Kinga Anna Gajda / Marta Pietras-Eichberger / Małgorzata Skawińska (eds.): Mediation as an Inclusive and Sustainable Method of Resolving Conflicts. 2025.

www.peterlang.com

www.ingramcontent.com/pod-product-compliance
Ingram Content Group UK Ltd.
Pitfield, Milton Keynes, MK11 3LW, UK
UKHW020834290926
15470UKWH00004B/1331

9 783631 922385